Mansions of the Spirit

Essays in Literature and Religion

Mansions of the Spirit

Essays in Literature and Religion

Edited by
George A. Panichas

Hawthorn Books, Inc. Publishers New York

Mansions of the Spirit

First Edition: 1967

Design: Gene Gordon

The epigraph is from *Selected Letters of Robert Frost*, copyright © 1964, edited by Lawrance Thompson, and reprinted by permission of the Estate of Robert Frost and Holt, Rinehart and Winston, Inc.

1840

To

CHARLES DRISCOLL MURPHY

"But we know when it has been given. We do not forget, though we may seem to. Kindness, more kindness, and even after that more kindness. I assure you it is the only hope."

To prayer I think I go,
I go to prayer—
Along a darkened corridor of woe
And down a stair
In every step of which I am abased.
I wear a halter-rope about the waist.
I bear a candle end put out with haste.
For such as I there is reserved a crypt
That from its stony arches having dripped
Has stony pavement in a slime of mould.
There I will throw me down an unconsoled
And utter loss,
And spread out in the figure of a cross.
Oh, if religion's not to be my fate
I must be spoken to and told
Before too late!

—Robert Frost

ACKNOWLEDGMENTS

The essays by Father Merton, Professors Cruickshank, Knight, and Pinto, and by Mr. Stanford were written especially for this volume. My own essay was first given as a public lecture sponsored by the Department of English at the University of Maryland. Subsequently it was published in *The Greek Orthodox Theological Review* and is reprinted here with the permission of the editor. The remaining essays appeared originally in two special issues on literature and religion which I edited, with the assistance of Martha Seabrook and Mary E. Slayton, for *Comparative Literature Studies* (II, No. 4 [1965]; III, No. 2 [1966]), published by the University of Maryland at College Park. To A. O. Aldridge and Melvin J. Friedman, editors of this quarterly, I am indebted not only for the idea of these special issues but also for permission to reprint the essays here. It is indeed gratifying for me to pay tribute to the Comparative Literature Department of the University of Maryland in recognition of its pioneering efforts in comparative literature and its contributions to American letters. To Professor Charles D. Murphy, Head, Department of English, I am indebted for his generous support and his many kindnesses.

The publication of this volume would have been impossible without the advice and the unfailing assistance of the editor's research associates: Martha Seabrook, who styled the essays, and Mary E. Slayton, who typed the manuscript. Their invaluable suggestions and criticisms, as well as their understanding of, and insights into, literature, have helped to stamp this volume with a clarity that otherwise might have been lacking. And for their personal encouragement, grace, and good cheer the editor renders his thanks superlative.

CONTENTS

PART II

IMAGINATION AND BELIEF

PREFACE

ALTHOUGH PROFESSOR RENÉ WELLEK COMPLAINS THAT RECENT LITERARY criticism has tended to abandon its central concern with the art, theory, and interpretation of literature by seeking to become sociology, politics, philosophy, or even mystical illumination, he nevertheless does not fail to stress that "criticism needs constantly to draw on [these] neighboring disciplines."

In a society that is dominated by science and technology, it is essential to effect a dialogue between literary and other scholarly disciplines. In this connection, the emphasis being given by critics to the organic relationship between literature and religion and to such special aspects as the "theological imagination" and the "religious meaning and dimensions" of literature gives cause for definite satisfaction—and hope. For the fact remains that any cessation of interdisciplinary dialogue in the world of letters would inevitably signalize the triumph of the mechanical mind, belonging to the spirit of time, over the creative mind, belonging to the spirit of eternity.

Of course, the fear is sometimes voiced that the attempt to explore the connections between literature and religion will lead to the conversion of criticism into theology. Those who express this fear contend that to judge literature according to whether it adequately illustrates religious doctrine, or whether it correctly captures the essential mood of a particular faith, would constitute an abrogation of the functions and the responsibilities of literary criticism. Critics as different in their approaches —and indeed in their religious backgrounds and positions—as F. R. Leavis and Joseph H. Summers indicate strong assent to the view that art must not serve a specific religion. Some years ago, Leavis clearly delineated his feelings in an essay "The Logic of Christian Discrimination." "As for Christian Discrimination," he noted, "it needs to be said that there can be no substitute for the scrupulous and disinterested approach of the literary critic. If Christian belief and Christian attitudes have really affected the critic's sensibility, then they will play their due part in his perceptions and judgments, without his summoning his creeds and doctrines, to the job of discriminating and pronouncing." More recently Summers, addressing himself to his fellow "Christian literary scholars," warned of the danger that, "concerned with our particular vision of orthodoxy, we may forget that our first duty as scholars is the discovery and communication of truth, and, instead, spend our chief energies as religious and moral cops and judges, rapping knuckles and heads, assigning sentences."

All the while, it is becoming increasingly apparent that the problems of the modern age will be solved neither by the doctrinaire man of letters nor by the doctrinaire man of faith. Understanding, not manifestoes, is what we need at present. If, moreover, we must be wary of those who would confuse literature with religion, we must also be wary of those who insist that criticism must concentrate solely on art-form and that literary values preclude religious values. D. H. Lawrence's well-known observation that "one has to be so terribly religious, to be an artist" would indicate certainly that there are levels of meanings and relationships existing between art and religion which can be neither escaped nor ignored. These thoughts should in no way imply that the strictly formalistic approach to literature is unimportant. They simply underscore its inadequacy. In fact, Nathan A. Scott, Jr., rejecting the notion that a work of literature should be treated "as a linguistic artifact that exists in complete detachment from any other independent existent reality," has declared that criticism today is "in something like a situation of crisis."

Now the qualities and the complexities of artistic vision are such that they cannot be contained by critical (or theological) dogmas. The truth of this statement has been singularly dramatized in the twentieth century, especially since the end of World War I, when, to quote Rainer Maria Rilke, "the world . . . passed out of the hands of God into the hands of men." As a result, in much of modern literature it is precisely the experience and consequences of the displacement that are re-created. Critics who are willing to examine this factor recognize the possibilities of extending our understanding of what is often spoken of as contemporary man's "cultural fragmentation and incommunicability" in a "desacralized world." That is to say, such critics, by rising above the obviously parochial limitations often imposed by schools of literary criticism and by remaining ever cognizant of artistic form which is expressive of meaning, are attuned to the cultural actualities and the temper of the times and to the ever-changing patterns of modern human experience. It is in the nature of this critical and synoptic awareness, then, to be able to "take account of secular man in all his dynamics," to quote a phrase of Amos Wilder.

Any preoccupation with the relations of literature and religion must not be construed as a development or a requirement of a point of view or of what might be called religious criticism: the kind of criticism, for instance, which chooses to view literature within the framework of Boris Pasternak's contention that "art has two constant, two unending concerns: it always meditates on death and thus always creates life. All great, genuine art resembles and continues the Revelation of St. John." No, it is not the religious critic who is needed but the critic who can discern spiritual sources of art and can communicate religious essences of art which are applicable and complementary to human existence. For such a critic there are no literary confines: His assessments of art are not dictated by adherence to tests of orthodoxy; nor are they restricted to the region peculiar to structural analysis, to matters of technique, style, and form. Concurrently, his sensitivity to language encompasses a sensitivity to other energies that consciously or unconsciously give shape and value to the creative imagination—e.g., the social, the historical, the ideological, and the moral elements that are continually at work in the thinking and creative processes.

Doubtless the growing awareness of significant relationships between literature and religion is symptomatic of the discontent some literary scholars are showing with criticism that is too professional, specialistic, or academic. Literary scholarship that limits itself to categories, criteria, and methodology—always in the name of "objective" truths, so we are told— may, to be sure, reveal a disciplined critical intelligence. But it does not have the breadth and the acuteness of vision that inhere in a critical sensibility: the sensibility that transcends the mastery of so-called methods and aims of criticism so as to embrace what Erich Heller has described as a concern "with the communication of quality rather than measurable quantity, and of meaning rather than explanation." In essence, then, literary theoreticians who very tidily dismiss a critical work dealing with literature and religion as, say, a mere religious-metaphysical study (we need not be bothered by the tone of the dismissal: it is a tone we have learned to bear with in pundits) deny the validity of the fact that the artistic imagination has important things to relate not only to the critic but also to the philosopher, the educator, and the priest. Critics who refuse to accept or to evaluate the place and the meaning of religious consciousness and convictions when they impinge on and inform the artistic imagination as a whole reveal a deficiency that impairs their study and appreciation of literature. (The study of literature, like the problem of education, must, as T. S. Eliot has declared, "be something more than the acquisition of information, technical competence, or superficial culture.")

The basic issue in the relationship of literature and religion, therefore, is whether or not a critic is prepared to admit the relevance of religious elements, aesthetically and intellectually, in art and to elucidate these in his interpretations. That literature and religion are not discrete entities, and that there is a living relation between them: these are truths that must be fully affirmed by a critic who in any way believes that criticism is the "pursuit of true judgment." Such an affirmation, on the other hand, in no way whatsoever posits the requirement that a critic should subscribe to an authoritative view, to a religious doctrine, or to particular theological tenets comprising an outlook on life. Orthodoxies and neo-orthodoxies have done damage enough in literary studies.

In religion one of the most welcome developments in recent years has been the willingness shown by different denominations to exchange views leading to harmony, even to unity. Above all, the ecumenical movement has indicated a realistic comprehension of both the momentous changes and the dangers that grip the modern world. The challenges of new ways to old have prompted a continuing exploration of religious issues, and more and more the theologian recognizes the secular realities of human experience and the need to cope with them. Thus dialogue has replaced the disputation that characterized religious discussions in the past. Both the beginning and the end of this dialogue rest in the realization that, as Martin Buber writes, "religions are mansions into which the spirit of man is fit in order that it might not break forth and burst open its world." To be sure, this is not the place for a discourse on ecumenism. These remarks are made only to point out that modern man is displaying a new readiness of sympathy for ways of finding understanding among people of conflicting religious beliefs. There is no reason why the literary critic should not also participate in the dialogue by directing his attention to art that contemplates and identifies itself with those universals in human life that are religious in origin: the meaning of the human predicament, the nature of evil, the fact of death, the concept of redemption.

More than thirty years have passed since T. S. Eliot's remarkable essay "Religion and Literature" appeared. In its implications and warnings, in its delicate and even prophetic insights, this essay showed a troubled awareness of literary scholarship which dispensed with a historical and traditional sense and which rejected religious apprehensions of the world found in creative art. "The 'greatness' of literature," Eliot insisted, "cannot be determined solely by literary standards; though we must remember that whether it is literature or not can be determined only by literary standards." The essays in this collection, written by scholars of different religious persuasions, remind us that Eliot has not been alone in his concern with literature and religion. At the same time these essays testify to modern literary scholarship that can enter into the mansions of the spirit, there to discover or rediscover the language of faith which coalesces with the language of art to work miracles of creation.

G.A.P.

INTRODUCTORY ESSAY

"Baptism in the Forest":
Wisdom and Initiation in William Faulkner

by

Thomas Merton

PERHAPS THE BEST WAY TO APPROACH THE RATHER TROUBLESOME QUESTION of literature and religion today is to begin with a typical case, an example not of "religious literature" but rather of the confusions surrounding it. When Camus undertook to adapt Faulkner's *Requiem for a Nun* for the French stage, there was a certain amount of gossip in the press: "Camus has been converted!" Why? Because the work of Faulkner was "religious." (Anything with the word "nun" in the title has to be Roman Catholic, you know.) In an interview published in *Le Monde*[1] Camus had to go through the usual tiresome business of explaining the fairly obvious. He was fascinated by Faulkner, "the greatest American novelist." To Camus, Faulkner was one of the few modern writers who possessed the "keys of ancient tragedy" and who was able to discover in the back pages of the newspapers myths embodying the essential tragedy of our time. Faulkner could place modern characters in conflict with their destiny and could resolve that conflict in the way classic tragedy had done. In a word, Faulkner made it possible to hope that the "tragique de notre histoire" would one day be made credible on the stage.[2] In Faulkner the theme of suffering was treated in a tragic, therefore (Camus thought) in a basically religious manner. Faulkner combined and concentrated in himself the "universe of Dostoievski and, besides that, Protestant rigorism." This was not at all a question of conventional moral sermons which (Camus admitted) bored him to death, but of the mystery of suffering as a dark abyss into which Faulkner saw a possibility of a little light sometimes filtering. Without being "converted," Camus was certainly fascinated by the "étrange religion de Faulkner," readily suggesting that it contained the secret of Faulkner's tragic power.

In a preface to the regular French edition of *Requiem*, translated by Maurice-Edgar Coindreau, Camus roundly asserted that the paradoxical religious outlook of Faulkner, which made a saint of the prostitute Nancy and "invested brothels and prisons with the dignity of the cloister," could not be dispensed with in an adaptation. "Ce paradoxe essentiel il fallait le conserver." Nonetheless, Camus admitted that he had shortened the meditative passages on God and faith.

Camus added sardonically, "If I translated and staged a Greek tragedy, no one would ask me if I believed in Zeus." At the same time, in the aforementioned interview, Camus repudiated a superficial "godlessness" which he considered "vulgar and threadbare." "I do not believe in God," he said, "but I am not for all that an atheist."

The purpose of these quotations is not to approve or to disapprove of Camus' evaluation of Faulkner or of "Faulkner's religion." The case is adduced as evidence of two facts: namely, that there does exist a consensus which admits the existence even today of "religious literature" and that there is also a disquieting, even annoying, popular tendency to look for "conversions" in connection with this literature. I do not say that these popular beliefs substantiate all that critics sometimes say about literature and religion. I am merely showing what seems to me to be the source of the problem with which the present book attempts to deal. Far from taking these popular opinions as proof of "Faulkner's religion," I will merely use them as a starting point for a more pedestrian investigation of themes in Faulkner which might conceivably be called "religious" but which, I think, can better be classified by another term.

Meanwhile, let us firmly repudiate those vices which make this whole question of "religious literature" so distasteful and so confusing. First, there is the often morbid curiosity about conversions and apostasies associated with the writing or the reading of this or that literary work. This curiosity is every bit as vulgar and tiresome as the aggressive religion and irreligion which often go with it. In large part the blame may well lie with the prevalence of another critical vice, that of "claiming for the faith" (see, in this connection, the essay by Hyatt Waggoner). This is the habit of searching authors for symptoms of belief—whether Christian, Marxist, or any other—and of forthwith enrolling them in one's own sect. John Cruickshank would call this "intellectual imperialism," and we can join him in finding it repugnant, especially when it claims to be "Christian." Unfortunately, the embattled inferiority complex of much nineteenth-century thought made this tendency almost second nature in some quarters. The dead, whose hash was definitely settled and who could not be discovered to have been deathbed converts, were nevertheless shown to have been secret believers in one way or another. The living were always rumored to be about to bow their heads over the font. Aldous Huxley, for instance, was repeatedly rumored to be on the verge of becoming a Catholic, perhaps because (as Milton Birnbaum shows) he once said that he disliked Catholics less than Puritans! Nor is there any need to recall the fury of conversions and apostasies which thirty years ago kept a ceaseless procession of intellectuals moving in and out of the Communist Party.

Further refinements in these matters can be left to the very competent treatment of the essayists in the first part of this volume. Is there such a thing as religious literature at all? What is meant here by "religious"? Does "religious literature" imply the author's orthodoxy, his belonging to a Church, or his commitment to a recognizable set of beliefs? The writers in this volume do not agree in their terminology, although they do in fact come to pretty much the same conclusions. "Literary" and "religious" values must not be confused. Obviously, religious orthodoxy or sincerity is no guarantee that a work is artistically valid. If, on the other hand, an understanding of the work implies some awareness of religious values, then one must be able to identify oneself to some extent with the author in holding these values to be "real." Otherwise, it becomes impossible to enjoy the work in question. But, again, what are "religious values"? Father Blehl, for instance, says that Graham Greene's whisky priest displays religious values, whereas in Faulkner's "The Bear" "the experiences have almost no intrinsic religious significance at all." Here, by "religious" Father Blehl evidently means "Christian" and "theological." The "religious" is "sacerdotal and spiritually redemptive" and "shows the operation of God in a world of sin." I would like to suggest later that Faulkner (at least in "The Bear") does have a "spiritually redemptive" view of the world, though it is not necessarily the orthodox Christian view.

Thomas L. Hanna would also like the range of "religion" in this regard severely restricted. For Hanna, a work is religious only if God is in the cast of characters. The fact that an author happens to have a coherent view of the world and of man's struggle with destiny in the world does not mean that he is giving "religious" answers. Perhaps, Hanna suggests, we should call his outlook a "metaphysic" rather than "religion." In such

a case Camus' statement about the "étrange religion de Faulkner" should
be emended to read "l'étrange metaphysique de Faulkner." I submit that
the idea is subtly transformed as soon as it gets into French. Hanna
is undoubtedly right in protesting against the naïveté of disoriented
Christians who, having no metaphysic and needing one badly, assume
that when they find a few ingredients for one, they have rediscovered
"Christianity." Still, this deficiency and this naïveté are perhaps more
apparent in America than in Europe. When in the very next essay
Edwin M. Moseley can speak calmly of "the essentially religious
content of serious drama in every age," he seems to be contradicting
Hanna; yet he is not. Moseley's statement is much more plausible in his
own context, since he starts out from Greek tragedy and talks the
language of people like F. M. Cornford. Here again our allusions to
Camus come in handy. Everyone can still respond to the great religious
and mythical motifs of Greek tragedy without being converted to a belief
in Zeus. As a matter of fact, Greek tragedy could imply a very definite
ambiguity toward the gods. Faith in the Olympians did not necessarily
imply a personal commitment to their service, and devotion to one of
them might bring the devotee into strained relations with another (as
Homer brings out). Aeschylus was not at all convinced that Zeus' rule
was beneficial or even fully justified. And the Zeus of *Prometheus* is
regarded as a usurper against whom Prometheus has a very plausible
case.

Nevertheless, there is no getting around the facts that Greek tragedy
deals religiously with the great basic problems of human destiny and that
one can accept this without committing oneself to a particular dogmatic
faith. The "religious" elements in Greek tragedy are of the same nature
as the "essential paradox" which Camus found in Faulkner's *Requiem*.
They lie embedded in different ground from that in which the revealed
truths of Christianity are found. They are embedded in human nature
itself, or, if that expression is no longer acceptable to some readers, then
in the very constitution of man's psyche, whether his collective unconscious or his individual character structure.

In this connection we can readily understand why the neopositivism
of Alain Robbe-Grillet rejects all tragedy as sentimental and false because
it inevitably implies certain basic religious postulates about the value of
life. But he assumes that these religious postulates are something *added*
to reality, not inherent in it. In his suppression of values he suppresses
something of reality itself. Hence his people are, as Fr. Jarrett-Kerr says,
like insects. Such is the fruit of a method which has triumphantly "made
tragedy impossible" and has, at the same time, rejected as irrelevant the

idea of human nature and, even more, that of the human person. But Father Jarrett-Kerr also raises the question whether there can be "Christian tragedy" in any context where the resurrection of the dead is taken for granted. "Theology," in I. A. Richards' words, "is fatal to tragedy."

But redemption is not automatic. "Salvation" can never be taken for granted. All the good potentialities in man can be irretrievably wasted and destroyed through his own fault. The Christian concept of damnation, whether one believes in it or not, is supremely tragic. When Camus (out of the bitterness of his experience under the Nazis and during the Algerian war) spoke of our time as "tragic," he was aware of the aspect of its *destruction of man*. And Camus excels in portraying the damned.

Greek tragedy is comprehensible irrespective of whether we "believe in" the Greek gods. It is so because it is not in fact concerned with truth about the gods but with truths about man. It is concerned with them in such a "classical," such a universal way that we, too, find ourselves involved in them without passing through the medium of a doctrinal explanation. This immediacy of Attic tragedy may be more obvious to us in the West because our whole culture is built on the basis of Greek and Hebrew literature and thought. But I think that with a very little initiation the Nō drama of Japan, for instance, or the religious drama of Bali[3] can have the same awe-inspiring and cathartic impact on a Western audience. In other words, once the ritual and symbolic language of gesture is grasped, one can participate in Oriental drama almost as well as in Greek tragedy. In either case, what is happening is not just that we are spelling out for ourselves a religious or a metaphysical message. Rather, the drama is having a direct impact on the deepest center of our human nature, at a level beyond language, where our most fundamental human conflicts find themselves not *explained*, not *analyzed*, but *enacted* in the artistic way which Aristotle tried to account for in his theory of catharsis, of pity and terror in tragedy.

In this way tragedy does not merely convince us that we ought to be resigned. Above all, it does not merely propose suitable reasons for resignation. Through its therapeutic effect it enables us to rise above evil, to liberate ourselves from it by a return to a more real evaluation of ourselves, a change of heart analogous to Christian "repentance." As we know, the mechanism of Greek tragedy is centered on *hubris*, that fundamentally false and arrogant estimate of one's self and of its capacities. The catharsis of pity and terror delivers the participant from *hubris* and restores him to an awareness of his place in the scheme of things—of his limitations as well as of his true nobility. It enables him to realize that "Puny Man," as Father Jarrett-Kerr says, "is still valuable for his freedom."

Now it is quite obvious that both Greek tragedy and Oriental ritual dance-drama were not merely presentations which an audience sat and watched. They were religious celebrations, liturgies, in which the audience participated. Thus, although we can still be immediately stirred by the impact of these archaic dramas even when we read them in translation, it does not take much imagination for us to represent to ourselves what would be the effect of our being present *then*, in those days, for instance in the theater at Delphi during the festival of Apollo. (Note what Father Jarrett-Kerr says about a recent performance of *Medea* before an African audience in Johannesburg.) We—our twentieth-century selves—might possibly have found the experience too powerful to bear. Or perhaps we would have undergone the sort of thing that happens now to the people who take LSD, which is presumably why they take it and why the taking of it has been invested with a quasi-religious ritual atmosphere.

The point is, I think, to realize that something of the same excitement and discovery remains accessible to us today in reading not only ancient tragedies but works of our own time. Faulkner is certainly one of those writers who possess this power to evoke in us an experience of meaning and of direction or a catharsis of pity and terror which can be called "religious" in the same sense as Greek tragedy was religious.

Unfortunately, as we have seen, the term "religious" is also very ambiguous, insofar as it as associated with many other things that have nothing to do with this basic experience. For example, the idea of religion today is mixed up with confessionalism, with belonging to this or that religious institution, with making and advertising a particular kind of religious commitment, with a special style in devotion or piety, or even with a certain exclusiveness in the quest for an experience which has to be sacred and not secular. In spite of all the talk of believers about breaking down the limits between the sacred and the secular, one still feels that there is a very obsessive insistence that one's whole experience of life has to be dominated *from without* by a system of acquired beliefs and attitudes and that every other experience (for instance, that of reading a novel) has first to be tested by this system of beliefs. Thus one has to read Faulkner with suspicion and enjoy only what conforms to one's own moral and religious code.

In order to make this simple and easy, one just proceeds to codify the novelists themselves. What did they believe? What was the preferred system of each? What in fact were "their messages"? But I submit that if you sit down to codify the "strange religion of Faulkner" and if you do so in terms of some other no doubt less strange religion of your own, you are likely to miss the real "religious" impact of Faulkner. His impact has all the directness of Greek tragedy because, although he works in words, he produces an effect that is somehow not explicable by an investigation of the words alone. He has a power of "enactment" which, if you are open to it, brings you into living participation with an experience of basic and universal human values on a level which words can *point* to but cannot fully attain. Faulkner is typical of the creative genius who can associate his reader in the same experience of creation which brought forth his book. Such a book is filled with efficacious sign-situations, symbols, and myths which release in the reader the imaginative power to experience what the author really means to convey. And what he means to convey is not a system of truths which explain life but a certain depth of awareness in which life itself is lived more intensely and with a more meaningful direction. The "symbolic" in this sense is not a matter of contrived signification in which things point arbitrarily to something else. Symbols are signs which release the power of imaginative communion.

The power of symbols is, I think, fully explicable only if you accept the theory that symbols are something more than mere artifacts of a few human minds. They are basic archetypal forms anterior to any operation of the mind, forms which have risen spontaneously with awareness in all religions and which have everywhere provided patterns for the myths in which man has striven to express his search for ultimate meaning and for union with God. Needless to say, these myths retain their power and their seminal creativity in the unconscious even after conscious minds have agreed that "God is dead." The myth of the death of God and of the void consequent upon it springs from the same archaic source as other myths. The conscious determination to deny that there is any void and to suppress all anxiety about it is another matter.

At the same time it must be quite clear that this imaginative and symbol-making capacity in man must not be confused with theological faith. But, because faith implies communication and language, the language of symbols is most appropriate in activating the deepest centers of decision which faith calls into play.

I would submit that the term "religious" no longer conveys the idea of an imaginative awareness of basic meaning. As D. H. Lawrence asserted, "It's not religious to be religious." And I would also say that the word "metaphysical" is not quite adequate to convey these values. There are other possibilities. One of them is the term *sapiential*.

Sapientia is the Latin word for "wisdom." And wisdom in the classic, as well as the biblical, tradition is something quite definite. It is the highest level of cognition. It goes beyond *scientia*, which is systematic knowledge, beyond *intellectus*, which is intuitive understanding. It has deeper penetration and wider range than either of these. It embraces the entire scope of man's life and all its meaning. It grasps the ultimate truths to which science and intuition only point. In ancient terms, it seeks the "ultimate causes," not simply efficient causes which make things happen, but the ultimate reasons why they happen and the ultimate values which their happening reveals to us. Wisdom is not only speculative, but also practical: that is to say, it is "lived." And unless one "lives" it, one cannot "have" it. It is not only speculative but creative. It is expressed in living signs and symbols. It proceeds, then, not merely from knowledge *about* ultimate values, but from an actual possession and awareness of these values as incorporated in one's own existence.

But *sapientia* is not inborn. True, the seeds of it are there, but they must be cultivated. Hence wisdom develops not by itself but in a hard discipline of traditional training, under the expert guidance of one who himself possesses it and who therefore is qualified to teach it. For wisdom cannot be learned from a book. It is acquired only in a living formation; and it is tested by the master himself in certain critical situations.

I might say at once that creative writing and imaginative criticism provide a privileged area for wisdom in the modern world. At times one feels they do so even more than current philosophy and theology. The literary and creative current of thought that has been enriched and stimulated by depth psychology, comparative religion, social anthropology, existentialism, and the renewal of classical, patristic, biblical, and mystical studies has brought in a sapiential harvest which is not to be despised. Let me mention some of the more obvious examples: T. S. Eliot both as critic and as poet, Boris Pasternak, St. John Perse, D. H. Lawrence,[4] and William Butler Yeats. Jacques Maritain's *Creative Intuition in Art and Poetry* illustrates what I mean, as do D. T. Suzuki's *Zen and Japanese Culture* and William Carlos Williams' *In the American Grain*. A great deal of what I call "sapiential" thinking has come out in studies of Melville and of the American novel in general, as well as in some of the recent Milton and Shakespeare criticism. I was fortunate to study in college under "sapiential" teachers like Mark Van Doren and Joseph Wood Krutch. In the classics Jane Harrison, Werner Jaeger, and F. M. Cornford have left us "sapiential" material.

The "wisdom" approach to man seeks to apprehend man's value and destiny in their global and even ultimate significance. Since fragmentation and objectivity do not suffice for this and since quantitative analysis will not serve, either, sapiential thought resorts to poetic myth and to religious or archetypal symbol. These must not be mistaken for *scientific* propositions. Symbols are not, here, ciphers pointing to hidden sources of information. They are not directed so much at the understanding and control of things as at man's own understanding of himself. They seek to help man liberate in himself life forces which are inhibited by dead social routine, by the ordinary involvement of the mind in trivial objects, by the conflicts of needs and of material interests on a limited level. Obviously, we do live in a world of things and institutions. We need to eat and to manage our everyday lives. But we also need an overall perspective to liberate us from enslavement to the immediate without taking us altogether outside the "real world." Sapiential awareness deepens our communion with the concrete: It is not an initiation into a world of abstractions and ideals. The poetic and contemplative awareness is sapiential —and it used to be, normally, religious. In fact, there is a relation between all "wisdoms." Greek wisdom was not out of harmony with that of the Bible. "Pythagoras and his disciples, and also Plato, followed that inward vision of theirs which was aimed at the truth, and this they did not without the help of God; and so in certain things they were in agreement with the words of the prophets."[5] So said Clement of Alexandria, hinting that all wisdom opened out upon true religion.

Wisdom, in any case, has two aspects. One is metaphysical and speculative, an apprehension of the radical structure of human life, an intellectual appreciation of man in his human potentialities and in their fruition. The other is moral, practical, and religious, an awareness of man's life as a task to be undertaken at great risk, in which tragic failure and creative transcendence are both possible. Another aspect of this moral and religious wisdom is a peculiar understanding of conflict, of the drama of human existence, and especially of the typical causes and signs of moral disaster. I might add that one of the characteristic qualities of this wisdom is that it goes beyond the conscious and systematic moral principles which may be embodied in an ethical doctrine and which guide our conscious activity. Wisdom also supposes a certain intuitive grasp of *unconscious motivations*, at least insofar as these are embodied in archetypes and symbolic configurations of the psyche.

Sapiential thinking has, as another of its characteristics, the capacity to bridge the cognitive gap between our minds and the realm of the transcendent and the unknown, so that without "understanding" what lies beyond the limit of human vision, we nevertheless enter into an intuitive affinity with it, or seem to experience some such affinity. At any rate, religious wisdoms often claim not only to teach us truths that are beyond rational knowledge but also to *initiate* us into higher states of awareness. Such forms of wisdom are called mystical. I do not pause here to discuss the validity of various claims to mystical wisdom. It is sufficient to say that certain types of wisdom do in fact lay claim to an awareness that goes beyond the aesthetic, moral, and liturgical levels and penetrates so far as to give the initiate a direct, though perhaps incommunicable, intuition of the ultimate values of life, of the Absolute Ground of life, or even of the invisible Godhead. Christian wisdom is essentially theological, Christological, and mystical. It implies a deepening of Christian faith to the point where faith becomes an experiential awareness of the realities and values of man's life in Christ and "in the Spirit" when he has been raised to divine sonship.

In this collection of essays only the last two raise the question of Christian wisdom in modern life. Robert Detweiler's study of Flannery O'Connor introduces us to the radically new character of a wisdom that is "from above" and is based on a Word which is an offense, breaking through the hierarchical orders of cosmic sapience and overturning every other form of knowledge in order to bring man into confrontation with a whole new kind of destiny, a destiny to freedom in Christ. (Flannery O'Connor well knew how to exploit the ironies of this shocking situation!) The essay by George A. Panichas, on the other hand, brings us into contact with the ancient contemplative tradition of the Eastern Church, which represents a much more peaceful approach to a Christian wisdom from which Hellenic elements have not been driven out. The story of the Russian Pilgrim that so impressed Salinger's Franny informs us of a sapiential technique first devised by the monks of Sinai and transmitted from there to Mount Athos and then to Rumania and Russia. The purpose of this elementary technique was to dispose the contemplative to a possibility of direct illumination by God in the *theoria* described by the Greek Fathers and further developed by Athonite hesychasm in the fourteenth century.

For my part, I am not concerned in this essay with specifically Christian wisdom. I want to discuss two examples of what I would call the natural sapiential outlook in Faulkner: in other words, two examples of a conscious and deliberate construction of myth in order to convey a sense of initiatory awakening into the deeper meaning of life in terms of a tradition of natural wisdom. In the two works I take as examples, *Go Down, Moses* and *The Wild Palms*, it seems to me that this sapiential use of myth and of symbolic narrative, culminating in a new awareness of the meaning of life in a historical situation, has to be appreciated and accepted if one is to understand what the author is trying to say.

Let me be clear about what I mean by "myth." A myth is a tale with an archetypal pattern capable of suggesting and of implying that man's life in the cosmos has a hidden meaning which can be sought and found by one who somehow religiously identifies his own life with that of the hero in the story. For example, the *Odyssey* shows life as a journey with many trials and perils typified by symbolic test-situations, a journey of return to one's home and one's place in the scheme of things. The ironic-epic journey of the tall convict on the flooded river in *The Wild Palms* is a mystical *navigation* of this kind, but other important mythical elements enter into it. The flood is indeed seen as an eschatological deluge. It is not only a mystical journey for the tall convict (whose name we never know and who is a kind of archetypal man), but also a parable of judgment and a revelation of the meaning or un-meaning of human destiny. But the journey of the convict is a spiritual one, and its goal is a deeper sense of his own identity and his own "vocation." What he finds is a more definite, and more ironic, certitude of his own measure and of his place in the world which, in this story, is absurd and void.

The part of *Go Down, Moses* that interests me most is, of course, "The Bear." There has been a great deal of exciting criticism written about this exploitation of the "Paradise theme" and the "Lost Wilderness,"[6] but I would add that the story of Ike McCaslin's novitiate and initiation in the wilderness life has to be seen in the context of the whole book, *Go Down, Moses*, since in fact Part IV of "The Bear" does not reveal its full meaning when "The Bear" is printed and read apart from the rest of the McCaslin story. The violation of the wilderness, symbolic of a certain predatory and ferocious attitude toward the natural world, is for Faulkner an especially Southern phenomenon here, because it is connected with slavery. Ike McCaslin's initiation, his "baptism in the forest,"[7] culminating in a "revelatory vision" followed by the death of the Bear and of Ike's spiritual "Father" and "Guru," Sam Fathers, leads to a religious decision, a monastic act of renunciation, by which Ike attempts to cleanse himself of the guilt that he believes to have become associated, like a classic "miasma," with the Southern earth. He renounces his ownership of land which, as he sees it, belongs to God and cannot be "owned" by anyone. But he finds that monastic poverty alone is not enough (note that he remains on his land but works as a carpenter, "like the Nazarene").

Poverty without chastity remains in some sense ambiguous and ineffective, as Ike's wife intuitively senses in the scene where she tries to bind him again, by erotic ecstasy and the generation of a child, to the earth he has tried to renounce. It is almost as if she has instinctively sensed the power of a counter-mysticism, another more elemental "wis-

dom," to cancel out the spiritual vision in the wilderness. And perhaps
she succeeds, for after this Ike McCaslin remains an ambiguous person-
age. At the end of Go Down, Moses (in "Delta Autumn") he reveals the
almost total loss of any prophetic charisma that might once have been
supposed his. We must not then forget that in spite of his initiation and
vision Ike McCaslin remains a failed saint and only half a monk.
(Speaking after twenty-five years in a monastery, I would like to add that
it is extraordinarily difficult for anyone to be more than that, and most of
us are not even that far along.)

However, it is the account of the spiritual initiation that seems to me
to be a particularly good, because evidently deliberate, use of the sapiential in Faulkner. It is clearly the story of a disciple being taught and
formed in a traditional and archaic wisdom by a charismatic spiritual
Father who is especially qualified for the task and who hands on not only
a set of skills or a body of knowledge, but a mastery of life, a certain way
of being aware, of being in touch not just with natural objects, with living
things, but with the cosmic spirit, with the wilderness itself regarded
almost as a supernatural being, a "person." Indeed, the Bear, Old Ben, is
treated as a quasi-transcendent being, like Sam Fathers and like Lion, the
fabulous brute of a hound that finally (when Old Ben has himself more
or less consented) brings the Bear down into death. It is as if the
wilderness spirit were somehow incarnated in Old Ben—as if he were a
wilderness god. The annual autumn hunting party of Major de Spain
becomes a more or less ritual performance in which Old Ben is ceremoni-
ously hunted; it is "the yearly pageant of Old Ben's furious immortality."
He is never seen and never expected to be caught, until the end comes for
the whole wilderness and Old Ben, we are led to believe, is ready to
surrender himself and the woods to the portentous ritual of desecration
that awaits them. This desecration signals the beginning of a new age, not
of gold or silver but of iron.

Thus the initiation of Ike McCaslin takes place precisely at a crucial
moment of religious history, a turning point when all that he has learned
and seen is to become obsolete. He will learn to be not only a wonderful
hunter but a contemplative and prophet, a wise man who has beheld the
real ground of mystery and value which is concealed in the Edenic
wilderness and which others can only guess at. But his skill and his vision
remain useless aristocratic luxuries. They are anachronisms in the modern
world, and he is helpless when, as an old man, he sees a young relative
getting involved in the ancient tragedy of miscegenation and injustice. He
has seen the inner meaning of the wilderness as an epiphany of the
cosmic mystery. He has encountered the Bear and had his "illumination."

In the light of this he has seen into the religious and historic mystery of the South which lies under judgment and under a curse. Yet there is nothing he can do about it, apart from his monastic gesture which remains ambiguous and abortive.

Worst of all, Ike McCaslin seems to have become oblivious of the one vital, indestructible force that remains in the world—the force of human love. "Old man," says the Negro mistress of Ike's nephew, "have you lived so long and forgotten so much that you don't remember anything you knew or felt or even heard about love?" The failure is typically monastic. Ike is concerned exclusively with the ritual handing on of General Compson's hunting horn, which belongs by right to the illegitimate son. Thus, there is after all a fruitful ambiguity in Faulkner's treatment of this wilderness-paradise wisdom which no longer has any real application in the world of our time, any more than the romantic gallantry of the Sartoris family has.

Nevertheless, the story of the boy's formation by Sam Fathers, his growing awareness of the Bear as spiritual reality and as "presence," his experience of the numinous mystery of the Bear as quasi-transcendent being, his decision to make the sacrifice which is necessary to see the Bear, and his consequent entering into a quasi-mystical relationship with the Bear: all this is told with an inspired mastery that betrays Faulkner's own enthusiasm, another evidence of "his strange religion." The story has Old Testament resonances characteristic of Faulkner everywhere, and the gradual ascent of the disciple to vision suggests the mystery cults of Greece; but what Faulkner actually celebrates is the primitive wisdom of the American Indian, the man who was *par excellence* the wilderness hunter and the free wanderer in the unspoiled garden of Paradise.

Countless mythical themes have been discovered in "The Bear." Everything is said to be there, from the Great Mother to the Holy Grail. There is no need to go into all that. I am primarily interested in Ike McCaslin's introduction to the wisdom of the wilderness and his initiation into it as spiritual mystery. This has the deepest possible resonances. It is not just a matter of knowledge or even of maturity. It is a question of *salvation*. This is not, of course, salvation and redemption in any Christian or theological sense, but rather a natural analogue of supernatural salvation: a man justifying his existence and liberating his soul from blindness and captivity by acquiring a deep and definitive understanding of his life's purpose and deciding to live in accordance with this understanding. This is not mere solipsism, but an illuminating and mysterious communion with cosmic reality explicated in mythical and symbolic terms. Though Ike becomes in the end ambiguous as a charis-

matic figure (and this is perhaps necessary because the wilderness itself,
which would be the very ground and source of his charism, has all but
vanished), there is no question, at least in my mind, that Faulkner
intended him to be one of "the saved."

This limited concept of salvation is not new, though it may seem so
to most of us who have forgotten the classic tradition. It is a humanistic
as well as basically a religious concept with an essentially ethical component, the same "old verities" which Faulkner said in his Nobel Prize
acceptance speech he had always been writing about: "The old verities
and truths of the heart, the universal truths lacking which any story is
ephemeral and doomed—love and honor and pity and pride and compassion and sacrifice." These Ike learns from Sam Fathers in the wilderness, along with humility and courage ("Be scared but don't be afraid.
. . . A bear or a deer has got to be scared of a coward the same as a brave
man has to be"). His wilderness life is essentially an education and a
spiritual formation: "The wilderness the old bear ran was his college,
and the old male bear himself . . . was his alma mater." The term "alma
mater" is not a mere cliché. It is to be taken seriously enough here (with
all its irony), for Ike is regenerated, twice born; he enters into a new life
because of the death of the Bear and of Sam Fathers. He becomes the
"child" and "heir" of the wilderness spirit which was in them and which
is passed on to him. (Note that there is another, less profound way of
participating in the wilderness spirit. To hunters, whisky—not women
—is a "condensation of the wild immortal spirit." This magic elixir is
also well known to have played a part in Faulkner's "étrange religion.")
This experience makes up not only an education but a spiritual and
religious formation—Ike's "novitiate to the true wilderness."

To understand fully this novitiate, we need to read "The Old
People," another section of Go Down, Moses, in which Sam Fathers is
shown introducing him into a kind of timeless contemporaneousness with
a largely vanished race. "Gradually to the boy those old times would cease
to be old times and would become a part of the boy's present, not only as
if they had happened yesterday but as if they were still happening and
more—as if some of them had not come into existence yet." This
extraordinary shift in consciousness makes Ike McCaslin aware that there
is a whole new dimension of being which is obscured by civilized assumptions and that in order to find himself truly he has to make an existential
leap into this mysterious other order, into the dimension of a primitive
wilderness experience. He will do so by "seeing" the Bear, an act of
initiation in which his own identity will be fully established.

The successive experiences of closer and closer awareness of the Bear are described almost like degrees of mystical elevation in which the Bear (acting not without a certain suggestion of spiritual initiative of his own) becomes more and more a real and finally almost a personal presence. The Bear is first experienced as an insurmountable void and absence, apprehended negatively in relation to the curious barking of the hysterically frightened hounds and then again in the silence created when a woodpecker suddenly stops drumming and then starts again. "There had been nothing except the solitude. . . ." The Bear has passed invisibly. Then Ike realizes that he is seen by the Bear without seeing anything himself. The Bear, he feels, now knows and recognizes him. In the end he resolves to go out into the woods without a gun and "prove" to the Bear that he is not an ordinary hunter. When this is not enough, he leaves his watch and compass hanging on a branch and lets himself get lost in the virgin forest. It is then that he finally sees the Bear in an instant of peaceful and Edenic revelation in which the Bear, incidentally, also brings him back to the place where his watch and compass are waiting. It is a description of the kind of "existential leap" which Kierkegaard demanded for any passage to a higher level of awareness or of existence. But what makes it possible for some critics to see the Bear as a symbol of Christ is the fact that in becoming *visible*, then *personal*, in manifesting himself to men, the Bear yields to a kind of weakness in his "supernatural" being, a kind of divine and *kenotic* flaw which will eventually make him vulnerable, destructible, mortal, and which will ultimately bring about his destruction. Hence I have no doubt that some will want to read "The Bear" as a fable of the death of God. Certainly there is good reason to see how Faulkner's myth *does* tell us something of the critical change in intellectual and spiritual climate, the irreversible mental revolution that has apparently made religious faith an impossibility for so many people. This could have been part of Faulkner's intention.

The wilderness-paradise in which Ike McCaslin receives his "baptism in the forest" is the archaic world of religious myth and traditional wisdom. Wisdom is perfectly at home in such a world. Initiation leads to a definite enlightenment which sets the seal of authenticity upon the communion of the initiate with the "gods" and "spirits" of the cosmic order which he now knows as a privileged and conscious participant. He has found his place in the hierarchy of being as a hunter who is worthy, who has earned his position by proving his respect and love for the other living beings in the forest, even those he must kill. In other words, the wisdom to which Ike McCaslin is initiated presupposes a traditional metaphysic, a structure which man can intuitively understand, which he can lovingly accept, and which is basically reasonable and right, with its own inner laws. The "wise man" knows these laws, knows the penalties for violating them, and knows how to avoid violating them. He lives in harmony with the world around him because he is in harmony with its spirits and with the Providence of God Who rules over it all. That Ike could pay homage to this underlying "will" by renouncing his property is, to him, a perfectly logical consequence of his enlightenment and a basically religious act of worship, though precisely *how* it has this religious character is not fully explained. Nor need it be. We know it to be more or less in the natural order, akin to the religious wisdom of primitive peoples and to classic stoicism. There may be biblical allusions here and there, but it is essentially a pre-Christian type of wisdom in an archaic and classic scheme of things which is supplanted as soon as Ike is initiated.

In *The Wild Palms* we are in a totally different world: the world of Pascal with its vast emptiness, its terrifying void, the world in which, in the words of Nietzsche's madman, someone has provided us with a sponge that has wiped away the horizon. This, in fact, is precisely the image we get in Faulkner's masterly description of the convicts arriving on the levee and seeing for the first time the vast expanse of the flooded Mississippi on which one of their number is about to be carried away on a helpless and fantastic odyssey. As J. Hillis Miller points out in the present volume, it is the world where God is not merely dead but murdered, and murdered not so much by willful malice as by a new mode of consciousness. The specific characteristic of this new consciousness, which if not *the* scientific consciousness is none the less *a* scientific consciousness, is that it excludes the kind of wisdom and initiation we have discovered in "The Bear." The wisdom of the Indian in the wilderness is a kind of knowledge by identification, an intersubjective knowledge, a communion in cosmic awareness and in nature. Faulkner has described it as a wisdom based on love: love for the wilderness and for its secret laws; love for the paradise mystery apprehended almost unconsciously in the forest; love for the "spirits" of the wilderness and of the cosmic parent (both Mother and Father) conceived as symbolically incarnate in the great Old Bear. But there is nothing of the kind in the new world. "This Anno Domini 1938," says Wilbourne in "The Wild Palms," "has no place in it for love." "If Jesus returned today we would have to crucify him quick in our own defense to justify and preserve the civilization we have worked and suffered and died shrieking and cursing in rage and impotence and terror for two thousand years to create and perfect in man's own image: if Venus returned she would be a soiled man in a subway lavatory with a palm full of French post-cards."

The new consciousness which isolates man in his own knowing mind and separates him from the world around him (which he does not know as it is in itself but only as it is in his mind) makes wisdom impossible because it severs the communion between subject and object, man and nature, upon which wisdom depends. In the new consciousness man is as radically cut off from the ground of his own being, which is also the ground of all being, as the struggling convict is cut off from a foothold on the solid earth of cottonfields by ten or fifteen feet of raging flood water.

Space does not permit us here to go fully into the problem of the person and society which is central in *The Wild Palms*. Faulkner faces a radical dilemma in modern life. Speaking of Sam Fathers and his wisdom in *Go Down, Moses*, Cass Edmonds says: "His blood . . . knew things that had been tamed out of our blood so long ago that we have not only forgotten them, *we have to live together in herds to protect ourselves from our own sources*" (my italics). But this does not imply that in order to return to vital contact with our own sources we need merely leave society. If people who have had the wisdom "tamed out of their blood" by civilization simply relinquish civilized society without being trained in the difficult work of recovering another wisdom, they will be as helpless as the convict in the flood and will be destroyed, in spite of themselves, like Charlotte and her lover.

But if the characters in *The Wild Palms* find themselves blind, helpless, and without wisdom, Faulkner, their creator, wants us to see them still from the point of view of classic tragedy and of an implicit wisdom. *The Wild Palms* is a mysterious pattern of fateful ironies which the characters themselves never see, or do not see until it is too late. Hence these characters remain starkly lonely and forlorn, struggling pitiably, full of determination and even of outrage, in a world they see to be absurd and against forces they cannot comprehend or manage in any way whatever, no matter how hard they try. The two "heroes," the lover Wilbourne and the tall convict, do end with a kind of dim and partially adequate illumination. But can we say that they have been initiated into wisdom, or that they have been reborn, or that they understand and fully accept their destinies? They do the best they can in their circumstances. Their best is not much. In one case it is a kind of comic return to a beginning which the convict never wanted to leave anyway—with an absurd bonus of ten more years of prison for "attempting to escape." In the other story the lover goes without resistance and without comment to the same prison, in a resignation that is not without nobility. In either case, the prison is the last refuge of provisional meaning in an otherwise meaningless world. And prison itself means little more than a place in which to "do time." The one thing this book has in common with "The Bear" is that the solution is ironically "monastic." The tall convict likes the peace and order of his secluded existence, and Wilbourne is determined at least to continue to exist and to grieve, rather than simply to let go and fall into total nothingness. To grieve, be it remembered, is the traditional function of the monk.

It is true that the saga of the tall convict, the story sometimes printed by itself as "Old Man," is able to stand apart from the other half of the novel, "The Wild Palms." But in actual fact the author's intention to play one against the other in counterpoint is not to be lightly dismissed. On the contrary, each section gains immensely in power when this counterpoint is perceived and appreciated. And it is precisely in the counterpoint of the two sections that the sapiential structure of the book is revealed.

It is true that the cosmos itself in *The Wild Palms* does not reveal a mysterious inner meaning. It remains a terrifying and inscrutable void speaking through its elements of water and air with no message that man can interpret. Yet man himself is still capable of giving his own life a meaning if he can grasp "the old verities" and be faithful to them. These "verities" are not arbitrary. One cannot simply select a value one feels to be appropriate and neglect everything else. Life is a balance of values and verities, and the true secret is in achieving wholeness and integrity. The two parts of *The Wild Palms* complete each other in a diptych which gives us the whole picture of man. Neither half is complete in itself. The wholeness of man is in the paradisal and integral union of man and woman, and in each half of the book one aspect of that union is sketched out. Charlotte and Wilbourne have erotic fulfillment, a passionately reciprocated love. The convict and the woman have no emotional relationship at all; in fact, they behave completely impersonally toward each other. They are pure archetypes. But what they do have is the complete moral responsibility toward each other and toward a basic truth of their relationship, which is almost entirely lacking in Charlotte and Wilbourne. It is almost as if the convict and the woman were the mystical embodiment of what was morally lacking in the two lovers, acting itself out on a mysterious transcendent plane. But there is a positive conclusion: Man does not necessarily have to be overwhelmed by the tragic forces which are let loose within him. There is an authentic and saving balance, an order and an integrity which he can discover and live by, in his right relation with woman; and this integrity is sapiential, in a sense salvific. It is centered on life, not on death. It is an affirmation of life, but an affirmation of a peculiar kind: "He that would save his life must lose it."

The saga of the convict with the nameless woman on the flooded river is a mythical and symbolic counterpart of the moral and psychological disaster of the lovers in "The Wild Palms." All the peril and evil are external to the man and the woman in the boat. Here we have an archetypal, larger than life, eschatological myth—the Deluge in fact— as commentary on the Judgment under which the lovers stand without knowing it at all because it is taking place within themselves. An explicit correspondence is suggested between the immanent will of Charlotte to seek an "absolute" love and the blind exterior force of the river that sweeps away the convict and the woman. As Wilbourne meets Charlotte on the train, which carries them away together, he is struck by her poise and by "that instinctive proficiency in and *rapport* for the mechanics of cohabitation even of innocent and unpractised women—that serene confidence in their amorous destinies like that of birds in their wings— that tranquil ruthless belief in an imminent deserved personal happiness which fledges them instantaneous and full-winged from the haven of respectability *into untried and supportive space where no shore is visible"* (my italics). Here, of course, the "supportive" element is air, not water. Maurice-Edgar Coindreau, the French translator and critic of Faulkner, has pointed out the evident balancing of mythical functions between "air" and "wind" in "The Wild Palms" and "water" in "Old Man."[8] But the sea as the mythical element of death plays an important part in "The Wild Palms" too. The lovers end like driftwood cast up on an evil-smelling, low-tide beach, helpless, exhausted, one of them about to die. They have been destroyed, in contrast with the completely unsinkable and indestructible pair in their rowboat, without oars on the worst flood in Mississippi history, who bounce off every danger unharmed and return to "normal life" with a healthy new-born baby.

In each story a man and a woman are more or less completely isolated from the rest of the world in situations that still somehow explicitly recall the paradise myth, though only in tragic or comic irony. For the convict, it is a daydream situation come true, and yet everything prevents him from taking advantage of it. First of all, the woman is pregnant. Besides, she repels him. Second, he has an obsessive sense of responsibility for her and for the boat which has been entrusted to him, and he still thinks he can rescue a man stranded on the roof of a cotton house and get back to the group of convicts with whom he belongs. As far as the woman is concerned, he wants only to get rid of her and the baby as soon as he decently and humanly can.

For the two lovers, Charlotte Rittenmeyer and Harry Wilbourne, there is also a daydream situation which has been made to come true by her determination (that determination which ultimately destroys her). Their love comes before everything else. Wilbourne cannot be persuaded to leave her even to save his own life. They live in order to make love together, alone, away from everyone else. They work only as much as is necessary to keep themselves alive and capable of making love. They intend explicitly to be *lovers* and not married people; hence they flee from any situation in which they find themselves settling down and living like secure and comfortable spouses. They accept absurd hardships in order to be left alone to their ritual erotic dream. Their life is consciously planned and patterned according to what one might call a certain level of wisdom, a certain understanding of man and of human destiny, in which sexual fulfillment is seen as the only real value worth living for. An erotic relationship between two passionately devoted partners then becomes an absolute, an end for which everything else can and should be sacrificed. There is nothing very esoteric about this "wisdom." It would probably be accepted as more or less axiomatic by a rather large proportion of Americans and Europeans today. You have one life to live; you might as well get as much out of it as you can. The best way to do this is to find someone with whom you really get on nicely in bed. And many would accept, in theory, the conclusion which these two carried out together in practice: you then spend as much time as humanly possible in bed together.

Wilbourne and Charlotte were able to do this because of her unwavering determination to sacrifice respectability, security, comfort, and all that is socially acceptable in order that they might give themselves with complete single-mindedness to their love. What remains a daydream for others became their life. Yet the blind force of cosmic tragedy bore down on them as the flood bore down on the convict and the woman in the drifting rowboat. Only here the force of tragedy was the destructive power of their own myth, or rather the inscrutable polarization set up between their personal myth and the trivial dreams which society has substituted for wisdom. Though they withdraw to a marginal life and try to construct for themselves a world of values which cannot be found in society, they do not succeed because it is not possible for man to get along without society. What is destructive is not their *eros*, but their determination to ignore an insoluble dilemma.

The judgment of Faulkner goes a little deeper than the general erotic daydream. "The Wild Palms" is neither homily nor casuistry. It is not a lesson in ethics. It is tragedy and myth, in a highly sophisticated artistic and sapiential pattern. The tragic death of Charlotte, as the result of an abortion which she forced her own lover to perform on her, is seen to be a consequence of the same passionate forces which drove her to run away and live with him. The seed of tragedy was present in the very nature of their love, in its psychology, in the strange disordered relationship between this willful, deeply erotic woman and the passive male she drew into a destructive and symbiotic relationship with herself.

Faulkner everywhere plays the deep, archaic, archetypal sapiential myths against the shallow and trifling mythology of modern society. This is explicit in "Old Man" where the convict realizes that he is in jail because he let himself be seduced and deceived by cheap crime stories. Wilbourne, at one point in his liaison with Charlotte, works by writing *True Confession* stories. He feeds daydreams to others and is aware of his bad faith in doing so. Yet he and Charlotte are dominated by the popular myth that when man and woman satisfy each other sexually, they have no problems. Everything is taken care of. This, as any analyst knows, is a gross oversimplification. But, for a vast number of people in the so-called civilized world, it is the most basic of all articles of faith. It is easy to confuse this superficial notion with the more profound mystique of sexuality which Vivian de Sola Pinto analyzes in his essay on D. H. Lawrence. But even in Lawrence's terms Charlotte, for all her sexual freedom, is "fallen" through willfulness and through the modern consciousness "into herself alone . . . a god-lost creature turning upon herself."

In "The Wild Palms" the love of Charlotte and Wilbourne is perfectly gratifying and in a sense happy. Yet their relationship is essentially destructive and death-oriented. From the beginning we are disturbed by the "bad smell," the classic miasma, which plays such an important symbolic part in their story and which is much more than unconscious guilt. It is the willfulness which is the direct result of that new consciousness which has isolated modern man from the world around him and from other human beings as an atom in the great void. The utter moral isolation of the modern character—Tillich and others would stress it as alienation, estrangement—leaves it no other way than to assert itself by pure will. In the void where there are no standards left (once one has broken away from the purely external and artificial ones imposed by society and which the characters of Victorian fiction could still take seriously) what is there left but to try to "get what you want"? But what do you want? How do you know what you want? You simply follow the incline down which you are already rolling. In other days one called it the "dominant passion," which you could accept or resist. But now who knows? Maybe it is your very identity which speaks, not just a tendency in you. When a person arbitrarily decides that a part of himself or herself is henceforth, for all practical purposes, *the whole self*, life will necessarily be lived destructively because of its radical bad faith. The power at work in Charlotte becomes as capricious, as arbitrary, and finally as devastating in its own order as the cosmic power of the flooding river. The tall convict saves himself and the woman by pitting all his strength against this power and by having miraculously good luck from beginning to end. Wilbourne has no strength to pit against anything, and his instinctive respect for love and for life that would have saved Charlotte is too weak to resist her will. He destroys her and in so doing destroys himself. Or rather, he completes the work of destruction which she has already made irreversible. Only in the end does he manage to salvage something from his own ruins by his refusal to escape or to commit suicide and by his determination to "grieve." Indeed, there finally emerges in him a kind of limited greatness, a tragic quietism, as if, sinking into his own nullity, he at last becomes united with the blind Tao of wind and finds in himself the acceptance of unbornness and unbeing which is for him his "salvation" and his entry into apophatic wisdom. Thus even Wilbourne is an "initiate" in a genuine traditional sense if we accept the idea that the devotee, as a Greek fragment says, is "not to learn but to suffer and to be made worthy by suffering."⁹ The power of the last section of "The Wild Palms," the eerie sound of wind in hospital and jail, makes it one of the most impressive things Faulkner ever wrote.

The wisdom of *The Wild Palms* is barely what one would call "religious" wisdom. The "gods" dealt with, if one could call them that, are malignant spirits, bent on destroying or at least frustrating man. The convict who wants nothing but to surrender to the police and get back to the prison farm which is "his place" is repeatedly thrust back, with all brutality and incomprehension, into the wild and hostile chaos of the flood. He feels himself to be up against "the old, primal, faithless manipulator of all the lust and folly and injustice," and his highest virtue consists in the cry of "final and irrevocable repudiation" of any such evil force. Here the "strange religion of Faulkner" becomes identical with the philosophy of Camus, his ethic of the absurd and of rebellion. But there is more to Faulkner's religion than this. It might be possible to interpret the voyage of the convict and the woman as a mythical "journey," like the medieval *Navigatio Brendani* with its visits to strange islands symbolizing spiritual states. The Indian mound where the baby is born is described as an "earthen Ark out of Genesis"; and its "cypress choked life-teeming constricted desolation," where the snakes respect the convict and

the woman and where nothing harms anything else, is a kind of eschatological paradise in reverse. But one would still have to stretch Faulkner's symbols a long way to find in this "deluge" an unquestionably
Christian meaning.

However, the wisdom of *The Wild Palms* and of *Go Down, Moses*
is not all of Faulkner, and it can be played in counterpoint to more
explicitly Christian themes in his other works. That exercise does not
concern us here. What matters is to show that a *sapiential* reading of
Faulkner's works is both possible and rewarding. Such a reading protects
the Christian against the temptation to claim Faulkner for the faith on
the basis of a mythical development like that in "The Bear." At the same
time it shows Faulkner's concern with the "old verities and truths of the
heart" which flow from his classic view of the world as endowed with
basic meaning and value. He embodies this view in symbols of a kind that
man has always spontaneously recognized to be "religious" in a sense that
is not confessional but sapiential.

What is the position of a believing Christian before the sick and
bewildering gnosticism of modern literature? First of all, while respecting
the truth and accuracy of his own religious belief, the Christian realizes
that today he lives in a world where most people find Christian doctrine
incomprehensible or irrelevant. Most modern literature speaks a language
that is neither Christian nor unchristian. It seeks to explore reality in
terms that are often symbolic, mythical, sapiential, vaguely religious. The
modern reader is intolerant of dogmatism, whether it be Christian,
Marxist, Behaviorist or any other; and he demands of the novelist, the
dramatist, and the poet that they seek their own kind of revelation. The
present book is a sympathetic and reasonable survey in which scholars of
varying beliefs and viewpoints have joined to explore this area in literature. Their studies show us that what we find in modern literature, when
we find any religious wisdom at all, is not a coherent intellectual view of
life but a creative effort to penetrate the meaning of man's suffering and
aspirations in symbols that are imaginatively authentic. If God does
appear in such symbols, we can expect to find Him expressed negatively
and obscurely rather than with the positive and rewarding effulgence that
we find in the poetry of other ages.

No sense can be made of modern literature if we are not willing to
accept the fact that we live in an age of doubt. But even in the midst of
this doubt we can find authentic assurances of hope and understanding,
provided that we are willing to tolerate theological discomfort. Derek
Stanford's quotation from Dylan Thomas sums up the casual but unim-
peachable sincerity of modern sapiential literature:

"These poems, with all their crudities, doubts, and confusions, are written for the love of Man and in praise of God, and I'd be a damn' fool if they weren't."

And many of our writers can be called, as Dylan Thomas is called in Stanford's essay, writers "of religious temperament nourished in a literary culture of doubt"; they make no commitments and they contrive to affirm and to deny the spirit at the same time.

Notes

[1] See the texts assembled by Roger Quilliot in Camus' *Théâtre, récits, nouvelles* (Paris, 1963), pp. 1855 ff.

[2] In his hope for a return of true tragedy Camus was influenced by the ideas of Antonin Artaud's manifestoes on "Le Théâtre de la cruauté." See Artaud, *Oeuvres complètes*, Tome IV (Paris, 1964), 101 ff. A reading of these helps us to appreciate what Camus saw in Faulkner.

[3] See Artaud, "Sur le théâtre balinais," *op. cit.*, 64 ff.

[4] Vivian de Sola Pinto's essay in the present volume brings this out well.

[5] *Stromata* V. 14. 116. 1.

[6] For example, R. W. B. Lewis, "The Hero in the New World: William Faulkner's 'The Bear,'" *The Kenyon Review*, XIII (1951), 458–474. This essay was reprinted in *Interpretations of American Literature*, ed. Charles Feidelson, Jr., and Paul Brodtkorb, Jr. (New York, 1959), pp. 332–348. For Lewis, "The Bear" is "Faulkner's first sustained venture towards the more hopeful liberated world after the Incarnation," a canticle celebrating the new life "not lacking in dimly seen miraculous events." He sees in Ike McCaslin's renunciation an intimation of "conscious Christ-likeness," and the wisdom of "The Bear" is " the transmutation of power into charity." It is true that there is a definite and perhaps intended Christ-likeness in Ike McCaslin; but it seems to me that the forces of "redemption" and "renewal" in "The Bear" are more on the order of a wilderness cult and identification with cosmic spirits than explicit Christianity.

[7] The words are those of an interviewer who admired Ike "because he underwent the baptism in the forest, because he rejected his inheri-

tance." Faulkner replied that rejecting one's inheritance was not enough: "He should have been more affirmative instead of just shunning people." Quoted in Michael Millgate, *The Achievement of William Faulkner* (London, 1966), p. 208.

[8] Maurice-Edgar Coindreau, "Préface aux *Palmiers sauvages*," *Les Temps modernes*, VII (janvier 1952), 1187–1196.

[9] Quoted in Hugo Rahner, *Greek Myths and Christian Mystery* (New York, 1963), p. 22.

Part I

THEORY AND AESTHETIC

"Point of View" in American
Literary Scholarship and Criticism

by

Hyatt H. Waggoner

THE PROPOSITION I INTEND TO DISCUSS AND, WITH CERTAIN QUALIFICATIONS, finally propose is that at the present juncture of affairs in American literary scholarship we want no more interpretations that depend for their interest primarily upon the point of view of the scholar-critic. Within this statement I mean to include all points of view insofar as they operate as guiding ideologies—Christian, naturalist-humanist, post-Marxist liberal, or whatever.

I was invited to contribute to this symposium not primarily, I can only suppose, because of my scholarly accomplishments, whatever they may amount to, but because my work is identified with a certain point of view, the Protestant Christian. Others in the volume will speak for and from within other points of view: the Catholic, the Jewish, the Orthodox, and perhaps others. It is gratifying, of course, to have been honored by being asked; but I cannot help feeling uneasy about the implications of being known as a "point-of-view" scholar.

Perhaps I will be pardoned, under the circumstances, for indulging in a little autobiography, in the hope both of throwing some light on what I have called my uneasiness and of developing, indirectly, the proposition I began with. When my first scholarly article, "Science in the Thought of Mark Twain," appeared in American Literature just under a quarter of a century ago, it was very warmly received by an eminent

scholar and damned by a well-known critic, specifically in the latter
instance for its point of view. Both the scholar and the critic at that time
were Marxists. My own point of view, so far as I was conscious of it, was
chiefly negative: that is, I was aware of myself as antimaterialist and
antimechanist, and thus as interpreting scientific philosophy differently
from the way my subject, Mark Twain, did (I had been influenced by
Whitehead and Bergson in college), but I held no very definite positive
beliefs. Certainly I had as yet come to no specific religious commitments.
Was it perhaps the fact that my point of view, so far as I had one, was
"antinaturalist," in the old-fashioned, pre-Whiteheadian, sense of "naturalist," that made my point of view unacceptable to the critic? Am I
wrong in thinking that of the two men, the one who held his Marxist
views lightly enough to approve of my article despite its non-Marxist
point of view was acting as the better scholar? (His name was Newton
Arvin, one of the great ones.)

Skipping some twenty-three years of repetitions of the negative half
of this incident, I shall mention the response of an eminent critic to one
of my latest efforts at careful and objective (yes, *objective*) scholarship.
Irving Howe, reviewing the recent *Hawthorne Centenary Essays*, which
in general he found dull and unnecessary, was kind enough to single out
my consideration of "Art and Belief" in Hawthorne for special mention,
along with several others, as being more interesting than the rest. I ought,
I suppose, to have been simply grateful for thus being noticed. But
gratitude was not what I felt: annoyance and depression, rather. For
these were the terms of Howe's praise: "Hyatt Waggoner's 'Art and
Belief' is an earnest and somewhat agonized reading of Hawthorne as a
Christian artist; and since Mr. Waggoner, though eager to claim Hawthorne for the faith, is equally honest in describing the difficulties of such
an enterprise, his piece becomes interesting for its revealed tension
between critic and subject."

If one were satisfied to be a "point-of-view" critic, content if one had
performed interestingly, this ought to be taken, I should suppose, as
sufficiently gratifying praise. But as I read it, the statement means that
what my piece says about the relations of art and belief in Hawthorne's
work is untrue, unsound, not revealing of anything about Hawthorne;
that my "point of view" unfits me to treat Hawthorne objectively; that
the "interest" in the piece is the interest one finds in a work of art, not
the kind of interest or profit one finds in a work of scholarship. I wish
Howe had had time and seen fit to say just which statements in the piece
are unverifiable and which conclusions do not follow from the evidence
available. I might then know whether he is objecting to what I say or

objecting to what he senses to be my point of view—Protestant Christian. If the former, we could then debate the specific differences; if the latter, then, of course, there is nothing more to be said. Only if he could show that my point of view, emerging in doctrinaire form, had biased my treatment of the evidence, making me overlook or suppress evidence contrary to my purposes and distort the evidence I treat, would my point of view be relevant to his assessment of the piece, so far as I can see.

The reason for this excursion into the personal, once again, is twofold: to explain why I am not happy when I find myself typed as "a scholar with a point of view" and to suggest why I opened this discussion by saying that I want no more "point-of-view" interpretations of American literature. Such interpretations are very likely to provoke the sort of assumption about motive that Howe makes. (I had not known that I was "eager" to claim Hawthorne or any other writer for the faith, but how can one deny his unconscious motivations?)

As I see it, good scholarship and good criticism equally—and they are not so distinct as has sometimes been supposed—demand humility on the part of the writer before his subject. Literary scholarship and criticism— to save time, I shall call them both just "scholarship" from now on—exist to serve literature, not the scholar and not some point of view extrinsic to the work being treated, not any point of view, including the Christian. It is not assimilating literary study to the exact sciences to say that the scholar must strive for objectivity, in the sense of transcending his own dearest beliefs if and when necessary. The more firmly he holds his beliefs as a private person, the more lightly he must hold them when he works as a scholar. A few years ago I would have thought it unnecessary to insist so much on what ought to be truisms, but I have the impression that in many quarters today they need to be emphasized.

I would suppose that any Christian—or Jew?—who held to his beliefs in an *essentialist* way might feel inclined to disagree with the argument I am trying to develop. If the Catholic—or whatever—view of life is true, he might say, as, of course, it is or I would not hold it, then is it a virtue to tolerate error or to forget the truth we know when we work as scholars? If some such question were asked me, I should have to reply that as far as Truth is concerned, I doubt that we—any of us—have any firm grasp on it, that while for the time being we must be content with little truths, we may hope to know more about Truth when we no longer see through a glass darkly but face to face; that believing that Christ is the Way, the Truth, and the Life does not in any way prejudice the answer to the question of whether, for instance, Hawthorne ought or ought not to be called a "Christian"; and finally, that to treat the faith as though it were an ideology (albeit the "true" one) is in fact to make it just one more competing ideology. I think we have had enough of ideologies for a while, for my time at least.

The religious scholar, as I see it, then, ought to pursue the truths of his immediate experience of literature, not being careful to avoid conflict between these truths and what he considers the Truth of the Faith. He ought to proceed with the confidence that the truths and the Truth will not ultimately conflict, even though he cannot see how the reconciliation is to be achieved. Another way of putting the same thing is to say that he must have faith enough to endure the anxiety of not knowing where he is going as he develops and grows in awareness of the truths offered him in his own experience. The impulse behind a doctrinaire attitude springs from the need for safety; which does not mean, of course, that we should all cease to hold whatever religious convictions have sprung from and justified themselves in our experience.

The great corrective influences in our tradition for the dogmatism of ideological scholars of whatever brand are Emerson and William James. Neo-orthodox Christians and secular humanists alike could learn from these two great spirits what they often need very badly to know. We shall, of course, continue to have our convictions, our points of view, even if they are only negative. We cannot escape them. But we might learn from Emerson and James to value openness and positively seek growth, too. Conviction and openness to new experience, new truth, must remain in some kind of balance if we are to be good scholars.

A decade or so ago there was a considerable output of "New Critical" interpretations of American literature, many of which were more or less clearly aligned with Christian points of view. Insofar as the point of view of these critics introduced a bias which prevented these critics from seeing the literary works they were examining in their fullness, an expectation which made them overemphasize some things and neglect others, "Christian criticism" has been justly rebuked in print by a number of scholars.

At present, in American literary studies, the trend seems to me to be the other way. Not only is "New Criticism" old hat, "neo-Christianity" as a governing point of view in criticism and scholarship is, too. Instead, two things now seem to me to be happening. On the one hand, the Higher Bibliography ("textual scholarship") attracts an increasing number of alert young men who sense the exhaustion of the critical impulse (for the time being, anyway) and need to find something to do that has not yet been done, if they are to make their reputations. This branch of literary study conceives of itself as a science; it intends to be value-free and completely objective, so that the point of view of the scholar will be totally irrelevant to the work he does. In part, certainly, this new Positivism in literary study springs from a recognition of the real subjectivity of the professedly "objective" methods of the New Critics.

The other current trend that I am aware of is made up of an increasing number of radical reinterpretations of standard authors from the point of view of naturalistic, or antireligious, humanism. The majority of such efforts that I am acquainted with I consider dubious scholarship and unsatisfactory criticism—and not, I like to think, simply because the point of view from which they are written is not mine. The naturalist-humanist point of view can have as warping an effect on scholarship as any other, if it is held as the Truth Revealed by Science. (Scientific philosophy has its fundamentalists, too.) Like any other point of view, it is more appropriate when applied to some subjects than to others. Whether it hinders or helps the scholar depends both on the way in which he holds it and on what subject he is treating.

But in general, it seems to me, the character of American literature is such that any point of view that may properly be described as tending to be positivistic and humanist in an antireligious sense is likely to hinder more than to help the scholar who wants to respond to and understand and evaluate justly the writers he studies. There is a persistent movement in our characteristic writers toward the metaphysical, which the humanist scholar may find difficult to deal with, perhaps even to understand.

Several years ago R. P. Blackmur wrote that most of our best poets belong to "the great wrestling tradition" of Western Christendom. As Jacob wrestled with the angel, so the poets wrestle "with God, with the self, with the conscience, and above all in our latter day with our behavior." Edward Taylor, Whitman, Dickinson, Eliot, Robert Lowell, Frost, and Stevens, all, according to Blackmur, "write poetry which *can be understood only if it is taken as religious*" (my italics). To which I should like to add, first, that the statement would be true of many more poets, especially in the nineteenth century, than are named here; and, second, that, with certain qualifications and exceptions, the same sort of statement could be made of many of our best prose writers.

A historian has recently made a statement on the subject that is at once narrower in the trait it ascribes to our literature and broader in the area to which the trait is applied. William G. McLoughlin, writing of "Pietism and the American Character," argues that pietist attitudes give our whole literature whatever uniqueness it has. He opens his discussion of what he considers the most important manifestation of our pietist temper by quoting Blackmur and borrowing from him the metaphor of spiritual wrestling. Then he has this to say:

> Our best poets and writers . . . are the ones who, like the Puritans, are not sure they are among the saved but who want desperately to establish some rapport with the absolute. . . . No doubt all great writers are fundamentally concerned with wrestlings, but I am convinced that this concern has been more pervasive and consistent in American literature than in that of any other culture in modern Christendom or post-Christendom. It is not just one theme of our literature, it is the theme. (*American Quarterly*, XVII [Summer 1965], 163–186)

Granted that attempts to define the uniqueness of a national character and a national literature always run the risk of ignoring too many exceptions or else of broadening the generalizations beyond the point of usefulness in an effort to include the recalcitrant exceptions, still it seems to me that Professor McLoughlin's statements cannot be easily dismissed. But I should like to put the matter a little differently, not for the sake of quarreling with the historian's analysis but simply of achieving a different focus. I shall return to Blackmur's word "religious" as including the attitudes and behavior McLoughlin relates to pietism but including other things besides. And I shall try to balance this inclusiveness by being as specific as possible about the writers to whom "religious" is intended to apply.

With very few exceptions our best writers, especially the poets, from the Puritans down through the first quarter of the present century, have written either from within the Protestant Christian tradition or against it. In either case, religious modes of thought and feeling have had an important, often decisive, part in their work. By the expression "from within," I mean that they have considered themselves to be speaking for, or interpreting or reinterpreting, their inherited faith. By the test of their own intention, that is to say, they are to be counted among the faithful. (Whether this makes them "orthodox" or not is beside the point. There is a good American tradition that every man is entitled to start his own church if he is dissatisfied—if necessary, a church with a membership of one.) By saying that other writers have written "against" their religious tradition, I wish to include two types: those who have opposed or combated their inherited faith, so that their own position is chiefly negative, and those who have defined their own positive faith, in part at least, by their opposition to the faith they equated with authority and convention.

Examples may give some substance to these generalizations. Emerson, Thoreau, Whitman (particularly in his early work), and Dickinson all belong in the second classification of those I have described as writing "against" the faith of the family or community. Religious experience and religious ideas are central and decisive in their work, so much so indeed that not to understand the "orthodoxy" they were reacting against and not to be responsive to the transcendental aspects of their own position is to fail to come to terms with their work. "They are religious—except me," Emily Dickinson wrote to Higginson; but the whole body of her work shows that she was using "religious" in *their* sense, her family's and Amherst's. *H*er religious experience and thought could not be fitted into the formulas of Trinitarian Congregationalism.

Mark Twain, in part of his work; Melville, with that part of his mind that carried on a quarrel with God; and Stephen Crane, in a good deal of his poetry and some of his stories—these would be examples of writers who wrote "against" in my first sense, the sense of primarily opposing or attacking the faith of the fathers. Perhaps Mark Twain is the only perfect example of the three, for Melville's work is surely not summed up by his quarrel with God, and Crane as often writes like an anti-Calvinist and an antiecclesiastic humanist as he does like one who ought to be called "antireligious." A writer who could blend the influences of Ambrose Bierce and Olive Schreiner is not easily typed.

Among those who wrote from "within" the faith, as they saw it, there are, after Edward Taylor, perhaps no really major writers until we come to Eliot. Hawthorne, as I have recently tried to show, was a special case, too ambiguously combining faith and doubt to serve as a clear example in an exercise in classification like the present one. Extended discussion would make it clear, perhaps, that he ought to be thought of as more "within" than not, but the matter is controversial, so I should prefer not to appear to be "claiming" him.

If there are few major writers who belong in the category I have called "within," there are, of course, many lesser figures. Whittier wrote as a Quaker; Holmes as a Unitarian; Cooper, Jewett, and Cather as Episcopalians. Still, it is clear enough that even among the minor figures, there are more who either ought to be called "against," in one sense or another, or else who are such doubtful cases that they resist any clear-cut classification. Longfellow and Lowell, for instance, were technically Unitarians, but Longfellow was so sad and Lowell so consumed by doubts that their private religious affiliations seem unimportant in their work.

I have not mentioned Poe because I am not sure what to do with him. Despite his concern with the "supernal," it is possible to read him as using religious ideas and emotions rather than being possessed by them. If so, his would be the ultimate sacrilege. There is, at any rate, not much in his work that a religious person in the Judeo-Christian tradition could take seriously as religiously meaningful. Henry James I have not mentioned, either, for a somewhat similar reason. He carried on Hawthorne's sense of the transcendent value of each self (Hawthorne's "sanctity of the human heart"), a value absolute and religiously grounded; but, at least until late in his life, he has always seemed to me one of the most secular of our writers, more so than his brother William, certainly. Though his stories often evoke religious associations, it is not clear that they ought to be interpreted in terms of religious ideas. In his very late essay on immortality, in which he rejected naturalistic conceptions of the self, he is not far from William's "Pragmatism and Religion" or from some of the ideas associated with William's conception of "radical empiricism"; and so he may be called "religious" to that extent. Still, stretching the word as far as this results in a loss of clarity, which I should like to avoid if possible. James strikes me as primarily a moral, rather than a religious, writer.

If that is so, he is an important exception, but still only an exception, to the statement that at least until quite recently, our writers have generally been positively religious (generally in an unconventional or "unorthodox" way) or negatively so, in the sense of being preoccupied with combating inherited religious ideas.

Emerson opens what strikes me as his greatest essay, "Circles," by saying that "the eye is the first circle" and then going on, in his third sentence, to quote a definition of God which he mistakenly (it would seem) attributes to Saint Augustine. God is a circle whose center is everywhere and whose circumference nowhere, he writes. Later in the essay he speaks of God as "the eternal generator of circles," which would add to God's immanence an element of transcendence. But it is the first definition that expresses Emerson's primary religious intuition. Doing so, it also expresses a feeling—one can hardly say a conviction—that characterizes the American religious consciousness, so far as it is unique.

For if God's center is everywhere, then He cannot be locked up as a "reserved sacrament"; He is not the property of specialists, the clergy; He is no more likely to be found in church than anywhere else—less likely, perhaps, if the church tries to *define* his circumference or limits. All experience is "sacramental" when properly "seen." If His circumference is "nowhere" (meaning not only not to be located in time and space but undefinable, ineffable, beyond our power to name and so to grasp and hold), then Whittier's idea that creeds are "husks" and Whitman's that all religions, regardless of their doctrinal differences, are really saying the same thing and that he could accept them all, would be justified by the nature of God.

This definition of God, which is the root idea of transcendentalism, was present in the thinking of the left wing of the Reformation. It implies "the dissidence of dissent." We need not think about it very long to see that its thrust is anti-institutional, voluntaristic, individualistic. "The priesthood of all believers" might be deduced from it. Exalting the individual's unmediated relation with God, it seems to imply just what Emerson thought it implied, that every individual is "in" God and God "in" him. The Revelation in the Bible is matched by the Revelation of Nature, perhaps indeed, as Emerson would have it, outdone by it.

Emerson had been influenced, in developing his transcendental doctrines, by reading and reading about George Fox, the Quaker mystic. Appropriately enough, the type of church—if there were to be a church— most clearly implied by the definition of God with which he opened "Circles" is that of the Society of Friends. Antinomianism could hardly concede more and remain itself. "Uriel," our greatest antinomian poem, concedes nothing at all.

The relevance of all this to the question I began with, of whether our writers lend themselves easily to interpretation in purely humanist terms, is this: the religious attitudes expressed in "Circles" and elsewhere by Emerson are those which characterize typical American religious experience. If this is so, then we are not far from Professor McLoughlin's contention that the pietist strain makes the American character unique. For pietism, radical Protestantism, and transcendentalism overlap, share many emphases. But because it would seem inappropriate and misleading to describe Emerson as either a pietist or a Protestant, since he did not profess to be a Christian, I have preferred to say just "religious," which carries no suggestion of sect.

And if the word chosen to describe typically American religious experience will not fit Emerson, I should like to avoid it; for Emerson is central, the fountainhead of the best and most characteristic American poetry of the nineteenth and early twentieth centuries. He is central both as representative man and as initiator, influence. He directly fathered Whitman and Dickinson, Robinson and Frost. Indirectly, he lies behind

Hart Crane, through Whitman. No other American poet is more relevant to us today, and perhaps no other thinker.

But Emerson, particularly in his early work, which is his most important, is profoundly religious. He was not exaggerating when he described transcendentalism as "a Saturnalia of Faith." Emerson in many ways anticipated Paul Tillich. He frequently reminds us of Eliot. His meanings and Hart Crane's are often the same. He often parallels the mysticism of Zen. He anticipates the openness to all religious experience of James' "radical empiricism." What he never sounds like is a "humanist," 1960's variety.

To the extent that there is validity in these speculations, it would seem to follow that a critical point of view that reduces everything to the "natural," the conditioned, the societal, as contrasted with the transcendental or religious, can be appropriately applied to only a minority of our writers, and those not the most typical. In a literature in which "Uriel," "Passage to India," "Faith Is the Pierless Bridge," "The Man Against the Sky," and "The Bridge" are typical poems, a point of view that finds the question "what is the meaning of human destiny?" in itself a meaningless question is not likely to enable the critic to do justice to our literature.

Examples at this point would surely do much to enliven, and I believe also to strengthen, my argument. I have a number of horrendous ones in mind, particularly in work that has been done recently on Hawthorne, Dickinson, and Frost. All three are deeply religious writers, though Frost, especially in the earlier part of his career, sometimes chose to disguise that fact, protectively; all three rejected institutional religion; all three were of a skeptical temper; all three wrote out of their faith, as well as out of their doubts. None can be understood by a critic who is blind to religious perspectives, or convinced that religious questions are meaningless, or determined to reduce all problems to the merely psychological.

It would be a trivial mind indeed that would arrive at a philosophic or religious point of view by considering what beliefs would be best suited to facilitate sympathetic understanding of most of the best American writers. But if one *had* to choose a position on that basis, one might well choose a "liberal" religious point of view simply as less likely to prove a crippling bias than a naturalist or humanist one. If I had to choose between the "New Critical," mythic, more or less neo-orthodox Christian kind of criticism that was so prominent a few years ago and the kind of humanist re-interpretation that seems to be coming to the fore today, I would still choose the older point of view and practice. I would choose it both for the reason that it would help me penetrate the meanings of the writers I work with and for another reason as well. Its tendency is to enhance its object, the literary work, whereas the tendency of the type of humanist criticism I am objecting to is to reduce its object.

To illustrate as specifically as possible without naming all the names, critics of Hawthorne of the former variety, including Fogle, Male, and the present writer, grant or even emphasize the psychological aspect of Hawthorne's fiction; but then they go on to show how myth, both classical and biblical, plays its part in that fiction, too, and how these mythic elements, seriously used by Hawthorne, enrich the meanings of his stories. A typical humanist reading takes a very different tack. It tells us, as a recent article did, for instance, of "Rappaccini's Daughter," that "except in a few moralizing lines that have a hollow ring" (to whom? why?), "we are never brought outside Giovanni's subjective plight," so that the story may not be said to have any religious meanings at all. "Here as elsewhere in Hawthorne," the writer concludes, "nothing whatever is asserted about the structure of the universe. For Hawthorne the problem of belief is psychological. . . ."

Note how this sort of humanist bias operates to rule out of consideration as evidence the narrator's comments on Giovanni's shallow empiricism and deficiency of character. The comments may sound "hollow" to this critic, but they did not sound hollow to Hawthorne: in his own person, outside his fiction, he made similar comments over and over. Are they not relevant to interpreting the story?

Note how the true statement about Hawthorne, made in effect by many traditional critics, to the effect that Hawthorne is chiefly interested, as a writer, in "belief as experienced" (the "psychological") gets twisted into the untrue one that "for Hawthorne the problem of belief is psychological." (Merely? Purely?)

Note how a doubtful reading of the story leads to a conclusion about Hawthorne that biographical evidence shows to be untrue to Hawthorne's conscious intention: the conclusion that "here as elsewhere in Hawthorne, nothing whatever is asserted about the structure of the universe." Have almost all of Hawthorne's critics in the past, except James, been simply wrong in seeing moral and religious, as well as psychological, meanings in his work?

As I said, if one had to choose between points of view. . . . But why should we have to choose? Let the scholar-critic hold whatever point of view he chooses to, or has to, to live and work by, but let him hold it lightly enough when he is at work, so that he can entertain opposing insights, take seriously feelings which are not his own, do justice to meanings which he does not, in his nonprofessional capacity, believe in. The scholar-critic who "re-interprets" everything he looks at to make it fit the shape of his own vision is not practicing an Emersonian subjectivistic self-reliance, though he may imagine he is. He is providing another, wholly unneeded, bit of evidence for the universality of what the orthodox call the fallen state of man.

Religion and Literature:
An Essay on Ways of Reading

by

Charles Moeller

Translated by Melvin Zimmerman

"LITERATURE DERIVES FROM THE SOUL AND IS DIRECTED TO THE SOUL," writes Charles Du Bos. "The subject of literature has always been man in the world," affirms Jean-Paul Sartre.[1] Confronted by these antithetical views, what should the stand of religion be?

On the side of the soul, the theologian would doubtless reply. The man in the street would probably agree with him, though with serious reservations. He would no doubt feel that the religious compass still points to the same North Pole, the point of inwardness and eternity, to the detriment of that oppressive, ambiguous, but daily reality in which nine-tenths of humanity spend their time. The question that Teilhard de Chardin asked Maurice Blondel as early as 1919 remains central: whether or not what nine-tenths of the human race do during nine-tenths of their time has any significance in respect to the Christian's professed hope for the Kingdom? Or, more broadly speaking, does human labor in the world have meaning in respect to religion—and not only through the religious intent that may inspire it?[2]

The man in the street is surely not mistaken in thinking that there is "religion" in the literature of "man in the world." That, in hypothetical form, is one of the main questions asked of self-proclaimed or would-be religious literature by twentieth-century man. It is equivalent to asserting that the "religion and literature" problem exists on a wider scale than has been assumed by a certain school of Christian humanism, which still ought not to be considered archaic. Rather than attempting to synthesize Du Bos and Sartre by "scholarly" reconciliation, showing how they complement each other within the framework of a fertile antinomy is a major task of the theologian who is concerned with literature, as well as of the writer who raises questions about the religious implications of his works. It is a question, not of the soul or the world, but of the soul and the world: the soul in the world. To be even more precise, it is a question of man in the world.

"All consciousness is consciousness of . . . ," says Husserl.[3] Man is a presence to the world; the world, a presence to man. Incessantly we create, we sketch, we outline, upon a backdrop of totality, the perspectives of our approach. "Neither with you, nor without you," the man in the world might say. Thus Paul Valéry's "Le Jeune Parque" knows that she will remain in a state of sterile purity, close to nothingness, as long as she does not wed the serpent. But she also knows that she will lose her purity and that undetermined potentiality of which it consists if she goes through with the nuptials.

If man is consciousness, open to the world—like an inclined plane that carries him outside himself toward the reality outside himself, as Sartre would say—he is at once immanence and transcendence, inwardness and outwardness. Du Bos thought that the main task of this century was the writing of a new De Anima, On the Soul. We would say that the main task is the writing of a De Homine, On Man. But man is simultaneously soul (inwardness, freedom, responsibility) and openness to the world—a world of matter, a world of others. God is the unconditional "you," calling out as much from within the self as from the apparent outwardness of the life of a man lost among others as he waits for the 7:49 bus at Saint-Germain-des-Prés.[4]

Until now it seems that "religion" has been more inclined to frequent the "serene temples of wisdom" which Lucretius speaks of, than the endless blocks of identical houses in London where Sartre saw "the human condition" conveyed better than in books, even the one bearing that title which Malraux published in 1933. But the time has come "to widen the brow of Pallas Athena,"[5] as well as to remind ourselves that there is a "hidden Christ"[6] in the world. Literature becomes increasingly the witness of one world and of the other.

In this perspective we must not only take an inventory of the explicit contents of literature, but at the same time compare them with the express affirmations of religion. We must also furnish a gloss of the implicit, uncover the secret sign, the watermark impressed into the pulp of the page, revealing the profound meaning. It is known, for instance, that Freud discovered the image of a swan or a vulture in a painting by Leonardo da Vinci. It is also known that after Freud came the abuse of this way of "reading" texts. Nevertheless, three complementary readings of a text are possible, especially when it is a matter of their relation to religion.

The first is the reading of the explicit text. In this sense there is a literature that is religious and another that is not. Claudel, Péguy, Julian Green, Bernanos, Graham Greene, and Heinrich Böll are "religious"; Camus, Sartre, Valéry, Broch, Thomas Wolfe, and Henry James are "nonreligious." In the beginning Gide was inspired by Christianity; he ended under the influence of positivistic atheism.

This approach is taken most frequently, it must be admitted. It is so "convenient"! Is it not perfectly clear to group the religious texts of India under the heading "littérature cléricale," as Étiemble did in the undeservedly famous *Encyclopédie de La Pleiade?* Once the sign is placed over the door, there is no danger of making a mistake: the consumers of "profane" literature will not go to the wrong wine cellar!

I do not say that this analysis is false, but only that it is incomplete. Faulkner is a case in point: Although "explicitly" a nonbeliever, he constantly uses, for example in *Requiem for a Nun*, a "religious" vocabulary borrowed from Christianity. It is enough to read the astonishing pages that prepare for the confession scene in the Governor's office, where, in a series of waves as in a new Flood, Faulkner evokes a kind of Genesis of the world, intermingled with that of the United States, symbolized by the creation and by sin.

I am well aware that this will prompt an objection: that every child whose mother tongue is English is twice baptized—first in the Bible and for a second time in the works of Shakespeare; and that the allusions cited do not go beyond the limits of an inevitable influence, a very literary one, all things considered. "All that is mere literature," Jean-Paul Sartre would say.

Doubtless. But I am convinced, if only by what Camus did with *Requiem for a Nun* in his French adaptation, that there is more here than mere literature. The same would hold true of works by Melville, by Robert Penn Warren, by Joyce. There is literature, fortunately, and of what genius, in Joyce; but there is also, and in equal measure, a profound, essential religious meaning woven into the very fabric of the works. The second way of reading them consists in uncovering their fundamental motivations in relation to the question of religion. It is now a matter of intuiting a "basic feeling of existence," what Max Scheler calls *Grund-gefühl*. This experience (*Erlebnis*) lies beyond consciousness; it subtly colors all sensations and decisions, all judgments.

Thus, beneath the religious denials of André Malraux, there is the primal experience of a threat, external and internal, in the face of which his characters have no other response than a "forward retreat" ("*fuite en avant*"). When Malraux corrects Heidegger's "*Der Mensch ist zum Tode*" by "*L'Homme est contre la mort*," when he sees the way of humanism as a challenge hurled against the absurd flux of history, as in the face of the very "drift of the nebulae," when in other words he imprints the stamp of human conscience into the consciousness of being mortal, he is elaborating a world-view much less than he appears to be. Rather, he is fleeing in a forward direction from the dread of death and madness which marks all his characters. That he could see in art, so conceived, "the money of the absolute," the only money that we can still hold on to after "the metamorphosis of the gods," is evidence of the presence of the religious problem beyond his explicit denials.

If the second approach is based on the experiences of literary heroes (or of their author when a work is autobiographical), the third is based on the work itself. But it is no longer a question of commentary on the explicit text, but rather of deciphering it, of reading it as a code, of finding a hidden meaning. To the degree that a literary work deserves the name, that is, to the extent that it transcends the projection of an atypical case or the demonstration of a thesis to attain some of the eternal symbols, it can lend itself to hermeneutics. Beyond its "words," whose deceit Sartre has demonstrated so well, true literature is the Word; it is Being calling out to man, as Heidegger puts it in his later writings. Paternity, guilt, and consolation are three themes that together bear witness to a vestigial memory, an oneirotic obsession of our childhood, and to the symbols of universal meaning in which we encounter some essential qualities of the religious problem.[7]

In *The Elder Statesman*, by T. S. Eliot, on another level than the amusing description of life in a provincial English nursing home, there is a retelling of the Greek myth of Oedipus at Colonus. Lord Claverton, at the end of his life, confesses his youthful follies to his daughter, Monica. In accordance with a very strong tendency in a part of English literature, we find here a repetition of the story of Oedipus, who, grown old, finds peace at Colonus through the mediation of his daughter, Antigone. But, on the third level of clarification, beyond the Greek myth, the Christian "myth" takes form: that of guilt, of paternity, which tries to purify itself in an avowal of its own weaknesses and finally achieves a glimpse of peace that passes all understanding.

In a way, this play is an answer, one that precedes the statement of the problem between Frantz von Gerlach and his father in Sartre's *Les Séquestrés d'Altona*. Here, apart from the brief moment when "the father" takes his guilt-ridden son in his arms, saying, "My poor little one"—a moment in which the infantile obsession of guilt is transcended —the final scene of the fifth act is a forward retreat, a "solution" that is not a solution, inasmuch as it becomes identified with a kind of second procreation of the son by the father, a kind of repetition of that unfulfilled life, that image without a future, in the bosom of the father and in the bosom of the death that they are going to seek together.

Whereas Eliot's work is "religious," Sartre's escapes for only an instant from the exhausting struggle against dreamlike memories, the fascinating images that paralyze Frantz.[8]

Reading the explicit, discovering the deep motivations, deciphering the religious symbols, whether present or absent (their very absence is significant): these three approaches are complementary, at the same time that each is autonomous. This point is essential, at least in literary scholarship.

As a matter of fact, it is possible that certain works are "religious" from all three approaches: for example, those of Péguy, as well as those of Bernanos and of Julian Green. It is likewise possible that a work is religious on only the explicit level, but much less so or not at all on the others. Claudel's works are religious on the level of explicit affirmation. I believe that they are much less religious on the level of fundamental motivation. In Claudel's heroes the commitment of faith coincides so perfectly with a solitary and powerful affirmation of individual will—it is enough to consider *Tête d'or*—that one is not always sure that the pure gold of the religious witness is unalloyed with ambiguity. On the level of symbols, Claudel's works show themselves to be even more problematical: a kind of exasperation from the secret omnipresence of male symbols and the quasi-absence of female symbols creates an opacity that becomes a screen. One need go no further in search of the reason for the annoyance that is felt by many "unbelievers" presented with the works of Claudel—masterly though they may be—as models of Christian poetry.[9]

On the other hand, certain works appear totally "nonreligious," like those of Camus. And so they are, on the explicit level and even on the level of fundamental motivations. But who does not see that the problems, so simple and so universal, of Tarrou in *La Peste*—to avoid the "plague," to be "a saint without God"—reappear in the "impenitent confession" of Clamence in *La Chute?* On the level of the basic symbols of guilt, judgment, and law, a deep religious meaning appears in this puzzling text. In the same way, too, the image of the mother in Camus' works, always a silent and benevolent presence linked with poverty and humility, gives to *L'Etranger, La Peste, Le Malentendu,* and *L'Envers et l'endroit* a human and religious resonance that goes far beyond explicit affirmations.[10]

Furthermore, it must be noted that an author is not always aware of the possible extensions of his works. I would even say that it is better for him not to be altogether aware of them. For it is precisely the presence of an experienced implicitness, transposed into symbols and myths, beyond the range of the explicit aims of the artist, which gives a religious resonance to a work. *Le Diable et le bon Dieu* seems to be the play by Sartre that is most "religious"—in an ironic sense, of course. Actually the margin of meaning beyond the explicit is extremely weak, if existent at all. On the other hand, Hugo in *Les Mains sales* and Sartre himself in *Les Mots* appear inaccessible on the explicit level, but infinitely "open" to a hermeneutics of the sacred, precisely because these two works go beyond their purely "exoteric" texts.

To be sure, each of the approaches remains autonomous in its domain. By this I mean that literary criticism as such, according to its concerns—chronology of texts, influences, construction of a work, etc.— must remain in the foreground of a critic's work. One can never dispense with it. Thus, the work of Joyce should be analyzed with all the resources of academic methodology. All the documents, in this case those that Richard Ellmann enumerates, should be kept in mind.[11] Similarly, the incomparable analyses based upon a mass of unpublished papers, such as those Jean Delay includes in *La Jeunesse d'André Gide,*[12] must never be neglected.

Indeed, such analyses do not take away one iota from the validity of other approaches, which are taken according to the criteria proper to themselves and which, of course, can never contradict the data of an analysis made on the level of the explicit. Concerning fundamental motivations, the most frequent, even obsessive, images are the ones to track down. Those of the mirror and the water—the first becoming the second—emphasize the sense of emptiness, the *vacio,* essential in Unamuno's works.[13] In Sartre's there are the images of carapaces and of stares; in Valéry's, of the black diamond and the serpent. For the symbols and myths that are latent, the reading ought to be altogether psychoanalytical, phenomenological, and existential. If it is subtle, it opens up astonishing perspectives.

I believe, for example, that a key to the works of Joyce is the breaking of the bond of paternity, rendered in *Ulysses* by Daedalus' search for a father (Daedalus being Joyce's double) and by Leopold Bloom's search for a son. But somewhere, in a time forgotten by the characters—if they ever did have any recollection of it, for here we are on the level of myth—the link of procreation has been broken. The break, moreover, coincides with a rejection of God. Thus, *Ulysses* is shown to be an odyssey that does not conclude with a return, even though for Joyce's characters the same things are always being renewed. It is precisely this ambiguous introversion of life, this unsuccessful attempt to give a linear sense to time, that is evident in the reverie of Molly, a Penelope of the atomic age.[14]

There is no question of justifying this reading, but merely of reminding the reader that he may very well accept or reject a religious interpretation of a work that is regarded as blasphemous, without diminishing the importance of the analysis of the work in its historical genesis and aesthetic structure. To put it another way, a religious reading of certain works does not short-circuit other readings. No criterion exists that might be imposed from without on a work to invalidate another approach to it. Here we see a literary application of a law governing the various approaches to reality: each considers man in his totality, but from a particular viewpoint, one limited to a given perspective.[15]

It is by now obvious that religious literature worthy of the name has nothing to do with didacticisms, a *fortiori* with moralizing. I do not claim that Paul Bourget's works—*L'Etape*, for example—are without artistic value. I simply believe that their artistic value lies elsewhere than in the moral and religious thesis that the novelist wishes to elaborate and even to prove. *Le Disciple* and *Le Démon de midi* possess merit through certain characters who are hard to forget; they are also impressive because of their power to evoke an intellectual and social milieu. The thesis of these books is worthy, and how essential it is to remember it; but the narrative appears more like a concrete illustration of a general truth than a universal symbol transcending particular situations.

Similarly, I am left quite unmoved by the hammering "demonstration" which D. H. Lawrence gives to his thesis in the third version of *Lady Chatterley's Lover*. This version, the crudest, is also the worst artistically, the least convincing, not because it is crude, but because the crudity is there only as "proof" of the author's thesis. Lady Chatterley appears as an abstract image, who would prove to herself that she is "living" by using words that the Victorian age disapproved of. Gudrun, however, in *Women in Love* is unforgettable. It is pointless to show that a constant tendency paralyzes Gudrun because, in the words of Lawrence, her sex is in her brain. Her characterization surpasses this diagnosis. Better yet, in *Sons and Lovers* Lawrence achieves some great symbols of the nonhuman world—the moon, the meadows, the river—and of the world of man, beginning with a primal one, the struggle between love of mother and love of woman. Works like these demonstrate nothing, fortunately, but they have infinite significance. I could never reread *Lady Chatterley's Lover*, but I have read *The Rainbow*, *Women in Love*, and *Sons and Lovers* three and four times.[16]

Obviously, we are beyond the problem of "literature and morals." Or rather, we are posing it in precise terms. Without repeating Gide's mot— "with fine sentiments one makes bad literature"—it is true that the works in which virtue is visibly rewarded and wickedness visibly punished are fastidious and false. This so-called morality does not appear in the Bible. It is built upon a discovery of the suffering of the just, whose ultimate image is the just man *par excellence*, Jesus, "the suffering servant," He whose "face had neither grace nor beauty," "for he bore our iniquities."

It is indeed necessary to point out that at present Christian novelists have almost reversed the terms of this problem! In the works of Graham Greene, for example, those who almost surely are damned are precisely those who never violate "the highway code." On the other hand, those who, like Scobie, appear to commit the worst sin of despair, suicide, seem to be surely on the road to salvation.

Doubtless my argument is a bit forced. But the essential here is a Copernican revolution, which is also a profound vision of the spiritual adventure. In the universe of a Bourget, a Bordeaux, a Bazin, the "Christian" is easily recognized by his behavior: He goes to Mass on Sunday, abstains from meat on Friday, has many children, etc. In a recent novel, *Boys and Girls Together*, by William Goldman, Ruth, one of the heroines, observes one day that her boy friend must be "a Catholic," because "he never touches me!" Too many "shocking" novels, coming out in great numbers these days, take the same view. All that is needed is to turn the tables, reverse the engines. The reverse of traditional morality makes for a "free," liberated novel, but one that is hardly better than the caricature which it would attack.

On the other hand, in the Christian literature that "is not for everyone's eyes," a Christian hardly recognizes himself. Whereas in Bourget the non-Christian immediately appears as "the bad driver" who violates the highway code,[17] in Julian Green the man going the wrong way down one-way streets would have the best chance of getting to Heaven.

It is obvious that excess in this direction would lead to a sort of new romanticism, a new version of the "prostitute with a pure heart" who moved Zola and before him Xavier de Montépin, with his unspeakable "bread-delivery girl." Nevertheless, the works of Bernanos, Green, Graham Greene, and Mauriac do set forth the mystery of the religious adventure. The old man of *Le Noeud de vipères* is in a sense closer to God than is his wife, Isa, who does not miss a Sunday after Pentecost but who is incapable of loving her husband. The priest who is not on the best terms with his bishop, who says to him one day, "You are kind," pierces the secret of this withdrawn man better than the docile ones do, they who among themselves refer to him as "the old crocodile," because of a resemblance that makes the nickname justifiable.[18] In the same way Temple Drake, the "perverse" girl of *Sanctuary* who lets a madman rape her, appears in *Requiem for a Nun* as a Lady Macbeth who can no longer sleep because of a certain small spot that all the perfumes of Arabia would never wash away; she is also a sinner who needs to "tell" her sin to somebody, who must hear from the lips of Nancy, a Negro who bears "the redemption of the white man," that somewhere there must be a place where children do not remember "even these hands that have smothered them."[19]

All this may not be reading matter for boarding-school pupils—if there are still any left—I do not disagree with that. But the subject of this inquiry is of another kind; artistically, metaphysically, and religiously. We are concerned with truly artistic works; we are concerned (at least I hope so) with an approach toward what appears to have to be the true religion: a dialogue, a summoning of the "I" by a sovereign "you" who does not appear as a means, a mere presence, that fills the gaps in our terrestrial knowledge. God is not a criterion of truth but a guarantee; He is not *given* but *giving*; He is not an alibi. If He is the necessary requirement of the absolute, He is still more "the absolute of a necessary requirement."[20] He is the judge and the father, but He also gives back life, renews it, as He does deep within the works of Kafka, that secular Moses, who points to a promised land which he himself never enters.[21]

If, going beyond the previous considerations, one asks oneself about the peculiarly *Christian* contribution to literature, I would say that it is found chiefly on the level of the meaning given to space and time. They must appear "open," like the progression of a birth and a maturation, always reaching a point at which the past attains awareness of itself in the present and is capable of being reassumed and projected into a future of hope.

The "new novel," by the spatio-temporal equations within which it encloses its characters and their adventures, implies a cycle. Time is somehow clogged up, turned back upon itself. Caught up in a space at present, in a here-and-now, not in the dimensions discovered by Einstein and Lemaître of an expanding universe but according to "the appearances" of continuously going back, time becomes enclosed. It becomes the site of a captivity, of an eternal return. One need only name *L'Année dernière à Marienbad* by Robbe-Grillet—Alain Resnais to grasp this imprisonment within a closed universe, a product of recommencement or noncommencement—perhaps nothing happened last year, perhaps there has been no last year—in the depths of a kind of nightmare rendered by a series of stills.

A cyclical vision is already present in Joyce. But in Joyce the vision of space and time remains problematical, enigmatic, dependent upon the break of the link of procreation. On the other hand, one need only read Marguerite Duras' *Moderato cantabile* to grasp a cyclical structure: there is a week in which the same events are repeated; the week opens with a yearly remembrance which will be relived; then, in a last sequence, which dilates the prison without opening it, beyond that year the other loves, identical yet different, which other women have had in the same room, take shape—all as in a play of mirrors.

It is clear that these characters are "in bondage under the elements of the world," as Saint Paul puts it. On the other hand, in the Marguerite Duras–Alain Resnais novel and film, *Hiroshima mon amour*, we watch a Frenchwoman's efforts to recapture the past. Her past of delight and guilt—her love for a German in wartime Nevers—comes back to her, evoked by her meeting a Japanese in Hiroshima. One then follows, with growing emotion, a reconstruction of memory. Through her confessions to the Japanese in the bar on the banks of the Ota estuary, the Frenchwoman evokes a sort of ectoplasm that is simultaneously the German whom she loved and who is dead, as her love is dead, and the Japanese, who is living but also dead, for she loves him only through her memory of her dead love. Instead of this memory's being assumed freely and knowingly; instead of its becoming an acceptance of death and of the limitations of time and space; and, so assumed, instead of its being regenerated in an undertaking that would impel the heroine into the future, toward hope, we see at the end of the film—as of the text—that oblivion again descends upon her. Memory becomes synonymous with oblivion, with a cutting off of the past, a repression of the past into the world of subliminal consciousness, into the archaic domain of pleasure and of guilt.[22]

"Hope is the same as reminiscence," says Ricoeur.[23] "Hope is the memory of the future," says Marcel.[24] Truly, it is. Not only psychology attests to this fact. Reminiscence, when it is open and searching, does not paralyze us; on the contrary, it opens to us a future that no longer appears to be a sterile repetition of the past. The Christian perspective postulates these truths. It announces hope. It is hope. Thus it speaks to us of our "past" of delight and of sin, hinging on original sin, only when it announces salvation in Jesus Christ. In other words, Christianity clarifies for us the meaning of the past, unveils its meaning in the midst of the present, which is rich with a coming revelation.

A literary work which gives a meaning to time, which sees in time something other than the occasion for monotonous repetition, is deeply Christian, even if it is otherwise "areligious," or even "amoral." Doubtless the ambivalence of symbols will always be with us. Time in this life is inexorably the occasion of a fascination—that of the eternal return; it is also the occasion of a summoning, of the Word, which disencumbers us, frees us from mediumistic conjuration, in order to impel us toward a creative future. It is at once the occasion of a *nekuya*, an evocation of the dead, of a "mediumistic objectification," and of a reminiscence, an invocation, a mediation, and a presence.[25]

Is it not evident that in this light the work of Proust appears deeply religious and even Christian? In Proust time indeed shows itself capable of being "found again," relived; it appears as the occasion of a moral, even religious, summoning, as in the famous scene of the "intermittences of the heart," in which memory and dream unite to bring the narrator back to a sense of the presence of his grandmother and to a feeling of remorse, for he knows that while she lived he did not do for her what she wished, namely, that he recognize her as a "you," requiring unconditional acceptance and giving.[26]

This paradoxical approach to Christianity permits us to return to the question with which this essay began. "The soul or the world?" we were asking. "The soul and the world," I proposed. Such is the answer. If, in Christian works time and space have meaning in the fundamental sense that I have spoken of—and therein lies the essential contribution of the Christian faith: to give meaning to human history in Christ risen, Lord of history, Savior of the world—if it is precisely in this that their Christian inspiration resides on an infinitely more essential level than all the explicit professions of faith, it is evident that the dilemma between, on the one hand, "inwardness, soul, contemplation, wisdom" and, on the other hand, "outwardness, action, commitment" in a historical process is a false dilemma. It is overcome, assumed, by the vision of the Christian sense of history. In fact, both the adventure of an individual and his participation in the history of salvation, or rather in salvation within history, come together here.

Again Claudel's works—and I am using those "Christian" works as a test, as a slightly scandalous test but one that will give rise to reflection— are only sometimes and partially Christian. In fact, Claudel never grasped the temporal, the historical dimension of the Christian revelation in the Bible. For him everything existed at the same time, in a kind of "octave of creation." His thought was much more influenced by the simultaneity of the Chinese cosmological view than by the biblical hope in the midst of a duration assumed by God, Who had "entered history." To be sure, this remark concerns the explicit aspect of the works. Fortunately, Claudel was also a poet of genius; and very often, surpassing his theories, he created some fundamental religious symbols. But I would call them more religious than Christian.[27]

If time and space are thus "saved," a Christian work will instinctively go beyond the destructive dualism that has often been a substitute for the true vision of man. In this connection, too, Péguy appears the most Christian of writers. But Proust can lead the way to a true vision by making a kind of evangelical preparation that Claudel, deeply impressed by the dualism of the Tristram and Iseult myth, never perceived.

Obviously, the complete Christian work would combine inwardness and outwardness. Does this work exist? It does fragmentarily: in Dante, especially in his *Paradiso*; in Cervantes' *Don Quixote*; in Shakespeare, embodied in characters like Richard II and Falstaff; in Dostoevsky, the Shakespeare of the novel; and lastly in Péguy. I have named only the greatest.

A word will conclude—my opening word. An essay like this is intended to show that religion in this context is universal and human, a confluence, and that Christianity is the ecumenical confluence among Christians, for its literary influence is revealed over and above the boundaries drawn by denominations. For me literature is religious and Christian when it is not just "words," but the circumstances of the Word, which summons us, like that word in *Varouna* which follows the chain of destiny and finally gives the key to the "*éternel retour*" of death and suffering by fastening them to the Cross that makes time unfold and the past give occasion for hope.[28]

Notes

[1] Charles Du Bos, "La Littérature et le spirituel," in *Approximations* (Paris, 1965), p. 1419. Jean-Paul Sartre, "Qu'est-ce que la littérature?" in *Situations*, II (Paris, 1948), 194.

[2] This Teilhard-Blondel dossier is available in *Archives de philosophie* (1961). Cf. Henri de Lubac, *La Pensée religieuse de Père Teilhard de Chardin* (Paris, 1962).

[3] Jean-Paul Sartre gave a suggestive commentary on this aphorism in *Situations*, I (Paris, 1947), 31–36.

[4] Jean-Paul Sartre, *Critique de la raison dialectique*, I (Paris, 1960), 308 ff.

[5] René Grousset, *Bilan de l'histoire* (Paris, 1946), concludes his first chapter in this fashion.

[6] Paul Tillich, *Christianity and the Encounter of the World Religions* (New York, 1963); one finds this idea at the center of this work.

[7] Paul Ricoeur, *De l'interprétation: Essai sur Freud* (Paris, 1965), pp. 521 ff.

[8] Cf. Charles Moeller, *L'Homme moderne devant le salut* (Paris, 1965), pp. 73 ff. and pp. 135 ff.

[9] Paul-André Lesort, *Paul Claudel, par lui-même*, Ecrivains de toujours, 63 (Paris, 1963), admirably demonstrates this point.

[10] Charles Moeller, *Littérature du XXe siècle et christianisme*, 10th ed., I (Tournai, 1964), 25–116, attempts to show the work of Camus within this perspective.

[11] Richard Ellmann, *James Joyce* (New York, 1959).

[12] Jean Delay, *La Jeunesse d'André Gide*, 2 vols. (Paris, 1956–57).

[13] Charles Moeller, *Textos inéditos de Unamuno* (Cartagena, 1965).

[14] Jean Paris, *James Joyce, par lui-même*, Ecrivains de toujours, 39 (Paris, 1957), makes this point.

[15] I have tried to make this point in "Religion and the Importance of the Humanist Approach," in *Religion and the University* (Toronto, 1964), pp. 65–111. Cf. *Truth and Freedom*, Duquesne Studies, Philosophical Series, 5 (Pittsburgh, 1954).

[16] Martin Jarrett-Kerr, C. R., *D. H. Lawrence and Human Existence* (London, 1951). I am planning to publish a similar study in Vol. V of *Littérature du XXe siècle et christianisme*.

[17] The expression is by André Blanchet, *La Littérature et le spirituel*, I (Paris, 1959).

[18] Moeller, *L'Homme moderne* . . . , pp. 116–121.

[19] Maurice-Edgar Coindreau, *Aperçus de littérature américaine* (Paris, 1946), pp. 111–147.

[20] Jean Lacroix, *Le Sens de l'athéisme moderne* (Tournai, 1958), pp. 55–66.

[21] Charles Moeller, "Franz Kafka et le terre promise sans espérance," in *Littérature du XXe siècle et christianisme*, 6th ed. (Tournai, 1963), pp. 195–320.

[22] Charles Moeller, "Le Temps et la mémoire dans *Hiroshima mon amour* de Marguerite Duras," to appear in *Mélanges in memoriam Charles de Koninck* (Québec, Presses de l'Université Laval).

[23] Paul Ricoeur, *Finitude et culpabilité* (Paris, 1960), pp. 218–243.

[24] Gabriel Marcel, "Essai d'une phénoménologie de l'espérance," in *Homo Viator* (Paris, 1944), pp. 39–95.

[25] *Hiroshima mon amour* appears to be a typical work in the sense of a "psychoanalysis" that is inconclusive.

[26] Marcel Proust, *A la recherche du temps perdu,* La Pléiade ed., II (Paris, 1961), 755 ff.

[27] Cf. Lesort, *supra,* n. 9.

[28] The novel Varouna, by Julian Green, reveals this Christian profundity.

A Question: What Does One Mean
by "Religious Literature"?

by

Thomas L. Hanna

QUITE CONCEIVABLY IN BELLES-LETTRES A LIVELY DISCUSSION OF SOME
topic might proceed for years, for decades, perhaps even for centuries
without anyone's being moved to ask whether the topic in question had
ever been clearly defined by its discussants. As a philosopher, I would be
foolhardy to suggest that this eventuality might take place only among
literary heads: it might, quite possibly, occur even among philosophers.
But this is not the task at hand. What is at hand is the duty of a
philosopher who has always had an interest in literary matters—and has
taken a particular interest in the discussions of religious literature—to
enter crudely into this lively discussion of religious literature and intrude
the tiresome question, "Can one legitimately say that there is such a
thing as religious literature, and, if so, precisely what is it that we are
indicating by this term?"

It is clear that this question can be asked with varied motivations,
not the least likely of which would be the possibility that contemporary
tools of analytic philosophy are being readied to reduce the term "religious literature" to the ashes of "meaninglessness" and perhaps throwing
in, for extra measure, the melancholic assertion that literature in general
largely shares this character of nonsignification. This is not the motivation here: the shiny cutlery of English and Austrian manufacture never
seems of much help in literary matters; such tools seem inescapably

destined not to elucidate literary matters but to defend against them. Instead, a relaxed and less stringent logic is much more in order, and it is just such a pedestrian inquiry which will now take place, seeking some lucidity through the search for logical consistency in the use of the term religious literature and setting this against such literary evidence as seems to justify this term.

Is there literature which is "religious"? If we think so, then this means that there is also literature which is nonreligious, unreligious, or perhaps antireligious; and it also implies that we are amply clear in our minds as to what nonreligious literature consists of. This appears a fateful distinction, and one would need to proceed cautiously in an enterprise which, categorically, splits literature in twain.

Or perhaps by religious literature we do not imply a species of literature distinct from a nonreligious species, but rather something quite different: an honorific term, denoting a level of literary achievement where literature truly fulfills itself in greatness, setting itself above that which is less than this fulfillment. In this sense, religious literature would be that which is "great," "serious," "classic," "the best," and nonreligious literature would be something less than these valuations.

Still, the expression religious literature could quite simply point to those literary pieces which overtly deal with religious topics, symbols, or personages, in which case the matter is simple and the use of the expression unquestionable. For in this case we have to do with a historical typology, and we could satisfy even the most obstreperous analytical philosopher by pointing out the presence of such topics as sin and redemption, such symbols as the cross or the dove, such personages as Luther or Thomas à Becket. But, however simple this might make matters, this also—according to the needs for thoroughness and preciseness—obliges one to make extensive tours through the myriad sub-branches of this same historical typology by pointing out that some religious literature is Methodist, some Jewish, some Mahayana Buddhist, some Abyssinian Baptist, etc.

Which, then, do we mean when we say religious literature? An autonomous structured category, an upper gradation of value, or an objective historical typology? Consider the last possibility: an objective historical typology. Even though this simplifies the problem, of what use is the term? Precious little, one must answer. If religious literature denotes those literary pieces which present to us clearly recognizable topics, symbols, or personages relating to some religious tradition or organization, then the term is not employable in belles-lettres per se but is purely an historically oriented term. It is historical because its very use involves pointing away *from* the literary piece itself in its own autonomy and pointing *to* matters of historical documentation. That is, if literary persons mean no more by religious literature than an objectively ascertainable historical type, then they are granting themselves a rather tedious and pointless exercise in historical classification. One need only set up the descriptive characterizations of each of the many branches of this religious type, and then the job is finished: simply run any literary work through the typology and automatically we will have it classified as to type. But besides providing an expenditure of time, such a procedure seems to have quite limited worth. One might well classify literature as to its implied philosophical position, or whether it is urban/agrarian, or has a hero or a heroine, or takes place on high ground or low ground, or in spring, summer, autumn, or winter. There are any number of computer classifications that can be run on literature according to objective classifications, and they all will have varying low-level interests; but does one have any literary purpose for doing so? Likely not: the double-sided reason being that not only is this a pointless historical exercise but also it is not a literary exercise—that is, it treats literature not as literature but as an aspect of history.

It is, then, evident that literature can be spoken of as religious in this obvious manner, and, for the amateur as well as a great many specialists in literary affairs, this is the ingenuous and immediate way in which this term is understood. The most natural of all reflexes is to reduce literature to something else, that is, something of personal or practical or historical familiarity, and by this reduction one is able to use literature for perhaps interesting purposes. This is natural, because any experience, such as the enjoyment of literature, which we have lived through with some intensity is an experience which, in reflection later, we attempt to profit from by relating it to the rest of our personal gamut of life experiences; and literature, as an artifact of human experience which one vicariously enjoys, is prey to this same understandable human reaction. But literature, as an artifact of life, is unique in that it is life lived according to possibilities which, taken together, are other than life as any of us has actually experienced in his own person. The ordering of its structural possibilities is different from any one person's life, and it is this difference which is the uniqueness of literature and its interest. It is the recognition of this uniqueness that lies behind the insistence in belles-lettres that literature is autonomous and self-justifying. And, because it is an autonomous artifact of life, it is to be *enjoyed* and not *used* or *reduced*. It cannot be legitimately used for the very good reason that it does not lend itself to a direct relation to one's personal and practical interests in the same way that raw personal experience does. It cannot be used or reduced, for this is to treat an artifact of life as if it were actual personal experience of life. Thus, to state the matter once more, if literature is considered to be religious in terms of objective historical comparisons, one has, by virtue of this viewpoint, left off dealing with literature; one has forsaken it, forgetting the very uniqueness which it represents for us. Religious literature as a typology? Yes, one can pursue this route, but to do so is to engage in matters of religious history, and rather barren ones at that.

To ascertain whether there is religious literature and *what* religious literature is, we are, then, forced to think of this term either as a category of literature or as an honorific valuation of certain types of literature—that is, in terms of distinctions which are, if you will, respectively horizontal or vertical. Either of these possibilities is promising because they both suggest a focus upon something in the literary piece itself and not upon its presumed relation to something extraliterary.

Then what about this vertical distinction which is qualitative in nature? Among those interested in what is termed religious literature, there are many who gravitate toward this viewpoint. They perforce feel that truly great literature, literature that has fully and triumphantly fulfilled its possibilities of creating an impressive artifact of life, is by the same token a literature which has religious dimensions, which has tapped some religious source simply by virtue of the magnitude and density of its literary fulfillment. This is a viewpoint which somehow espies a direct relation between the ultimate aims of literature and the ultimate apprehension of reality which is called religious. Indeed, this attitude is possible only with just that prior assumption: that the implicit purpose of literature and the fulfillment toward which it fitfully strives are the creation of an artifact of life which transparently incarnates that which is held to be the religious dimensions of life in this universe.

To term this a vertical conception of religious literature is not, it would appear, a misnomer, for even if such literature is not exactly thought of as moving heavenward, it certainly is felt to embrace those highest values and ultimate insights toward which the religious man believes he must strive or leap. There is no doubt that this conception of religious literature can be argued in a highly sophisticated manner, but, whatever the discursive level of this conception, there is equally no doubt that it rests upon the simple belief that "If it's really good, it's got to be religious."

For the religious man, such a belief and such a conception of religious literature is, in a great number of cases, inevitable. It is natural for the literary amateur to use his literary experience for other and extraliterary purposes; it is also natural for the religious man to hold that the ultimate fulfillment of literature is the literary representation of the ultimate religious dimensions of life as he, the religious man, sees them. This is the equation of religious assertions about reality with literary representations of reality, and the rationale behind this equation has considerable persuasiveness. The rationale would be something like this: "Through the eyes of my faith, I know or feel—as far as man is permitted to know or feel—the ultimate nature and destiny of men's lives in this universe, even though this is a vision of faith and not something encountered in human history; and inasmuch as literature is the occasion in which men fashion artifacts of particular human history in this universe, I am able to recognize truly great works of literature to the extent that they embody in their artificial reality that ultimate vision of man's nature and destiny which I otherwise see only through the eyes of faith." The rationale of this equation is persuasive not alone because it engagingly relates the dimensions of religious life to the dimensions of the literary depiction of life, but also because it entails a conception of literature which respects not only its scope and autonomy but also its immediate value as something to be enjoyed per se. Ideally, such a man would find his life and faith affirmed and reinforced by the vicarious experience of great literature.

With this much said, we must admit that the question before us is a sticky one. Is there a work of literature which is, while being a depiction of a specific human situation or destiny, at the same time a depiction of the final verities of life recognized by the eyes of faith? This would be difficult to argue against, for the religious man "sees" this equation and he can but feel a certain bewilderment and pity in the face of those who are so blind as not to be able to see this same vision. It is, as we remarked, natural for him: it is a very real and undeniable equation, founded upon the comparison of his own reality of faith with the witnessed literary reality. And in terms of this very real experience, he cannot help seeing what he calls religious literature as, qualitatively, the highest exemplification of literature.

The obvious problem with this conception is that it makes of religious literature a topic which is discussable only by those who share the same vision of faith. As such, it is a literary attitude that is parochial rather than universal. Its parochialism—and therefore its insufficiency as a belles-lettres conception of literature—is demonstrable by the fact that, for one holding this attitude, it is not possible to apprehend the greatness of those classics of religious traditions exotic to his own. If he is a Christian, the literary achievements of a humanist culture, of a Hindu culture, or of a Buddhist culture do not, in all honesty, seem to measure up to the standards of truly great literature—something is lacking, something is not quite achieved, not fully representative of the real and ultimate nature of things. Of course, by the same token, the humanist or Hindu or Buddhist may have the same parochial conception of literature, each seeing great literature as that which displays the ultimate nature and destiny of man as each has come to envision it. The proof that such a conception of things is parochial and limited is always the comical situation of several men of mutually exclusive faiths claiming in good faith that the others simply cannot see what is "really there" and each, in his heart of hearts, knowing that the others are parochial, blind, and not really as fully "human" in perception and emotion as he is himself.

But the patent parochialism of this conception of what is religious in literature is not the only reason for its insufficiency as a useful literary expression. Even though this view is fatally constricted by an implied tyranny of values which insists that *this* kind of literature is truly great and none other, there is yet another consideration to be set forth: namely, that in this attitude there is implied as well an insistence that literature, as an artifact of life, must by its nature move toward conformity with certain modes of life. Such an insistence ignores that a literary piece is not the artifact of an *actual* personal life but is the representation of a *possible* career of life and that, as a projection of possibilities, a literary work creates a unique structure and denouement which stand in clear, autonomous detachment from the modes of actual life against which and beyond which the religious man projects his vision of faith. To insist that an autonomous literary piece, thus understood, follow out the vision of reality which he has, in faith, projected is to insist that this piece not be the free structuralization of human possibilities but, instead, to demand that it be the deliberate choice of human possibilities in order to structuralize them according to a final specific pattern. The tyranny of this attitude not only is founded upon a misunderstanding of the unique nature of literature but compounds itself through its pretension that, in the acquisition of a specific religious vision, one has transcended historical process and has already seen the actualization of all possibilities and therefore already knows the final structure toward which all possibilities move. Such pretense is not simply absurd, but has no direct contact with the enterprise of literature, which takes place now rather than ultimately and which deals with the humanly artificial unfolding of possibilities in an artificial present and not with the divine finalization of actualities in a divine timelessness.

But, if no valid grounds have been discovered for justifying the term religious literature either as a historical type or as an honorific gradation, then—given the normal expectations of reasonable men—it would appear likely that our intention has been to save the best till the last and that our two initial defeats are about to give way to a tertiary victory. If there is such a thing as religious literature, then, by a satisfying and assiduous process of elimination, are we not forced to conclude that there *is* religious literature because it is certain to be a category or genre of literature? But we should not be precipitant, stampeded by the pressures of logical sequentiality. Instead, we should proceed to this last possibility cautiously, suspensefully (and open-mindedly), entertaining the possibility that religious literature may very well be a meaningless and unusable literary term. If the term religious literature is an expression to be employed in the belles-lettres area, then it must point to some aspect of a literary work which is autonomous to that work and which is neither parochial to a particular group nor recognizable only by reference to some extraliterary topic. There must be something about the literary artifact itself—as a unique representation of life—that one can specifically characterize as religious. With these simple ground rules—namely, that we must deal internally with the given nature of the literary work—we can proceed to explore the third possibility which seems to be offered us.

The most likely approach to this third possibility would be to consider a work of literature to be religious when and if it exhibits the visible or invisible presence or potency of the divine. This would seem a *sine qua non* of the religious, for, without it, we would not in a presumed religious work appear to have something clearly religious but, at best, we would have perhaps a literary work concerning moral behavior conditioned by social mores and expectations. And, if we do in fact seek for the presence of the divine within a literary situation, the task is not so difficult as would first seem. Certainly, we are all aware of the myriad subtleties bequeathed us by the millennia of speculations about the varying fashions in which the divine might penetrate into human history, and there are, of course, an extraordinary number of conceptions of the nature of the divine; but, when we have to do with works of literature, it is not necessary in this instance that we catalogue all of the hidden and oblique manners in which a possible divinity might secrete itself into the literary situation. On this level the situation is much simpler. It is plainly a matter of determining whether the divine is a member of the dramatis personae or not. Literature is rather simple in this respect: either there is a potent divine presence actually affecting the internal literary situation, or there is not. The tightness and economy of the literary artifact allows us only this either/or. The historical typologists and the parochialists may speculate as much as they wish on whether the divine is symbolically or soteriologically present in a literary work, but the man of belles-lettres may not: he cannot deal with what is extraliterary or esoteric in nature, but only with the given internal life of the literary work in question.

So, then, are there works where the divine is such a potent presence, a member of the dramatis personae? There are. Such a literary device is as old as the *Mahabharata* and the Homeric epics and as recent as T. S. Eliot and Graham Greene. God or gods appear visually, auditorily, tactilely, or as hidden but logically certain manipulators of scenery and events —this is an ancient and continuing tradition in literature, and such literature, internally considered, is religious. Here, then, we have a clear and indisputable hold on an internal, belles-lettres conception of religious literature, and we can point to epics, tales, narrative poems, ballads, short stories, dramas, and novels which fully bear us out. Our search is thus ended: we have found out that there *is* religious literature and *what* it is.

Theoretically, our inquiry is ended, and all the proponents of religious literature should be both justified and satisfied. But only theoretically. Among many of those proponents there is perhaps a distinctly flat feeling about the inquiry's result. Like Prufrock's disappointed antagonist, they likely mutter, "That is not what I meant at all. That is not it, at all." In this day and time no one is so intrepid as to lack respect for any antagonist of Mr. Prufrock, and so, accordingly, we must ask ourselves, "What is it that they meant?"

The explanation of what "they meant" is, from this point onward, speculative—even as much of what follows is also argumentative in respect to this pure speculation. But speculate and argue we must, in order to press beyond that flat feeling which is so unsatisfactory.

The speculation is this: the only persons who might be left feeling flat after this quite successful—though logically pedestrian—discovery of the nature of religious literature are likely those of American background and education. We can push the speculation further and specify that these discomfited persons are not only Americans but Americans of serious Christian backgrounds of a Protestant nature. And as a final push to the speculation we might suggest that these are American Protestant Christians of an intellectual bent who have struggled away from the theological convictions of an earlier generation and have thoughtfully and tenuously embraced those innovations of the Christian tradition which are variously associated with Christian humanism, liberalism, existentialism, etc.

There. The speculation has been blindly thrust forth, not cognizant of those on whom it might land. But since it has now landed upon the present reader who knows himself and knows those of his fellows who are interested with him in religious literature, there is no choice but to assume, speculatively, that the speculation landed as programmed and to proceed from that point.

So I suggest to you, my friend the American Protestant Christian humanist, etc., that your lack of interest in literature which has the divine as one of its dramatis personae is owing to the fact that you are unable to think of God as a member of a dramatis personae or even as a persona. For you, the divine is not a person or a "what" but, instead, a "how," or condition, or *telos*, or primal order, or Being, or Ground of Being, or something of that order. You are in possession of a novel and searching conception of the divine, and it is, by no coincidence at all, a conception which, by the way, fits very well into the nature and structure of literature.

This is the terminus of the speculation. Now, going on the only presumption that we can—namely, that the speculation has been correct—we should make the attempt to explain why this speculation is correct and bring in as well some comment upon the significance of this situation.

Holding to our logical 1-2-3 procedure, we would insist that the third possible conception of religious literature which was left us was correct: namely, that a work of literature becomes categorically religious when, as a potent member of the dramatis personae, we have the presence of the divine. What the speculation has sought to point out is that those anti-Prufrockian littérateurs who have a flat feeling about this third conception have this feeling not because they believe that religious literature does not have the presence of the divine but because they honestly cannot conceive of the divine as a persona. What is at issue is a matter of disagreement over the nature of the divine. Those committed to the humanist, liberal, existentialist, etc. innovations of the traditional and popular conceptions of the divine are quite unable to accept the traditional notions of a divine, superpersonal being or substance. And, in this refusal, they are—if it helps to add something—on the forward edge of history, for among the peoples of this earth there is manifestly a rampant decline in open-hearted adherents to this older theological conviction. And, riding this forward edge of history, the innovators of the Christian conception of the *theos* have, with radical and even desperate good faith, sought to reaffirm the Christian *theos* in a strikingly different fashion. This fashion is to conceive of the *theos*, not in static and/or substantial terms, but in temporal and/or relational terms—a matter of turning the sack inside out. As a result of this innovation, the presumption is that Christian theory is both transformed and renewed. And, however true this presumption may be, it is, at the least, quite true that it opens up a fresh interest in and approach to the structure of literature which is our concern at the moment.

In literary terms, what this innovation means is the following: if the divine is thought of as immanent in the relational structures of human and/or natural life, either as a special situation (e.g., as love, peace, harmony, etc.) or as a teleological *aboutissement* (redemption, forgiveness, grace, etc.), and if a work of literature is thought of as an artifact of human and/or natural life, then those works of literature which show, in their artifact of life, these particular relational structures or temporal denouements embody the presence of the divine and are, therefore, to be considered categorically religious. This would seem to be the simple belles-lettres syllogism of those who would hold that certain categories of literature can be analyzed as religious, purely from the standpoint of their internally given structure, even though the divine is not effectively present as a persona.

This is a conception of religious literature which has considerable concern for the autonomous nature of a literary piece and can, accordingly, deal with such a work in terms of its thematic and structural givenness. But it must be pointed out at the same time that this is a literary conception which is thoroughly motivated by a specific theological viewpoint, a viewpoint without which neither the motivation nor specific analytical interest in such works of literature would be possible. Putting this in a more direct manner, we should say that this is a theological interest *in* literature, an interest which is an extension of theological concerns. In a word, it is plainly a theology *of* literature which seizes upon and uses literature for exegetical or apologetical purposes rather than for the purpose of self-enjoyment within literature.

Well, then, what could be wrong with this? What could be wrong with a viewpoint which accepts literary works as autonomous artifacts representing life and analytically reacts to certain of these artifacts as if their thematic and relational structure embodied the same immanent theological structures which they apperceive in life itself—a structure which they can point to publicly (not parochially)—and which is immanent within the work, clearly present without the private vision of faith. Such a viewpoint would, as has been said, open up a quite fresh approach to literature, a line of attack which could develop an agreed-upon literary methodology around which an entire discipline could be formulated.

What could be wrong with this? In truth, nothing. It is impeccable and eminently proper, and one can wholeheartedly recommend it if one adds a significant qualification: namely, that, in all honesty, the name for this fresh discipline should be changed to what it actually is: a metaphysics of literature. To term this point of view "theological" or "religious" is, after all, to use a misnomer; it is—despite whatever its proponents might wish—a metaphysics of literature, based upon a specific metaphysical viewpoint.

We should notice that the peculiar rationale of this viewpoint is to view a literary piece in its internal givenness and to descry there the very immanent presence of conscious wrongdoing, guilt, judgment, redemption, etc., and then transpose these immanent events in terms of "religious" name changes, so that all of these immanent events become functions of a theological name-system. That these immanent events are what they are is indisputable; but that these same events are functions of a theological situation is disputable. Yet it is just this kind of transmutation which takes place in a "theology of literature," an attitude which is, in fact, a metaphysics of literature seeking systematically to identify itself with a Judaic-Christian nomenclature. That a work of literature may have a specific structure and teleology is a matter of public analysis and not, as such, subject to debate; but that a specific structure and teleology is divine or religious in nature is not a matter of public analysis and verification and is subject to vigorous theological debate, a debate in which the more numerous defenders of the orthodox conceptions of the Christian faith would themselves point out that such a viewpoint is not the function of a religious faith but the function of a metaphysical system.

What we are saying, then, is that it is possible to have an approach to literature which isolates certain categorical types of literature according to immanent themes and structures which display certain aspects of the nature and limits of men as they move through a background of the nature and limits of their social and natural world; but this approach to literature—which brings with it specific conceptions of the nature of reality, time, process, and human and natural possibility—is unquestionably a metaphysics of literature. Its claim to be a theology of literature or a literary approach to religion is a claim only and is an assertion within the midst of an internecine dispute within theology that is only tenuous.

Weighing our words thoughtfully, we can see no other course than to conclude that there is, in belles-lettres, no theology of literature and no specific type of literature that can be categorically religious other than those literary works which overtly deal with a publicly recognizable presence of the divine. That there is such a thing as a metaphysics of literature is not only possible, but is actual, and it is actually this that seems to be put forward by the proponents of a literature which is, presumably, internally structured in a categorically religious manner. This is not to suggest that a specific metaphysics of literature is improper. To the contrary, it is likely that to approach literature with a broad and self-conscious metaphysical attitude is the most fruitful way to draw out the maximum richness of any major literary work. But there are any number of possible metaphysical attitudes, and the attempt of proponents of one such attitude to argue that that attitude is Christian and religious is an extraneous and debatable claim, which adds nothing to the value of a metaphysical analysis and only befogs its purpose.

The upshot of this pedestrian line of reasoning is not, in any fashion, to undermine the Christian faith and its theology, but, rather, to delineate the limits of its authentic application. Nor, at the same time, does this line of reasoning undermine the contemporary concern for an analysis of literature which is more exhaustive than the prevailing formal and historical modes of analysis. To the contrary, it is just this concern that should be encouraged, at least in those persons capable of thinking structurally and metaphysically about literary theme and structure; and such thinking must be lucid about what it is actually doing, without being burdened with the apologetic attempt to translate metaphysical insights back into a pre-existent system of theological terms. Neither literature nor theology could authentically benefit from such a procedure.

That such a procedure is, however, adopted is testimony to the honest difficulty in which many find themselves when they have become personally or professionally habituated to calling themselves Christians. Troubled souls and searching minds, they reach out into the many currents of contemporary philosophical speculation and gather together those strands of thought which seem to embody more of the truth than any previous theological formulation they have known. This becomes their truth; and, inasmuch as Christianity *is* the truth, this truth they have found is, *ipso facto*, the very truth of Christianity: it is Christian truth; it is a deepened understanding of the Christian faith. That men with troubled hearts should, in faith, embrace the truth of Christianity, not really knowing what that truth is, and that they should subsequently take this word, Christianity, and all it entails and identify it with the metaphysical conceptions that have satisfied their intellects—this is a natural and understandable mistake. But it *is* a mistake: a personal commitment is mistaken for a random metaphysical position, and a random metaphysical position is mistaken for a personal commitment of faith in the divine. Such a mistake is of no ultimate enrichment to a metaphysical understanding of reality, and it would seem as well that ultimately it could be of no enrichment to a serious human appreciation of the terribly human marvel of literature.

Religion and the Literary Genres

by

Edwin M. Moseley

THE RELIGIOUS ORIGINS OF THE DRAMA OF EVERY CULTURE ARE ACCEPTED, even though in the passing of time they are forgotten. One comprehends Greek tragedy more fully through some awareness of its original purpose as part of the Dionysian festival, but a neglected corollary is that we understand the religion of the Greeks with a natural and nonacademic empathy because even now, some two thousand years later, the well-produced Greek tragedy achieves its originally intended cathartic function. Its effectiveness as drama continues not simply because, to be redundant, its themes are universal and its representations or imitations of human behavior are valid, but because its form, its structure, its pattern of words and action reduce timelessness to the time the theater-goer can give to attending a performance.

I have written elsewhere that in this very containing of timelessness in time is the essence of art:

> Selection, the symbolic short cut, careful manipulation of structure allow us to live a lifetime in two hours in the theater or through thirty pages or a thousand in fiction. It is literally time and space that are shortened for us so that we suspend our disbelief and accept the eternal and the universal which endure beyond all time and space. In these terms, Greek tragedy is perhaps the epitome of art in that it juxtaposes the vastest of themes with the greatest limitations of time and space. There is something here subtly akin

to the essential pun [at the center of much great literature]: timelessness is effectively proclaimed in a short time! At the beginning of
the play, Oedipus seems to be on two feet. The attaining of his lofty
position even from birth is traced for us in summary after summary:
the very technique of the delved-out memory is essential to the
central narrative. Before the day is done Oedipus has moved from
innocence and pride to experience and humility. He leaves the stage
virile and kingly in appearance, though aged now in spirit, and
returns suddenly and shockingly a broken old man, the guise of the
flesh compatible with the state of the soul. As if this were not
enough, now old, he is for the first time truly young; now blind, he
at last sees. All of this literally and artistically in less than an hour![1]

     An irony that I did not pursue is that this supreme artist, this
Sophocles, this Euripides, this Aeschylus, could and did accept without
questioning something nonartistic, something nonintellectual, something
nonliterary: a ready-made, an appropriate, a faith-provoking ritual which
celebrated each spring the resurrection of Dionysus after various associations with persecution and death and assured the audience of the spiritual
rebirth of man made in the image of God. A literary tradition circumscribed by ritual for its form and by myth for its content is constraining
by definition, but it frees the artist within the tradition to achieve the
highest possible polish of his art without the random and noneconomic
distraction of the modern writer's passionately literal pursuit of realism.
Maud Bodkin writes that "the nature of the ritual dance, as communication of a complete experience . . . makes it an illuminating prototype of
the various differentiated modes of art."[2] She compares the dance with
its "sequence of bodily attitudes so related that each, within the total
rhythm, enhances the experience of the rest" to drama, music, visual art,
and poetry with "the sensible object created by the arts—the spatial form
seen, the sequence of sound, or of action sensuously imagined—that
serves as a vehicle of a vision, intuition, or emotional understanding, of
certain aspects of our common reality." The closeness of Greek drama to
the ritual dance was an advantage denied writers in later cultures concerned with law, with exploration, with scientific discovery, with man's
freedom on earth, with accumulation, with technocracy. Paradoxically, as
dramatists have drifted further away from the ritual at the source of their
genre and willingly so as reflectors of their respective ages, they have
remained consciously and unconsciously nostalgic for the artistic economy
to which the Greeks were in a sense born. As a culture becomes more
sophisticated and the religion becomes either more elaborate or less

ritualistic, the neatness of the primitive ritual is lacking. Drama may still serve its religious function directly or implicitly, but the central "sensible object" may be obscured, for example, in scenes of comic relief and details for the achievement of psychological and social realism as ends in themselves.

Still, out of the subplots and the realistic details the critic or the playgoer in his retrospective quest for meaning may abstract the essentially religious pattern. Note the critics' application of what Herbert Weisinger calls "the myth and ritual approach to Shakespeare."[3] Theodore Spencer declares "birth, struggle, death, and revival" to be "not only the themes of the individual final plays" but also "the themes which describe the course of Shakespeare's work as a whole, from his earliest plays through *King Lear* to *The Tempest*." E. M. W. Tillyard describes the pattern of the last plays in a way significantly suggestive of Greek tragedy: a "general scheme of prosperity, destruction, and re-creation. The main character is a King. At the beginning he is in prosperity. He then does an evil or misguided deed. Great suffering follows, but during this suffering or at its height the seeds of something new to issue from it are germinating, usually in secret. In the end this new element assimilates and transforms the old evil. The King overcomes his evil instincts, joins himself to the new order by an act of forgiveness or repentance, and the play issues into a fairer prosperity than had first existed." And G. Wilson Knight finds the "habitual design of Shakespearean tragedy" to be "from normalcy and order, through violent conflict to a spiritualized music and then to the concluding ritual."

About these and a number of other comments recognizing patterns of myth and ritual in Shakespeare, Weisinger raises several questions. A predictable one paying homage to old-line scholarship is: but "there is no satisfactory way of explaining how Shakespeare got at it." The traditional scholar asks for proof of historical continuity from Greek drama to Roman drama to the medieval pattern of out-of-the-church, to the churchyard, to the town square, to the inn, to the theater constructed like an inn, or for evidence of a specific influence, such as Sophocles on Seneca on Kyd on Shakespeare; but even if proof of development or influence did exist, it would somehow be beside the point. Serious drama treats the fact and the mystery of life and death—that is, man's physical birth, his rise into manhood, his physical death, his spiritual rebirth— regardless of the particular moment, the particular tradition, the particular roots, literary or religious. Lord Raglan's fascinating study has defined the fundamental pattern of the hero in "genuine mythology, that is, mythology connected with ritual" and with "the imitation mythology" that grows out of them:[4]

(1) The hero's mother is a royal virgin; (2) His father is a king, and (3) Often a near relative of his mother, but (4) The circumstances of his conception are unusual, and (5) He is also reputed to be the son of a god. (6) At birth an attempt is made, usually by his father or his maternal grandfather, to kill him, but (7) He is spirited away, and (8) Reared by foster-parents in a far country. (9) We are told nothing of his childhood, but (10) On reaching manhood he returns or goes to his future kingdom. (11) After a victory over the king and/or a giant, dragon, or wild beast, (12) He marries a princess, often the daughter of his predecessor, and (13) Becomes king. (14) For a time he reigns uneventfully, and (15) Prescribes laws, but (16) Later he loses favour with the gods and/or his subjects, and (17) Is driven from the throne and city, after which (18) He meets with a mysterious death, (19) Often at the top of a hill. (20) His children, if any, do not succeed him. (21) His body is not buried, but nevertheless (22) He has one or more holy sepulchres.

He might have pursued his study further from ritual to mythology to imitation mythology to conscious literature. This is simply another way of saying that the pattern of man is timeless, that great themes are archetypal, that effective literature is universal and enduring. If the pattern of Shakespearean tragedy or of the tragedy of any other time is reminiscent of the pattern of the hero in myth or, more fundamentally, of the structure of religious rituals which preceded even myth, the answer lies in the unchanging nature of man, of nature, of the universe, not in how the author "got at" the myth and the ritual which seem to lie beneath and to give order to the richness of his literal details. To be sure, the artistry lies in those details: the distinction of Greek tragedy from Shakespearean tragedy from whatever may pass for modern tragedy; but the significance is in the meanings that transcend the moment which determined the particular details and the particular traditions.

We are here emphasizing the essentially religious content of serious drama in every age: depictions of the physical rise of man, which is life, and of the physical fall of man, which is death, and assurance of the spiritual rise of man, which may suggest that man is greater than the physical forces which contain him, either by his very actions on earth or his rebirth into a life beyond earth. These depictions may be of a god, any of the great scapegoats for human frailty, whose story gives man a way of coping with life and with death (the ritual, the religious literature itself, such as the Bible). Or they may be of heroes part god and part man, who demonstrate the physical weakness and the physical strength of man but also the spiritual strength of the god-in-man (the center of classical tragedy and of the epic, the former one step away from the ritual in both form and content, the latter one step away in content but further, much further away in form). Or they may be of man, imagined or historical, whose inevitable pattern through life to death receives the consolation of the reminders in various ways that man is created in God's image, comes from Him, and will return to Him (the extension into modern tragedy, the development of the historical hero into the legendary hero, the elegy in verse and the eulogy in prose). Dionysus, Mithra, Christ may serve very well as examples of the great scapegoat gods; Oedipus, Beowulf, Arthur, as examples of the great tragic and epic heroes; Willy Loman, Becket, Edward King of Milton's "Lycidas," as examples of man saved by tragic treatment, by movement from history into legend, by elegiac transcendence.

What then of the religious form when the total rhythm of the dance which originally circumscribed the content has been submerged or forgotten? The rhythm of the dance may emerge in the strict pattern of the content, the highly stylized and selective nature of the action, the resultant economy of the unities of time, place, and action; or it may emerge in the rhythm of the verse, a matter of form in the most exact sense of the word. If we refer to audience or readers, who after all give life to any art form, we can say with Aristotle that tragedy is *cathartic*, or we can say more broadly that verse is essentially incantatory. The most effective religious art combines inseparably the structure of content and the structure of form; and as we have suggested above, the writer closest to ritual, the writer taking for granted the incantatory nature of verse, that is, the writer nearest to form in its essence, has a remarkable advantage in conveying his basically religious content.

Eliot's *Murder in the Cathedral* is a marvelous example of the intellectually achieved, though certainly sincerely felt, intertwining of ritual, verse, and content. A former student of mine has pointed out that the play is essentially a liturgical drama taking for its basic structure the form of the Mass in the Roman Catholic Church:

The first and perhaps the most striking feature of the drama is its structure. It is written in what is actually two parts which are separated by an interlude: Part I, the return of the archbishop to

England and his temptation; Part II, the murder of the archbishop.
The Interlude which separates the two is written in the form of a
Christmas sermon. . . . The mass itself is divided into parts as is
the play. The first part of the mass is called the "Mass of the
Catechumens." The second part of the mass is called the "Mass of
the Faithful" and it is in this part that the sacrifice of the mass is
actually performed. These two parts are separated by what is not
really a part of the mass but is often included, the sermon. These
parts correspond directly, both in function and overall structure,
with the divisions that Eliot uses in his drama. Both the Mass of the
Catechumens and the sermon are preparations for the second, the
part in which the victim is offered. It is with this in mind that Eliot
places the actual murder in the corresponding part of the drama.
One specific example that will demonstrate these observations more
clearly is the last chant of the chorus, which Eliot uses as a sort of
choir in his "mass":

> Lord, have mercy upon us.
> Christ, have mercy upon us.
> Lord, have mercy upon us.

which in the liturgy of the Church has its specific correlative:

> Kyrie, eleison.
> Christe, eleison.
> Kyrie, eleison.

The structure of the drama is also based upon the two dominant
facets of the life of Christ on earth: namely, his coming, advent; his
"going," the crucifixion.[5]

Consider by contrast a second modern play, Robert Bolt's *A Man for
All Seasons*, which treats Sir Thomas More, another clergyman who
achieved martyrdom in the face of temporal pressures. The basically
religious content is present; nothing distracts from the pivotal pattern of
man's rise to temporal power, man's fall from temporal power, and man's
transcendence beyond the temporal. The form to be sure is in the skillful
structure of the content, in the author's adherence both to the tradition
of English tragedy and the pattern of the sacrificial archetype. But do
the absence of a containing ritual and the use of prose compatible with its
psychological and social realism interfere with the achievement of the
cathartic and incantatory function, that is, result in a play comparatively

prosaic and mundane in both the literal and the metaphorical senses of the words?

I am not asking for verse drama, for literally poetic drama, if the religious function of tragedy is to be fully achieved. The poetry can lie in the concentration and suggestiveness that are the essence of poetry even if, indeed particularly if, they are achieved in prose. Arthur Miller's *Death of a Salesman* may be an excellent example of poetry achieved not through the rhythm of verse but by the rhythm of movement back and forth through the past and present of Willy Loman's career in Brooklyn, New York, and Boston, of the careers of his two sons and his neighbor, so much a part of Willy's consciousness, and of the perhaps imagined career of his brother, through time and through space, from one age to another, from coast to coast, from continent to continent, all without moving an iota of scenery and all within the short time spent in the theater. Stepping through walls and stepping through time free the stage from the confines of modern realism and move it back to Shakespeare, who changed scene after scene with a word, or to Sophocles, who without changing a scene delved out the memory endlessly in one spot.

Critics argued at length as to whether Miller actually returned tragedy to the modern stage.[6] Miller made several pleas directly to the audience to accept the play as tragedy, one of the most moving through a speech of Linda, Willy's wife, who in effect pleads for the acceptance of what Ivor Brown called the "tragedy of the stool" instead of the "tragedy of the throne":

> I don't say he's a great man. Willy Loman never made a lot of money. His name was never in the paper. He's not the finest character that ever lived. But he's a human being, and a terrible thing is happening to him. So attention must be paid. He's not allowed to fall into his grave like an old dog. Attention, attention must finally be paid to such a person. . . . A small man can be just as exhausted as a great man.

No god, no hero, only a small man, but a human being to whom attention must be paid—that is, to whom admiration of a sort must be added to the pity and the horror. If it is added, man, not a god yet somehow more than man, is effectively portrayed, and the religious function of a literally nonreligious play is served.

The question of whether Miller achieved tragedy, which is religious in its origin and its point, or pathos, which may have the same origin but implicitly mocks the religious point, raises the larger question of the closeness of tragedy and comedy. Both reveal the ridiculousness of man, but tragedy nevertheless gives him a place, however small, in the vast scheme of things, whereas comedy gives him his place, small to be sure, in the small scheme of things, and perhaps even this ironically or romantically. That is, in comedy we are not even asked to suspend disbelief. Wylie Sypher in his brilliant essay "The Meanings of Comedy"[7] reminds us that both tragedy and comedy derive from the same sacrifice and feast which were the ritualistic center of "some sort of fertility rite—Dionysiac and phallic." Following Cornford,[8] he describes the ceremony familiar to every culture, "the death or sacrifice of a hero-god (the old year), the rebirth of a hero-god (the new year), and a purging of evil by driving out a scapegoat (who may be either god or devil, hero or villain)," along with its variations, its peripheral actions, its extensions. Cornford and after him Sypher point out that the accompanying drama included a contest between the old and new kings, a slaying of the old, "a feast and marriage to commemorate the initiation, reincarnation, or resurrection of the slain god, and a final triumphal procession or komos, with songs of joy." The conclusion is interesting that tragedy kept only that part of the ritual portraying the suffering and death of the god or hero, whereas comedy kept both sacrifice and feast, "retaining its double action of penance and revel." Again, we are talking primarily about content, but I find especially meaningful Sypher's point that comedy, attempting to balance its opposites, to attain unity out of a difficult dichotomy, "remains an 'improvisation' [Aristotle's word for the beginning of all Greek drama] with a loose structure and a precarious logic that can tolerate every kind of 'improbability.'" One might contrast rather the ritual of the sacrifice with its strict and predictable order which gave to tragedy both its content and its form with the revel of the feast, the disorder of which effused the entire comedy, even the part recalling the sacrifice, with an atmosphere of looseness. The corollary may be that form and reverence, formlessness and irreverence go together to make up the dramatic whole. The ritual dance, poetry, and tragedy have for the other side of the coin the revel, perhaps prose, and comedy.

Tragedy and poetry, comedy and prose as the two sides of the same coin are strikingly apparent in English drama, primarily, of course, Shakespeare's, in the sixteenth and seventeenth centuries. We are accustomed to saying that the low scenes, the scenes of comic relief, are in prose by contrast to the dignified, the majestic, the seriously moving, fundamentally the incantatory verse as if the prose said: here is what man is in this our world, vulgar, mocking, ridiculously imitative of the ideal, in contrast to the poetry's: here is the promise of man in spite of his involvement in the world, in spite of his excesses from which his godlike nature will ultimately save him. The prose scenes of Marlowe's *Dr. Faustus* in which the servant Wagner re-enacts almost precisely the verse scenes of Faustus' dealings with the devil are reminders of ritual in content but a denial in form and tone and hence a reversal of content. They are a kind of black mass presided over by a god of misrule—revel in effect, yes, but hardly in form, for the mockery of the ritual is too circumscribed, too strict. In all literatures the development of prose as a vehicle of expression, ironically since man supposedly *talks* in prose, is slower than the development of verse, reminding us once more of the ritualistic, the unsophisticated origins of drama, the incantatory nature of poetry. For reasons we shall pursue below, in Western literature the use of prose extensively did not develop until the Renaissances of the respective countries. Marlowe is literally Shakespeare's contemporary, but to move from Marlowe to Shakespeare is to cover practically an entire history of drama from the morality play to modern realism. Shakespeare can use prose to invert the poetic scenes, to mock his ritual, but at times he succeeds in freeing it from certain confines to give us a deep and awful look into the true nature of man, indeed into man's very nonpublic, subconscious self. Peter's vulgar prose remarks to the Nurse in juxtaposition to Romeo's high-flown and poetic wooing of Juliet is *public* enough because that is what we expect of the lowborn, but Iago's prose plotting with Roderigo and, more frightening yet, Hamlet's obscure and prose bewilderment of Ophelia are *secret* scenes in which a god of misrule takes over, Iago an extensionally allegorized one (as if Shakespeare has separated every man into an Othello or an Iago) and Hamlet expressive of some other side of his princely public self (a mad side? a repressed side? a true side?). One can hardly say here the *improvisation* of the revel instead of the *form* of the sacrifice—*improvisation* rather than *form*, yes, but of revel only in the sense of frightening chaos, of repressed evil rearing its head to subsume public order. The realism achieved by the prose is much more than the realism of possible and probable action. It is the psychological realism of man's hidden and awful self for a moment without the assurance of salvation that the total drama, the containing ritual, the prevalent rhythm of the verse leave with the audience.

All that we have been saying about the relationship of formlessness and irreverence, further about the relationship of the revel, prose, and comedy, and finally about the relationship of comic improvisation to psychological realism, revealing the unrevel-like chaos within man, suggests the entire history of the novel from its random beginnings to its flowering in the Renaissance and indeed to its emergence as the domi-

nant literary form in both quantity and quality in our time. Any attempt
to place the precise beginning of the novel is difficult because the novel,
defined loosely as a long prose narrative, is delimited neither as to form
nor as to content. The literature of every culture contains prose tales of
varying lengths, but these universally tend to be *outside* the ritual-based
literature which affirms man's tie to some god or other or even counter to
the implications of such literature. Petronius' *Satyricon*, often referred to
as an early example of a novel, is a medley of prose and verse describing
through a series of loosely connected episodes the adventures of three
rogues in southern Italy. The tone is unredeemed mockery; the content
or butt of the tone is the materialism of an entire age found both in the
aristocracy and in the upstarts who threatened and imitated the aristocracy. Again, formlessness and irreverence characterize this work by a man
who spent his time at Nero's loose court as a self-appointed Master of
Revels, a kind of god of misrule in the flesh. The pastoral Greek
romances of two centuries before Petronius, such as Longus' *Daphnis and
Chloë*, are characterized by formlessness in that their narratives are far
from being the necessary series of events that warrant the name of plot or
attain the unity of emotional impact at which ritual aims. The idealistic
presentation of characters in idyllic settings is far from irreverence but
just as far from any imitation of human behavior that would achieve the
cathartic function of serious or significantly comic literature. Actually, the
improvisations presided over by a god of misrule are ironically stronger
reminders of ritual celebrating God's order than pastoral fantasies and
romantic adventures which have no relationship to man's confessed
failures and man's painful redemption. One could continue a consideration of isolated examples of prose narratives that superficially point
toward the novel, but the prose tale was not produced in any number
until a large public was able to read without effort. This condition came
to pass during the Renaissance, when printing resulted in mass production of books at prices within the public's reach. The technical development of printing, then, encouraged the emergence of the novel, but this
development both provoked and was provoked by an increased freedom
of individuals, of which increased literacy was only one evidence.

Writing elsewhere on the development of the novel in quite a
different connection, I have summarized: "An author's contribution to
the development of the novel is his particular addition to the previously
established ways of describing individual behavior. In this connection it is
natural that the English prose tale had its beginning in the Renaissance,
when attention to the individual in contrast to the social organism was
becoming a characteristic attitude."[9]

Medieval man conceived of the universe as an organic whole with every part in its ordained place, serving its ordained function. Of society it was similarly believed that each "member," that is, class, whether the nobility, the merchants and artisans, or the serfs, was essential to the whole and therefore that all were equal in the sight of God. Each individual was bound by divine law, reflected, of course, in natural and human law, to perform his duty within the class of his birth. A man might change his station within his class: the gradations of the guild system, from apprentice to journeyman to master, allowed for this possibility, and a nobleman could acquire more land, hence higher status. But to move from one class to another, to assume pretentiously the manners of the class above or to debase one's self by marrying into the class below, was sacrilegious as a defiance of God's will and treasonable as a denial of the stated and tacit mores which manifested His will. The metaphor of the organism and its necessary members was derived from the physical being of the human individual, for whom, paradoxically, the medieval climate of opinion had so little concern.

Attention to the individual was a conscious concept of the new humanism, which was as much a nostalgic as a progressive, intellectual movement; the individual was also the chief emphasis of the new bourgeois climate, which questioned and looked forward from the feudal milieu. The Renaissance as a revival of learning found its most zealous expression in the humanists. They approved of the translation of the classics, including the Bible, into the native tongues of the Western world, and they aimed at the creation of literature worthy of comparison with that of ancient Greece and Rome. Still, their motivation was more moral than aesthetic: they desired to arrive at ethical direction other than that laid down by the medieval Church and consequently at a new definition of the individual in relation to his society. But the humanists were not radical in their demands for social change: they worked for the purification rather than the destruction or replacement of existent institutions; they were in effect the liberals of their time, wanting to analyze the discrepancy between current myths and actual behavior and to eliminate pretense. They constantly asked the questions: what is *true* nobility, what is *pure* Christianity, what is *ideal* kingship? using the familiar concepts of feudal organization and objecting only to the refutation of words by acts. They attacked ignoble noblemen, un-Christian Christians, and unruly rulers, but they approved of each group in the ideal. They described seriously or they ridiculed abuses: they wrote essays on morality, dramatized utopias, satirized corruption, and even recorded behavior realistically, often by way of pointing out moral lessons.

That humanistic criticism contributed to changes more drastic than the humanists intended is the familiar irony of the liberal position in every age. Wycliffe, the English churchman of the fourteenth century, would still describe himself as an advocate of the true Church rather than an originator of European Protestantism. Sir Thomas More, preaching the sacrifice of the individual to the common good, consistently criticized abuses which were deviations from the feudal system and literally lost his head in defense of the medieval Church. Spenser lamented corruption at court but blamed it in part on change, and Shakespeare judged tragic heroes whose flaws were usually sins against the medieval values. Even Caxton, the first English printer, whose very trade helped to make literature available to the middle class, romantically yearned for the good old days before the disintegration of King Arthur's Round Table, dramatic symbol of the ideally functioning feudal system. It is, then, in spite of such conservative allegiances that the humanists contributed to a fresh conception of the individual so necessary for the development of the novel as we think of it.

The entire context of the novel's development was a questioning of established form in society, in religion, in government, that is, a kind of figurative formlessness, and the tone was repeatedly irreverence, intended or not. Significantly, the medieval climate of opinion which was being questioned had as its pivot faith and ritual, whereas the modern climate which succeeded it took as its slogans *individual* responsibility, *individual* endeavor, *individual* revelation, the very denial of form becoming the theme of the content.

To put it simply, the long prose tales, the creation of which was encouraged by and the circulation of which was made possible by the invention of printing and the growth of literacy, were at first mockeries of feudalism and implicitly of the feudal rituals, social and/or religious, and of the keepers of the feudal rituals, the landed knights and the priests. The form they tended to take, paradoxically an inversion or a complete neglect of form, came soon to be known from its Spanish origins as the picaresque novel, a genre which has pervaded the development of the novel from its strong emergence in the Renaissance both on the Continent and in England until well into the nineteenth century and indeed in isolated but significant examples in our own time. The center of the usual picaresque story is the picaro, or rogue, a fellow of low birth, often of uncertain origins, or at least in temporary low position. His lack of status in society allows him the advantage of having nothing to lose and therefore considerable freedom of insight and comment. Armed with this freedom from vested interests, he is exposed to the world and soon taught that professed morals and actual behavior have little to do with each other. Then, with this additional weapon of knowledge gained from experience, he proceeds on adventures of his own. This picaresque pattern has the panoramic advantage as a vehicle of social comment because the picaro in his movements usually covers considerable territory, but it has the truly dramatic disadvantage of trying to cover so much literal space that attention is paid primarily to things external, to a journey through some defined world so very literally that any journey of learning for the central character is beside the point. It is everything that Aristotle's tragedy is not: the character at the center is self-consciously nonheroic; the development of character from physical birth through the stages of life to physical death and at least the promise of spiritual birth, the very point of most ritual, is a concept of man's nature precisely denied by the picaresque; and the unities of action, of time, and of place, which in a sense reflect the form of the original ritual and determine the form of the literature which derived from it, are flagrantly disregarded. The conspicuous characteristics of the picaresque are irreverence and formlessness. If the picaro seems to arrive at some moral re-evaluation from his experience, as we are told that he does at the end of such works as the Spanish *Lazarillo de Tormes* or *The Unfortunate Traveller*, by the English writer Nashe, the learning does not dramatically develop out of his experience step by step; it is arbitrarily tacked on. The adventures may go on until the author chooses to stop or at least so long as anything in society remains to be mocked, and furthermore they may go on in any order the author wishes: that is, they lack the necessary order known as plot.

The picaresque is mock-heroic, or with specific reference to its antifeudal origins mock-chivalric, and some examples are self-consciously mock-epic. Aristotle, comparing and contrasting tragedy and the epic as to length (essentially a matter of content) and meter (essentially a matter of form), criticized the writers of epic who neglected the very unity of action which he considered essential to effective drama. The same criticism could be made severalfold of such deliberate mock-epics as *Don Quixote* and *Tom Jones*. The communal epic and the effective literary epic contain and are contained by the recurrently emerging pattern of the hero which Lord Raglan found in his "genuine mythology . . . connected with ritual." (Aristotle refers to epic content as matter for a series of tragedies.) One does not expect a precise repetition of the hero's pattern in ages less susceptible to what Aristotle called "the marvelous," but since the hero's pattern is symbolically the pattern of every man's life, which in turn gives ritual its symbols, the narrative lacking the control of the original ritual, however far away, whether respectful or inverse and mocking, may deny emotional closure to its readers. Many of the famous eighteenth-century English novels, not only *Tom Jones* but also, say, *Moll Flanders, Roderick Random, A Sentimental Journey,* interest us historically and delight us part by part but admittedly lack the sustained and single impact of works in which nothing is wasted. The improvisation of the irreverent, then, continued to be encouraged by a society which mocked form in every fundamental context, including the religious, even when it paid attention to the superficial form of manners and dress.

There was, of course, another kind of narrative emphasizing not the individual's questioning of or rebellion against society, not, that is, negative in its tone, but extolling the positive values of the new individualism at the center of the bourgeois climate of opinion. According to this set of values, every man was endowed with the capacity for endeavor and obligated to use this capacity in the employment of resources about him. Each man had equal opportunity on God's earth to use his natural industry to reach the goal at which he aimed without fear of class restrictions. The bourgeois virtues of diligence, thrift, and morality, which came naturally to him, would protect him from seeking the vain goals which characterized the decadent feudal aristocracy. Economic success was considered evidence of man's thorough exercise of his natural virtues and hence a symbolic promise of the religious salvation which he had earned. These ways of thinking, condoning as just and natural the economic revolution of the middle class and the concomitant Protestant Reformation, gave the condemned *avarice* of the Middle Ages the admirable name of *ambition.* This social philosophy suggested the entire structure of a prose tale in which the central character journeyed through trial after trial, contest after contest, adventure after adventure, always with success until he ended with a climactic reaching of whatever earthly goal he had before him, his success, of course, proving his righteousness. Excellent examples are the tales of Deloney, Bunyan's *Pilgrim's Progress,* Defoe's *Robinson Crusoe,* and Richardson's *Pamela.* In contrast to the picaresque mockery, the tone is prevalently positive, but as in the pastoral romances of the Greeks, if irreverence is absent, so is the convincing imitation of human behavior that achieves catharsis; the reader cannot with any honesty identify with the optimistic experience described. Too, though the direction of the journey is, so to speak, upward in such success stories, the order of events toward the final goal is generally random. Again, the concept of character and the economy essential respectively to the content and form of ritual are lacking. The mockeries of the bourgeois climate, from much of Dickens and *Vanity Fair* to Lewis' *Babbitt* and Dreiser's *The Financier*, are in effect the picaresque novels of the modern age, with irreverence as their unifying intention and formlessness as a function of their attempt to cover society thoroughly.

At the end of the nineteenth century the irreverence was abetted by the new scientism in the center of which Darwin, Marx, and Freud were the gods, and the formlessness was abetted by the deterministic denial of "God's in His Heaven,/All's right with the world." As the humanists' brave new look at man in the Renaissance resulted in a redefinition of his nature and in experimentations in art to represent this nature, the determinists freed the characterization of man from both the romantic emphasis on his basic goodness and the bourgeois emphasis on his pre-destined capacity for success. By the beginning of our own century, however smothered in naturalistic details of social and psychological realism the novel had become, novelists were not afraid to treat man's failures and not afraid to seek ways to transcend them.

Whereas the irreverence of the picaresque story lies in its comprehensive mockery of social and personal values and the irreverence of the success story lies, dichotomously, in its refusal to admit the limitations of society or of man, the failure of both as significant literature was usually the absence of any journey of learning for a central character or a central intelligence to give meaning to the external journey about society or upward through it. One can, of course, point to earlier examples, but as novels continued to be produced in great number throughout the nineteenth century, authors gave increasingly greater attention to the development of central characters or to the maintenance of a central point of view. Steps in the extensional journey in society became subordinate to, dependent upon, or actually symbolic of steps in the intensional journey of the protagonist or the focus of narration. The journey of learning, then, subsumed the journey in time and space just as in Greek drama the unity of action subsumed the unities of time and place. For the last hundred years, in significant story-telling on the Continent, in England, and in America, though it may provide a particular author's special richness, movement through a setting has been secondary to the coming of age of the pivotal character, to his movement from innocence to experience, to—as we have said—his journey of learning. Examples are too abundant and too rich to discuss or even to list with any thoroughness here, but I have been thinking of such novels as Dickens' *Great Expectations* (a mockery of the bourgeois success story, yes, but a kind of rites of passage for Pip, the central character, as he moves from innocence to experience, from pride to humility), Twain's *Huckleberry Finn* (a truly

picaresque journey baring in its movement down the river the pretenses
of mankind in America and everywhere else at all times, but more than
that, as an endless number of critics have pointed out, a ritual journey of
the coming of age in any time), James' *The Ambassadors* (the journey of
Strether, the middle-aged innocent, from the optimistic illusions of
America to the awful truths of Europe, again from innocence to experience and perhaps self-understanding), Flaubert's *Madame Bovary*,
Joyce's *Portrait of the Artist as a Young Man*, Turgenev's *Fathers and
Sons*, the early Hemingway, Fitzgerald's *The Great Gatsby*, Camus' *The
Stranger*, and so on even unto Salinger's *The Catcher in the Rye*. The
lessons learned in these journeys and the many other possible examples
may vary; some may be negative and some may be positive in implication;
but they are all achieved by a step-by-step, stage-by-stage, carefully
structured look into the self on the part of the central character.
Whether there is the seemingly irreverent discovery of no promised
salvation for man or the universally reverent one of salvation out of
suffering, in novels of the kind which I mention there has been a remarkable emergence of form, conscious or not on the authors' part. Rituals
dramatize the cycle of man and of nature, and in the emergence of
attention to man's development, authors have shown a striking awareness
of ritual in a supposedly nonritualistic age.

I am not neglecting, say, the despair of Hemingway's *The Sun Also
Rises*, the disillusionment of Fitzgerald's *Tender Is the Night*, or the
secular existentialism of Camus' *The Stranger*, for in these novels and in
many others in our time the denial of God's order is most firmly dramatized by the inverted ritual, the mock sacrament, the correlative of the
mythic quest unfulfilled. Nor am I neglecting in a consideration of form
the impressionistic or stream-of-consciousness novel which may take
advantage of the flexibility of prose to desert entirely the extensional
journey for the intensional one, making the subconscious and unconscious levels of action even more important than the conscious ones. We
have referred before to the Renaissance dramatists' adventurous use of
prose to reveal the unravel-like chaos within man, a kind of foreshadowing perhaps of the novel completely subjective in its technique. But,
interestingly enough, the novels accused of betraying the very genre by
their disregard of ostensible action achieve their order implicitly from the
timeless symbols, the archetypal shapes, the unchanging myths which
persist in man's dreams and in the rituals which precede and transcend
time. Joyce's *Ulysses*, with the *Odyssey* for its paradigm, and Faulkner's
The Sound and the Fury, with the story of the Passion Week for its

paradigm, are highly experimental in style; but myth and ritual give them a stronger order than does the syntax of a particular language.

Whatever the multiplicity of reasons, the novel in the last century has become a tighter form artistically and a more intense genre in its content. Is the tightening of content as well as of form simply a natural refinement of a genre after several centuries of extensive practice with it? Did a disillusionment with the values of the modern world lead to a gradual resurgence of belief in man's ennobling capacity for suffering or at least to an unashamed lament for the passing of his heroic qualities? Or does the archetypal pattern of man, celebrated in ritual, by its very definition endure and by its very endurance recur, however the peculiar expressions of a particular age may seem to have obscured it? Has the novel in our time moved toward serving the communal religious function of ritual-based drama and achieved it, without help from the incantatory nature of verse, through an intensity of content and an economy of structure? The ritual dance is hardly just off stage, as it was and occasionally is even now with significant drama; but nevertheless in the modern authors mentioned and in many others the action is "sensuously imagined" and conveyed with nothing wasted. Somehow form and reverence converge often indeed in a prose genre, the very beginnings of which were a denial of them.

The development of an effective literary form in our time is assuring aesthetically and—if one likes—spiritually. I have suggested before that the great religions and the great literature which dramatizes them evolve from a profound sense of personal and social end; and I wondered then, in recognition of the strength of the novel in our time, "what manner of end are we experiencing?" In his fine essay "The Spiritual Problem of Modern Man" Jung quotes Hölderlin's "Danger itself/Fosters the rescuing power."[10] With the public ritual of the communal drama no longer available, has the structured and intense novel come to the religious rescue with a private ritual offering personal drama, with a form, that is, to contain and convey reverence?

Notes

[1] Edwin M. Moseley, *Pseudonyms of Christ in the Modern Novel* (Pittsburgh, 1963), p. 95.

[2] Maud Bodkin, *Archetypal Patterns in Poetry* (New York, 1958), p. 314.

[3] Herbert Weisinger, "An Examination of the Myth and Ritual Approach to Shakespeare," in Henry A. Murray, ed., *Myth and Mythmaking* (New York, 1960), p. 132.

[4] Lord Raglan, *The Hero: A Study in Tradition, Myth, and Drama* (London, 1949), p. 178.

[5] William James, "History, Religion, and Literature: Eliot's 'Murder in the Cathedral,'" *The Wall* (Winter 1958–1959), p. 22.

[6] Reviews of *Death of a Salesman* by Brooks Atkinson, Ivor Brown, John Mason Brown, Eleanor Clark, and Frederick Morgan, in Eric Bentley, ed., *The Play, A Critical Anthology* (New York, 1951), pp. 729–747.

[7] In Wylie Sypher, ed., *Comedy* (Garden City, N.Y., 1956), pp. 214–226 *passim*.

[8] Francis M. Cornford, *The Origin of Attic Comedy* (London, 1914).

[9] Edwin M. Moseley, "Introduction," in Robert Ashley and Edwin M. Moseley, eds., *Elizabethan Fiction* (New York, 1953), p. i.

[10] C. G. Jung, "The Spiritual Problem of Modern Man," in *Modern Man in Search of a Soul* (New York, 1933).

Literature and Religious Belief

by

Vincent Ferrer Blehl, S.J.

THE RELATIONSHIP BETWEEN LITERATURE AND RELIGIOUS BELIEF IS A PHILO-sophic question, just as theoretical criticism is really a branch of philosophy. Theoretical criticism is not literature but aesthetics. Even practical criticism is not literature unless it possesses such remarkable literary qualities as to become itself a work of literature of the nonpure type.[1] Some philosophers, such as the logical positivists, assert that both literature and religious belief have only emotive, not cognitive, value. But even among the practitioners of linguistic analysis there has been a reaction against this view, which is really an assumption rather than a reasoned philosophic judgment. This is not to deny that both literature and faith have emotive values, but to affirm that they have other values as well. The reflections which I am going to set forth in the following pages will be concerned mainly with the cognitive aspects of literature and religious belief, and I will conclude with a consideration of the problem which religious faith presents to those theoretical and practical critics who hold that literature has a genuine cognitive value but consider Christian beliefs on the same level as the myths of ancient Greece and Rome, that is to say, that they possess only imaginal, not objective, cognitive value.

In speaking of the relationship between literature and religious belief, I will be concerned mainly with Western literature and with religion in the Western world. This is not to deny that there are authentic values to be found in all religions, but simply to say that the religions of Judaism and Christianity are more relevant to Western literature. Religious belief is a commitment which arises from a personal and intersubjective encounter with divine realities as these are revealed by God. The ground of this commitment is God revealing. The resultant act is called faith. Now faith has its own understanding in which the believer attains to God in religious acts such as prayer, meditation, sacrifice; and this understanding is commonly called religious knowledge. It is personal and individual. When, however, a man who believes begins to reflect upon *what* he believes and gives an answer to that question, he is giving a theological answer. Beginning with faith and remaining close to faith, the believer uses his rational discursive intelligence illumined by faith to seek a greater, fuller, and more systematic understanding of the content of his belief. In this process of theologizing, the human mind makes use of rational categories, particularly those supplied by philosophy. But in the great systems of theology, such as in those of St. Augustine and St. Thomas, the authors allowed the data of revelation to correct, enlarge, and inwardly transform their philosophic categories. Every conceptual or metaphysical transposition of Christian teaching was recognized as falling short of the divine message which is grasped in faith. The theologian, therefore, ultimately returns to the word of God, but at the same time the word of God is clarified by theology. Meanwhile, difficulties have been resolved and obscurities clarified, and unity is discovered amid diversity. Since theology is an activity of the discursive intellect illuminated by faith attempting to understand the truths of revelation, it is distinguished from theodicy or natural theology, which is a purely philosophic knowledge of God without revelation.

A further distinction may be made between religious and theological knowledge. The religious imagination discerns, rests in, and appropriates as a living reality what is held as a truth by the theological intellect; but there is no real opposition between these two modes of apprehension and assent. Every religious man insofar as he reflects on his beliefs is a theologian, and no theology can either begin or be constructed without the initiative and abiding presence of religion. Nevertheless, there are two distinct habits of mind: the theological, discursive, intellectual, and systematic; and the religious, imaginative, affective, and intellectual. As Newman pointed out

> The formula, which embodies a dogma for the theologian, readily suggests an object for the worshipper. It seems a truism to say . . . that in religion the imagination and affections should always be under the control of reason. Theology may stand as a substantive science, though it be without the life of religion; but religion cannot

maintain its ground at all without theology. Sentiment, whether imaginative or emotional, falls back upon the intellect for its stay, when sense cannot be called into exercise; and it is in this way that devotion falls back upon dogma.[2]

Finally, religion involves not merely a set of beliefs but a way of life, that is, the continuous struggle to live an authentic existence in the light of what God has revealed. Religion, consequently, is more experiential and is a wider term than theology. Though the analogy should not be pressed, one might say that theology is to religion what criticism is to literature, with this exception (among others): that whereas religion cannot maintain its ground without theology, literature can maintain its ground without criticism. Nevertheless, both criticism and theology are abstractive, discursive, and systematic; literature and religion are concrete, experiential, imaginative, and affective.

The simplest way of discussing the relationship of literature to theology and religious belief is to follow the accepted types of criticism and in so doing to point out how a knowledge of theology and religion can be of some value to the critic. The act of criticism is a judgment following upon an intelligent and sensitive encounter with the values inherent in a work of art. This involves two levels of knowledge, which may be called apprehension and understanding. Apprehension is knowledge on the level of experience. "Men of experience know that a thing is so, but they do not know why."[3] To know why is the result of an analytic reflection upon experience. To have any sort of adequate knowledge of a thing, according to Aristotle, one must first apprehend it and then discover its origin, its essential structure, and its finality.[4] In fact, the ordinary types of criticism have more or less followed the steps which he laid down.

The starting point of criticism, consequently, is an adequate comprehension, "the endeavor," in Matthew Arnold's phrase, "in all branches of knowledge to see the object as in itself it really is." At this point criticism attempts a description of the experience which has been communicated in a literary work. Usually this is accomplished by means of a paraphrase of the meaning of the work and through a description of the emotions which accompany it. But since a work of literature cannot be adequately described nor its effect presented in any terms other than those which the original artist has employed, this type of criticism, if it can be called criticism, is never entirely successful. Like all impressions, this type of criticism gives highly selected aspects of the work and tends to subjective and excessively relativistic judgments.

Since a work of literature is a historical record to the extent that it was composed at a particular time in history and in a particular cultural milieu, a critic will find it helpful to know something of the cultural background which determined the experiences, the associations, the habits of expression, and the interests of the author. Secondly, a knowledge of the biography of an author will help to determine his predominant habit of mind, his preoccupations, his particular ethos, the reasons which caused him to react in a certain manner, with a particular tone, and with a certain hierarchy of values. For the understanding of a number of works of literature, a knowledge of the theologians of the period will prove immensely rewarding. For example, one's understanding of Spenser, Milton, and Bunyan will be enriched by some familiarity with the specific doctrines of Luther, Calvin, and Hooker. Or, to take a more recent work, Auden's *For the Time Being* yields a more intimate understanding when read in the light of Kierkegaard, who explicitly influenced Auden's beliefs as expressed in this poem. A proper understanding of this work demands as well some knowledge of the problem of belief in the modern world.

Two remarks are appropriate at this juncture. First, this kind of criticism, if it is valuable, should be concerned with the forces operative in the composition of the work, not in the abstract but rather in the concrete. It should as far as possible keep really close to the work of literature itself. Such knowledge can be valuable, as G. Ingli James has remarked, "in precisely the same way and to the same extent that one's knowledge of a person's background can be. 'Background information' can enormously enrich our total understanding of both persons and poems; and without it we are liable to make the most elementary errors."[5] It is one of the deficiencies of the modern university that it has excluded theology from the standard curriculum of the liberal arts, a defect which incidentally is coming, at least in America, to be more explicitly recognized and in some instances even remedied. A lack of theological knowledge has led to some rather arid nonsense being written, especially about Shakespeare's theological views. The theological shallowness of such critics has been ruthlessly exposed by Roland Mushat Frye in his *Shakespeare and Christian Doctrine* (Princeton, 1963). To take a negative example, William Whitla in *The Central Truth: The Incarnation in Robert Browning's Poetry* (Toronto, 1963), by not paying sufficient attention to the evangelical character of Browning's beliefs, conveys the impression that Browning is a more orthodox and systematic religious thinker than he actually was. I would also endorse James' further statement that such background information "becomes a dehumanizing distraction only when we cease to use it to illuminate the living entity and begin to use the poem (or person) to illustrate our familiarity with the background."[6]

This leads me to a second remark: that genetic criticism is not criticism in the full sense of the word. Its relationship to criticism proper is rather like the function of Henrietta Stackpole in Henry James' *Portrait of a Lady*. In the preface to that work James remarks that, though she may be one of the wheels, she does not belong to the body of the coach, nor is she accommodated with a seat inside.

When we pass from genetic criticism of the substance of the literary work itself, the problem of the relevancy of theological or religious beliefs becomes more complicated. Here I must first recall some general ideas about the nature of a literary work. The mode of existence of a literary work is that of an act of the intentional order. By "intentional" I do not mean something done on purpose, which is obviously the case with a work of art; but I use the term to designate the realm of conscious, meaningful relation to objects. A work of literature is not simply the written or printed text. Literary discourse is essentially a structure of meaning. For practical purposes, critics distinguish in the literary work form and matter, technical from cognitive values, while affirming that actually matter and form are one. Literature communicates through the instrumentality of language not merely an experience but a *significant* one. It communicates a uniquely personal insight into reality, particularly into the human condition, but one which the educated reader or critic recognizes as both new and somehow known. The structure and patterns of words, the symbolic character of language and the images conveyed through the language, the connotative meanings and associations of words, not only in themselves but as these acquire further meanings through their sequential arrangement into patterns of images—all these technical aspects of a literary work—have been determined by and made subservient to the creative intuition of the artist. The intuition is said to have been completely realized, or rendered communicable, when the form of the work has been organic, that is to say, when the whole has been so fashioned and designed as to convey an integral and unique experience, leaving in the mind a sense of completeness and harmony. "Organic form is both a function of the experience communicated and the instrument of its communication."[7] In the former case, it has avoided mere subservience to convention, which would have denatured the experience; and on the other, mere idiosyncrasy, which would have rendered it incommunicable. In the latter case, *i.e.*, as instrument, it has eschewed mere virtuosity, which distracts from the significance of the words, and at the other extreme, a blunt presentation of ideas without care and concern for the expressiveness latent in the sounds and associations of language. Thus organic form is considered to be the adequate expression of a theme. The full actualization of the theme is the entire experience rendered communicable through the instrumentality of the patterned word structure of the entire literary work.

Here it must be recalled that organic form is really not a cause of the literary work but rather its formal effect. The formal cause is the creative intuition of the author which has determined (1) his mode of apprehending his theme; (2) the attitude he assumed toward the values of good and evil in his theme, which led to his writing tragedy, comedy, pastoral comedy, lyric, satire, popular romance, or any other type; (3) his attitude toward his audience and toward his medium of communication. The more concerned the writer is with self-expression than with contact with other minds, the more he tends to depart from conventional usage in vocabulary and syntax, so as by "literary language" to communicate his vision more adequately. What the language has lost by way of precise denotation is counterbalanced by a richness of intuitive knowledge. Concrete symbols are capable of expressing many levels of meaning and shades of value that are inaccessible to the abstractive or discursive intelligence. Not only sensible objects have this representative power but actions and situations as well. Among the latter may be placed myths, *i.e.*, stories of particular events that represent some basic phase of man's encounter with life, whether his origin, his struggles, or his destiny.

This is a rather compressed and perhaps unnuanced summary of much present-day critical theory, but it will serve to recall some basic principles which must be explicated if the relationship of religious and theological beliefs to images and symbols is to be understood. And here I would suggest that the beliefs of the writer could not help affecting the meaning and content of his symbols and myths and that this is particularly true of religious symbols in literature. Let me first illustrate this in a work of nonpure literature and then in works of pure literature. Modern biblical scholars, whether Catholic or Protestant, are agreed that the Bible presents the kerygma, or message of belief of the biblical writers and therefore of the community of believers to which the writers belonged. There are in the Old Testament many symbols, myths, and archetypal images that are also present in nonbiblical literature: origin myths, saviors, floods, etc. There was on the part of the biblical authors an extensive borrowing of images and myths from the surrounding environments, but there is also a radical discontinuity between the biblical and the nonbiblical usage of symbols and myths. The Babylonian creation story, for example, presents a luxuriant polytheism, whereas the biblical creation is monotheistic in its outlook. Similarity amid radical differences of theological outlook has been shown in the Babylonian and the Genesis flood stories. So also there is a differentiation of meaning in the use of images, such as light and darkness, height and depth, king and kingdom. A comparison of the imagery of light and darkness in the *Manual of Discipline*, one of the Dead Sea Scrolls, and the imagery of light and darkness in St. John's Gospel reveals that the imagery of the former is moralistic and legalistic, the imagery of the latter, theological. In the *Manual of Discipline* one is a son of light or of darkness, insofar as one is a faithful observer or nonobserver of the laws of the community. In St. John's Gospel one is a son of light if one has a new nature in Christ, if one participates in the Divine Nature.

Now a nonbeliever is free to say that the biblical writers were deceived, that the contents of their symbols are not what they thought they were, because objectively they are not true; but then such a critic is not comprehending the work as it is in itself. Moreover, as a reader he is not undergoing the same experience as a believer who reads the Bible. The significance of the symbol depends upon what the author intends it to convey.

Let us now look at some examples in creative literature. Steinbeck in *The Grapes of Wrath* employs a mythic structure based on Old Testament imagery: a chosen people, wanderings toward a Promised Land, a Babylonian captivity. Jim Casy, who expressly rejects Christian belief in favor of humanitarianism and a nature religion, is presented as a Christ-like figure, especially in his sacrificial death for the community. Steinbeck uses these devices in a purely external, metaphorical way. Now I suggest that if Steinbeck had conceived Jim as a more orthodox Christian, he would have presented a different characterization and hence a different experience, and the meanings which would have emerged from these symbols would have been different from those which do emerge. As Robert Detweiler has pointed out, the modern fiction writer generally "utilizes the accumulated connotative—not the denotative—potential of the Christ story to reflect his own values."[8] The Christ figure in American literature is not one with the Christ of the believer. The Christ figure of modern literature in his moral actions often does not reflect Christ at all. The writer is free, of course, to make whatever use he wishes of the Christ figure, but the writer's beliefs will determine the significance of his imagery and symbolism. Another example will reinforce this assertion. The priest in Graham Greene's *The Power and the Glory* is both an outlaw and a scapegoat. He is an outlaw from the state, but he has also defied some of the laws of the Church. Starving, driven from village to village, he nevertheless continues to act as a priest until he is finally betrayed and executed for his faith. His influence is felt almost immediately after his death. On another level, however, the priest is the object of another pursuit, the pursuit by God through the labyrinthine ways not only to his own salvation but to his sanctification. Suffering and penitent, the priest lives according to the highest demands of Christian charity.

> The Priest as scapegoat images the high priest, Christ. In imitation of Christ, whose sense of eternal responsibility for others was demonstrated on Calvary, this meek Mexican curate withdraws the claims of self. In enduring sacrificial suffering for others he becomes Christ-like. The events in *The Power and the Glory* preceding the execution of the Priest intentionally imitate the actions that led up to the crucifixion: the ignoble half-caste betrayer is a yellow-toothed Judas; the agony in the cell block, Gethsemane; the temptation to escape to Las Casas, the temptation of Christ in the desert; the solace the Priest offers the dying Yankee murderer, the solace Christ offers the good thief; the Lieutenant's stronger desire to destroy the Priest than the Yankee murderer, the multitude's stronger desire to shed Christ's blood than Barabbas'; craven Padre José's refusal to shrive the Priest, the denial by Peter. Unimaginable glory pools around the Priest's death, because he dies not for the good and the beautiful but for the half-hearted and the corrupt, just as Christ died for all the depravity in the world. Thus the power and the glory of the Father bursts forth from the whisky priest with the bastard child.
>
> The Priest's outlaw status and his scapegoat status stem from the fact that he is a priest. The salvation the outlaw priest offers the people is love and the death of the scapegoat priest is an act of love, but, since he is a man first of all, his own evolution in love is the story of man in the world.[9]

Greene uses religious symbolism to alert the reader not to accept the priest's self-evaluation; and he contrasts the whisky priest, who responds to God's overtures, with Padre José, who resists them. So also by introducing a scene in which a pious lady is reading a life of a saint, Greene throws into relief the truth about a real flesh-and-blood saint.

Greene's pattern of events, his juxtaposition of character, his symbolism, and his occasional authorial intrusions add a dimension of religious meaning which is quite different from and beyond that of novelists who, like Faulkner in *The Bear* or Steinbeck in *The Grapes of Wrath*, use Christ simply as an archetypal person in situations which represent eternal patterns of existence, without necessarily incorporating within their lives the spiritual and moral values of Christ and without their participating in the sacerdotal and spiritually redemptive function of Christ. Indeed, in these authors the experiences have almost no intrinsic religious significance at all, whereas Greene, on the other hand, is trying to show the operation of God in a world of sin.

An orthodox religious author, therefore, in using religious symbolism gives to these symbols a content beyond the mere humanistic understanding of archetypal patterns, symbols, and myths. He adds a further dimension of meaning to his symbols, and literary critics should apprehend and comprehend these meanings and not reduce them to the mere univocal level of analogy, even if they themselves cannot give an assent to this further dimension of meaning. This is not to say that a critic judges the literary value of the work on this basis, for technical literary values relate to the efficacy of the instrument of communication, which, as has been noted, is ideally an organic form, a structure which presents the successive phases of the author's experience in such an order and economy as to communicate it to a reader as fully as possible. Organic form also postulates a language and diction which convey the quality of the experience with a minimal dilution or distortion. These technical values (which are not the only values of a work of literature) proceed from craftsmanship and inhere in the structure and texture of the work itself, and they determine whether the work is a work of literature, and, if so, to what extent the writer is competent. These specific literary values are the special province of the critic, and upon his competence to understand and evaluate them rests his competence as a literary critic. But since the cognitive elements are intrinsically united with the technical, a critic is failing to judge the work as it is in itself if he ignores, dilutes, or distorts the meaning of the work as that has been determined by the creative intuition of the author.

The finality of a literary work is its potentiality to induce in a reader of some taste an aesthetic experience, and in this perspective the question of literature and belief is sometimes formulated as follows: "At what point, in short, does our disagreement with a writer's ideas interfere with our appreciation of his work as imaginative literature?"[10] Since this question usually arises with reference to religious beliefs, I should like to take a religious poem to illustrate the problem. Francis Thompson's

"Hound of Heaven" employs a metaphor of a chase which ends in the surrender of the poet. Its theme is basically the same as that of Graham Greene's *The Power and the Glory*, namely, the pursuit of the individual soul by God and the surrender of the antagonist to His love and kindness. Must one share Thompson's belief in a personal and solicitous God in order to enjoy and appreciate his poem? I think it may fairly be presumed that many readers of Thompson have enjoyed his poem without sharing that belief. To them his symbol of pursuit and salvation evidently remains a mere exercise of imagination, since they must assume that the situation could have no actuality and so could offer no other pleasure than the pleasure of contemplating an imagined possibility. To those, however, who share Thompson's belief and accept the entire experience of the poet's discovering a profound reality expressed through the fiction of the hound and the hare, it seems safe to assert that the pleasure which the poem gives will be greater.[11] The reason for this would seem to be that such pleasure proceeds from the fullest harmony of the intellect with the other faculties and the fullest acceptance of and response to the values presented, and hence the resulting pleasure is greater, more intense, and more completely satisfying. But this would depend upon one supposition, namely, that the aesthetic distance is equal in the believer and in the nonbeliever. A conscience-stricken Christian might find in the poem an excessively personal reference which would create an anxious state of concern, which in turn would disturb the free play of imagination and dilute the feeling of disinterested pleasure. To such a reader the poem would afford a less purely aesthetic experience than it would to the sympathetic atheist or agnostic.

What has been said does not, however, answer all the questions which can be raised. The question of the suspension of assent is usually asked with reference to religious or theological views, such as one finds in Milton. But the question can be pursued further. Cannot a reader suspend assent to all the views which a poet such as Milton implies in his work? Why is it necessary simply to state the problem in terms of a reader's inability to accept Milton's religious beliefs? Yet critics who raise the problem with respect to religious views assume that readers precisely because they are *men* (not every one is a Christian, but every one is a man) will accept Milton's presentation of the human condition as authentic and objective. The following statement about *Paradise Lost* will illustrate this:

As a poem its subject is not the justification of the ways of God to men, but the essential and tragic ambiguity of the human animal.

Expanding his meaning, by means of images, similes, and sheer choice of vocabulary, to include all that Western man had thought and felt, pivoting the action on a scene which, as Milton describes it in the poem, illuminates immediately the paradox of man's ambition (at once good because noble and bad because arrogant) and human love (both bad because selfish and because passion clouds the judgment and good because unselfish and self-sacrificing), linking the grandiose action at every point to images suggestive of man in his daily elemental activities in fields, cities, and on the ocean, developing, as in his picture of ideal nature in the early scenes in Eden, all the implications of man's perennial desire for a better world with the continuous awareness of man's tendency to trip himself up and turn his very virtues into snares—achieving all this in spite of the plot, as it were, by placing an image where it will sing most eloquently and by linking each unit to others so that the chorus of implication grows ever richer, reverberates ever more widely, Milton, by operating as a poet rather than as a theologian and moralist, in spite of himself probes deeper into man's fate than his former scheme would seem to allow and in the magnificent close sums up in one climactic image all that has ever been said about man's capacity to hope in spite of despair, about loneliness and companionship, about the healing effects of time and the possibility of combining bewilderment with a sense of purpose, giving us, in fact, his final echoing statement about man's place in the world.[12]

Are not judgments made here which are a response of the individual writer of these lines to the experience conveyed in Milton's poem, namely, that man's ambition is good because it is noble and bad because it is arrogant, that love is bad because it is selfish and because passion clouds the judgment and good because it is unselfish and self-sacrificing? Could not an individual reader challenge these statements? And if one replies that Milton's view of the human condition has been experientially confirmed, could not a reader reject the experience of the Western world just as easily as the modern reader has rejected Christianity and religious beliefs? Could not a modern reader say that man is not good; that every man has his price; that therefore ambition is not selfish but that it is simply action according to nature? The reader is always free to assent or not to the views presented by an individual writer. But surely Mr. Daiches is saying more than that he assents to Milton's views of the human condition. If I interpret him correctly, he is affirming that on the experiential level through literature he has gained a genuine knowledge of the human condition, that he has perceived values and disvalues such as good and evil, selflessness and selfishness, and that he holds these to be objective. That they are objective is confirmed not only by the testimony of the whole Western literature but by the critic's personal experience as well. In other words, though literature is imaginal, it is not merely fictional in the sense that it presents objects which exist only in the mind and are entertained by the mind only as fictions. Justice, mercy, love, selflessness are something objective and autonomous: they have an intrinsic necessity and intelligibility independent of their existence in a fictional or real person.

I am in fundamental agreement with Daiches' views thus interpreted. The awareness of values which literature gives is a prephilosophic one, because knowledge of values is communicated in literature on an experiential level. It is knowledge resulting from a lived (though imaginal) contact with being. The full intellectual grasp, however, of the nature of the datum given in a literary experience is a philosophic task, and Daiches is presenting philosophic, not literary, judgments when he affirms that literature gives an authentic knowledge of man and of values that are truly objective. He perhaps assumes that any person who reflects upon his prephilosophic experience will agree, but it is obvious that at least some persons read literature and undergo a genuine aesthetic experience without "believing" that literature gives the type of knowledge which he asserts. Let us not assume, therefore, that modern man, who is without religious belief simply because he is a man (and literature deals with man), will admit that authentic knowledge is conveyed through literature. Literature as literature does not nor can it guarantee that the knowledge conveyed through it is objective. Such a task is a philosophic one. When it arises, let us recognize it as a philosophic question to be dealt with by rational discursive analysis and argumentation.

Many values encountered in literature, such as beauty, honesty, selflessness, reverence, fortitude, temperance, justice, reverence for truth, as well as many disvalues such as injustice, pride, and untruthfulness, have been recognized by the human mind without the aid of revelation. Since these values were understood by Aristotle, Plato, Socrates, and many other Greek writers, a knowledge of a personal God is not a prerequisite for the knowledge of and response to these values. Nevertheless, the Christian philosopher holds that "every value response, but above all every response to a morally relevant value, is an implicit, indirect response to God."[13] The reason for this is that "as soon as one philosophically contemplates and analyzes the message embodied in moral values, in their unique gravity, in the categorical character of the obligation which can be grasped by us, we discover that only the existence of a personal God who is the Infinite Goodness can fulfill the message of moral values or can ultimately justify the validity of this obligation."[14]

On the other hand, the Christian philosopher holds that some virtues are "fruits" of the Holy Spirit and possible only in "the new creature in Christ." These would include virtues such as contrition, mercifulness, patience, meekness, and peacefulness and are possible only as responses to the God of Christian revelation and to a world seen in the light of such a response. So also a genuine love of one's neighbor, not a vague humanitarianism, responds to the dignity and beauty of a human person as created in the image of God, redeemed by Christ, and destined for eternal union with God. The Christian philosopher sees these virtues as the fulfillment of all natural morality. As regards natural virtues, the Christian also affirms that these are incorporated and therefore transformed in a new way in Christian morality and that all the virtues manifested in the lives of the saints are now open to philosophic analysis. Thus Bergson as a philosopher and not a believer acknowledged that the morality of the mystics differs from all morality without Christ and that the former is clearly the more exalted and authentic. It is possible, therefore, for the mind which does not accept Christianity to uncover and recognize Christian values in literature, indeed even to respond to them.

The Christian natural philosopher affirms that in addition to the proofs for the existence of God and the manifold avenues to a knowledge of God, there is a prephilosophic approach in which a knowledge of Him is attained in a prereflexive or implicit fashion. Such approaches include the first choice of good, the response to beauty, indeed the response to any authentic value.[15] The problem for the natural theologian, therefore, is to attempt to bring to awareness this prephilosophic or implicit awareness of God. H. E. Root affirms: "The best text-books for contemporary natural theologians are not the secondhand theological treatises but the living works of artists who are in touch with the springs of creative imagination."[16] Literature, therefore, though it is not philosophy nor religion nor theology, can place a reader in contact with God on a prephilosophic level, the level of experience of genuine values and especially of moral values.

By way of conclusions I should like to add that a double danger should be recognized in the current interest in literature as a source of values. On the one hand, students ignorant of theology and religion may seek in literature what actually only religion, theology, or philosophy can explicate and justify. On the other hand, theologians wishing to communicate on a more concrete level than the abstractions of theology may be tempted to use literature simply as illustrative of theological ideas, while bypassing the arduous task of literary criticism in its technical aspects. It is well to recall that, though, as Newman said, all knowledge is one, still, as he also said, every body of knowledge is autonomous within its own boundaries and uses its own methodology. While seeking relationships, let us keep in mind that "good fences make good neighbors."

Notes

¹ I use the words "pure literature" to denote works which are primarily products of the creative imagination; "nonpure literature" to refer to those works primarily intended to communicate facts or ideas but so artistically composed as to communicate, in Walter Pater's phrase, not merely facts but the author's sense of fact.

² John Henry Newman, *The Grammar of Assent* (London, 1889), p. 121.

³ Aristotle, *Metaphysics*, Book I, Section 1.

⁴ *Ibid.*, Book I, Section 3.

⁵ G. Ingli James, "The Autonomy of the Work of Art: Modern Criticism and the Christian Tradition," *The Sewanee Review*, LXX (April–June 1962), 316–317.

⁶ *Ibid.*, p. 317.

⁷ With the gracious permission of Joseph Slattery, S.J., Professor of English, College of Philosophy and Letters, Fordham University, I use in the following remarks on organic form some material from his unpublished manuscript and literary criticism.

⁸ Robert Detweiler, "Christ and the Christ Figure in American Fiction," *The Christian Scholar*, XLVII (Summer 1964), 120.

⁹ Francis L. Kunkel, *The Labyrinthine Ways of Graham Greene* (New York, 1959), pp. 117–118.

¹⁰ David Daiches, *A Study of Literature for Readers and Critics* (New York, 1964), p. 212.

¹¹ For the following explanation I am once again indebted to Joseph Slattery.

[12] Daiches, pp. 217–218.

[13] Dietrich von Hildebrand, *Christian Ethics* (New York, 1953), p. 457.

[14] *Ibid.*, p. 456.

[15] See, for example, Robert W. Gleason, *The Search for God* (New York, 1964), Chapter 11, "New Approaches to God's Existence."

[16] "Beginning All Over Again," *Soundings,* ed. A. R. Vidler (Cambridge, England, 1962), p. 18.

The Conditions of Tragedy

by

Martin Jarrett-Kerr, C.R.

"WHAT THEN IS TRAGEDY? IF NO ONE ASKS ME, I KNOW; IF I WISH TO explain it to one that asketh, I know not." So might one paraphrase St. Augustine's famous remarks about time.[1] Maybe our best approach to an explanation is to see what are some of the conditions which, in the main traditions of literature, are essential to or destructive of the composition of tragedy.

We can recognize perhaps two boundaries: to the left and to the right. The boundary on the left is that of dehumanization. It is represented, some will feel, in an extreme form in the French "anti-novel." Alain Robbe-Grillet, a scientist by training (expert in tropical agriculture, which is not irrelevant to his writing), obviously owes a great deal to Sartre's *La Nausée* and his well-known distinction between the *en-soi* and the *pour-soi*. But Robbe-Grillet criticizes Sartre (and Camus too) for yielding to sentimentality. They are guilty, he says, of using metaphor; and a metaphor is either a capitulation or a falsehood.[2] When you talk of the "majesty" of a mountain or of a village "nestling" in a valley, you are writing anthropomorphically, *i.e.*, you are guilty of the pathetic fallacy. But it is just this that leads to tragedy and ultimately to the illicit creation of a God: if you begin by using metaphor, you may end by believing in God, because God is no more than the most generalized form of the pathetic fallacy. God is a projection of the human sense of misery:

I call out. No one answers. Instead of concluding that no one is there—which might be quite simply an ascertainable fact, dateable, localised in space and time—I decide to behave as if someone were there, but someone who, for reasons unknown, refused to answer. From now on the silence which follows my appeals is no longer a *true* silence: It is endowed with a content, a depth, a soul. . . . Ought I to go on calling out? . . . Should I use a different set of words? Again I try . . . but I very soon realise that no one will answer. Yet the invisible presence that I continue to create by calling out forces me to go on forever breaking the silence with my unhappy cry. . . . In the end, my distraught consciousness translates my exasperated loneliness into a high fatality and a promise of redemption.[3]

The kinship between this mood and that of Samuel Beckett's plays and novels is clear, but it is precisely this that Robbe-Grillet wants to deliver us from. Instead, he offers us *le nouveau roman*, which is written in such a way as to discard the old "sacrosanct psychological analysis" and invites the reader

to look at the world which surrounds him with entirely unprejudiced eyes. . . . Around us, defying the clutter of our animistic or protective adjectives, things *are there*. Their surfaces are clear and smooth, *intact*: neither doubtfully glittering, nor transparent.[4]

This is why the cinema is the most authentic art form today, for it moves us away from the "universe of signification" (psychological, social, functional) and can stress the sheer thereness of familiar gestures and objects. Instead of what the Marxist critic Roland Barthes has called "the romantic heart of things," a dubious kind of inwardness, ordinary objects lose their ambivalence, their secrecy. The hero of this new kind of novel, too, is, literally, "all there." The traditional hero is constantly being distorted, overwhelmed, even destroyed by the author's interpretations of him; he is never fully there—he is "relegated to an intangible *elsewhere*, ever more remote and indistinct, the hero of the future"; but the new hero will "stay put"—it is the commentators who appear to be otiose, even dishonest. Away go the old myths of profundity—"Ah, vous croyez encore à la nature humaine, vous!" cries Robbe-Grillet contemptuously. Man is just a behavior-pattern at a given moment. "Soul-states"—hate, love, etc.—are sloppy metaphors. The artist's business is not to provide an explanation but to "create an object."

The result in Robbe-Grillet's novels is predictable. Every event, object, person in them is described as with a slide rule on a drawing board. For instance, this scene, visible from the dining room in *La Jalousie:*

> The corner window has both leaves open—at least partly. The one on the right is only ajar, so that it still covers at least half of the window opening. The left leaf, on the other hand, is pushed back towards the wall. . . . The window therefore shows three panels of equal height which are of adjoining widths: in the centre the opening, and on each side, a glass area comprising three panes. In all three are framed fragments of the same landscape: the gravel courtyard and the green mass of the banana trees. . . . Franck's big blue sedan, which has just appeared here, is also nicked by one of these shifting rings of foliage, as is A. . . .'s white dress when she gets out of the car.[5]

This is not the place for a lengthy discussion of Robbe-Grillet. But it is significant that even Marxist critics disagree among themselves about him. Roland Barthes praises him, precisely because he rejects tragedy: "Tragedy is merely a way of retrieving human unhappiness, of subsuming it, and thus of justifying it in the form of necessity, wisdom or purification. It is precisely this process that we must reject today: we must search for a technical method of avoiding the traps which tragedy lays—for nothing is more insidious than tragedy."[6] On the other hand, the East German Marxist critic Ernst Fischer finds fault with this *nouvelle vague* for the same reason. He points out—referring to modern cybernetics for comparison—

> how closely the "anti-novel' corresponds to these neo-positivistic ideas and to what a striking extent the people in these novels are reduced to the "black box" of cybernetics, where only the relations of input and output matter and never the nature and essence of man. False philosophical conclusions from the revolutionary discoveries of cybernetics have linked up with a literary method which, in certain individual instances, may be useful as behaviorism is in science but which, as a whole, not only describes the dehumanization of man but actually invests this dehumanization with the character of inescapable finality.[7]

Whether, then, we praise or blame Robbe-Grillet for inventing a method which makes tragedy impossible, he clearly provides us with the

left-hand boundary. There is no tragedy possible where there is no
"human nature" distinct from the rest of nature. Actually, in his attempt
to escape anthropomorphism, Robbe-Grillet gives us, I think, only a sort
of flat, universal theriomorphism—or better, entomomorphism: his eye
for insects is significantly acute.

The boundary on the right is marked by any doctrine which makes
suffering and sorrow ultimately unreal. It is, for instance, often held that
Christian doctrine does so and that, therefore, no Christian tragedy is
possible: "An actor who has often played the role of Becket (in *Murder
in the Cathedral*) put the matter succinctly: 'I know I am being
murdered on the stage, but not once have I really felt dead.' "[8] I do not
know that Eliot ever claimed that his play was a tragedy. There is no
doubt, however, that the anonymous author of the eleventh- or twelfth-
century play *Christus Patiens* thought it a proper Christian successor to
Euripides. And Milton thought so, too. In his Preface to *Samson
Agonistes, i.e.,* in his own defense, he says that "Gregory Nazianzen, a
Father of the Church, thought it not unbeseeming the sanctity of his
person to write a Tragedy, which he entitled, *Christ Suffering*." (Perhaps
it does not much matter that Milton is some eight centuries out.) The
play is called a "Passion according to Euripides," is 2,640 lines long, and
is made up of lines (about one in three) ingeniously lifted from seven of
Euripides' plays. It begins after the betrayal of Christ and ends after the
Resurrection; it has a chorus of Galilean women; there are five messengers, one of whom recites a dialogue between Pilate, the chief priests,
and the guard from the sepulchre. The Virgin is the main figure, but
Christ, St. John, St. Joseph of Arimathea, Nicodemus, and Mary
Magdalene also appear. The play opens with a travesty of the Prologue to
Medea. Medea had said:

> Ah would that Argo ne'er had winged her way
> To Colchis through the blue Symplegades,
> That ne'er in glens of Pelion had fallen
> Those pines likewise beneath the axe!

In *Christus Patiens* the Virgin's opening speech is:

> Ah would the snake had never entered Eden,
> That in its glens the serpent ne'er had hid!

For the trial of Christ some of the lines are borrowed from the trial of
Orestes, and (even more daringly) for Christ on the cross, the lines

describing Peleus caught up in the fir tree (from *The Bacchae*). The Epilogue ends with the unambiguous words:

> Here is a drama true, not wrought of lies,
> Nor smeared with the dung of half-wit tales of old.[9]

No doubt the play is worthless. But even if it were not, it would raise the question whether a drama which includes a hero's death, but ends with a resurrection and a vindication, can be a tragedy. I think that we certainly have to contest Corneille's description of *Polyeucte*—"Polyeucte, Martyr: Tragédie Chrétienne en cinq actes." For, even more explicitly than Becket, Polyeucte desires martyrdom:

> J'ai l'ambition, mais plus noble et plus belle:
> Cette grandeur périt, j'en veux une immortelle,
> Un bonheur assuré, sans mesure et sans fin,
> Au-dessus de l'envie, au-dessus du destin.

The hero's death not only assures him heavenly bliss, but also effects the conversion of his wife Pauline, who is literally baptized in his blood; the conversion of his father-in-law, Felix, who then spares Pauline the death penalty; and the softening, if not (one is led to expect) the ultimate conversion, of Sévère himself, to whom Polyeucte bequeaths his wife.

The play is skillful, powerful, and moving; and the poetry is both resonant and sharp. But there is a tension, if not a contradiction, at the heart of it. Insofar as it has a certain classical, tragic grandeur, it is because Polyeucte has a Promethean kind of defiance, if not bravado, which is less than fully Christian. (Give him a chance, you may say: he is baptized only between Act II and Act III, an hour or so before his death. He has hardly had time to grow into Christian humility! But that is to bring Bradleyan psychology to a classical drama.) On the other hand, insofar as the notion of martyrdom is linked to the notion not only of heavenly glory but also of spiritual effectiveness in this world—the blood of the martyrs is the seed of the Church—that is, insofar as the play is authentically Christian, it ceases to be a tragedy in the classical sense. It may be this very tension which gives the play something of its unique greatness in the Corneille corpus. But at least it defines for us the right-hand borderline of tragedy.

But granted that tragedy must operate within these two boundaries, does this help us much in defining it? Let us try working toward the center from the borders.

First from the left. We have seen that Robbe-Grillet deliberately rejects tragedy and, with it, the notion of the personal. But is there not an element of the "impersonal" in great classical tragedy? Is this not the meaning of the swing away from Bradley: for instance, in Professor Stoll's denial of all relevance of psychology to Shakespeare's characterizations? Critics, says Stoll, have overlooked "a central Aristotelian principle and indulged too much in thoughts about Shakespeare's characters."[10] No doubt this extreme view overlooks the extent to which Aristotle's own principles logically lead to some concern for characterization. "There should be nothing improbable among the actual incidents" in a tragedy; and though the plot is more important than the characters, these must be "good," "appropriate," "lifelike," and "consistent." True, "a convincing impossibility is preferable to an unconvincing possibility."[11] But the wholly unbelievable or monstrous character would not do. There is indeed something of a swing back toward Bradley today. Professor Empson says, "There was a fashion for attacking 'character-analysis,' especially in Shakespeare, which I have taken some time to get out of."[12] And John Bayley has even defended the kind of question represented by Morgann's "Was Falstaff really a coward?" and ridiculed in Professor L. C. Knights' *How Many Children Had Lady Macbeth?* Is this sort of query

> really quite so absurd as it sounds? Its great virtue . . . is that it takes for granted the scope and completeness of Shakespeare's tragic setting. . . . There is a sense in which the highest compliment we can pay to Shakespeare is to discuss his great plays as if they were also great novels.[13]

This involves Bayley in defending *Othello* against its detractors—particularly Eliot and Dr. Leavis. Their premise is

> that a great play should be impersonal, that the quirks and under-currents of individual psychology should be swallowed up in a grand tragic generality. It is significant that admirers of this impersonality in Shakespeare find it at its height in *Antony and Cleopatra*, which is of all his plays the closest to its source. The admired qualities are already implicit in Plutarch. . . . Already the theme is noble, archetypal, while that of *Othello* might well have been turned into comedy, as Shakespeare converted similar tales in *Much Ado* and *All's Well*. The nature of this gap between story and play, and the steps taken to span it, are ignored by the purists of tragic completeness.[14]

This is percipient. Yet I believe that the "purists" were basically right. It was Shakespeare's peculiar genius to lift the naturalistic, without too much disturbance or distortion, into the conventional and thereby to give it a greater, because a more classical, stature and at the same time to bring the conventional, by natural touches, down from the pillared archways and pediments into living contact with surrounding human existence. The gap between his sources and the plays he makes of them does not consist in that the sources are conventional, stylized, whereas Shakespeare's resulting plays are concrete, psychologically convincing. The gap consists in that the sources are (usually) trivial, pedestrian, or artificial (whether naturalistic or conventional), whereas the plays are resonant with the music of greatness and permanence. It *is* a distraction to ask how many children Lady Macbeth had, just as it would be a fatal distraction to ask whether Jocasta had had any husbands before Laius and Oedipus. And if one looks at *Oedipus the King*, and then at what Seneca, Corneille, and Dryden made of it, one sees that it is the compression, the simplicity, the lack of irrelevant incident or psychologizing about incident and character which give it its greatness.

I conclude that, though the total depersonalizing of man marks the left boundary of tragedy, a relative "impersonality" or distance—by which themes loom larger than the men who play in them—is not destructive of tragedy, but indeed has been (so long as the men are recognizable as men, and not puppets or symbolic ghosts) a mark of the greatest tragedies we have known.

We have worked toward the center from the left boundary. Now let us move in from the right. The boundary itself has been expressed in different ways:

Goethe: Tragedy disappears to the degree that an equitable settlement is possible.

Karl Jaspers: The believing Christian no longer recognizes tragedy as genuine. Redemption has occurred and is perpetually renewed by grace.

I. A. Richards: The least touch of any theology which has a compensating Heaven to offer the tragic hero is fatal.

We have agreed that a *Polyeucte* or a *Murder in the Cathedral* is outside the bounds of genuine tragedy. But the relevance of Christian (or of any "redemptive") theology to the possibility of tragedy is a more delicate issue.

George Steiner states roundly that "the Christian vision of man leads to a denial of tragedy"[15] and that "real tragedy can occur only where the tormented soul believes that there is no time left for God's forgiveness."[16] But the implication of this, as Professor E. J. Tinsley acutely points out, is that "Christian orthodoxy is universalist." Indeed, he suggests that

> Some sense of original sin is essential to the tragic sentiment, which sees man as both victim and culprit. The weakening of this doctrine inside theological circles because it was thought to be tied up with the literal acceptance of the Adam and Eve myth and incompatible with the idea of evolution, and outside because it was often confused with Augustinian notions of original guilt, has been a potent factor in making the present climate of thought much less favourable to the tragic sense.[17]

To put the point—or rather, the two points—concretely: a martyrdom can never be a tragedy, but a damnation can. *Doctor Faustus* can be regarded as a fair sample of Christian tragedy, as, indeed, can *Macbeth*, because they both carry a great load of Catholic dogma on their backs and yet do not flinch at the full tragic possibilities of man. There is, of course, a difference between *pre-* and *post-Christum*, in the nature of tragic expression: but it is a difference within the notion of tragedy, not a difference between tragic and non-tragic. Steiner, for instance, contrasts the Greek view of destiny with that of the Old Testament:

> The wars recorded in the Old Testament are bloody and grievous, but not tragic. They are just or unjust. The armies of Israel shall carry the day if they have observed God's will. . . . They shall be routed if they have broken the divine covenant. . . . The Peloponnesian Wars, on the contrary, are tragic. Behind them lie obscure fatalities and misjudgments.[18]

This may be true of the wars; but I do not believe it proves that there can be no tragedy except where there is a Greek notion of atē. Indeed, when he later compares the Elizabethans with the Romantics, Steiner says that in the former, "a tragic rift, an irreducible core of inhumanity, seemed to lie in the mystery of things. The sense of life is itself shadowed by a feeling of tragedy. We see this in Calvin's account of man's condition no less than in Shakespeare's."[19] Yet some accounts of the difference between Greek and Elizabethan would imply that tragedy is possible only with the former. W. H. Auden says:

Greek tragedy is the tragedy of necessity: *i.e.*, the feeling aroused in the spectator is "What a pity it had to be this way"; Christian tragedy is the tragedy of possibility, "What a pity it was this way when it might have been otherwise." . . . The hubris which is the flaw in the Greek hero's character is the illusion of a man who knows himself strong and believes that nothing can shake that strength, while the corresponding Christian sin of Pride is the illusion of a man who knows himself weak but believes he can by his own efforts transcend that weakness and become strong.[20]

Auden is actually contrasting Greek tragedy with a novel like *Moby Dick*; but what he says would apply equally to Shakespeare, and indeed he does later mention *Macbeth*. His conclusion is that Greek tragedy is inescapably pessimistic:

The pessimistic conclusion that underlies Greek tragedy seems to be this: that if one is a hero, *i.e.*, an exceptional individual, one must be guilty of hubris and be punished by tragic fate; the only alternative, and not one a person can choose for himself, is to be a member of the chorus, *i.e.*, one of the average mass; to be both exceptional and good is impossible.[21]

The mention of the chorus is interesting, because in quite another context the theologian Reinhold Niebuhr had asked:

What would the hero of tragedy do without these weeping, appreciating and revering spectators? This necessity of pity from the lesser who keep the law for the greater who break it out of inner necessity, is the symbol of an unresolved conflict in the heart of Greek tragedy. It does not know where the real centre of life lies, whether in its law or in its vitality. Therefore the weak law-abiders must honour the strong law-breakers, lest the latter seem dishonourable.[22]

Now this judgment of Greek civilization—for that is what it is—seems to me a theological judgment which does not arise out of the situation of the Greek theater as such. I happen to agree with it, but it is an extraneous judgment, not a literary one. The same is true, though less so, of Auden's description of the essential "pessimism" of Greek drama. If we could put ourselves in the sandals of the Greek spectator at a performance of Oedipus or Medea, should we come away at the end with "pessimism" as our prize? If by "pessimism" we mean "despair of the world, of fate, of the gods," surely this is the emotion to which catharsis is supposed to be applied. Perhaps in the long run it is not the rather abstract and generalized notions of a particular people's theology that will best illuminate the works of art they produce, but the more hazy, symbolic forms through which they think their theology. And these may be similar to those of other peoples in a way which brings an imaginative agreement over a wide area.

Let us widen the area still more and see what happens. Teilhard de Chardin as far back as 1923 wrote: "I feel more and more strongly the necessity to free our religion from everything in it that is specifically Mediterranean."[23] This goes for more than religion. It is significant that Brecht drew, for some of his plays, on Japanese and Chinese sources. Let me take an Indian one, Kalidasa's Shakuntala (probably fifth century). (I read it twelve years ago or more but was fortunate to see a performance of it by an Indian cast in Johannesburg in 1956.) It is based on a legend from the Mahabharata, but the legend has been expanded, embroidered, and made more dramatic. It may seem irrelevant to a discussion of tragedy, for it is a kind of fairy-tale comedy—indeed, all Indian plays must traditionally have a happy ending, and this puts them outside our right-hand boundary. But, abstracting from that convention for a moment and disregarding the deus ex machina conclusion (a charioteer of Indra comes down to take the hero, Dushyanta, off to battle with demons, and it is in the land of the gods, apparently, that the recognition and the reconciliation between Dushyanta and Shakuntala take place), we can in fact find potentially tragic moments in the play. Shakuntala, a lovely virgin, has married King Dushyanta, who saw her when he was hunting in the forest. When pregnant, she comes to the capital to remind him of their marriage. But because of a curse put on them both by an irascible sage, Durvasas, who was annoyed about a minor failure in hospitality, the King does not recognize Shakuntala. When he does remember her, she has departed from the court and has been snatched into Heaven.

In spite of this supernatural conclusion and the reconciliation, the play does show some of the characteristics of Greek drama. King Dushyanta, looking back at the crisis, says of his wife, Shakuntala: "My memory failed me, and I rejected her. In so doing I sinned against Kanva [i.e., Shakuntala's ward]. . . . But afterwards when I saw the ring, I perceived that I had married her." (The ring was to have been the means by which Shakuntala would prove to him her identity, but part of the curse was that she should lose it in the Ganges. After she has vanished, the ring is found and brought to the King.)

> KASHYAPA (*father of the gods: reassuring him*): My son, do not accuse yourself of sin. Your infatuation was inevitable. . . .
> DUSHYANTA: Then I am free from blame!
> SHAKUNTALA (*to herself*): Thank heaven! My husband did not reject me of his own accord. He really did not remember me. I suppose I did not hear the curse, in my absent-minded state, for my friends warned me most earnestly to show my husband the ring.

The supernatural element is not surprising, since Shakuntala herself was half-supernaturally born: A royal sage was getting so holy with ascetic practices that the gods became jealous of his sanctity. They sent a nymph, Menaka, to tempt him, and Shakuntala, born of this holy man and the nymph, was the result! Yet basically the ingredients are those common to all classical drama: Fate decrees the original situation; then, not fully aware of what you are doing, you break a law; and then Nemesis (a henchman of Fate) guides the course of events within the given situation. Finally there is a *dénouement*, which may be tragic or happy, and though you will be blamed only for that segment of the resulting evil for which you are really responsible, you will suffer out of proportion to that blame. But take courage! For either the sorrow will be lifted (comedy), or at least its significance for man will be shown and can be accepted (tragedy).

I know nothing of Japanese and Chinese drama. But I do know that African folklore and ritual can throw an interesting light on our European dramatic tradition. Dame Sybil Thorndyke has written of the remarkable reception she and her husband had from Africans (Negroes of South Africa) when playing *Medea* in Johannesburg, and I can confirm this, having sat among the African audience at the time. Back in 1899 Mary Kingsley wrote about the African convert to Christianity who was troubled by the theme of Job—why do the righteous suffer?—

> I see the temptation to return to those old gods—the gods from whom he never expected pity, presided over by a god that does not care. All that he [the African, in his anxiety] had to do with them was not to irritate them, to propitiate them, to buy their services when wanted, and above all to dodge and avoid them, while he fought it out and managed devils at large.[24]

And an anthropologist, Professor Meyer Fortes, has written an illuminating study, *Oedipus and Job in West African Religion*,[25] which shows the form of and the social way of coping with the themes of Oedipus and Job among the Tallensi of West Africa. He says that the central conception of Oedipus, the "Oedipal principle," "is best summed up in the notion of Fate or Destiny" and the "Jobian principle" is summed up in that of "Supernatural Justice."[26] Now among the Tallensi many evils (accidents to men, above all barrenness in women) are due to an evil prenatal Destiny; this can be met only by sacrifices to the paternal ancestors, who will put things right. The parallel with Sophocles is exact—up to a point; but beyond that point there is divergence. For whereas for Oedipus there is no reconciliation possible, the Tallensi victim has a chance, viz., by restoration of the right relationship to his ancestors. Of Oedipus, Professor Fortes says:

> His fate is evil; it enters into his life at the very beginning through his being rejected by his parents when they cast him away. He survives only because he is accepted by substitute parents. . . . But his fate catches up with him. He is finally overwhelmed by his fate because he unknowingly violates the basic norms of filial relationship. His tragedy can be described as that of a man blindly seeking to achieve his legitimate place in society, first as son, then as husband, father and citizen, against the unconscious opposition of an inborn urge to avenge himself by repudiating his parents, his spouse, and his children. When he succumbs to this fate he shows his revulsion against himself by mutilating his own eyes, and so blotting out his relationship with his kin and his society. He dies in exile, almost like a ghost departing from this world rather than like an ordinary man.[27]

But the Tallensi would provide a means of countering Oedipus' prenatal Fate. And so, perhaps, like the Indians, they would not have allowed of ultimate tragedy.

What is common to these diverse examples are the two elements: (a) you are not wholly responsible for your fate; therefore your suffering is undeserved, quixotic from man's point of view. *Moral*—puny man must respect what is greater than he. But (b) you are partly responsible for what you make of your fate, even for part of the fate itself; therefore if you are to keep your self-respect, you must do something about it (repent, sacrifice, accept). *Moral*—puny man is still valuable for his freedom.

And this is relevant to the last question we must ask: What is the future for tragedy in the West? Steiner reminds us that the main reason for the decline (he calls it the death) of tragedy is the coming of Rousseauist optimism, which

> cannot engender any natural form of tragic drama. The romantic vision of life is non-tragic. In authentic tragedy, the gates of hell stand open and damnation is real. The tragic personage cannot evade responsibility. To argue that Oedipus should have been excused on grounds of ignorance, or that Phèdre was merely prey to hereditary chaos of the blood, is to diminish to absurdity the weight and meaning of the tragic action.[28]

And he says percipiently of Ibsen that, though the greatest dramatist of the past two hundred years, he

> starts where earlier tragedies end, and his plots are epilogues to previous disaster. Suppose Shakespeare had written a play showing Macbeth and Lady Macbeth living on their black lives in exile after they had been defeated. . . . We might then have the angle of vision that we find in *John Gabriel Borkman*.[29]

And the reason why the tragic dimension is missing from Chekhov is simply that Chekhov was a physician, "and medicine knows grief and even despair in the particular instance, but not tragedy."[30] If the recent past is thus unpromising, what of the future? Mr. Raymond Williams, critic, historian, and novelist, has put the contrasting views in a dialogue. First, the view that tragedy has no future:

> When man is his own measure, or, worse, when the attributes of God are transferred to man or to life, you simply cannot have tragedy. . . . Tragedy [in the sense of] the bare facts of suffering and death, of course still exists. But tragedy as a form which can interpret them significantly is only a memory. When, as with the Greeks and Elizabethans, there was an order beyond human life, the bare facts could be illuminated and transcended, because there were facts beyond them to which they could relate.[31]

But another character replies:

> We have abandoned the tragic universe, and we've lived past the tragic hero. [But] we have reached, definitively, the tragic society.

. . . Tragedy has, if you like, broken out of its frame. . . . Yeats
spoke of tragedy as breaking the dykes between man and man, and I
have always remembered the phrase and been moved by it. But did
he only mean sympathy? . . . That is real, but not only that. And I
have been moved . . . by men's actual solidarity in suffering: a
coming together, and a giving, that seem absolute, while they
last. . . . [In this shared suffering] which of these, in the end, can
be individual, and which society? . . . The tragedy seems to be, our
tragedy seems to be, in the images of connection.[32]

Something of the same emphasis is in Brecht, who replaces human *nature*
by human *relations:* who claims in his plays to offer us his personages in
such a way that we deduce their character from their actions—instead of
the traditional theater "which derives its action from the nature of the
characters."[33]

The reason, again, why *Waiting for Godot* is the one play of Samuel
We have, however, seen reason to doubt whether this account of
"the traditional theater" does justice to it—whether Brecht is not reacting against the idealistic-psychological interpretation of romantic criticism. Brecht's own program for his theater would, if carried out, take him
over our left-hand boundary of tragedy—the depersonalized. His success
as a playwright lies in the fact that he does not carry out his program:
that his sense for the human person in the human situation is too
powerful to remain trapped in the bulldozer jaws of doctrinaire Marxism.
The reason, again, why *Waiting for Godot* is the one play of Samuel
Beckett's that stands out from the sad ash cans (and audiences have
registered this) is that here, in the face of Beckett's metaphysical
conclusions, his sense of human life, his sheer power to make people
laugh (not just sick laughter, either) are at full play and show Beckett to
be imaginatively still within the human family.

The banal conclusion is this: that tragedy will survive only so long as
the artist does not work against the grain of common human nature;
conditions of man and society may be such that it can survive even then
only in an attenuated form; but survive it will, so long as man is man.
And perhaps we shall find it re-emerging most forcefully in those
countries where a total political authority tries to encompass the total
human person—tries and fails. For—and it is a Marxist critic who writes
this—"Man, being mortal and therefore imperfect, will always find
himself part of, and yet struggling with, the infinite reality that surrounds
him."[34]

Notes

[1] *Confessions*, Book XI, Part XIV.

[2] See his articles in *Nouvelle Revue Française:* "Une Voie pour le roman futur," *NRF*, IV (July 1956), 77–84, and "Nature, humanisme, tragédie," *NRF*, VI (October 1958), 580–604. See also J. G. Weightman, "Alain Robbe-Grillet," *Encounter*, XVIII (March 1962), 30–39.

[3] "Nature, humanisme, tragédie," 590–591. Cited by Weightman, 32.

[4] "Une Voie pour le roman futur," 80–81.

[5] *Jealousy* (New York, 1959), pp. 47–48.

[6] Cited by Weightman, 31.

[7] *The Necessity of Art, A Marxist Approach* (Baltimore, 1963), p. 200.

[8] George Steiner, *The Death of Tragedy* (London, 1961), p. 341.

[9] Cited in Frank L. Lucas, *Euripides and His Influence* (New York, 1963), p. 86.

[10] See Elmer E. Stoll, *Art and Artifice in Shakespeare* (Cambridge, England, 1934) and "Poetry and the Passions," *PMLA*, LV (December 1940), 979–992.

[11] Humphry House, *Aristotle's Poetics* (London, 1956), *passim*.

[12] *Milton's God* (London, 1961), p. 69.

[13] *The Characters of Love* (London, 1960), pp. 41 ff.

[14] *Ibid.*, p. 137.

[15] Steiner, p. 6.

[16] Ibid., p. 332.

[17] Christian Theology and the Frontiers of Tragedy (Leeds, 1963), pp. 19 ff.

[18] Steiner, p. 6.

[19] Ibid., p. 16.

[20] "The Christian Tragic Hero," New York Times Book Review, December 16, 1945, p. 1. Cited in William K. Wimsatt, Jr., and Cleanth Brooks, Literary Criticism; A Short History (New York, 1957), p. 55.

[21] Ibid.

[22] Beyond Tragedy (New York, 1937), p. 165. Cited in Thomas R. Henn, The Harvest of Tragedy (London, 1956), pp. 160–161.

[23] Letter of May 27, 1923.

[24] West African Studies (London, 1899). Cited in Olwen Campbell, Mary Kingsley (London, 1957), p. 130.

[25] Cambridge, 1959. Professor Fortes is Professor of Social Anthropology at Cambridge University.

[26] Fortes, p. 11.

[27] Ibid., pp. 70 ff.

[28] Steiner, p. 128.

[29] Ibid., pp. 296 ff.

[30] Ibid., p. 302.

[31] "Dialogue on Tragedy," New Left Review, Nos. 13–14 (January–April 1962), 26–27.

[32] Ibid., 34–35.

[33] Martin Esslin, Brecht: A Choice of Evils (London, 1959), p. 118.

[34] The Necessity of Art, p. 223.

The Fall: Christian Truth and Literary Symbol

by

Frederick W. Dillistone

AT THE END OF JULY, 1965 THE REGULAR SATURDAY COMMENTARY IN THE London *Times* on the week's broadcasting was devoted to the first teach-in which had been staged on television—an exercise described by the critic as the most protracted and colossal bore in the history of British broadcasting. But some of the phrases used in the commentary were intriguing. This was a kind of "tribal conclave," similar to a Red Indian "pow-wow," to consider the basic question, "how to get Britain moving." Many walks of life were represented, but "their total contribution to the problem set was disappointing. The spokesmen of management and labor wrangled about their familiar differences, and doled out the blame to each other. Most of the eloquence was at least ten years old and there was a woeful shortage of constructive comment about how to get out of the hole we are in."

I have begun by referring to what may seem a trivial event and a lighthearted commentary in order to draw attention to a ritual form and a verbal symbolism that have characterized human life from the dawn of history. Men get together to consider what has gone wrong in their common life and to ask what may be done to improve their present condition. And in the attempt to describe this condition no picture comes more readily to the imagination than that of a *fall*—a fall into a hole, a trap maybe devised by an enemy, or simply a natural pit unforeseen because of overgrowth or darkness. Man has fallen. He is immobilized. How can he get out of the pit? How can he get moving again? The question of how he ever came to fall into the hole may be secondary, but it may also be of great importance when it comes to the search for a way out, for a reversal of the unhappy disaster.

This simple imagery is not, of course, the only scenery associated with the drama of a fall. Man may fall from a tree, from a great rock, or even from a tower of his own construction. This can be still more disastrous than the act of stumbling into a pit. It can easily be inflated in the imagination until it becomes a fall from the skies or from some celestial realm. Heights have exercised a strange fascination over the human psyche, and yet man has been quick to recognize that the greater his achievement in climbing to the heights, the more serious will be the hazard of falling to the depths. "Humpty-Dumpty had a great fall." From the most elementary nursery rhymes to the most complex dramas of sophisticated culture, the fall theme retains its popularity and its moving appeal.

What is true of life in general has certainly been true of the life of religion. Until comparatively recently, a coming-together to consider the ills afflicting a community would have felt bound to ask whether something had gone wrong in the relation between the seen and the unseen worlds, between the human and the divine, between man and the supernatural forces which surround him on every side. Had man "fallen" out of favor through some trespass? Had he "fallen" into a condition of helplessness through the malevolent trickery of some evil spirit? Had he, through aspiring to some "higher" level of existence, exceeded his limits and been therefore cast down to something "lower" than he had known before? Such questions were incapable of what we should call "rational" answers. Answers, rather, were framed in terms of "myths, dreams, and mysteries," to use the title of one of Mircea Eliade's books. There was no single myth of the Fall. But the stories which we in our Western civilization have inherited from Greece and Rome and Israel directly, as well as those which have come from Egypt and Babylonia and Persia indirectly, have had as one of the constantly recurring themes the hole into which man has fallen and the way in which he may get moving again.

Within the Christian tradition, which dominated Western culture at least until the beginning of the nineteenth century, the biblical fall stories were those most widely known; and they provided a natural background for man's imaginative thinking. It is true that at the time of the Renaissance the Greek myths and tragedies began to make their impact upon limited circles of the intelligentsia. But any poet or painter or

dramatist who wished to appeal to the general conscience of his contemporaries turned almost instinctively to the great themes which had
been vividly portrayed to successive generations of Christendom through
sculpture, through stained glass, through mystery plays, and above all
through the simple recital of the biblical stories themselves. Through the
Bible an authoritative divine revelation had been given to mankind. It
was man's duty, whether he were statesman or poet or peasant, to pay
heed to this revelation, both for the saving of his own soul and for the
carrying out of the particular function he was called to fulfill in the life of
the society to which he belonged.

Now, although there was constantly the need to consider what could
have brought about the immediate ills of the community—defeat at the
hands of an enemy, plague and sickness, drought and flood—there was a
constant reminder, through the Church's living representatives and institutional forms, that there was an ultimate condition whose seriousness
transcended all immediate ills, however unpleasant they might be. In the
past there had been a Golden Age and a Garden of Blessedness. Man had
enjoyed that high estate until the primordial disaster had overtaken him
when, assailed by temptation, he had fallen into the sin of radical
disobedience and had consequently been expelled from the paradise in
which he might have lived forever. Yet even in that dark hour there had
come the promise of a way out, and it was the Church's task to proclaim
that way as it had been inaugurated by the Divine Redeemer and
continued through the sacramental system, which brought life and
healing to mankind.

This was the background myth of the human situation which maintained its hold on the Christian imagination for some 1600 years. Yet,
strangely enough, there is no direct use of the imagery of *falling* in the
foundation story of Genesis 3. There are a state of innocence, an invitation to pass beyond innocence to a knowledge of good and evil (though
this advance had been forbidden by a divine fiat), the fateful act of
grasping the forbidden fruit, the loss of innocence, the involvement in
toil and pain, and the expulsion from the garden of immortality. The
obvious imagery is that of being shut out, excluded, repulsed rather than
of falling or descending to a lower level. "The presumption of man and
his exclusion from Paradise" is in a sense a more accurate title for the
myth than simply "the fall of man." But somehow the language and
imagery of "fallenness" came to prevail.

For this I suggest two or three possible explanations. First, there is
the fact to which I have already drawn attention: that to fall is one of the
commonest and most shattering experiences of life. A glance through a

concordance reveals constant reference to "falling" in battle in the Old Testament. "How are the mighty fallen!" occurs twice in the moving lament over Saul and Jonathan. It is always distressing to fall. To fall in death is the final disaster—and in later theology the sin of Adam and his death were inextricably interrelated. Again, in the Apocryphal Book of Wisdom a Greek word meaning literally a fall or a falling aside is used as a summary description of the defection of the first-formed father of mankind; and this word was later taken up and used by St. Paul in his exceedingly important and influential commentary on Adam's transgression in the fifth chapter of the Epistle to the Romans.

But more significant still is the vivid language of the prophets employed to denounce the tyrannous powers of their day. Nineveh, Tyre, and above all Babylon are seen as guilty of the fearful sin of *superbia*, of proudly exalting themselves in defiance of the living God. Yet their glory lies in ruins, and some of the most magnificent dirges in all literature are those in which the prophets look either back upon the fall which has already come to pass or upon the downfall which they regard as inevitable in the future. And in one oracle, perhaps the most influential of all, the prophet links the collapse of the Babylonian empire with the fall of the Prince of Evil from the bliss of heaven itself:

> How hath the oppressor ceased!
>   the golden city ceased!
> Hell from beneath is moved for thee
>   to meet thee at thy coming.
> How art thou fallen from heaven,
>   O Lucifer, son of the morning!
> How art thou cut down to the ground,
>   which didst weaken the nations!
> For thou hast said in thine heart,
>   I will ascend into heaven;
> I will exalt my throne above the stars of God;
> I will ascend above the heights of the clouds;
> I will be like the most High.
> Yet thou shalt be brought down to hell,
>   to the sides of the pit.   (Isaiah 14:4 ff.)

Though the first reference to Lucifer may have been to an imaginative astral counterpart to Babylon, it was easy for later generations to read it as referring to Satan, the angel who had exalted himself against God and for this reason had been cast out of heaven. In an unusual but striking outcry

Jesus is recorded as having said, "I beheld Satan as lightning fall from heaven"; and the theme recurs in the great visions of the Apocalypse, when Satan's final overthrow is envisaged. This I think is one of the great archetypal pictures which have become engraven upon the imagination of the West: the rebellious angel in heaven tries to exalt himself and, instead, falls headlong to earth; this same angel now in earthbound disguise tempts man also to exalt himself that he may be "like God"; and man shares, though in a less dramatic way, the fate which overcame Satan himself. The total universe of man is now a "fallen" system, doomed to final destruction unless somehow a champion intervenes to rescue man from his prime adversary and to remove the incubus of his folly which weighs so heavily upon him. This is the picture of fallenness which Christendom accepted and made normative for both its theology and its culture.

Even the revolutionary changes brought about by the Reformation did not seriously affect the general view of the Fall. They may have resulted in a new emphasis in some sectors of Christendom on the heinousness of man's crime and the helplessness of his condition. They may, in Reformed circles through the new acquaintance with the text of the Bible, have led to a more widespread knowledge of the details of the Fall and a more literalistic interpretation of its place in human history. Certainly a major division arose between those who believed that the effects of the Fall had been undone for all men by the work of the Redeemer and that all could enjoy the benefits of His redemption by being incorporated into the Church which He founded and those who believed that God had from all eternity chosen certain men unto salvation and that only those who were joined to His Christ in faith and love would be rescued from the fallen world of darkness and given an inheritance among the sons of light. But whatever theories of grace and redemption and the church and the sacraments were entertained, the background picture of man's condition and the fundamental analysis of how he came to be in such a situation were common to all. Man was a fallen creature and in need of redemption to eternal life—this was the conviction of Augustinian and Pelagian, Calvinist and Arminian alike.

With this common conviction so securely held, the Fall theme could provide a natural background for literature as well as for theology. It is not necessarily elaborated: it is simply assumed. In Dante, for example, references to "Adam's evil brood," to "our first parent" confined to Limbo, to the tree pleasant to taste from whence "the appetite was warped to evil," to the nature which

> Created first was blameless, pure and good;
> But, through itself alone, was driven forth
> From Paradise, because it had eschewed
> The way of truth and life, to evil turned;

perhaps above all to Adam's own imagined confession:

> Not that I tasted of the tree, my son,
> Was in itself the cause of that exile
> But only my transgressing of the mark
> Assigned me:

all these reveal a general background of the human imagination to which the poet could appeal and be assured of immediate response. Even in Shakespeare, who is far more concerned with man in history, his possibilities, his achievements, his conflicts, his disasters, there is one moving passage which indicates that the imagery of a primal Fall was tacitly assumed—though it could be claimed that man has far greater power to deal with his own inheritance and to shape his own destiny than any Augustinian tradition would allow.

The passage to which I refer is at the conclusion of Act 3 in *King Henry VIII*. First Wolsey alone meditates on the state of man: tender leaves of hope, blossoms of honor, then the killing frost: "and then he falls as I do." Like little wanton boys that swim on bladders he has ventured far beyond his depth; his high-blown pride has broken under him:

> And when he falls, he falls like Lucifer,
> Never to hope again.

Now Cromwell enters, "amazedly," but Wolsey asks:

> What, amazed
> At my misfortunes? can thy spirit wonder
> A great man should decline? Nay, and you weep
> I am fallen indeed.

Cromwell gives news which makes Wolsey's future even darker, but the great man fallen will not allow him to stay by to assist or defend. He must seek the king and enlist in his service, yet not until he has heard a concluding charge wrung from his former master's bitter experience:

> Mark but my fall and that that ruin'd me.
> Cromwell, I charge thee, fling away ambition;
> By that sin fell the angels; how can man then
> The image of his Maker, hope to win by't?
> 　Be just and fear not,
> Let all the ends thou aim'st at be thy country's,
> Thy God's and truth's; then if thou fall'st, O Cromwell,
> Thou fall'st a blessed martyr! Serve the king.

As is clear, the mythology of Lucifer and his angels, of man created in the image of God and tempted to presume, is taken for granted, though far more is included within the individual's responsibility than would have been allowed by the Puritans of Shakespeare's own time. For them mankind in general was in a state of complete fallenness: only the mercy of God could draw individuals out of the pit. For Shakespeare, on the other hand, the primordial picture of the Fall presented man with the warning not to exalt himself above measure lest the same disaster should overtake him as had been the case with the Prince of Darkness.

The translation of the Bible into the common tongues, the distribution of books through the coming of the printing press, and the general advance of the new learning resulted in a still more extended popular familiarity with the great drama of the rebellion in Heaven, the fall of Lucifer, the creation of man and his subsequent capitulation to the wiles of the fallen angel, and the still greater redemption of man, the harrowing of hell, and the restoration of Paradise. Writers in many European countries saw the possibilities of expressing this all-powerful theme through the media of epic poetry and tragic drama, and their works still bear witness to the universality of interest which it evoked. But it was the destiny of one outstanding Englishman to sum up, as it were, in one great epic poem the assumptions of European culture in a pre-scientific, pre-critical age. Deeply versed in the classics and natural philosophy, Milton had virtually committed the Bible to heart. Because he also possessed an almost unparalleled genius for the composition of rhythms and cadences of language, no other man could have been better qualified to construct the imaginative work which was to magnify the wisdom of God and to expose the tragedy of angels and of men. And it has I think been rightly claimed that Milton did more to engrave the Fall drama upon the English imagination than did even the Bible itself.

It would be superfluous to quote at length from Milton's great work. Within the first fifty lines occurs one of the most magnificent passages in all literature. Here is the age-long question—"What could possibly have caused mankind to 'fall off from their Creator' "? The answer is expressed in unforgettable words:

> The infernal Serpent, he it was whose guile
> Stirred up with envy and revenge deceived
> The mother of mankind, what time his pride
> Had cast him out from Heaven, with all his host
> Of rebel Angels, by whose aid, aspiring
> To set himself in glory above his peers,
> He trusted to have equalled the Most High,
> If he opposed, and, with ambitious aim
> Against the throne, and monarchy of God,
> Raised impious war in Heaven and battle proud,
> With vain attempt, Him the Almighty Power
> Hurled headlong flaming from the ethereal sky,
> With hideous ruin and combustion, down
> To bottomless perdition, there to dwell
> In adamantine chains and penal fire
> Who durst defy the Omnipotent to arms.

Milton rose to the heights in expressing the Fall in terms of the Ptolemaic world-picture at the very time when that picture was being severely threatened (and it seems clear that Milton felt the threat himself) by Copernicus and Galileo. He reached a similar eminence in describing the great Rebellion in terms of the Hebraic picture of absolute Divine sovereignty at the time when that picture was being threatened by new ideas of human freedom and responsibility (and this threat must also have been present to Milton's mind). The poem coincided with the end of a theocentric, theonomous universe. The question was what would happen to the imagery of the Fall as the new scientific and new libertarian notions gained increasing acceptance in Western culture?

It is almost exactly three hundred years since *Paradise Lost* was published. During that period enormous changes have taken place in the Western world, the most obvious of which has been the advance of science in theory and in practice. The whole temper has been empirical, and this has brought about a gradual loosening of all close ties with traditional theological disciplines. As science has grown in confidence, theology has adjusted its sights, re-examined its presuppositions, clutched eagerly at an alliance with historical research, and, broadly speaking, tried to retain its autonomy over whatever its rival might discover about the universe in which we live. Yet at one point the two disciplines were bound to confront and challenge each other. This point was the doctrine of man—his nature, his potentialities, his limitations, his destiny. What effect would the scientific investigation of man's past and the technological direction of his present capacities have upon the Christian doctrines of the Fall and Original Sin? What effect, if any, would the theological affirmation of man's createdness and necessary limitations have upon the progress of science?

It is already clear that this has been a very one-sided encounter. Science has marched triumphantly forward, little troubled by notions of a Fall or inherited sinfulness. Theology, on the other hand, has seemed constantly to be fighting rear-guard actions or to be withdrawing from the conflict into some fastness of its own. By 1924 a position had been reached which was brilliantly summarized by N. P. Williams in his Bampton Lectures delivered at the University of Oxford and bearing the title "The Ideas of the Fall and Original Sin":

> There was a time when the scheme of orthodox dogma appeared to all as an unshakable adamantine framework, resting upon the two pillars of the Fall and of Redemption. These two complementary conceptions—that of the great apostasy which defaced the image of God in man, and that of the great restoration through the Incarnation and the Atonement, which revived it—were universally taken for granted as the twin focal points which determined the eclipse of traditional theology: and the imagination of Christians loved to play around the parallelism of Adam and Christ—of the deathbringing Tree of Knowledge and the life-giving Tree of the Cross. But the days when this conviction reigned unchallenged were days when most men believed that they dwelt in a comparatively small, geocentric universe. Since then the world in which we live has expanded like a wizard's creation, at the touch of the magic wand of science. The imagination is staggered by the illimitable leagues of interstellar space and the uncounted aeons of geologic time.
>
> It is not too much to say that, whilst for professed and genuine Christians, the second great pillar of the Faith, the doctrine of Redemption, remains unshaken, founded upon direct experience of the redeeming love of God in Christ, even they have the uneasy

feeling that the first pillar, the doctrine of the Fall, has been irretrievably undermined, and totters on its base, no longer capable of bearing its former share of the super-incumbent weight. There are indeed those who urge that it is now a source of weakness rather than of strength to the fabric which it supported for so long and should be razed to the ground.

But if this was the situation in the relationship of theology and science, what was the attitude of literature and the arts? They for their part could certainly not be indifferent to the doctrine of man. In fact, their abiding concern has been to interpret the actions, the perceptions, the sensitivities, the anxieties of man through symbolic forms. Normally, as I have suggested, until Milton's time this was done against the background of the general assumption of a Fall and its legacy of evil to posterity. But if this assumption were to be doubted or denied, what would take its place?

It can be said at once that poetry and drama and the novel were almost as disinclined as theology was to accept the presuppositions and outlook of science. Yet at the same time they had no wish to be hampered by any kind of orthodox theology. So we see the emergence in the nineteenth century of various doctrines of man, doctrines described by Norman Nicholson in his book *Man and Literature* by such titles as "Liberal Man," "Natural Man," and "Imperfect Man." The study of history suggested a picture of a gradual ascent upon an inclined plane rather than a fall into a hole from which no ordinary escape was possible. Or it suggested a picture of conflicting elements on a lower plane, ultimately finding a creative synthesis on a higher, rather than of continuous fighting in a cockpit from which a limited number of combatants were snatched by the exercise of some supernatural fiat. There was a richly varied output of literature in the nineteenth century, and generalizations about it are highly dangerous. Obviously Browning was deeply concerned about the liberalistic and idealistic assumptions which were gaining credence in his time. Hawthorne and Melville had little doubt about the fallenness of man. Yet it can at least be said that the old assumptions were being questioned and modified even when they were not abandoned. There was no longer any single myth undergirding literature. Man's growing knowledge of his universe, his increasing power to organize his social environment, his developing ethical insights—these were themes which the sensitive artist tried to represent in word and action and pictorial form without necessarily setting them within any all-inclusive world-picture. Above all, there was uncertainty about the existence of transcendent elements, whether of good or of evil, of wisdom or of irrationality, within the range of human experience. That there was room for improvement in man's condition few could doubt. But could this not be achieved by man himself, given time and patience and cooperation and fuller knowledge and a removal of the prejudices and dogmas and restrictions of the past?

"In or about December 1910," Virginia Woolf once wrote, "*human nature changed.*" The question immediately arises: Why this particular date? Here Walter Allen, from whose recent book *Tradition and Dream* I have quoted this statement, comes to our aid. He points out that December 1910 was the date of the opening in London of the Post-Impressionist Exhibition: a wide public became aware of the paintings of Van Gogh, Gauguin, Cezanne, Matisse, Picasso. Dostoevsky's novels, which had been appearing in French translations, began to be made available in English in 1912. Twelve volumes of Frazer's *Golden Bough* were published between 1911 and 1915. Most important of all, both Freud and Jung had been lecturing in America in 1909; and by 1913 *The Interpretation of Dreams* could be read in England. So, Walter Allen concludes, the men of 1914—writers, critics, interpreters—"all break up the accepted realistic surface of things and emphasize, at the expense of the rational and mechanical, of the scientific in its simpler manifestations, the irrational, the unconscious, the mythical." Yet had human nature really changed? Or had the Western view of human nature begun to change?

Let us look in another direction—to a recent poem by Philip Hobsbaum:

The Beginning of a War

That Sunday I was at classes, I remember,
But we didn't do much work. The teachers all
Were clustered in another room listening—
We clustered round the door, listening—
To tones which trembled as a life's work fell:
"That Note has not been received. . . . War is declared."

War is declared, they said: the words seemed tame.
So many things had been declared of late.
We thought the teachers' faces were absurd
As solemnly they sent us home. The sun

Shone and the park was leafier than the street.
I went the long way round. A siren wailed.

My street had changed. No neighbours were in sight.
I found my mother rushing up and down.
She clutched me to her as I came and glanced
Rapidly up at the sky as we ran in.
The gestures, clear to her, were vague to me.
It seemed the threat was only in her head.

That innocence has gone, stately, primal.
Signs leap out at us from every page,
Rumble in the air over our heads, are breathed
In with the air we breathe, wake when we sleep—
We would call back our innocence again,
So troubled is the air after the fall.

Did a Fall, the second Fall, the ultimate Fall, take place in September 1939?

I take one more example: "On the 10th of September 1945," Edith Sitwell tells us, "nearly five weeks after the fall of the first atom bomb, my brother, Sir Osbert Sitwell, and I were in the train going to Brighton, where we were to give a reading. He pointed out to me a paragraph in *The Times*, a description by an eyewitness of the immediate effect of the atom bomb upon Hiroshima. That witness saw a totem pole of dust arise to the sun as a witness against the murder of mankind—a totem pole, the symbol of creation, the symbol of generation." And out of that experience the poem "The Shadow of Cain" took shape.

"The poem," she tells us, "is about the fission of the world into warring particles, destroying and self-destructive. It is about the gradual migration of mankind, after that Second Fall of Man that took the form of the separation of brother and brother, of Cain and Abel, of nation and nation, of the rich and the poor, the spiritual migration of these into the desert of the Cold, towards the final disaster, the first symbol of which fell on Hiroshima."

The living blind and seeing dead together lie
As if in love— There was no more hating then
And no more love. Gone is the heart of Man.

Did human nature change at eighteen minutes past eight o'clock on the morning of Monday, the 6th of August 1945? Was this the inexorable outcome of the Second Fall which took place when Cain sought to obliterate Abel? Was Hiroshima the ultimate Fall, the death of the heart of Man?

1910, 1914, 1939, 1945. What is the significance of dates such as these? I have drawn attention to three remarkable attempts by modern writers to interpret the character of the age in which we are living. There is obviously no certainty, no precision here but rather agonizing questions: What has gone wrong? Where did things begin to go wrong? Has the final wrong-turning been taken? It would be easy to adduce other examples of this desperate anxiety: T. S. Eliot and *The Waste Land*, W. H. Auden and *For the Time Being*, Arthur Koestler and *Darkness at Noon*, George Orwell and *1984*. Man is sick, hollow, sterile; man is frantic, bewildered, lost; man is in bondage, enslaved by the fabrications of his own intelligence and imagination. C. S. Lewis deliberately chose as the title for his Riddel Lectures "The Abolition of Man." Man as evolution has produced him, man as history has recorded him, man as Western civilization has disciplined him, this man has fallen, has been ruined, has been abolished. Can this be true? Has human nature really changed?

It is evident that this change of emphasis or direction in the world of letters has been motivated by two main factors: (a) the open recognition of irrational and unpredictable elements in human nature to which testimony has been borne so massively by modern psychological investigation and (b) the grim awareness of the violent and destructive elements in human nature to which similar testimony has been borne by twentieth-century world wars and concentration camps. Internal and external, psychological and historical factors, these combined have caused men to speak again in terms of fall and corruption, of human depravity and transcendental evil, in ways which echo the theological pronouncements of an earlier age. At the same time the two factors which I have mentioned have strongly affected theological discourse. There has been a marked tendency to turn from the literalistic and chronological to the psychological and existential, even to rehabilitate the mythical. If the traditional doctrines of the Fall and Original Sin and corporate guilt are to mean anything to the contemporary mind, they must, it is recognized, be expressed in the light of the new knowledge which has been made available to us by psychologists, social anthropologists, and existential thinkers.

Perhaps this new attitude can best be summarized by quoting a passage from a notable series of open lectures given at the University of Cambridge some fifteen years after Williams' lectures at Oxford. "The idea of a Fall from an original state of perfection," the lecturer, J. S. Whale, said, "is not a scientific statement about the dawn of history. The Fall is symbolism, necessary to the intellect, but inconceivable by the imagination. It involves no scientific description of absolute beginnings. Eden is on no map, and Adam's Fall fits into no historical calendar. Moses is not nearer to the Fall than we are because he lived three thousand years before our time. The Fall relates not to some datable aboriginal calamity in the historic past of humanity but to a dimension of human experience which is always present—namely, that we who have been created for fellowship with God repudiate it continually; and that the whole of mankind does this along with us. Paradise before the Fall . . . describes the quality rather than the history of 'man's first disobedience.' "

This brief statement received ample and learned expansion almost at the same time in Reinhold Niebuhr's Gifford Lectures and has been reinforced since by a man well versed in depth psychology and existential philosophy—Paul Tillich. For him any ideas of an origin in time or of stages in time within which the Fall can be set are meaningless. The Fall is entirely concerned with what Tillich calls the transition from essence to existence, the passage from "the dreaming innocence of undecided potentialities" to self-actualization. This transition "is a universal quality of finite being. It is not an event of the past; for it ontologically precedes everything that happens in time and space. It sets the conditions of spatial and temporal existence. It is manifest in every individual person in the transition from dreaming innocence to actualization and guilt." In other words, the Fall story is a cosmic myth interpreting universal human existence and is in no way patient of a purely logical or historical analysis. Human freedom, responsibility, anxiety, and alienation all gain meaning in the light of the Fall myth, and the re-establishment of categories such as these opens the way to the reinterpretation of redemption, the second pillar identified by Williams as essential in the Christian structure of faith.

In the realm of literature, besides those attempts to identify certain events as critical turning points in the development of human nature to which I have already referred, there have been imaginative reconstructions of the Fall story in existential and psychological terms. The most obvious example of the former is Albert Camus' *The Fall*, of the latter William Golding's *Free Fall*.

The central figure in *The Fall* is Jean-Baptiste Clamence, a name which is almost certainly linked with that of John the Baptist, the man whose cry in the wilderness defined the desolation of the human spirit in its estrangement from its true meaning and destiny. His story, told as a monologue, is of the passage from what Tillich calls "dreaming innocence" ("I was in perfect harmony with life. I blended with its entire being and avoided no part of its irony, its grandeur and its demands") to one of conscious despair ("Things kept slipping. Yes everything slipped past me"). The moment of crisis came when a young woman threw herself from a bridge into the Seine ("fell"), but he, Clamence, did nothing to help: he passed by on the other side. Henceforward he himself was not so much fallen as *continually falling*. There were no longer any securities. The self in which he had trusted had failed him. He acknowledged no standards of judgment save his own, and these had proved impermanent. So at every moment human existence is the experience of falling. The only relief that Clamence can find is to talk continuously, particularly by buttonholing others and by confessing to them his own cowardice in order to convict them of their own. But even with that relief, the haunting cry of the drowning woman may be heard at any moment—and then he falls—forever.

William Golding wrote *Free Fall* some five years after *Lord of the Flies*, a book in which, Angus Wilson has suggested, he solved the problem of expressing transcendent evil and good more successfully than has any other living English novelist. There the theme is essentially that of the transition from dreaming innocence to conscious freedom, responsibility, guilt. In *Free Fall* it is worked out in terms of the autobiography of an individual rather than in the form of a universal fable. An artist, Sammy Mountjoy, incarcerated in a Nazi prison camp, goes back over his past life trying to determine when exactly he *fell*, when, that is, he lost the buoyant sense of inner freedom and became aware of something not only holding him fast but dragging him down. He pursues a ruthless self-analysis, punctuated by moments of crisis when he asks:

"Is this the point I am looking for?
No,
Not here."

until at length he reaches the point of no return.

Golding will not allow that heredity—a fatherless bastard—or environment—a rural slum—is the necessary background of the Fall. Sammy is exposed to influences good and bad in his early years. There is nothing to suggest that the scales are unduly loaded on the side of evil.

But a moment comes when he is confronted by a choice which has within it the potential of an ultimate. As he left school his headmaster spoke these words: "I'll tell you something which may be of value. I believe it to be true and powerful—therefore dangerous. If you want something enough you can always get it provided you are willing to make the appropriate sacrifice." Sammy knew what he wanted. He deliberately made the sacrifice. And the chain of events was set in motion which ended in stark and unrelieved tragedy, not so much for Sammy himself but for the one he had wronged.

In his most recent book, *The Spire*, Golding returns again and again to the symbolism of falling. Dean Jocelyn is obsessed with the vision of the tower rising above his cathedral. But the master-builder knows the plan is sheer folly: "I tell you—whatever else is uncertain in my mystery —this is certain, I know. I've seen a building fall." One after another of the characters falls. Yet this time the tragedy is not unrelieved, for the book ends with the vivid symbol of the apple tree (the tree associated with the original Fall myth) standing and growing (the tree of redemption), glittering like a waterfall but an *upward* waterfall, breaking all the way to infinity in cascades of exultation.

To sum up: Theology and imaginative literature will always have this in common: each is concerned with the nature and experience and destiny of man. Neither has been prepared to accept (I am speaking of Western culture) an exclusively scientific view which would regard man as an object in nature to be observed, experimented with, manipulated, and conformed to some arbitrarily chosen standard. Any kind of consistent materialism, mechanism, or automatism leaves no room either for a theological or for an artistic interpretation of human existence. If, however, the extremes such as I have mentioned are rejected, how will the theologian and the artist go about their task of constructing a modern doctrine of man?

On the theological side there are still those who cling to literalistic interpretations of the biblical stories, to traditional formulations of Original Sin or to the belief in a Fall crisis which can somehow be located in history, even though this may be placed in some remote past. On the literary side there are those who seek to interpret man in terms of nineteenth-century liberalism, or of twentieth-century eroticism, or of some general philosophy of existentialism or nihilism such as have been in vogue in this mid-twentieth century. Between these two groups a wide and seemingly impassable gulf is fixed.

On the other hand, there has been a powerful movement in theological circles toward a re-interpretation of the traditional doctrine of sin and the Fall by the aid of insights derived largely from the research of psychologists and social anthropologists. And the same may be said, I think, of those whose interests are primarily literary and artistic. They too have in many cases become aware of the importance of psychological insights and anthropological research for their own continuing task. Through both of these disciplines we have learned how significant a place is occupied in human experience by the myth and the symbol, the dream and the image, the parable and the ritual pattern. These may appear in different forms in the course of man's historical development, but certain archetypal symbols seem to be indestructible. One such, I have suggested, is the Fall; and for this reason it has renewed its appeal to theologian and artist alike.

From the psychological side the Fall has been seen to express a dimension of human existence which is powerfully present from the beginning to the end of life. The fear of falling is one of the earliest forms of anxiety in the human psyche, and it is never finally overcome. In a certain sense all life is a falling—a falling below and away from one's aspirations, one's ideals, one's hopes, one's intentions. Falling short is a reality even if the ideas of an aboriginal Fall and inherited guilt seem unimaginable and are virtually meaningless. From the side of social anthropology the Fall has been seen to express a crisis in social development which again constitutes part of the experience of any society wherever found. As I have shown, modern artists have made attempts to identify such crises in modern times—turning points in human affairs brought about by the onset of new knowledge bringing untold possibilities of good or evil. Even if the possibilities for good are kept in view, there cannot fail to be a sense of lost innocence, of a fall from a state which was easier to cope with and in which no such fearful possibilities threatened.

All this in no way constitutes a new dogmatism. Rather, it is a new openness to interpret human existence not as a closed system—moral, logical, historical, or scientific—but as related to transcendent categories and values. If it is possible to speak imaginatively and convincingly of a fall or of falling, then a context of height or "aboveness" must be inferred. And if it is man himself who has *fallen* or is *falling*, the height or the "aboveness" is not a part of man's own self-contained existence. In other words, some recognition of transcendence, however this may be interpreted, is involved. Further than this it does not seem to me that we can at present go. But it is by paying attention to the symbols and myths and archetypes which have captured the interest both of theologians and of artists in our contemporary world that we may hope to make progress in constructing a doctrine of man which is true to the heights and depths of universal human experience.

Part II

IMAGINATION AND BELIEF

Three Masters: The Quest for Religion in Nineteenth-Century Russian Literature

by

Georges Florovsky

. . . *Quia fecisti nos ad te et inquietum est cor nostrum donec requiescat in te.*

—St. Augustine, *Confessions*, I.1.

P. N. SAKULIN IN HIS WELL-DOCUMENTED BOOK *Russian Literature and Socialism* makes an important observation: "The Russian intelligentsia of the thirties [1830's] was, on the whole, undoubtedly religious."[1] The word "religious" is used here in a comprehensive sense, covering a wide "variety of religious experience." The religion of the early Russian intelligentsia was frequently quite unorthodox, vague, dreamy, erratic, syncretistic. It was often a psychological mood, or an aesthetic rapture, or else a kind of moralistic psychoanalysis, rather than a sober and firm belief. (The same is true of the religious situation in the West today.) We should recall that even Rousseau pleaded for "a religion," that the deism of the Enlightenment was still a kind of religious option, and that sentimentalism, in life and in literature, was a metamorphosis of a long mystical tradition. The role of German Pietism and of Freemasonry, including the cult of the Rosicrucians, in the formation of modern Russian culture and literature was conspicuous. In this connection the names of Novikov, Kheraskov, Karamzin, and Zhukovsky must be noted. The mystical movements of the time of Alexander I cannot be dismissed as just obscurantism and reactionary extravagance. Their psychological impact on the intellectual and emotional character of Russian society was strong and lasting. Russian romanticists derived much of their vision and pathos, as well as much of their imagery, from precisely that mystical agitation of the preceding age and from its Western sources. The best example of such influence can be found in the literary work of Vladimir Odoevsky, one of the first Russian idealists. Believers were also not unusual among the Decembrists, who included Alexander Odoevsky, Kuechelbecker, G. Batenkov, and probably K. Ryleev. It was by no means an accident that in the thirties many of the future leaders of the radical intelligentsia (Herzen, Belinsky, and—most conspicuously—Michael Bakunin) passed through a protracted period of intensive religious, or quasi-religious, exaltation. This mood was characteristic of the epoch. The heritage of that "remarkable decade," as it was styled by a contemporary, remained for long an integral component of Russian culture and of Russian psychology. It is significant that socialism itself first appeared in Russia under a religious guise and in the halo of prophetic enthusiasm; among its proponents were Vladimir Pecherin, Herzen, Ogarev, and the young Dostoevsky and several of his friends in the circle of Petrashevsky. It has been rightly suggested that it was precisely as a "Christian socialist" that Dostoevsky came to a sharp clash with Belinsky in the late forties, when the latter had lost or renounced his earlier idealistic or "romantic" convictions.[2]

Impending since the late forties, the crisis came in the sixties. It was a violent explosion, a radical break, a kind of conversion. From that time we date the "retreat" of the Russian intelligentsia from Christianity and, indeed, from any religion or "metaphysics," a "retreat" in variable and fleeting versions, from indifference to revolt. As a matter of fact, the Russian movement was a continuation or repetition of the simultaneous shift and crisis in Western thought; and foreign sources of the Russian inspiration can be easily identified. Yet the Russian response to the new message or challenge of the West was spontaneous, passionate, and elemental: it was a kind of wild emotional storm. Indeed, it was rooted in emotions, not in ideas. The ideological equipment of the Russian radicals was rather flat and meager; and there was in it a poisonous alloy of cynical disregard for any cultural concerns. Here lies the sting of Russian nihilism of the time. Existentially it was a transfer of allegiance. There was a kind of new creed to be adopted. There was a new commitment, a new engagement, and a thirst for substitutes. Psychologically it was a change of faith. Dostoevsky was undoubtedly correct when he identified the major theme of his time as religious. It was the problem of faith and unbelief, in their confrontation and conflict. But unbelief itself is a religious phenomenon and a religious option in the direction of ultimate negation; it is a kind of inverted religion. There were different shades of Russian radicalism and different stages in its development. Occasionally religious motifs can be found even in radicalism itself. And there was a new movement in the early seventies, with the rise of Populism. There was a new search for religion, or a search for a "new religion." It was again utterly unorthodox: a "religion of the heart" or a "religion of humanity"; but even there one can observe a resurgence of certain evangelical motifs.[3] The Russian intelligentsia was inwardly split at that time. And the movement itself was dialectical; it was a "retreat" counterbalanced by a "return."

The quest for religion is a distinctive feature of all those periods in history which are usually described as "transitional" and which are actually "critical"—when "the time is out of joint" and "walls are crumbling." In such situations the quest for faith assumes inevitably a dramatic and even a tragic turn. Not all who seek find. Yet for believers all epochs are, in a sense, "critical" and problematic. Faith is in no case an easy venture; it has its own internal obstacles and temptations, even its own discomfort—its "dark nights." It is a venture of hope and courage. It is an incentive, an urge. A quest itself is an ambivalent exploit: it may be a symptom of failing or shaken belief; it may also be a token of spiritual vigilance.

The greatest Russian writers of the nineteenth century (Gogol, Dostoevsky, and Tolstoy) were deeply concerned with the problem of faith. As writers they were and wanted to be interpreters of life, of human existence, with all its predicaments and with all its promise. Their ultimate problem was the problem of man and of his destiny in the double dimension of personal and corporate life. Gogol was acclaimed by his contemporaries as a genial master, and his influence in literature was decisive and enormous. In fact, he was probably the central figure in Russian literature of his century. But the intimate message which he wanted to communicate was misunderstood in his own time, through his own fault, and rejected even by his close friends as an unhealthy aberration, as a deception or an illusion. This message was rediscovered, with astonishment and even with alarm, by the end of the century. At last his voice was heard. Notwithstanding, Gogol is still an enigmatic figure, a tragic figure indeed. Dostoevsky walked in his steps, but in his own peculiar manner, and rather critically, with caution and reservation. His message was heard in his own time, but it was hardly understood in full and by all. He was a disquieting spirit in Russian literature. His prophetic soundings in depth-psychology were moving and imposing. He raised and discussed perennial problems, "the damned problems," but always in the perspective of his own time. He interpreted current events, but always in the perspective of the ultimate. All his writings were "situation-conditioned" and need historical commentary. And yet they were focused on recurrent themes of human existence. Although many of his prophecies were false and delusive, he had the full stature of a prophet.

The position of Leo Tolstoy was always peculiar. He was forever in opposition: in opposition to any particular historical situation, actually to history itself. His concern was rather with man as man, *in nudo, in puris naturalibus*. In a certain sense, of course, such an approach is quite legitimate and even necessary. Man stands naked before God; and human life with its toil and tribulation is, in a certain sense, dust and vanity in God's sight. Nonetheless, this is but one dimension of man's existence and of his relationship with God. The real man is always a "historic man" with concrete and personal needs and failures, as well as with concrete and diversified tasks in a particular historical setting. It is unrealistic to subtract all "historicity" from human existence and to regard it as an aberration, not as the fulfillment of human "nature." And Tolstoy was persistently doing precisely this, in spite of his great skill in depicting life in its concrete shape and variety. Ultimately he was dealing with a schematic man in certain typical situations, so that, strangely enough, the real mystery of the human personality was lost. Indeed, moral principles and standards are always essentially the same; and it was timely in an age of irresponsible relativism to remind men of that fact, which may explain the wide response to Tolstoy's moral, or rather moralistic, preaching at home and abroad. Still, it also explains the sterility of this preaching. Tolstoy was able to teach one to evade the present, but he could not teach how one had to wrestle with it on its own level. Moreover, he stubbornly refused to do so: Evil, he contended, should not be resisted but only condemned and disavowed—and endured. His rigoristic radicalism led him, ultimately, to passivity. At this point he was the antagonist of Dostoevsky. The contrast in their views was illustrated at a later date in the remarkable literary dialogue between Vjacheslav Ivanov and Gershenson, embodied in their *Correspondence from Two Corners*.[4]

These three masters were not basically in agreement. They differed deeply in their analyses and in their conclusions. Gogol wanted to reform the "inner man" without any change in his environment, although he was extremely concerned with social issues. Dostoevsky dreamed of an historical renewal, of a coming Kingdom on earth. Tolstoy simply disregarded history; on this point he was strangely close to Gogol. But there was a common element in their divergent endeavors. It was their conviction that human life without faith is a perilous adventure which is bound to end in disaster. Man without God cannot remain truly human; he sinks and decomposes. This joint preaching, in spite of all divergences, alerted those who were willing to listen to the responsibilities of the higher calling of man: to faith, to obedience, and to service. But there were many who simply did not want to listen.

In his late years Gogol made the following significant statement about himself: "I came to Christ rather by a *Protestant* than by a *Catholic* way." At the time Gogol was residing in Rome, and his friends in Moscow suspected that his new religious views had been derived from Catholic sources. He was prompted to deny the charge sharply and emphatically. His phraseology, however, is rather obscure. Indeed, there is no evidence of any interest taken by Gogol at that time in the Protestant Reformation, with its specific and distinctive issues and options. Gogol, on the whole, had little interest in doctrine and doctrines. Probably he should have said that he came to Christ by an "evangelical" or even by a "pietistic" way, which, it seems, is precisely what he meant to say. In fact, he continued: "His analysis of the human soul, in a manner in which others do not make it, was the reason that I came to Christ, being struck in Him first by His human wisdom and unprecedented knowledge of the soul, and only then proceeding to worship His Divinity."[5] Gogol elaborated on this testimony in his *Confession of an Author*, a kind of apology. Here he stressed once more the fact that his primary and initial interest was in man, in the human soul. He was searching for those "eternal laws" by which man is governed. He was studying human documents of all kinds. And by this road, "imperceptively, almost without himself knowing how," he came to Christ and found in Him "the key to the soul of man." In other words, Gogol came to know Christ by way of a peculiar psychological analysis. He did not expect to meet Christ on this road. In fact, he came to Christ by way of that *pietistic humanism* which was typical of the epoch of Alexander I. He was himself a belated representative of that age. He seemed archaic to his own generation, wrestling alone in his own universe of discourse.[6]

Gogol was well acquainted with romantic literature. But he was hardly touched by the philosophical movements of his time. His first stories were written in a romantic way that was not an imitation and was much more than just a literary manner. His own vision was romantic; he had "romantic experience." The world of men was sharply divided for him in a distinctly "romantic" manner: there were strong men, with

clearly defined personalities, and there were "common men." He was
never really interested in the strong men, or heroes; his occasional
attempts to depict such men were never successful. But he was desperately concerned with those ordinary people who fill the whole stage of
human life. If these people are amusing or picturesque, their existence is
nonetheless meaningless, monotonous, and futile. They are trivial and
petty, and they dwell in their own narrow and secluded little worlds
without any perspective. Although Gogol was ready to sympathize with
poverty and hardship, with sorrow and misfortune, he could be only
frightened and shaken by this vision of empty life—almost subhuman
and, at its worst, even beastly. In this stagnant world there are "passions,"
but these "little passions" or ambitions only reveal the utter corruption
and debasement of human nature. It may seem that Gogol took pleasure
in drawing his comical, grotesque, and ridiculous figures or, better,
figurines. There was, of course, some epic charm in his early stories. Yet
even in these stories, allegedly humorous and sentimental, there is often
heard a strongly tragic note—a note of boredom. As Gogol matured, this
feeling grew in him, until it overwhelmed him completely by the end of
his life. In this connection it has been suggested that Gogol apprehended
life *sub specie mortis*,[7] which does not mean simply that death is the
inevitable end of each individual life. Rather, it means that life itself is
deadly and deadening, a sort of impasse or illusion. Life stands under the
sign of frustration—not because hopes are not fulfilled, but because there
are no hopes. "The earth is already inflamed with incomprehensible
melancholy. Life is becoming more and more hardhearted. Everything is
getting smaller and smaller. Only the gigantic image of boredom is
growing in the sight of all, reaching day by day beyond all measure.
Everything is hollow, and graves are everywhere." The wording is hyperbolic indeed! But these words are well chosen to render the real vision of
Gogol, a vision that was apocalyptic. Merezhkovsky compared Gogol to
the hero of one of Hans Christian Andersen's fairy tales, who had the
misfortune to get a piece of an accursed mirror into his eye, with the
effect that he could see only distorted and disfigured things. But was the
sight of Gogol really distorted? Or was it not sharpened to enable him to
perceive reality beneath the veil of conventions, to grasp the impending
catastrophe beneath the veil of stagnation? Gogol described fallen men;
and his "caricatures," like those of Goya, are utterly "realistic" in this
perspective. Professor Viktor Vinogradov has recently contended that in
Gogol's writings men are presented as things, that they are, as it were,
"reified."[8] And Rozanov suggested that the human figures in Gogol are
not actually living persons; instead, they are marionettes, "wax figurines"

moved on the stage by the hidden hand of a skillful master who is able, by certain devices, to create the impression that they are alive. They have no spontaneous motion—they are static and fixed.[9] The question remains: was this striking peculiarity of Gogol's art a symptom of his distorted sight or a sign of his deep insight? Indeed, he never dwelt on the surface—he was always digging and sounding in depth. Under the veil of banality he detected the dark underworld. Emptiness itself was an obvious evil. But it was more than just a human defect or failure: a great Adversary could be discerned behind his victims.

The demonology of Gogol's early stories was probably not quite serious, being derived from the Western romanticists, including Hoffmann, and from folklore. The devils here are only grotesque and amusing. Still, in *The Terrible Revenge* and even more so in *Vij*, the intrusion of evil spirits into human life is presented with tragic sobriety. In the major works of Gogol evil spirits do not appear in person, but their presence is assumed. They are operating everywhere, if usually in disguise. By the end of his life he was overwhelmed with the feeling that evil, or the Evil One, was omnipresent, as it were. Satan, he thought, had been unbound and released so that he might appear in the world without even a mask. Although one may be embarrassed by Gogol's phraseology, there can be no doubt that evil was for him a superhuman reality charged with enormous power which could be conquered only "by the mysterious power of the unfathomable Cross," the sole hope of Gogol in his later years.

In spite of his grim vision of reality, Gogol was, except in his very last years, optimistic. He believed in the possibility of conversion, of renewal and regeneration. Moreover, he expected it shortly. Over this very point his difficulties began. In his early years he believed in the redemptive power of art and felt that man could be awakened by a vision of beauty. This hope was frustrated. He soon discovered the ambiguity of aesthetic emotions, the ambiguity of beauty itself. In this respect he was followed by Dostoevsky and by Vladimir Soloviev, who, with him, believed that Aphrodite is ambiguous and unprotected against corruption. And still the hope for conversion was not lost. Strangely enough, Gogol expected that when his famous play *The Inspector General* was performed on the stage, it would effect widespread awakening and conversion. He believed that people would be moved by the vision of human misery, of human nothingness, of human absurdity. And he was once more grievously disappointed. The play was received as an entertaining comedy, as an invitation to laugh. It did not evoke any deep moral emotions; it did not move people's hearts. Gogol's later attempt to explain the moral significance of the play and to interpret it symbolically was hardly convincing. Yet he firmly believed that he had been called from above to the ministry of persuasion. In this mood he conceived the plan of his greatest work, a "poem," *Dead Souls*.

The title *Dead Souls* was chosen for its symbolic connotation. In this work Gogol intended to deal with the deadly condition of man. The poem was to be in two parts: the "dead souls" depicted in the first part were expected to come to life in the second. The internal pivot of the poem was the concept of "conversion." There was to be a confrontation: "Dead Russia" and "Russia Alive."[10] Only the first part was published by Gogol, who was rather disappointed with the response of readers— they did not understand his intention. And probably their inability to understand was inevitable: the first part could not be properly assessed before it was supplemented by the second, in which the true meaning of the story was to be disclosed. Indeed, Gogol engaged in a description of human pettiness and vice only in order to demonstrate finally that even misers and crooks can be saved or healed. He wanted to show the transformation of the human soul. Although the second part was to be much more important than the first, unfortunately it was never completed, and Gogol was unable to achieve his purpose. He wrote his *Paradise Lost* but failed completely with his *Paradise Regained*. He worked on it intensively, obstinately, desperately, but he was increasingly dissatisfied with the results. The story of his work is still rather obscure; the published text of the second part is only one of the versions of the poem. In it no "conversion" has taken place. Instead, some new persons are introduced to illustrate the way of goodness. They are the least convincing of all Gogol's figures. For Gogol this failure was more than a disappointment: it was a terrible shock. Awakening or conversion proved to be a much more complicated matter than he had expected. Man could not be moved to conversion simply by aesthetic emotions or by moralistic reasoning. He could not be moved by any of his own resources; he could be moved only by the grace of God. In order to become a "new man," the old man had to turn to God, Gogol concluded. The whole problem had to be thought over afresh. But there was another difficulty of which Gogol himself was not fully aware. In spite of his intensive study of the human soul, he was not a master of psychological analysis. His men and women were simply marionettes: they could not be brought to life by any device.

The last book that Gogol published, *Selected Passages from Correspondence with Friends*, was probably his greatest "human document." And yet it was an unfortunate book. It was unfavorably received even by his most intimate friends and was violently attacked from all sides, as evidenced by Belinsky's famous letter. In any case, it was not understood by anyone at the time of its publication. Later on, however, it was heartily appreciated by Leo Tolstoy, when he was himself engaged in a religious quest. The book was, in fact, a program of social Christianity. Conceived as a kind of ideological preface to the second volume of *Dead Souls*, it describes in advance what Gogol sought to prove by the images of his still unfinished poem. ("To prove" is his own wording: artistic images were regarded as proofs.) It was by sheer misunderstanding that the book was interpreted as an essay on personal piety; its pathos is practical, even utilitarian. On the whole, it is a call to social and public action: Gogol's basic category is *service*. He does not call for retreat and seclusion; the monastery is now Russia itself. Gogol is still frightened by her present situation; he does not try to defend it. Those who are not yet in service must take jobs. Only by doing so can one be saved, for salvation depends upon service. Service itself is understood as work within the state structure. But the state itself has been transformed. Therefore, one has to serve as a member of "another heavenly State, or Kingdom, the head of which is Christ himself"; no one can serve as he would have served in "the former Russia." Gogol's phrase is striking: "the former Russia" is already unreal for him; he finds himself in "another world," in a new *theocratic* dimension. The phrase reminds us of the Holy Alliance: it was, in fact, a solemn invitation to realize that earthly kingdoms have been fused to constitute a new Celestial and Sacred Kingdom of which the only Sovereign is Christ. Accordingly, the state assumes all the functions of the church. Christian work must be done more by laymen than by the clergy; and the laity must guide the clergy, Gogol insisted. The monarch himself must understand that he is and must be "an image of God on earth." Gogol's biblicism reminds us of the epoch of the Biblical Society in Russia: the Bible must be read as a contemporary book. In it all current events can be found, as well as the Last Judgment, which is already going on. On the other hand, the Bible is a book for kings: the pattern of contemporary kingship is set in the story of the ancient theocracy of Israel. The king's vocation is to be on earth an image of He Who is Love. The same paradoxical and utopian image of the theocratic Tsar dominated the mind of Alexander Ivanov, who was quite close to Gogol at the time of their stay in Rome and who was going through his own religious crisis. Much later one hears echoes of the same conception in Vladimir Soloviev: the Tsar's vocation is to forgive and to heal by love. All these motifs should be traced back to the time of the Holy Alliance and its popularity in Russia. It is significant that Gogol's friends of that old generation did actually welcome the book. His own generation would not follow him; even the Slavophiles' concept of theocracy was quite different, as was their idea of the state.

Gogol regarded the Eastern Church as the church of the future. Up to the present she had been hiding herself, "like a chaste virgin." Now she was called to meet the needs of the world. (The church in the West was hardly prepared, in his opinion, for new historical tasks.) Everyone, in his own place, was called to action. Indeed, Gogol even had practical advice to offer and often went into minor details. Most of this advice seems naïve and casuistic. That he tended to treat all problems as moral problems, without much attention to their other aspects, is especially true of his new "economic utopia," to use a phrase of Father Zenkovsky's. Still, the moral aspect of the economic problem cannot be disregarded. Gogol continued to believe that social renovation could be achieved by preaching alone. But now, more than ever before, he was stressing the power of Christian love. He was deeply distressed by the fact that the contemporary world had lost the spirit of brotherhood. At this point he was close to early French socialism and to Lamennais, who believed that brotherhood had been forgotten for the sake of equality and freedom. Gogol further remarks, "Christians! Christ has been expelled to the streets, to infirmaries and hospitals, instead of being invited into private homes—and people still think that they are Christians." Such words express more than philanthropy or sentimental truisms: to recognize Christ in all one's neighbors, the true name of every man to be simply "brother," was for Gogol the first step on the road to perfection. *First of all* one had to learn love for one's brethren, and *only then* was one enabled to love God. There is no trace of personal piety in this sharp claim. It is true that Gogol took no interest in social or political reforms and that he was therefore attacked as "a reactionary" by Belinsky. But in no sense was he an apologist for the current situation; he was sharp and sensitive on that point. The world, which he saw crumbling, stood under an apocalyptic sign. Nonetheless, there were bright omens: youth were striving now to embrace all men as brothers and to reform mankind. It was suggested that everything must be owned in common, even houses and land—a daring viewpoint in Gogol's time.

Various and often discordant motifs were intertwined in Gogol's last book, which may be regarded as his spiritual testament, his last will. Apocalyptic alarm and utopian expectation of a speedy resurrection of Russia and the coming of a Sacred Kingdom of Christ on earth could not be easily reconciled, although this paradoxical combination is not quite unusual in the history of human thought: it was rather a typical phenomenon in the pietistic age. Fear and love were strangely synthesized in Gogol's own religious experience. Above all, he was at the same time sincerely humble, even inclined to an excessive self-denigration, and intolerably ambitious, almost intransigently proud—and this odd mixture irritated his best friends in Moscow. From his early years Gogol regarded himself as an instrument of Providence. He was certain that he had been chosen for some high and exceptional mission in the world, that he was predestined for some high task. To an extent, this feeling was character-istic of all people in the romantic epoch. In Gogol self-confidence grew at times into a real obsession: "The invisible One is writing before me with a mighty rod." Gogol often claimed a kind of infallible authority for his words. "My word is now charged with supernal power," he exclaimed on one occasion, "and woe to any one who will not listen to it." It is for that reason that Gogol expected so much, too much, from his writings; and for the same reason he apprehended painfully his failures. He wanted to act as an authoritative counselor of friends and acquaintances through pre-tentious imposition and claimed infallible authority for himself even in private affairs. This inner contradiction, this unresolved tension, was the root of his personal tragedy and collapse. By nature Gogol was an extrovert, although he used to mix together dreams and reality. On the other hand, he claimed to be a student of the human soul, of man's inner life, which was precisely his weakest point. His prophecy was often little more than sheer rhetoric. And yet he had genuine prophetic insight. In his own generation he was one of the few who were able to perceive and to understand that the whole historical world was on the eve of a crisis, that it was already entering into a "revolutionary situation" and was in a state of danger and impasse, a perception which was both a true prophecy and a timely warning.

In spite of his glamorous literary fame, Gogol is a lonely figure in the history of the Russian mind. His literary heritage has been grievously misinterpreted. He is regarded mainly as a great humorist, although his laughter is always bitter, and as the pioneer in the realistic trend in literature. His religious ideas are commonly disregarded or dismissed as nonsense and superstition. It should not be forgotten, however, that Dostoevsky stood in direct succession to Gogol.[11]

All his life Dostoevsky wrestled with a basic problem, the problem of human freedom. It was his starting point, his primary intuition, his central theme. The dignity of man, his human identity, is perilously grounded in his freedom. The loss of freedom is the major human grief. But freedom is at once a privilege and a burden, an endowment and a task. The highest human achievements and the most hideous failures are rooted in the exercise of freedom. Freedom is intrinsically dynamic. It is given to man, it is inherent in the human constitution, but it must be vigilantly maintained. Strangely enough, freedom can be lost, for the world of freedom is problematic. Freedom is always at a crossroads, which confronts us with a crucial antinomy: by nature man is a free being, but in empirical reality he usually appears as enslaved. What is the cause of this bondage? Is there any safeguard for human freedom?

Early in life Dostoevsky discovered the mysterious paradox of human freedom. All the meaning and all the joy of human life lie precisely in man's freedom, in the freedom of his mind, of his will, of his actions. All the values of human existence presuppose freedom. And yet, paradoxically, freedom itself may become an instrument of bondage. Moreover, man is able to enslave not only others, but also himself. On the other hand, free will may degenerate into "self-will," causing the suicide of freedom. The root of human tragedy is not so much in man's clash with a blind and inexorable *fatum*, as was assumed by the ancient tragedians, but rather in the aberration of man's own will and in the conflict of discordant "self-wills." This perception was probably the deepest insight of Dostoevsky. The theme can be traced through all his writings. Indeed, he knew well that man is often enslaved by social pressures, by violence and constraint, by tyranny and neglect, by poverty, and by many other forces—in short, by the environment, the outer life. Dostoevsky was always ready to intercede for all those who were humiliated and debased, for the offended, and for the oppressed. He was fully aware of social ills and horrors and could describe them with incomparable power and pathos and with shocking realism. It suffices to recall that his *Winter Notes on Summer Impressions* is truly prophetic and that he began his literary career with a moving plea for the "poor folk." But he came to believe that the root of human bondage is not in the environment but primarily in man's inner world. It is significant that, after having written his first "philanthropic" story, Dostoevsky immediately turned his attention to another side of the problem on a deeper, psychological level. He was concerned now with the peculiar phenomenon of human estrangement, of self-imposed solitude. It was probably from French socialists (particularly from Fourier and George Sand) that Dostoevsky first learned that the ultimate source of all social ills is the spiritual disintegration and dissociation of human life, the decay or decrease of brotherhood among men. Indeed, that was the initial assumption of the French socialist school. The theme of estrangement was also a characteristic theme of romanticism. Man detaches himself from his environment in protest, or in order to preserve and protect his individual independence.

He hides himself in a secluded world of which he seems to be the only master. Now he may perhaps set himself free from outer pressures or from interference by this shift, but only at a high cost. He is in danger of losing all contact with objective reality. He becomes his own prisoner, the captive of his own passions and thought, over which he has no control. His experience is reduced and impoverished. His personality may break down at any moment. Such was Dostoevsky's firm conviction from the time he wrote *The Double* and *White Nights*. The problem of the "dreamer" became the center of his thought. All the major figures of his later great novels are "possessed," are swallowed, as it were, by ideas. Dostoevsky was tracing the transformation of the dreamer into the "superman." Dreamers become aggressive and want to impose their dreams and their own "self-will" on other people and on external reality. They tend to regard their ideas and passions as absolute authority; and at the same time they suffer from an incurable schizophrenia, as witnessed in Raskolnikov, Stavrogin, Ivan Karamazov. A claim for ultimate authority is inherent in the "self-will." It begins with detachment from historical reality and ends with rebellion against God. There is a threatening consistency in this development. It is the destiny of the uprooted man. Solitude and rebellion are intrinsically correlated.

Man is a social being meant for communal life. But the "community" itself has been broken. It has lost its "organic" character. Cohesion is now maintained only by "ideas," that is, by abstract principles. It has become a sphere of coercion, a threat to the personal freedom of man. In this situation the revolt of individuals seems to be justified. This much Dostoevsky could learn from his early socialist inspirers. But he inherited from them also the conviction that a normal or perfect community can be built only on love or brotherhood. Equality and freedom have to be supplemented by brotherhood, which has to be more than just a principle.

Planning for the new society tended to impose new abstract schemes on reality which promised to be no less prescriptive and oppressive than the ancient order itself. The concept of order dominated all these schemes. But the real question concerned not so much the new order as the new man. Dostoevsky's early doubts were confirmed by his experience in the "house of the dead." Indeed, there he could well observe the fatal power of evil over man, with all its existential consequences. But his major discovery there was something else. The common life of the criminals was horrible enough, but the real torment lay in the fact that the common life was *compulsory*. It is significant that it was precisely in his *House of the Dead* that Dostoevsky for the first time introduced the image of the palace: it is beautiful in itself and everything there has been provided for man's happiness and prosperity. Only one thing is missing— freedom. In his later writings Dostoevsky elaborated on this image in his vigorous protest against any schemes of an ideal society. From the House of the Dead there remained but a step to the Underworld. At this point the tragic antinomy of the human dilemma appears in full light. It cannot be solved either by individualistic detachment or by inclusion in any order, however "perfect" it may be. In both cases human freedom is curtailed or threatened. Could this antinomy be solved at all? From the humanistic concept of brotherhood Dostoevsky moved to organic theories of society. They were in the air at that time in Russia. A return to "nature" or to "the soil" could be regarded as a remedy against individualistic dissociation and against the threat of dreams and ideas. Dostoevsky could not be satisfied with this solution for long, however, although certain elements of the organic view remained in his later attempts at synthesis. Moreover, a return to organic wholeness was impossible because the world was in a crisis. The real question was how one could get from under the ruins of the old world. At this point Dostoevsky could not take that way which was adopted by Leo Tolstoy at approximately the same time. Dostoevsky looked forward to the future and could not be satisfied with references to the static structures of human existence *in abstracto*. Moreover, he did not believe that human problems could be solved at the personal level alone by individual conversions. His thinking was essentially social; he had to have a social ideal. By the end of his life his suggestion was, as Vladimir Soloviev formulated it, that human problems could be solved only in the church, which he regarded as a "social ideal."

Dostoevsky was referring, of course, to the Eastern Orthodox Church. He did not believe that Western Christianity was able to overcome with its own resources the crisis in which it was at that time involved. Concerning this point he was sorely prejudiced, and there was a great deal of wishful thinking in his predictions. But such a prejudice should not obscure the validity of his basic option: only in the church of Christ can human freedom be reconciled with the living brotherhood that brings persons together in Christ. Actually, his thinking evolved from two different questions, related but not identical. On the one hand, he believed that the church as a divine establishment is the realm of redemption in which man's existential predicament is being solved: the wholeness of life is restored and the freedom of man is rehabilitated there. On the other hand, he continued to believe in the possibility of an ultimate historical solution for all human contradictions. There was an obvious utopian alloy in his belief in the coming general reconciliation, as is movingly professed in his great Pushkin speech. Still, Dostoevsky's Christianity was in no sense "rosy," as Constantine Leontiev quite unjustly insinuated in a way that betrayed only the limitations of his own view. Dostoevsky's vision of life was much more tragic than Leontiev's, and he had much more courage in dealing with it. He apprehended history as a kind of continuous apocalypse in which God and evil were struggling against each other. The world of human values was being destroyed by demonic counterfeits. The new Tower of Babel was in the process of construction. Apollo would once more stand against Christ. And if Dostoevsky still believed in the power of love, it was the love of Christ that he was preaching, Crucified Love.

From his youth Dostoevsky was aware of human tragedy. He could discern the symptoms of spiritual anxiety, of intensifying anguish and despair in human hearts, in human societies, on all levels of human existence. Modern man is an arrogant, rebellious creature; he may even make blasphemous claims and assign a Godlike dignity to himself. And yet this rebellious creature is a troubled and suffering being. In the turmoil of contemporary history, in the face of growing revolt and apostasy, Dostoevsky could discern the anguish of unbelief. It was his deep conviction that it is unnatural for man to deny God's existence: *quia fecisti nos ad te.* Man ceases to be truly human when he retreats from God and claims to stand alone. On the other hand, Dostoevsky knew only too well how difficult it is for man to believe. He claimed that his own faith was in no sense "naïve" or unaware of difficulties and objections, that his hosanna had passed through the crucible of trials and temptations, had been tested and proved. Indeed, he was himself affected by the doubts and hesitations of his own turbulent and skeptical age. It was a long and arduous way from his early vague and sentimental commitment to the Christ of history to his definitive belief in Christ's Divinity, in the decisive role of the Incarnation in the redemption of man. But in his presentation of skeptical or atheistic arguments he was speaking not always of himself or out of his own personal experience. He was able to speak with such unparalleled insight, honesty, sympathy, and precision only because his own faith was strong. Dostoevsky was not a theologian, although he was a Christian visionary and prophet in his own style; and he never claimed authority or competence in this field. One should not look in his novels for pondered and accurate doctrinal statements, as some have done, unfortunately, for polemical purposes. But he was a believer who had not only the right but also the duty to render a responsible account of his faith and beliefs. He claimed that before him nobody, even in the West, had been able to present the atheistic case with the same fullness and with the same power as he had presented it. And he did so deliberately and conscientiously in order to demonstrate its fallacy. He felt that there was no sense in asking about the origins of nihilism in Russia, because everyone was nihilistic. It was a strange and unexpected contention. What Dostoevsky meant to say was rather simple: People in general tend to be negligent about faith and usually reduce it to certain propositions. Therefore, unbelief can be overcome not by arguments but by internal evidence, by an encounter with the living God. It may seem that Dostoevsky presented the case of faith less convincingly than the case of unbelief: the arguments of Ivan Karamazov are not refuted in the novel. In fact, they can be dismissed only by the act of faith—they cannot be refuted in the "nihilistic" universe of discourse. Experience itself must be widened; the proud man must humble himself.

Dostoevsky was, first of all, an interpreter of a crisis. He was wrestling not so much with metaphysical problems as such, but rather with the existential situation of man. Accordingly, he described metaphysical options primarily in relation to their impact on man's destiny. Freedom was at the center of his query. It is the theme of his great "Legend of the Grand Inquisitor" (probably the greatest of his achievements and at the same time the most controversial and enigmatic). Is this work just an exposition of Ivan Karamazov's views? Or is it Dostoevsky himself who is speaking in disguise? Is the image of Christ an "orthodox" image, or is it reduced? Was the Legend written, primarily or even exclusively, about the Roman Church, and the Inquisitor presented as her authorized spokesman? And who, after all, is the winner in the story which ends so abruptly and so unexpectedly? There is no unanimity and no consensus on any of these questions. It may be contended, however, that none of them really touches the core of the story. The true sting of the Legend lies in the alternative: *freedom*, with all its uncertainty, dangers, and risks, or *satisfaction*—it is difficult to find the right word for that option which the Inquisitor adopts, proclaims, and imposes. Dostoevsky's own option is obvious, even if he is speaking on behalf of Ivan. Actually, the alternative itself is false. No genuine satisfaction is possible for man outside of freedom. Any other kind of satisfaction would reduce him to a subhuman status, which is precisely what the Inquisitor is doing. Here lies his crucial fallacy, the main deceit and counterfeit of the Wise Spirit. Even if we could trust his sincerity and admit that he is really moved by compassion for the frail and the weak, the love which fails to respect freedom and is ready to eliminate it from human love is a demonic counterfeit. What is really exposed in the Legend is the tragedy of a misguided philanthropy. It is a new variation

on the old theme of Shigalev in *The Possessed*: to begin with unconditional freedom for the few in order to end with unconditional bondage
for all. It may seem paradoxical that Christ in the Legend gives no answer
to the invectives of the Adversary except the silent kiss. But probably it is
the only truly divine answer to the challenge. Did not Christ come into
the world to redeem the blind and the lost? Certain basic motifs of the
Legend, and the scheme of temptation itself, were already anticipated in
the earlier writings of Dostoevsky, beginning with *The Possessed*; and at
that time Dostoevsky was thinking of the socialist utopia in which
priority was given to order and prosperity at the expense of freedom. In
any case, the Legend, as well as Dostoevsky's own attacks on the Roman
Church in his *Diary of a Writer*, must be read in the context of the time
in which they were written—soon after the Syllabus and Vatican Council
I, when the common impression in Europe was that Rome stood against
freedom. It may be that this impression was erroneous or grossly exag-
gerated; but it should not be forgotten that at that time it was shared by
many faithful and honest members of the Roman Church herself.

It is obviously impossible, in a brief survey, to exhaust the whole
wealth of Dostoevsky's observations and suggestions. Nor is it possible to
translate his experience from the language of images into the language of
concepts. No logical summary of his visions is even desirable. As a seer
and prophet Dostoevsky became a guide for later generations in their
religious quest, a guide not only in Russia.[12]

D. N. Ovsjaniko-Kulikovsky, a renowned literary critic and historian
of Russian literature, made a startling statement in writing about Tolstoy
in 1908. He strongly contended that Tolstoy was not, in any sense, a
religious man and even claimed that he had no gift for religion. Tolstoy's
alleged "religion" was just a substitute. "His teaching was dry, rational,
and rationalistic. It was not a religion of soul, but a religion of syllo-
gisms."[13] Ovsjaniko-Kulikovsky was a scholar of positivist persuasion who
had no religious convictions himself but who did have a keen interest in
the psychology of religious experience. Thus, his impression cannot be
simply ignored; and he was struck by the total absence of *transcensus* in
the vision and experience of Leo Tolstoy.

Tolstoy himself described his religious crisis at the end of the
seventies in his *Confession*. It is a peculiar book—an interpretation, not
just a narrative. It is built on the scheme of "conversion." That is,
Tolstoy was a libertine, but then an awakening occurred and he understood his depravity. It is a typical revivalist theme. No doubt Tolstoy was
profoundly shaken at the time; it was, however, not the first time. It was
a trying experience, but there was hardly any change of convictions.

Tolstoy himself stresses two main aspects of the conversion. The first was a feeling of bewilderment: Was there any meaning in life? The second was a craving for death, an aversion to life, a fear of life. Everything seemed but a lie; only death was true. Was there any meaning in life that could survive death? In Tolstoy's words, it was the feeling of being abandoned, lonely, lost. Then the crisis was solved by understanding. Tolstoy understood that he was not alone in the world. And he underlined the fact that the strength of life did come back to him, not as a new power but precisely as the same old power which had always been in him. There was no change, except in his attitude. There was no encounter in this renewal, no "mystical" experience, no new disclosure or revelation. Everything suddenly became clear and comprehensible: God is life. After this major crisis Tolstoy continued his religious search. Actually, he was not searching—he was testing the beliefs of others, at the present and in the past, making his own selection and brutally dismissing everything which he could not understand or was unwilling to accept. The Gospel itself was subjected to the same testing. In one of his late essays Tolstoy recommended a method of reading the Scriptures: take a pencil and mark all passages that you can understand, "what is simple and fully comprehensible." Tolstoy was sure that everyone would make approximately the same selection, because reason is identical in all men. One has to believe in reason, first of all, and then one may select passages from any scriptures: Hebrew, Christian, Moslem, Buddhist, Confucian—whatever is in agreement with reason, and then reject whatever does not agree with it. This process is exactly what Tolstoy was persistently doing himself in disregarding completely the context from which he was detaching his selections. What is puzzling in his method is Tolstoy's naïve confidence in the infallibility of reason, of common sense. Mistakes, he thought, can occur anywhere except in reason, which is given to man by God. Let people follow reason, and there will be no dissension. Tolstoy undoubtedly had a thirst for the spiritual life, but it was poisoned and distorted by his unbridled rationalism. He was able to appreciate as excellent the *Invisible Warfare* of St. Nicodemus Hagiorites, a favorite guide of the Athonite monks; but he measured it also by the criterion of "comprehensibility" and wanted to omit the "superfluous." He would read the lives of the saints, the writings of the fathers and masters of spirituality; but, again, he was selective, omitting miracles and whatever pertained to dogma. Christianity was not his starting point. He was essentially pre-Christian in his mentality and could accept the Gospel only in his own expurgated version. (He was sympathetic to Stoicism and admired both Epictetus and Seneca. In them everything was "comprehensible.")

In 1852 he wrote in his diary: "I believe in one, incomprehensible and good God, in the immortality of the soul and in the eternal reward for our deeds. I do not understand the mystery of the Trinity and the genesis of the Son of God, but I respect and do not reject the faith of my fathers." (Later the phrase "do not understand" would become his main weapon in the destruction of "the faith of my fathers.") In 1855 he mentioned in his diary his new and formidable idea of establishing a new religion, adjusted to the contemporary stage in human development—it would be the religion of Christ, but cleansed of faith and mystery, and would not promise any future happiness but would bestow happiness on earth. All men might be united in this religion. In 1860 he decided to write a "materialistic Gospel," a "life of Christ the materialist." It is not easy to detect the sources of all these passing plans and ideas. But it is obvious that his later "faith" was prepared for by his searching in the years before his alleged "conversion." He was psychologically and ideologically rooted in the Enlightenment and in sentimentalism. Reading his early diaries and his lengthy intimate letters, one gets the impression that they were written by a contemporary of Zhukovsky, or even of Karamzin. Tolstoy did not belong psychologically to his own generation; he was much behind it. He was in permanent opposition to the course of history.

War and Peace was originally conceived as an attack on history; and this tendency is still strongly felt in the definitive version: historio-philosophical digressions, which many readers simply omit, were, in the conception of Tolstoy, an integral part of the story, a kind of running commentary. According to these digressions, history has no meaning; it is an irrational stream, intrinsically indifferent to human striving, to human aims and purposes. Meaning can be found in the private lives of men and women, not in great historic events. Ovsjaniko-Kulikovsky described *War and Peace* as a "nihilistic epic." No doubt such was the initial intention of Tolstoy, who stressed that nothing really valuable happens or is achieved in history. One may happily get out of it. Accordingly, Tolstoy was bound to reject culture, in the manner of Rousseau, for the same reasons and probably under the direct influence of the French master for whom he always had profound admiration. Culture is indeed an artifact of history, an historic superstructure to nature and common sense. It is grounded in tradition, in the accumulation of human achievements and experience. Tolstoy regarded culture as a corruption, a burden, a waste of energy and time. As he could not get out of history, even by retiring into private life, he hoped at least to get out of culture, to return to the simplicity of the precultural stage. B. M. Eikhenbaum, one of the most competent students of Tolstoy in recent years, has aptly described

Tolstoy's position as a *nihilism of common sense*, in which common sense is pitted against history.[14] It is because of his radical "antihistoricism" that Tolstoy was unable to "understand" Christianity: Christianity is essentially a historic religion, appealing throughout to historical revelation at sundry times and in diverse fashions. An appeal to historical revelation had no meaning for him. Nor could he admit any Christian metaphysics, since all philosophy was for him just nonsense and illusion.

Of all modern philosophers Tolstoy respected only Kant and precisely that part in Kant's system which is its weakest—his philosophy of religion. Tolstoy was more than influenced by Kant; he shared with him an identity of conception of purpose: *Religion innerhalb des blossen Vernunft*, with the excision of everything "mysterious" or "miraculous," with a deadening regimentation and legalism. Of course, Kant's *Vernunft* and Tolstoy's "reason" are not quite identical. But the regard for legalism was the same in both cases. Tolstoy had the temperament of a moral preacher; but his moral vision was strangely reduced. The highest moral category for him was law. He persistently invited people to do not what was "good," but what was "lawful" or prescribed. Only the fulfillment of the law gives satisfaction. Only this fulfillment is necessary and joyful. God to Tolstoy was not a Heavenly Father, but a Master for whom man must work. It is curious that even as a youth Tolstoy was inclined to a minute regimentation of his life and conduct, although he had little success with it. He wanted to live according to a schedule, recording his progress or failures day by day. He kept this habit until his very last years. Moral behavior, in his opinion, could be reduced to a schedule, a simple and reasonable scheme.

In spite of all his obvious limitations, Tolstoy was widely acclaimed in his day as a moral guide, as a teacher of the righteous life—although few were prepared to follow him to the end. The strength of Tolstoy was in his radicalism, in his polemical frankness, in his vehement and outspoken exposure of human ills and contradictions. His voice was heard as a call to repentance, to a renewal of life. Yet his positive program was poor and somewhat superficial, in spite of his radicalism. He never went beyond an invitation "to understand" and "to withdraw." Strangely enough, Tolstoy was not aware of the depth and the potential of evil in the human soul. Sometimes his artistic insight was ahead of his moral analysis: he could depict the devastating growth of the passions and the burden of temptation. Discovering pollution in human life, he spoke of it with scorn, disgust, and aversion. Still, shame is not yet repentance, although it may lead to repentance. In *Resurrection* his attempt to describe the renovation of broken souls is hardly successful, because his conception of the human person was inadequate. His explanation of the origin of evil in human life is flat and naïve: evil things are born out of mistakes, out of somebody's mistakes or deceptions in the past, out of somebody's fraud or stupidity, out of a malicious lie. Such thinking was exactly in the style of the Enlightenment. The deeper aspects of the human dilemma escaped Tolstoy's attention. He could not understand the problem of man's social existence: he was an incorrigible individualist. There was a paradoxical disproportion in his moral teaching between the aggressive maximalism of his invectives and the striking poverty of his positive program. Actually, his ethics were reduced to common sense and practical prudence. He was able to suggest that even Christ taught simply that one should do no silly things. In Tolstoy's digest of the Gospel, Christ was often presented as just a teacher of the happy life. The doctrine of nonresistance was a capitulation or an impasse. Even Maxim Gorky was shocked by the lack of enthusiasm and inspiration in Tolstoy, who spoke of Christ without any fervent spark.[15]

It seems that in his very last years Tolstoy was becoming increasingly aware of that impasse which he himself had created. Maxim Gorky speaks of the "infinite, irresistible despair and loneliness" which he discerned at the bottom of Tolstoy's radical negation.[16] In any case, Tolstoy's dramatic exodus was a pathetic epilogue to a long life of gropings and ramblings.[17] The rest is silence.

The 1890's were a critical period in the history of Russian thought and literature. In this period of renascent romanticism and of symbolism, motifs of hope and resignation, of expectation and despair, of faith and disillusionment were strangely amalgamated in a new manner. By the end of the century religious themes had become conspicuous. The trend reached its peak in the first decade of the new century, on the eve of World War I. N. A. Berdyaev has rightly called the whole movement the Russian Religious Renaissance.[18] On the whole, it held an odd mixture of insights and illusions, of honest search and irresponsible vagaries, in which were integrated various impulses from philosophy, art, and literature. As the heritage of older masters was rediscovered and reassessed in a changed situation and in a new perspective, the religious and prophetic message of Gogol, Dostoevsky, and Tolstoy came alive in the consciousness of the Russian intelligentsia. Later it assumed a new significance during the Revolution.[19] One of the distinctions of the great Russian literature of the last century, the religious and prophetic note, was a mighty stimulus in the quest for ultimate reality and truth.

Notes

[1] Pavel Nikitich Sakulin, *Russkaja Intelligentsia i Sotsialism* (Moscow, 1924), p. 89.

[2] Vladimir Leont'evich Komarov, "Junost' Dostoevskogo," *Byloe*, No. 23 (1924), 23.

[3] See Nadejda Gorodetskaya, *The Humiliated Christ in Modern Russian Thought* (London, 1938), and Gregorii Petrovich Fedotov, "The Religious Sources of Russian Populism," *Russian Review*, I (April 1942), 27–39.

[4] Cf. Georges Florovsky, "Michael Gershenson," *Slavonic Review*, No. 14 (London, 1926), 315–331.

[5] Letter to Shevyrev (February 11, 1847) from Naples, quoted in *Polnoe Sobranije Sochinenij*, XIII, 214.

[6] Cf. Georges Florovsky, *Puti Russkogo Bogoslovija* (Paris, 1937), pp. 260–270, and D. Tschizhevsky, "Neizvestnyj Gogol," *Novyj Zhurnal*, XXVII (New York, 1951), 126–158.

[7] See Boris Fedorovich Schloezer, *Gogol* (Paris, 1933).

[8] Viktor Vladimirovich Vinogradov, *Evolutsija Russkogo Naturalisma* (Leningrad, 1929).

[9] Vasily Vasilevich Rozanov, *Legenda o Velikom Inkvisitore*, 3rd ed. (St. Petersburg, 1906).

[10] Cf. Andrzej Walicki on Gogol.

[11] Vasily Vasilevich Zenkovskij, *N. V. Gogol* (Paris, 1961).

[12] Cf. the recent book by Ryszard Presybylski, *Dostojewski i "Przeklete Rproblemy"* (Warsaw, 1964).

[13] Dmitry Nikolaevich Ovsjaniko-Kulikovsky, *L. N. Tolstoy* (St. Petersburg, 1908), p. 24.

[14] Boris Mikhailovich Eikhenbaum, *Molodoj Tolstoy* (St. Petersburg, 1922), and *Leo Tolstoy*, Vols. I and II (Leningrad, 1928 and 1931).

[15] Maxim Gorky, *Vospominanija* (Berlin, 1923), p. 69.

[16] *Ibid.*, p. 45.

[17] See Nicolas Weisbein, "Quelques précisions sur le 'Depart' de Léon Tolstoi,"*Revue des Etudes Slaves*, XXXVIII (1961), 223–229.

[18] Nikolai Aleksandrovich Berdyaev, "Russkij Religioznyj Renessance nachala XX veka," *Put'*, No. 49 (1935), 3–22, and Georgy Petrovich Fedotov, "Le Renouveau spirituel en Russie," *Cahiers de la Quainzaine*, Série 22, Cahier I (Paris, 1932).

[19] See the remarkable article by Berdyaev on Gogol, Dostoevsky, and Tolstoy: "The Spirits of the Russian Revolution," first published in the symposium *Iz Glubiny* (Moscow–St. Petersburg, 1918) and recently reprinted in *Novyj Zhurnal*, LXXIX (New York, 1965), 211–252.

The Search for Forgiveness in Some Nineteenth-Century English Novels

by

William A. Madden

> . . . We have lost track of the light, the mornings, the holy inno-
> cence of those who forgive themselves.
>
> —Albert Camus, *The Fall*

THE SEARCH FOR FORGIVENESS APPEARS IN NINETEENTH-CENTURY ENGLISH
fiction with what might be considered, for that "secular" century, surprising frequency. The importance of this theme and the direction in
which the English novel moved at the time in handling it may be indicated by two quotations. In Scott's *The Heart of Midlothian* Effie
Deans tells the Scottish judges who have condemned her to death:
"God forgive ye, my Lords . . . and dinna be angry wi' me for wishing
it—we a' need forgiveness. —As for myself I canna blame ye, for ye act
up to your lights. . . . But God is mair mercifu' to us than we are to
each other."[1] And in Conrad's *Lord Jim* the narrator, Marlow, reflecting
upon the predicament of the novel's hero, comments:

> These were issues beyond the competency of a court of inquiry: it
> was a subtle and momentous quarrel as to the true essence of life,
> and did not want a judge. . . . He wanted an ally, a helper, an
> accomplice. . . . He burrowed deep, deep, in the hope of my
> absolution, which would have been no good to him. This was one of

those cases which no solemn deception can palliate, which no man can help; where his very Maker seems to abandon a sinner to his own devices.[2]

In the first passage a merciful God is spontaneously and confidently invoked against another, less merciful, external agency, but in the latter, human as well as divine forgiveness seems either unavailable or unavailing to men whose attention is directed inward.

Forgiveness, of course, implies guilt, and guilt implies a law to be transgressed, the most profound guilt traditionally attaching, as the Conrad quotation indicates, to transgression of a divine law. Correspondingly, the supreme forgiveness is that bestowed by God. When there is no God, there is no forgiveness, perhaps no need for forgiveness in this ultimate sense. D. H. Lawrence acknowledged the connection in a negative formula that expresses a point of view widespread in twentieth-century literature: "For man, there is neither absolute nor absolution." For *modern* man, we should add, since forgiveness in the religious sense for centuries meant precisely "absolution," a Christian forgiveness resting upon belief in man's freedom to violate a divine law which he is capable of knowing and in a God whose mercy is above all His works. Over the centuries Christian theology has not been very consistent in its opinions regarding the extent of man's freedom and guilt, but the possibility of divine forgiveness has never been questioned. St. Augustine exhorted:

Have compassion on man, O man, and God will have compassion on you. You are a man and the other is a man: two who are unhappy. God is not unhappy; He is merciful. If the unhappy have not compassion on the unhappy, how can he ask for mercy from Him Who shall never know unhappiness?[3]

The link between the divine and the human in Christian forgiveness asserted by Augustine has been central. Another influential Church Father wrote:

Let us then take refuge in the ever present mercy of God, and . . . let all the faithful seek to make holy their own hearts. Let harshness give place to mildness, let wrath grow gentle, forgive one another your offences, and let him who seeks to be forgiven be not himself a seeker of vengeance. For when we say: *Forgive us our debts, as we also forgive our debtors* (Matt. VI. 12), we bind ourselves in the most enduring bonds unless we fulfill what we profess.[4]

A twentieth-century commentator reaffirms the tradition in distinguishing between Christian and other kinds of forgiveness:

> Christ's exhortations [to forgive] are founded neither on social nor ethical nor any other worldly motives. We are told, simply, to forgive men as our Father in heaven forgives us. He is the primary and real Pardoner, and man is his child. Our powers of forgiveness are derived from his.[5]

Thus Christian forgiveness, in Augustine's words, "has its place in the soul," is related to and dependent upon an order of grace which is its motive power, having no limits set to its exercise. It is the absence of this kind of forgiveness which Lawrence notes and Camus so searchingly explores ("They believe solely in sin, never in grace. . . . Grace is what they want"[6]), the consequences of which were dramatized earlier by nineteenth-century English novelists.

In focusing upon the theme of Christian forgiveness as treated in the nineteenth-century English novel, the following remarks indicate that the English novel has been less purely secular than its eighteenth-century origins and much twentieth-century novel-writing and criticism would lead us to expect. The point I would like to make is that even though, as the nineteenth century progressed, Christian forgiveness became more and more difficult to lay hold of, the English novel persistently concerned itself with forgiveness in a religious sense, the search ending in the shocking discovery that divine forgiveness was no longer available, perhaps no longer relevant.

We may recall that the great Evangelical Revival in England during the eighteenth century did not make itself felt in the English novel until late in the century. Even then it did not, as Wesley had hoped, stem the tide of Pelagianism that had shaped the novel in its beginnings.[7] Rather, the two incompatible currents of English Pelagianism and English Evangelicalism grew up alongside one another, the complications in thought and feeling which resulted, evident in relatively simple ways in Defoe and Richardson, being felt in the early 1800's in more complex ways, notably in a new awareness that the naïve consciousness of medieval Christianity had been irrecoverably lost. These complications are everywhere evident in the literature of English Romanticism and nowhere more conspicuously than in the novels of Sir Walter Scott, the father of nineteenth-century fiction.

In the passage from *The Heart of Midlothian* cited above, Scott confronts the reader with a model act of Christian forgiveness as it might have occurred in early eighteenth-century Scotland. The passage is taken from the speech that Effie Deans addresses to the Scottish judges who have just condemned her for child murder and which conforms to a general Christian strain that runs through the novel. In their explicit appeal from a human to the divine tribunal, Effie's words recall the staunch Cameronian Christianity of her father, Davie Deans, whose training lies behind her utterance of them, anticipate the longer and more famous speech of her sister Jeanie in the presence of Queen Caroline, and direct the reader's attention laterally, as it were, to the tragic career of Madge Wildfire, a mad young vagrant girl who, like Effie, was seduced by the outlaw Robertson and was to suffer grave reprisals.

The most obvious connection is with the career of Jeanie Deans, the novel's main character. Effie's condemnation and brief speech serve merely as a prelude to the climactic event in the novel, Jeanie Deans' appeal to Queen Caroline. Significantly, Jeanie's initial resolve to make the pilgrimage to London to seek the King's pardon for her sister crystallizes around an ancient maxim which comes into her mind immediately after the court's condemnation of her sister: "The king's face gives grace." This maxim evokes for the reader the medieval-feudal-Christian world in which kings, as anointed ministers of God, served as vehicles of grace, the kind of world in which Davie Deans so cantankerously grew up. Having said a prayer that apparently confirms her resolve, Jeanie completes the hazardous journey from rural Scotland to urban London and obtains, through the good offices of the Duke of Argyll, an interview with the Queen, to whom she addresses a speech couched in terms as explicitly Christian as those which Effie employed earlier in speaking to the Scottish judges. Jeanie reminds Caroline that royalty too must die and that on her deathbed the pardoning of a poor peasant girl will stand Her Majesty in good stead both with her own Christian conscience and before God.

> O, my Leddy, then [*i.e.*, at death] it isn'a what we hae dune for oursells, but what we hae dune for others, that we think on maist pleasantly. And the thought that ye hae intervened to spare the puir thing's life will be sweeter in that hour, come when it may, than if a word of your mouth could bring the haill Porteous mob at the tail of ae tow.[8]

The Queen, astonished and impressed, remarks to the Duke, "This is eloquence," and promises to speak to the King on Effie's behalf.

Up to this point *The Heart of Midlothian* exhibits a persuasive consistency. Not only does Jeanie's successful pilgrimage verify her sister's earlier distinction between secular and Christian judgment, but events consistently occur in a world in which divine and human forgiveness are available, in which Wilson, a contrabander sentenced to death, forgives Porteous, his cruel guard, Effie forgives her seducer and her judges, Jeanie forgives Effie, and the Queen exercises her prerogatives as a Christian monarch to help free Effie from the sentence of death passed by the secular court in Edinburgh. All of this is presented by Scott in the circumstantial, episodic style of Defoe. The combination of Christian theme and realistic technique works perhaps most powerfully in Scott's portrayal of Madge Wildfire, who operates in the novel as the moving emblem of a victimized humanity in search of love and absolution. Pushed by her early suffering at the hands of her avaricious mother and the "respectable" George Staunton, alias Robertson, into the twilight realm of insanity, Madge preserves an essential innocence which in its haunting simplicity and implicit indictment of man's cruelty to man might not unwarrantably be called Shakespearean.[9] Having forgiven those who did not forgive and would eventually destroy her, Madge dies singing, among other things, fragments of a Christian hymn.

At the beginning of the nineteenth century Scott thus introduced into the form of the novel, by means of the realistic technique that he had inherited from the eighteenth century, a religious element that shapes the dense mesh of character, event, and symbol which he weaves out of the related lives of simple Christian people. What disconcerts the reader is that the climactic event in *The Heart of Midlothian*, Jeanie's winning of the Queen's pardon, comes just a little more than halfway through the novel and that the remainder of Jeanie's story is both anticlimactic and unconvincing. Why Scott found it necessary to depart from history and human experience in the latter part of the novel is explained, in part, by the nature of the world which Jeanie enters when she goes to London. This world is radically secular, a fact established very early in Scott's contrasting of Scotland and England and verified in the King's other pardon, this time for Captain Porteous, who, like Jeanie, was modeled by Scott upon a real figure.[10] Porteous is described by Scott as a personally vicious man, although he heads the forces assigned to protect law and order in Edinburgh. In the pursuit of his duty he precipitated the great civic rebellion—the Porteous Riots of 1736—which Scott describes early in the novel. In her speech to the Queen, Jeanie specifically distinguishes between the Queen's forgiving Effie and the Queen's desire to defend Porteous by way of hanging the mob which attacked him, a distinction which rests on two different conceptions of kingship, the medieval conception of the King as an anointed minister of God and the commercial conception of the King as a parliamentary protector of middle-class property rights. According to the new commercial ethos, Effie's allowing herself to be seduced was not, as Effie herself and her Christian family saw it, a transgression of the divine law, forgivable by God, but a devaluation of her negotiable virginity in the marriage market, in the eyes of the middle class an unforgivable "crime." Thus in pardoning Effie, the King acts in a capacity incompatible with that which obliges him to uphold the law of property and to pardon the unscrupulous Porteous for firing upon a mob. In the former case he acts as a sacramental instrument of divine grace: his pardon of Effie is, in the religious sense, a form of absolution; Effie has really sinned and is really forgiven. In the latter case he acts as the legally appointed protector of middle-class property rights, declaring, in effect, that Porteous has committed no crime.

The greatness of *The Heart of Midlothian* is that in the first half Scott could allow the ancient biblical law and the new secular law to work against one another in an objective portrayal of the tensions, complexities, and ambiguities that were inherent in the historical clash between the feudal past represented by Jeanie and the commercial present represented at its best by men like Mr. Middleburgh. The interplay of the two elements as rendered in Scott's circumstantial style was itself a major discovery in technique, enabling Scott to objectify as a novelist his discovery that history moves and basic assumptions change. The scene in which Jeanie Deans confronts Queen Caroline is, in this perspective, among Scott's great achievements as a novelist, for the reader can accept both the genuineness of Jeanie's Christian faith and the essential irrelevance of that faith in the new commercial order. The Queen's willingness to urge the forgiving of Effie thus becomes for the reader, even while it remains for Jeanie a pure act of Christian forgiveness, the whimsical act of a capricious woman, decent enough to be moved by Jeanie's eloquence, womanly enough to be engaged by the Duke's charm, and shrewd enough to recognize the Duke's political power, who allows herself to be surprised for a moment into playing the archaic role of anointed instrument of God's mercy. But once Scott has finished his great "scene," in which Christian faith triumphs over worldly realities, he cannot face the actual consequences as he knows them: Helen Walker's return to suffering, obscurity, and isolation.

In the first half of the novel Jeanie moves from the archaic, dying, feudal world of rural peasantry into the modern, urban, commercial world of Edinburgh-London. Both worlds are real, and their juxtaposition enables Scott to dramatize his discovery that Scotland in 1736 was caught up in a momentous, painful crisis of change. In the latter part of the novel, unable to conceive a role for his Christian heroine in the newly dominant commercial world run by the respectable Mr. Middleburghs and populated by the Ratcliffs and Sharpitlaws, who connive their way to money and respectability, Scott translates Jeanie, through the agency of the Duke's magic wand, into an unreal pastoral world that is the literary product of a debased romanticism. Relative to the theme of forgiveness, the novel reveals that the only form of forgiveness available to the new commercial civilization is the impersonal, capricious "charity" of the two lawyers who in the opening chapter of the book "save" the wretched pauper Dunover from death in the Tolbooth for the "crime of poverty," a gesture which foreshadows the Queen's equally capricious forgiveness of Effie. Thus, in the very act of nostalgically celebrating Jeanie Deans' Christian heroism, Scott also writes its epitaph.

Read with *The Heart of Midlothian* in the background, Dickens' *Pickwick Papers* and Thackeray's *Vanity Fair* confirm Scott's historical intuition regarding the effect of the triumph of the middle-class commercial ethos upon the exercise of forgiveness. The affinity between Dickens' and Scott's novels lies in the plot movement of *Pickwick*, which is away from the eighteenth-century Comic Garden of Dingley Dell, with its harmless fun and Falstaffian analogues of grace,[11] into the nineteenth-century Wilderness of London, the Fleet, and a ubiquitous legal system that enforces the commercial law of property. In the course of moving from one world to the other, the amiable Pickwick readily forgives the faults of Jingle and other individuals, but finds it impossible in the latter half of the novel to forgive the system which produces and then brutally punishes these people. In fact, in the first half of the novel no forgiveness is really necessary, because in a "Pickwickian" world no guilt is incurable. Pickwick and his companions consistently move in a prelapsarian world of play whose capital is Dingley Dell. By the time Pickwick encounters Jingle and Job Trotter in the Fleet, however, this comic world is much diminished, guilt has been incurred, and hence forgiveness becomes necessary.

"Come here, sir," said Mr. Pickwick, trying to look stern, with four large tears running down his waistcoat. "Take that, sir."

Take what? In the ordinary acceptation of such language, it should have been a blow. As the world runs, it ought to have been a sound, hearty cuff; for Mr. Pickwick had been duped, deceived, and wronged by the destitute outcast who was now wholly in his power.

Must we tell the truth? It was something from Mr. Pickwick's waistcoat-pocket, which clinked as it was given into Job's hand, and the giving of which, somehow or other, imparted a sparkle to the eye, and a swelling to the heart, of our excellent old friend, as he hurried away.[12]

Although the forgiveness here is of an altogether lower order from that evidenced by Effie's speech to her judges, it is not yet the impersonal, capricious "charity" of Scott's lawyers or of Queen Caroline.

How far Dickens' novel has moved in its latter sections from the pleasant, harmless folly and foolery of Mr. Wardle's country retreat is evident in Dickens' description of London as seen, or rather as heard, from within the Fleet:

Above the hoarse loud hum, arose from time to time a boisterous laugh; or a scrap of some jingling song, shouted forth by one of the giddy crowd, would strike upon the ear for an instant, and then be lost amidst the roar of voices and the tramp of footsteps; the breaking of the billows of the restless sea of life that rolled heavily on, without. Melancholy sounds to a quiet listener at any time; how melancholy to the watcher by the bed of death![13]

The whole passage is a curious blend of Fielding's bright world of a roisterous, innocent humanity and the somber impression of human life suggested by Wordsworth's "still, sad music of humanity." Though wedding bells ring in profusion at the end of the novel, it is clear that there is no room for Pickwickian innocence in a metropolitan wilderness of legalized, institutionalized greed, any more than there was room for Jeanie's Christianity.

The ambiguity in Dickens' handling of forgiveness appears in the frightful projections of revenge which are contained in the interlarded Tales that punctuate the novel so disconcertingly, of the Stroller, the Inn Client, Lobbs and his daughter, the Methodist Preacher, Tom Smart, the Madman, and others. The depths of Dickens' rage against the commercial world and the inadequacy of Pickwick's sentimental goodheartedness as an antidote for its brutalities can be measured by these repeated fantasy projections of vengeance. The split between Pickwick's benevolent forgiveness of Jingle and the undisguised desire for revenge evident in the Tales recurs in Dickens' later writing, in Pip's differing attitudes toward Magwitch and Orlick, for example, in *Great Expectations*, a split

which is transcended only in the Dostoevskian figure of the holy fool, Joe
Gargery, an angel of a different order from Pickwick.[14]

With Thackeray's *Vanity Fair* we come to a world from which
forgiveness is totally absent. As the title of the novel indicates, Thackeray's vision of post-Waterloo Europe is that of a civilization in which
Bunyan's Vanity Fair has filled the whole earth, driving from it every
vestige of faith, hope, and charity. The extent of the change since Scott,
both in society itself and in the recording sensibility of the novelist, can
be seen in Thackeray's presentation of what amounts to a terrible parody
of Queen Caroline's forgiveness of Effie Deans. In *Vanity Fair* the king's
face bestows grace, but the face is that of a debauched and despised king,
the woman pardoned is the corrupt Becky Sharp, and the ritual of
absolution is a travesty appropriate to a society in which nations and
empires are up for grabs. Thackeray renders this grotesque ritual of
forgiveness as a parody of Christian baptism:

> At last Becky's kindness and attention to the chief of her husband's
> family, were destined to meet with an exceeding great reward. . . .
> If she did not wish to lead a virtuous life, at least she desired to
> enjoy a character for virtue, and we know that no lady in the genteel
> world can possess this desideratum, until she . . . has been pre-
> sented to her Sovereign in Court. From that august interview they
> come out stamped as honest women. The Lord Chamberlain gives
> them a certificate of virtue. And as dubious goods or letters are
> passed through an oven at quarantine, sprinkled with aromatic
> vinegar, and then pronounced clean—many a lady whose reputation
> would be doubtful otherwise and liable to give infection, passes
> through the wholesome ordeal of the Royal Presence, and issues
> from it free of all taint. . . . This angel was admitted into the
> paradise of a Court . . . her sister-in-law acting as her godmother.
> . . . Becky felt as if she could bless people out of the carriage
> window, so elated was she in spirit. . . .[15]

The only kind of forgiveness available in *Vanity Fair*, Thackeray suggests,
is that which Becky, an orphan of dubious background, can extort from
"genteel" society by virtue of her skill and courage in playing expertly and
successfully the game of appearances, sustained ultimately by money, in
which that society lives and moves. Because most of the players are
hypocrites—as well as inexpert in playing the game—the reader, along
with Thackeray, can relish Becky's triumph with something like moral

satisfaction, but it is a grim and bitter satisfaction which Thackeray's solemn moralizing does nothing to alleviate.

In *Pilgrim's Progress* Bunyan has Evangelist observe, "He that will go to the Celestial City, and yet not go through this town [where Vanity Fair is kept], must needs go out of the World." For Thackeray there is no Celestial City, no heroine like Jeanie Deans, and no place to go out of the world to. (Effie Deans enters a convent.) There is only the "gentleman's" code of manly honesty and courage represented by Major Dobbin, who by the end of the novel finds himself married to the mindless Amelia and living on the fringes of Vanity Fair in utter loneliness. All alike are guilty, at the least of stupidity, and there is neither forgiveness nor escape for anyone. Because in *Vanity Fair* self-interest, sustained by appearances, is everything, Becky's fall from "grace" is as far removed from moral realities as was her "absolution" in the presence of George the Good. Thackeray emphasizes the point by showing that neither the motive for nor even the fact of Becky's adultery need be unequivocally established by those who condemn her: as her own husband remarks, she's "as good as guilty."[16] The clash between the feudal past and the commercial present which preoccupied Scott has thus ended in the total victory of commerce and in moral bankruptcy. Thackeray was no happier in witnessing this triumph than Scott had been in foreseeing its possibility, but the relative clarity of Thackeray's vision, based on his helpless resignation before a *fait accompli*, enabled him to sustain an ironic detachment which Scott and the early Dickens achieved but rarely. There was no longer a feudal Jeanie Deans and a Duke of Argyll, or a comic Mr. Pickwick, to complicate Thackeray's vision.

Wuthering Heights appeared in the same year as *Vanity Fair*, and from the moment in the third chapter when we hear the Reverend Jabes Branderham's sermon during Lockwood's dream-vision and witness its results, we are aware that the novel has forgiveness as its central theme. At the same time, in its development of a realistic technique which enabled Emily Brontë to explore the psychic origins of vengeance and forgiveness in much greater detail and with much greater precision than earlier novelists had done, *Wuthering Heights* marks a major shift in perspective in the treatment of the theme. In Scott, Dickens, and Thackeray, both guilt and forgiveness, where they exist, are described in the externalities of appearance, speech, or act; the inner lives of Effie and Jeanie Deans, of Pickwick, of Becky, and of Major Dobbin remain closed to us. Emily Brontë, through dreams, letters, and speeches that expose the inmost feelings of her characters, explores the timeless world of psychic impulse where the historical conflict of cultures, nations, or classes treated by the earlier novelists becomes an inward conflict of "dark" and "light" forces that originate in the unconscious. Relative to *The Heart of Midlothian*, Arnold Kettle's suggestion that "The Whistler," Effie Deans' illegitimate son who slays his father and at the end of the novel flees to the wilderness, turns up in *Wuthering Heights* as Heathcliff is pertinent here. Heathcliff is the embodiment of an undifferentiated power for good or evil which it is in civilized society's hands either to channel and make creative or to thwart and make destructive; and the key to his future has to do with forgiveness.

The internalizing of forces which previous novelists had treated in external, historical terms can be seen in Emily Brontë's treatment of forgiveness. *Wuthering Heights* is an astonishingly detached double parable of vengeance, hate, isolation, and death, on the one hand, and forgiveness, love, integration, and life, on the other hand, in which Emily Brontë not only asserts man's imperative need to give and accept forgiveness, but discriminates between forms of behavior that masquerade as forgiveness and the real thing. Catherine Earnshaw, who in a moment of euphoria claims, "I'll take no revenge on his [Edgar's] folly—I can afford to suffer anything hereafter," and who in a moment of self-pity later tells Heathcliff, "I won't upbraid you! I forgive you. Forgive me!"[17] does not in fact forgive either man; rather she withdraws from the conflict which they provoke within her. Thwarted in her search for fulfillment, Cathy exerts her revenge through self-destruction as Heathcliff exacts his through the destruction of others. Unable to blend the "dark" Heathcliff impulses and the "light" Edgar impulses, Cathy gradually regresses to the security of the remembered joys of childhood integrity when these alien impulses had not yet become fatally separated. "You and Edgar have broken my heart, Heathcliff! And you both come to bewail the deed to me, as if you were the people to be pitied! I shall not pity you, not I" (p. 135). Her beauty in death testifies both to the reality of the integration she knew in the childhood world to which she returns—"No angel in heaven could be more beautiful"—and to its inadequacy; in her death mask there is the peace of inexperience and stasis, not of moral maturity. For the latter we must turn to the second half of the novel and to the younger Catherine, offspring of Cathy and Edgar Linton, who forgives the wretched Linton Heathcliff—"I felt I must forgive him again" (p. 215), confronts and endures Heathcliff's campaign to make her hate—"I don't hate you. I'm not angry that you struck me. Have you never loved anybody . . . ?" (p. 234), and redeems the brutalized Hareton—"Say you forgive me, Hareton, do! You can make me so happy, by speaking that little word" (p. 267).

Christian as well as seasonal imagery is brought to bear upon the double rhythm of *Wuthering Heights*—Heathcliff's alienation is finally determined on Christmas Eve, and Hareton's integration commences on Whitsunday—but Emily Brontë is not writing a Christian parable. Rather she is translating into the novel form, through the sophisticated use of point of view, irony, symbol, and circumstantial realism, the aspiration toward wholeness which informs her best poetry. This aspiration, the novel affirms, can be realized only through recognizing that the only unforgivable sin is the refusal to forgive. But while to be able to forgive is a sign of redemption and the badge of psychic maturity in the novel, the sanction for forgiveness is not the example and command of a loving Father, but Nature. That is why it would be misleading to call *Wuthering Heights* a Christian novel, although it is certainly a religious one.[18] Indeed Emily Brontë does not attempt to tell us what the ultimate sources of grace, of psychic health, are—why the older Cathy should be unable to forgive, and as a result should regress, is no more explainable than the younger Cathy's capacity to forgive—but the symbolic genealogy of the younger Cathy does indicate the conditions for such forgiveness, the blending of the "dark" Earnshaw energy with the impulse for order represented by the Lintons. If the former by itself produces chaos and destruction, the latter by itself produces sterility, and of the two perhaps the former enjoys priority, since it is better to act than simply to exist. But whether we love and forgive, or hate and seek vengeance—and both for Emily Brontë are always possible—certain consequences inevitably follow. Such is the law of nature for both persons and societies, a law based not on faith but on experience.

In George Eliot's *Middlemarch*, also, forgiveness is the moral center of the novel, and it is again seen as a function of interior wholeness, in this case the integration of what George Eliot would call the spiritual and the sensual. Although, like Emily Brontë, she offers no divine sanction for forgiveness, treating it rather as an ethical imperative, there is nevertheless, as in *Wuthering Heights*, a residue of Christian feeling in *Middlemarch* which enables us to say that George Eliot's treatment of forgiveness, although non-Christian in its philosophical premises, is Christian in derivation insofar as it is made the center of a wholesome moral life. Dorothea Brooke, whose forgiveness of Rosamund Vincy is the climactic event in the novel, is a modern-day St. Theresa, George Eliot tells us; without the saint's "coherent social faith" or a social medium adequate to a heroic external work, she is a heroic woman nonetheless in her interior conquest of self and her "reaching out" to others in sympathetic forgiveness, an achievement paralleled in the novel by the heroic forgiveness extended by Mrs. Bulstrode to her husband and the more amiable forgiveness extended by Mary Garth to her fiancé, Fred Vincy.

It would be as misleading, therefore, to call *Middlemarch* a secular novel as it would be to call *Wuthering Heights* a Christian novel. Both are opposed to the self-assertion and material acquisitiveness celebrated by Defoe; both emphasize the central need for giving and receiving forgiveness; both are interested in the consequences of forgiveness, not only for the individual who practices it but for its effects upon the lives of those who are touched by it; but neither seeks a sanction beyond that of experience and man's sense of what is right. It is as though in response to Thackeray's despairing vision of modern man living without God in the world that these sensitive women, reared in an atmosphere of a defensive introverted form of Christianity, turned inward to seek a fresh source of hope and forgiveness in humanity itself, Emily Brontë in the world of preconscious impulses where the Dionysian and Apollonian instincts that compete for expression and domination are "educated" by the responses they meet with in society, and George Eliot in the minute discriminations of man's moral consciousness as it labors to bring these forces to harmonious joint fulfillment under the aegis of a powerful sense of duty.

Yet there is a subtle and important difference between the two novels. For George Eliot the exercise of fellow-feeling has about it a sufficiency in itself which is alien to the world of Emily Brontë, a sufficiency made necessary, perhaps, by George Eliot's deep sense both of the fallibility of mortals and of the absence of anything more perfect than other mortals to satisfy man's need for completion in something larger, better, and higher than himself. Stated differently, Emily Brontë's religious thirst for some transcendent Other that would fully satisfy her never abated; George Eliot decided, on philosophical grounds, that her own similar thirst would have to be content with something less. Hence the curious ineffectiveness of Dorothea's splendid character and actions, her failure to change anyone, and the reasonableness of arguing that she simply exercises within the fictional provincial world of Middlemarch the kind of sympathetic understanding which her creator exercised in the world at large and which is a good in itself, whatever its effect upon others. For the most impressive act of forgiveness in *Middlemarch* is that of George Eliot herself, whose imaginative capacity to find an "equivalent center of self" even in a Casaubon acts as a kind of perpetual benediction on everything and everyone it touches. The forgiveness that is measurably most productive and creative in the modern world, then, is that exercised by the artist. It is in this sense appropriate that at the end of *Middle-*

march Dorothea should marry art in the guise of Will Ladislaw. George Eliot concludes:

> Her full nature, like that river of which Cyrus broke the strength, spent itself in channels which had no great name on earth. But the effect of her being on those around her was incalculably diffusive: for the growing good of the world is partly dependent on unhistoric acts. . . .[19]

Or, we might add, on fictional acts. What George Eliot questionably claims for Dorothea—that she was "incalculably diffusive"—is certainly applicable to George Eliot herself, and what she hoped to diffuse through her art was man's need and capacity for forgiveness even though the Christian sanctions for it had apparently disappeared.

With Hardy and Conrad the nineteenth-century search for forgiveness concludes on a note of despair, for to their more logical and masculine minds the disappearance of God made the universe itself problematical. Hence in their novels the treatment of forgiveness becomes a questioning of its moral relevance. In a simultaneous narrowing-in of the novel's focus upon an individual human consciousness and an expansion of its implications through the reading of cosmic meanings in the light of that consciousness, both Hardy and Conrad dramatize the prior question of whether or not man is in fact guilty.

The tragic plot of *Tess of the d'Urbervilles* hinges upon Angel Clare's inability to forgive Tess, or rather upon his inability, rooted in prejudices which he has absorbed from his environment, to see that Tess is in fact innocent, that her seduction by Alec d'Urberville was simply part of a young girl's "liberal education"[20] in a universe where pain is ubiquitous. Recognition of this truth, added to the practice of loving kindness, Hardy implies, might have averted tragedy and given Angel and Tess a modicum of happiness. Thus Hardy, although sharing up to a point George Eliot's Religion of Humanity and her belief that by practicing loving kindness and thereby changing society man might attain the only happiness he could be confident of on this planet, is much closer to Emily Brontë than to George Eliot in his concentration upon the archaic, simple, instinctive impulses rather than upon the power of the human will to harness and direct these impulses creatively. As E. M. Forster has remarked, Hardy's characters seem peculiarly volitionless, dependent upon Fate as the ultimate enabling or frustrating power; and because Fate seems blind, if not actually malevolent, Hardy is profoundly pessimistic. On a "blighted" planet the heightening of self-awareness and sensitivity recommended by George Eliot becomes simply a heightening of man's capacity to suffer, a heightening of his sense of irony.

Hardy saw man's inextinguishable vision of and thirst for beauty, wholeness, and joy as a fundamental datum of experience, whether produced by love, or music, or, like the lovely landscape projected by the drunken farm hands returning from the fair, by alcohol. But Hardy also believed that contacts with such a world are rare and transitory. The moon-world of the imagination for a moment transfigures Tess into a Demeter and Angel into an Apollo, but the vision is proved hallucinatory by the dominant sun-world, or reality; Tess is eventually sacrificed on an altar built for sacrifices to placate the sun. Hardy's prevailing despair is projected in the scene in which Tess and her alcoholic friend crawl across a wintry landscape of stones and rubble shivering like two minuscule animals, framed between a great slab of gray sky above them and the brown slab of earth beneath, while over their heads fly strange polar birds made crazy and empty-eyed by cosmic encounters beyond human imagination. The guilt is not man's but rests with the "circumstantial will" of the cosmos; and if it was difficult for Dickens and Thackeray to forgive a whole society, it was impossible, not to say irrelevant, for Hardy to forgive the President of the Immortals, whatever or whoever that might be. Human forgiveness, therefore, has lost for Hardy not only its religious sanctions but its deep moral relevance; at best it is a sensible strategy for meliorating pain.

With Lord Jim we come to the second quotation cited at the beginning of these remarks and to the final confrontation in the nineteenth-century drama of guilt and forgiveness. The hero of Conrad's novel is distinguished both from those whose roots remain fixed in Western civilization and from those in the seafaring company he keeps, who drift from port to port hauling the goods of civilizations with which they have no moral relationship, by his inability to rationalize or forget his sense of guilt. The guilt originated in Jim's instinctive leap from the Patna, an act which shattered the romantic dreams of glory and honor which he had derived from his boyhood reading and induced a restlessness that eventually drives him to an island in the Southeast Asia archipelago where he meets his death.

The interest of the novel is centered entirely upon Jim's endless self-searching in his attempt to settle the question of whether or not he in fact is guilty, and if so what might be done about it. As told by Marlow, Jim's tale is that of a puzzled Ancient Mariner who confides his story to the one person who will listen. To those who are unaware of his criminal leap from the Patna he seems naïvely good: "I am unable to imagine him guilty of anything much worse than robbing an orchard."[21] Yet, like St. Augustine before him, whose motiveless robbery of an orchard led him to a profound exploration of the nature and meaning of guilt, Jim's instinctive abandoning of an endangered ship induces a restless questioning which gives him no peace. Was he guilty? Marlow refers at one point to Jim's "strange illusion of passiveness, as though he had not acted but had suffered himself to be handled by the infernal powers who had selected him for the victim of their practical jokes" (p. 79); to his illusion later that "a fellow could begin with a clean slate" (p. 133); and finally, when Jim has created a community of peace among the natives on Patusan, to his talk about "being done with it—with the bally thing at the back of my head . . . forgetting. . . . Hang me if I know! I can think of it quietly. After all, what has it proved? Nothing" (p. 219). What Jim cannot do, that is, is accept and live with his sense of guilt, because, as Marlow tells him, he cannot forgive himself.

It is true that his later deliberate and courageous leap into Patusan is, in Jim's own mind, meant to expiate the guilt of his instinctive and cowardly leap from the *Patna*. Moreover, as a result of his second leap he succeeds in winning the respect of the island natives, creating a circle of trust symbolized by the ring given him by his native friend Wain Daris. Yet the latter leap of courage proves to be far more destructive to others than did the first leap of fear, an irony worthy of Hardy. And the native girl Jewel, who dwells at the center of the circle of love and trust that Jim had created on Patusan, finds it impossible in the end to forgive him for abandoning her. ". . . He was blind and deaf and without pity, as you all are. He shall have no tears from me. Never, never. Not one tear" (p. 251). Marlow appeals the case: " 'You must forgive him,' I concluded, and my own voice seemed to be muffled, lost in an irresponsive deaf immensity. 'We all want to be forgiven,' I added after a while" (p. 252). Yet at the end Marlow, who knew Jim best, comments: "He goes away from a living woman to celebrate his pitiless wedding with a shadowy ideal of conduct. Is he satisfied—quite, now, I wonder?" (p. 300). Marlow can neither extend the absolution Jim seeks for his early betrayal of a "shadowy" ideal nor tell us whether Jim had found a clue to the origin and expiation or even the existence of guilt. Jim dies looking about him into the uncomprehending faces of the natives, his hand over his lips, still searching for the understanding and forgiveness that a "deaf immensity" fails to yield up. "Nobody, nobody," Marlow tells Jewel, "is good enough" (p. 229).

From our contemporary vantage point one might say that in *Lord Jim* Conrad anticipated the paradox which later obsessed Kafka, who wrote: "The state in which we find ourselves is sinful, quite independent

of guilt."[22] Where can man find forgiveness for those "falls" that induce
a sense of guilt and yet seem instinctive and unavoidable? In the
character and remarks of the French Lieutenant, Conrad indicates that,
living in a universe without God, contemporary man must forgive himself
if he is to go on to win that final courage which alone creates, however
precariously, a community of faith among men. But, as in Hardy, such
forgiveness, with no sanction other than man's own needs, seems incapable of satisfying and has its own grave self-deceptions. "Incurable
romantics" like Lord Jim, all those, that is, who refuse both to ignore evil
and to accept reality as it is, find it difficult to forgive themselves when
they fall, since they can find no signs of forgiveness in their fellowman,
and, more especially, because their "exalted egoism" finds no response at
all from the "deaf immensity."

The strategy adopted by twentieth-century authors like Kafka and
Camus to meet this predicament was beyond the imagination of the
nineteenth-century English novelists whom we have examined. As the
narrator of Camus' *The Fall* puts it: "Is not the great thing that stands in
the way of our escaping [judgment] the fact that we are the first to
condemn ourselves? Therefore it is essential to begin by extending
condemnation to all, without distinction, in order to thin it out at the
start." This is not only the beginning, but, in the absence of a merciful
God, as far as the Western conscience can go. Camus insists: "We
cannot assert the innocence of anyone, whereas we can state with certainty the guilt of all. Every man testifies to the crime of all the others—
that is my faith and my hope. . . . No excuses ever, for anyone. . . .
With me there is no giving of absolution or blessing."[23] Yet as Effie
Deans says, "We a' need forgiveness," and as Marlow says, "We all want
to be forgiven." It thus appears that "the light, the mornings, the holy
innocence of those who forgive themselves" is related to faith in a God
Who is more merciful to us than we are to each other or even to ourselves. The nineteenth-century English novel, at least, constitutes an
impressive record of Western man's compelling need to find, in society or
in nature or, latterly, in himself, some source of grace equivalent to that
offered in the Christian conception of forgiveness. In the course of this
quest his self-awareness has expanded enormously, and along with it his
conviction that his Maker, if there be a Maker, has abandoned him to his
own devices.

Notes

[1] *The Heart of Midlothian*, ed. D. Daiches (New York, 1948), p. 257 (Chapter XXIV).

[2] *Lord Jim*, ed. M. D. Zabel (Boston, 1958), p. 71.

[3] M. F. Toal, *The Sunday Sermons of the Great Fathers* (Chicago, 1958), II, 278.

[4] *Ibid.*, II, 127.

[5] Romano Guardini, *The Lord* (Chicago, 1954), p. 302.

[6] Albert Camus, *The Fall*, trans. Justin O'Brien (New York, 1958), p. 135.

[7] Rebecca West provides a working definition of Pelagianism: "the theory that man is free equally to choose good and evil, and that, should he choose good, his own natural ability will enable him to reach moral perfection, and that our race could be changed and made innocent without search for a higher authority and submission to it." See *The Court and the Castle* (New Haven, 1957), p. 71. In his excellent study *The Rise of the Novel* (Berkeley and Los Angeles, 1962), Ian Watt has described the radical secular bias which shaped the English novel as it emerged in the eighteenth century. The writings of Defoe indicate that by 1750 Bunyan's fictional vision of the Christian Celestial City had lost its hold upon the imagination of a society dominated by the middle-class ethos of "getting on" in the world. Despite his invocations of Christian maxims, Defoe's sensibility was as secular as that of his hero Robinson Crusoe, whose "original sin" of having abandoned his family became, as Watt points out, his salvation, his restless discontent being blessed by the wealth which natural acquisitiveness drove him to amass. Defoe's importance in the history of the novel rests upon his discovery of a realis-

tic, circumstantial, episodic technique which was admirably suited to expressing the new ethos and which has characterized the novel as a form ever since. So essential has this combination of a secular orientation and a realistic technique been to the novel that Northrup Frye has concluded that "the supernatural or the suggestion of it" can be got into a novel only with great difficulty. How, then, can the novelist assimilate a religious experience such as Christian forgiveness into his art? The answer is implied in Watt's observations that realism as a literary technique, despite its historical link with secularism, is morally neutral. Defoe's use of it to express a secularist view of life by no means exhausted its potentialities.

[8] *The Heart of Midlothian*, p. 405 (Chapter XXXVII).

[9] Scott uses lines from *Hamlet* on Ophelia as an epigraph to Chapter XVI, which is concerned with Madge.

[10] In a brief preface to the novel Scott informs his readers that Helen Walker, the woman on whose career Jeanie's story was based, returned to Scotland to a life of penury, spinsterhood, and menial drudgery; in the novel he would persuade us that Jeanie returned to an edenic married existence in the pastoral surroundings of the Duke of Argyll's estate, Roseneath. The contrasting of Scotland and England is on pp. 12–13 (Chapter 1).
Alexander Welsh has documented Scott's preoccupation with property and commerce in *The Hero of the Waverley Novels* (New Haven, Conn., 1963), esp. Chapter IV.

[11] On Falstaff as a comic analogue to the saint, see W. H. Auden, "Some Notes on the Comic," *Thought*, XXVII (1952), 69–70.

[12] *The Pickwick Papers*, ed. Joseph Mersand (New York, 1960), p. 640.

[13] *Ibid.*, p. 672.

[14] See Julian Moynahan, "The Hero's Guilt: The Case of Great Expectations," *Essays in Criticism*, X (January 1960), 60–79.

[15] *Vanity Fair*, ed. Geoffrey and Kathleen Tillotson (Boston, 1963), pp. 458–460.

[16] See, on this point, G. Armour Craig, "On the Style of *Vanity Fair*," *Style in Prose Fiction: English Institute Essays* (New York, 1959), pp. 87–113.

[17] *Wuthering Heights*, intro. by V. S. Pritchett (Boston, 1956), pp. 85 and 128. (Subsequent page references are in parentheses in the text.)

[18] For a discussion of the religious element in *Wuthering Heights*, see Derek Traversi, "The Brontë Sisters and *Wuthering Heights*," in *From Dickens to Hardy*, ed. Boris Ford (Harmondsworth, 1958), pp. 256–273.

[19] *Middlemarch*, ed. Gordon S. Haight (Boston, 1956), p. 613.

[20] *Tess of the d'Urbervilles*, ed. William E. Buckler (Boston, 1960), p. 87.

[21] *Lord Jim*, p. 134.

[22] *The Great Wall of China*, trans. Willa and Edwin Muir (New York, 1946), p. 270.

[23] *The Fall*, pp. 110, 131.

Some Implications of Form
in Victorian Fiction

by

J. Hillis Miller

THE SPECIAL PLACE OF JOSEPH CONRAD IN ENGLISH LITERATURE LIES IN the fact that in his work a form of nihilism covert in modern culture is brought to the surface and shown for what it is. I am using the term "nihilism" here to describe two related forms of nothingness. First, nihilism is the emptiness left after what Nietzsche calls "the death of God." This emptiness is figured in the vacancy of astronomical space. It undermines man's values by depriving them of extra-human foundation. Second, nihilism is the hollowness of human consciousness itself. The second aspect of nihilism is associated with a tendency to define man in terms of his self-sustaining strength of will. The relation between these two aspects of nihilism is implicit in the speech of the madman in Nietzsche's *The Joyful Wisdom*. This text announces the death of God and defines it:

> "Where is God gone?" he called out. "I mean to tell you! We *have killed him,*—you and I! We are his murderers! But how have we done it? How were we able to drink up the sea? Who gave us the sponge to wipe away the whole horizon? What did we do when we loosened this earth from its sun? Whither does it now move? Whither do we move? Away from all suns? Do we not dash on unceasingly? Backwards, sideways, forwards, in all directions? Is

there still an above and below? Do we not stray, as through infinite nothingness? Does not empty space breathe upon us?"

The death of God is not the same thing as the loss of faith in God's existence. Nor is it the same thing as a willing withdrawal of God from the world. God is dead because man has killed him. Man has killed God by dividing existence into two realms, subject and object, mind and world. This dualism, already implicit in Descartes' *Cogito ergo sum*, is present in many forms of modern thought and art, even in those forms which try to deny it or transcend it. It is, for example, the latent presupposition determining the forms of Victorian fiction, and it is these I shall discuss in this essay.

Descartes' hyperbolic doubt establishes the priority of consciousness over its objects. It leads to the notion that things exist, for man at least, only because he thinks them. When things exist only as represented or reflected in man's consciousness, then man has drunk up the sea and has become himself the measure of every coordinate of space. God was once seen as the power establishing the horizon which divides heaven from earth; but when man becomes the measure of all things, he drinks up the sea. In doing so he also drinks up God, the creator of the sea. God now becomes an object of thought like any other. It is in this sense that man, for Nietzsche, is the murderer of God. After this catastrophe, as the first sense of exhilarating freedom begins to wear off, man wanders "backwards, sideways, forwards, in all directions," through an "infinite nothingness" which is both within him and without. It remained for Conrad, in English literature, to bring to the surface in his own way these implications of modern subjectivism, but Conrad is the culmination of a development which can be traced through previous novelists.

This development is particularly well-marked in English fiction, though of course it is present in Continental fiction too. Though it exists alongside the drama of the attempt to recover an absent God in mid-nineteenth-century poetry, Victorian fiction follows a different track. The novel shows man forgetting the death of God and attempting to establish a purely human world based on interpersonal relations. In the novel the secret nihilism accompanying man's new role as the source of all value is gradually revealed. Conrad is part of European literature and takes his place with Dostoevsky, Mann, Gide, Proust, and Camus as an explorer of modern forms of experience. Within the narrower limits of the English novel, however, he comes at the end of a native tradition leading from Dickens and George Eliot to Hardy and James.

Dickens begins his career as the inheritor of eighteenth-century conceptions of man and society. These assume that each man has a fixed nature, given to him by God. All men are naturally good, but the goodness in some men is invulnerable whereas in others it can be corrupted by the world. *Oliver Twist* takes up themes Dickens inherited from Fielding and Smollett. Oliver manages to protect his goodness from the stains of the world's evil and thereby earns the place which is waiting for him in the society of the good. His destiny is secretly manipulated by a Providence which is the presence of God in the world. But even as early as *Oliver Twist* Dickens sees the city as a place from which God is absent. Only in the country is God a sustaining presence in nature, the support of individual and social goodness. As Dickens' work progresses, there is a gradual widening of this split between the small communities where God is present and the vast city, teeming with people separated from God or touched by Him only intermittently. The central issue of *David Copperfield*, for example, is a metaphysical or even theological problem: What is the source of the pattern of David's life, as he presents it in retrospect? Is the structure a merely human one of memory, free choice, and linked associations, or has David's life been the gradual revelation of a destiny secretly prepared for him by a benign Providence? The old objective world, ordered by a living God, is delicately balanced against the new subjective one in which man gives pattern and value to the world by seeing it from a certain point of view and assimilating it into his mind, as all the world of *David Copperfield* exists in the reconstruction of David's first-person narration.

Dickens' last work moves toward a recognition of the hollowness which undermines a society constructed freely by men and women living together in the city. His last completed novel, *Our Mutual Friend* (1864–1865), goes furthest toward recognizing the nihilism emergent in English culture. It is a novel about "money, money, money, and what money can make of life." Dickens sees that money is the collective ascription of value to what has no value in itself, but the "Society" of *Our Mutual Friend*, in forgetting this fact, has allowed itself more and more to be measured by the nullity of money. The result is a progressive emptying-out of the characters, as they are gradually more cut off from any extra-human reality. In the absence of any such reality, society becomes the scene of a spectral battle of vacuous wills struggling for dominance. In *Our Mutual Friend* Dickens sees that a human society cannot be self-generating. Values created entirely out of the interaction of one consciousness with another can have no authenticity. They are the reflection of nothing by nothing, as the Veneering dinner parties are reflected in the great looking glass over the sideboard and shown to be a vain pretense.

Salvation is possible in *Our Mutual Friend* only for those characters who can break through the façade of mediated reflections and reach a reality, whether material or spiritual, beyond the human world.

If Dickens' last novel approaches a confrontation with nihilism which is something like Conrad's, the derivation of the formal conventions of Victorian fiction from an assumption of the separation of subject and object appears with great clarity in the work of George Eliot. The aesthetic and metaphysical presuppositions of the art form inherited by Conrad are already well developed in her novels. Her work is a deliberate attempt to construct a viable human world after the death of God. Following Feuerbach, she sees God as the projection of collective human values and tries to show that mankind can, as Barbara Hardy puts it, "be its own providence." George Eliot's novels are a full working-out of what follows from the assumption that each consciousness is a separate sphere, a "centre of self," as she puts it in *Middlemarch* (1871–1872), "whence the lights and shadows must always fall with a certain difference." Everything exists as an appearance in some "centre of self." Nature, like God, is subjectivized and made over into a reflection of the qualities of human life. Each mind is cut off from other minds and has no natural access to them. The dramatic action of George Eliot's novels tends to develop from the obdurate opacity of minds to one another. Self-centered egotism is the great danger to man and the source of evil. Good follows from the enhancement of man's power of self-denying sympathy.

There is, however, an apparent contradiction in the form her novels take. They presuppose that every human being is imprisoned in his subjectivity, limited to his own perspective on the world. The lesson of life, even for so intelligent, so "ardent and theoretic" a person as Dorothea in *Middlemarch*, is a lesson of renunciation. Each man or woman must accept a narrow lot, both in power of vision and in range of effective action. But the narrator of the novels claims for herself precisely that all-embracing breadth of vision, that intimate access to the hearts of others, which is denied to the characters. If the acceptance of a separation of subject and object leads the novel inevitably to the technique of limited point of view as it is practiced by James or Conrad, George Eliot seems old-fashioned and naïve in her assumption of the possibility of angelic omniscience for the narrator. To borrow another phrase from *Middlemarch*, the narrator of her novels is related to the world of the novels in a way like that of "Uriel watching the progress of planetary history from the Sun."

Nevertheless, in spite of her appeals to a seemingly "realistic" theory of fiction, George Eliot is the most subjective of novelists. This can be

seen in the fact that there is throughout *Middlemarch* a constant parallel-
ing of the scientist's work and the novelist's. As the scientist investigates
physical nature, so the novelist investigates society and human nature,
and a good novel is an "experiment in life." A shift from one group of
characters to another, for example, is justified by an appeal to scientific
method: "In watching effects, if only of an electric battery, it is often
necessary to change our place and examine a particular mixture or group
at some distance from the point where the movement we are interested in
was set up." The parallel between scientist and novelist would seem to
make George Eliot an objective writer, effacing herself before external
reality like a good scientist and discovering laws which are independent of
her own mind. On the other hand, the characters in *Middlemarch* and all
their world have no such objective existence as that of an electric battery.
Even though the characters may be based in part on real people, these
have been transposed into a purely fictive realm. George Eliot has in-
vented all the novel, and the town of Middlemarch exists nowhere but in
the words on the page. This seems to show her once more inconsistent.
She claims scientific objectivity for what is in fact a fictitious invention.

Science, however, is not the effacement of the subjective before the
objective. It is just the opposite: an assimilation of nature into an interior
realm where everything can be manipulated as number and calculation
and where the energies of nature can be "harnessed" to human ends. A
remarkable passage in *Middlemarch* shows George Eliot's recognition of
this, and gives, in a description of the subjectivity of correct scientific
method, a covert description of her own method as a novelist. Proper
imagination is no mere inventive fantasy, concocting ideal realms that
never were. The imagination necessary for both scientist and novelist
presupposes a turning inside-out of the objective world and its assimilation by the mind. When the world has been taken into the mind, then
the scientist can follow sequences of causality otherwise hidden, just as
the novelist can know the hearts of her characters in all their subtle
interactions. The consciousness of the narrator is an all-embracing vessel
which contains the characters and their world, bathing them in its
permeating medium. George Eliot's description of the subjective realism
of Lydgate the scientist is an exact description of her own "arduous
invention" as a novelist:

Many men have been praised as vividly imaginative on the strength
of their profuseness in indifferent drawing or cheap narration:—
reports of very poor talk going on in distant orbs; or portraits of
Lucifer coming down on his bad errands as a large ugly man with

bat's wings and spurts of phosphorescence; or exaggerations of wantonness that seem to reflect life in a diseased dream. But these kinds of inspiration Lydgate regarded as rather vulgar and vinous compared with the imagination that reveals subtle actions inaccessible by any sort of lens, but tracked in that outer darkness through long pathways of necessary sequence by the inward light which is the last refinement of Energy, capable of bathing even the ethereal atoms in its ideally illuminated space. He for his part had tossed away all cheap inventions where ignorance finds itself able and at ease: he was enamoured of that arduous invention which is the very eye of research, provisionally framing its object and correcting it to more and more exactness of relation. . . .

This admirable passage is a full statement of the aesthetics of that form of the novel which develops from modern subjectivism. The suprasensible world no longer exists. It is mere fantasy, product of a bad imagination diseased or drunken in its dreamings. The physical world is all that remains outside the mind. This world as it is in itself is an outer darkness, unknowable by any objective lens. Things can be known only as they are transformed into objects, that is, taken into the ideally illuminated space of the mind. When things have been absorbed into that inner space, their exact relations can be understood in finest detail and in necessary sequence. All things now are of the same nature as the mind and lie open to that searching inward light which is the substance of the mind's power piercing through every darkness to make its own contents transparent. The eye of research is turned inward, not outward, for nothing can be known which is not already inside the mind.

In *Middlemarch* or in *Daniel Deronda* (1876) the embracing consciousness of the narrator is the inner space in which all the characters dwell, as in a fluid, continuous, permeating medium. The minds of the characters are contained within the narrator's mind. That mind binds everything together in time and space and is the reader's guarantee that he can move freely from one mind to another, knowing them all completely. The narrator's mind is subtle, tactful, sensitive to delicate nuances, conscious that any process may be subdivided indefinitely into ever more minute parts. The greatness of a late novel like *Middlemarch*, as well as its advance over earlier works like *Adam Bede*, lies in the substitution of the image of an immense moving system, "a play of minute causes," for the simpler image of a chain of single causes used in the earlier novel. *Middlemarch* is an enormously complicated network of relations. On whatever moment in whatever mind the narrator focuses, the reader is constantly made aware of a multiple complexity: the complexity of the single mind in any moment, the complexity of that mind in relation to its own past and future, the complexity of the co-presence of all the minds, all misunderstanding one another, each living in its own world, and each with its own past and future—the whole making a dynamic web of interwoven influences. Any particular mental state participates in the "embroiled medium" of the whole and is inevitably "a part of that involuntary, palpitating life." This vision of society as a structure of reciprocal effects is achieved only through the subjectivizing of the world, its assimilation by the inward light of imagination. George Eliot's novels are the triumph of her will to understand the world. The ideally illuminated space we enter when we read one of her novels is sustained by nothing but her mind, just as her religion of humanity proposes that men in their living together can create their own God.

Like other mid-nineteenth-century writers, George Eliot was not fully aware of the implications of her humanism, and, as Nietzsche saw, attempted the difficult task of upholding the Christian morality of altruism without faith in the Christian God. "When one gives up the Christian faith," says Nietzsche in a paragraph on George Eliot in *Twilight of the Idols*, "one pulls the right to Christian morality out from under one's feet. This morality is by no means self-evident: this point has to be exhibited again and again, despite the English flatheads. Christianity is a system, a *whole* view of things thought out together. By breaking one main concept out of it, the faith in God, one breaks the whole: nothing necessary remains in one's hands. Christianity presupposes that man does not know, *cannot* know, what is good for him, what evil: he believes in God, Who alone knows it. Christian morality is a command; its origin is transcendent; it is beyond all criticism, all right to criticism; it has truth only if God is the truth—it stands and falls with faith in God."

Another of the "English flatheads," Anthony Trollope, begins, like George Eliot, without full recognition of the implications of his vision, but his later work moves toward such recognition. Trollope's fanatical commitment to the writing of novels as a daily routine grew out of an early habit of daydreaming. His novels, like those of George Eliot, exist in a subjective inner space which is the consciousness of the omniscient narrator. Trollope's characters, however, unlike George Eliot's, are as transparent to one another as they are to the inward vision of the narrator. This transparency follows naturally from the fact that the characters live in a humanized world. In spite of the fact that many of

Trollope's best novels are about clergymen and their wives and daughters, these novels do not center on religious themes. All ladies and gentlemen will go to heaven, but heaven is a long way off, beyond the barriers of death. It does not exist within the confines of the story, which are the confines of the narrator's mind. In the same way, nonhuman nature does not exist except as a sign of some subjective or social quality, as a man's estate signifies his wealth or as the rooms in *The Warden* are perfect expressions of the people who live in them. Trollope's novels concentrate on minds and their interactions; and, since the characters share the assumptions and moral judgments which define their society, they can usually see perfectly into one another's hearts.

The dramatic action of a novel by Trollope can therefore rarely derive from that interplay of appearance and reality which arises when minds are opaque to one another and which is central in the work of a novelist like Jane Austen. The clarity with which the characters in Trollope's novels understand one another means that the drama often arises from a conflict of wills. His characters are distinguished by the strength and quality of their volition, and each novel is a kind of game in which each character plays with all his energy the role in which he finds himself cast. Trollope is a striking example of the way a definition of man as subjective ego leads to a definition of him as will. In Trollope's early fiction, however, there is no understanding of the autonomy of the will, or of the way society as a whole rests in consequence on nothing but human volition. This understanding is made impossible by the lack of abstract self-consciousness in the characters, the utter spontaneity with which they make the decisions which allow them to go on being themselves. They are able instinctively to decide to be true to themselves, and this keeps secret the fact that they could decide to be different. If their selfhoods are sustained only by acts of will, then those selves are in fact nothing but will. Continuity, self-consistency, is therefore the supreme virtue in Trollope's world. As long as the characters remain true to themselves, the fragility of their society will not appear. As long as the game does not appear as a game, its arbitrary quality will stay hidden. So Lily Dale sticks to the decision made in *The Small House at Allington* not to marry Johnny Eames and in *The Last Chronicle of Barset* writes herself down as "Lilian Dale, Old Maid." If she were to betray her earlier commitment and choose to marry Johnny, the earlier decision might appear to be gratuitous. If man is nothing but will, then he may change as often as he wills; and if a man recognizes this, he may become the shape-shifter of one form of twentieth-century existentialism.

The emptiness of a self-sustaining society never appeared in such stark terms to Trollope, partly because of his native English faith in the permanence of each man's character; but one of his last novels, The Way We Live Now (1874–1875), moves toward an understanding of the latent implications of his earlier ones. The Way We Live Now denies all the laws of Trollope's earlier novels. It shows the new way of life in the city destroying the old provincial society. But in being the end of the apparently stable society of small communities, the new city life shows that society for what it secretly was all along: unstable because resting primarily on human wills. A community of such wills is a game held together by the fact that people go on obeying rules which are "absurd" in the sense that they might have been different, and they might be different now, if the characters should choose to play the game by different rules. Lack of detached self-awareness prevented the people in earlier novels from recognizing this, but many characters in The Way We Live Now have a new self-consciousness.

In place of the continuity usual in Trollope's fiction, The Way We Live Now shows sudden changes in society and in the individuals who make up society. The new men and women are radically different from Lily Dale. Instead of remaining true to themselves at all costs, they betray themselves and their allegiances to one another. They waver from moment to moment, make a decision and then reverse it. The novel's many plots are unified by the theme of betrayal. Society as a whole in The Way We Live Now is no longer moving in a gradual curve of change, the result of the tension of opposing forces. Now change comes suddenly and makes a radical break with the past. A fellow like Melmotte, who comes from nowhere, can get into Parliament and become a great power in the city.

The Way We Live Now also lacks the transparency normal in Trollope's novels. It is full of mysteries and opacities. The characters are again and again said not to be able to understand one another. Melmotte is the center of fascinated attention just because nobody knows whether he is a scoundrel or a great financier, as in The Last Chronicle of Barset the blank place of the Reverend Crawley's loss of memory is the center of concern for the community. In The Last Chronicle the blank place is opened at last to everybody's gaze, and what is revealed there sustains the homogeneity and safety of Trollope's world. In The Way We Live Now the opposite is the case. Melmotte is a great thief, as most people come to suspect, but in his suicide he takes his secrets to the grave and remains a mystery to the end.

As in Our Mutual Friend, money is the paradoxical agent of the degradation of society. Though it is in itself transparent, it is the source of secrecy. Since the appearance of money is as good as the real thing and since money is a zero which may through speculation multiply itself to infinity or disappear in a moment to nothing, it makes people opaque to one another and creates the possibility of discontinuity: Melmotte's rise to power or the marriage of aristocrats with parvenus. Money as an instrument of the will to power reveals in *The Way We Live Now* the ungrounded nature of the human will.

This is shown even more directly in the development of Marie Melmotte, the daughter of the central character. Marie is a Lily Dale brought into the full light of self-consciousness. As she gradually discovers the power of her own will, she finds at the same time its complete freedom. Instead of using her will to remain true to her original choice, as Lily Dale did, she takes possession of the freedom of her will and uses it to emancipate herself from all commitments. Like the fiery American Mrs. Hurtle, she becomes a creature of dangerous strength of will. She decides to remain her own woman and to act only for herself. "Feeling conscious of her own power in regard to her own money, knowing that she [can] do as she [pleases] with her wealth," she tells the man she decides to marry that if she finds anything to induce her to change her mind, she will change it. She frees herself from all allegiances, even the allegiance to her own past self, and becomes, in her modest way, like her father before her, an embodiment of the will to power sustained by nothing but itself. In becoming so, she brings into the open latent implications of Trollope's earlier fiction.

George Meredith's characters, too, though they seem at first to be the offspring of an evolutionary naturalism, are ultimately dependent on only their own wills. The question in *The Ordeal of Richard Feverel* appears at first to be whether man's continuity with nature means that he must be thought of as a repeating mechanism or as a developing organism. Richard's original "choice" of Lucy is a spontaneous action of his nature and therefore not a free choice at all, but he discovers that he is free to remain true to Lucy or to betray her. The choice made spontaneously must be reaffirmed, consciously and deliberately. It is in this sense that "we make our own fates, and nature has nothing to do with it." *The Egoist* (1879) initiates that series of late novels in which Meredith takes full possession, in his own way, of the new novel, the novel which focuses exclusively on the conflict of consciousness with consciousness, will with will. Meredith has an extraordinary sensitivity to the pressure exerted on a mind by the mere presence of another person. In his fiction is already present that drama of mediated desire and that attempt of one consciousness to found itself on the enslavement of another person's freedom, which Sartre and others have explored in the twentieth century. Clara Middleton in *The Egoist* must discover that her "nature" is her freedom, the "whims, variations, inconsistencies, wiles" of her "currents of feeling." "Her needs [are] her nature, her moods, her mind." As a result, "her free will [must] decide her fate." In a proper relation between two minds, each person respects the freedom and individuality of the other, as Vernon Whitford says to Clara: "I wish you to have your free will." For Meredith, selfhood is freedom.

If Meredith believes that a happy love is possible because two people can sustain one another in their freedom, Hardy also begins with the notion that each human being is a freedom which must found itself on its relations to others; but he sees that if consciousness is defined as the will to possession of others, then that will can never be satisfied. Though Hardy and his characters try to place the blame for their sufferings on society, on man's biological nature, on the "crass casualty" of external nature, on absurd coincidence, or on the blind determinism of the immanent will, the secret source of pain in Hardy's intuition of existence is consciousness itself. Each man's mind is a hollow space between him and things, an annihilating power which nullifies whatever it touches. In *The Mayor of Casterbridge* (1886) Henchard hates and repudiates all those people and things he comes to possess. He repudiates them because he finds that he does not really possess them. His tragic grandeur is his persistence in the search for a happy possession of another person, but the climax of his story is his recognition that the "emotional void" in his heart can never be filled. When he sees this, his will turns in on itself, the only thing it truly possesses. The reflexive will in Hardy is not the will to will of Nietzsche. It is the suicidal will not to will. In Henchard's plea for annihilation in his testament ("& that no man remember me"), as in Jude's Jobian curse on himself in *Jude the Obscure* (1894–1895) ("Let the day perish wherein I was born"), latent implications of the subjective bias of the novel come fully into the open. If man's thinking ego is the source of everything, then he can never encounter anything but his own mind and things which have been turned into objects by that mind. The isolated ego is nothing but an empty will, nothing, to borrow Matthew Arnold's words in "Empedocles on Etna," but "a devouring flame of thought," "a naked, eternally restless mind." If the subjective ego is for man the ground of all things, then all things are ultimately swallowed up in the ego's vacuity.

Henry James' fiction, to discuss briefly a final novelist, is continuous with Trollope's both in aesthetic presuppositions and in themes. James' novels, like Trollope's, limit themselves rigorously to encounters between one consciousness and another, and the theme of renunciation in James is, like similar themes in Trollope, a covert recognition that society is sustained in its continuity only by the free decisions of the characters to remain true to themselves. Catherine Sloper in *Washington Square* (1881) "sticks" to her love for Morris Townsend even when she discovers that Morris has betrayed her. Her allegiance is supported by nothing outside herself and preserves only the virtue of consistency. In the same way Isabel in *Portrait of a Lady* (1881) and Strether in *The Ambassadors* (1903) renounce new possibilities of life for the sake of remaining true to earlier choices made in ignorance. Human existence is necessarily tragic for James, since the good life can be discovered only by commitment to life. Initial commitments are always made in ignorance, therefore wrongly. Ultimately a person is faced with the choice either of betraying his first commitment in order to seize the good life or of renouncing happiness in order to remain true to an earlier self. That James' characters so often choose the second course shows that for him continuity in the self, the will willing to will itself as the same even in altered circumstances, is the supreme value. It is the supreme value because only through such consistency can a person avoid falling into that version of nihilism which is the evaporation of the self into an endless series of different selves, chosen arbitrarily, as a weather vane turns in response to the slightest shift in the wind. James' interest in the histrionic personality and his understanding of its dangers is shown in *The Tragic Muse*. For James, too, measuring man in terms of the strength of his will tends to lead to an evaporation of his substance.

From Dickens and George Eliot through Trollope, Meredith, Hardy, and James, the implications of subjectivism become more and more apparent. It remained for Conrad to explore these to their depths and, in doing so, to open the way for the transcendence of nihilism in the writers of the twentieth century. But the overtly "metaphysical" quality of Conrad's fiction, its grappling with experiences which take a man outside the safe bounds of civilized society, is, as I have tried to suggest in this essay, a development of themes and aesthetic conventions which were already present in Victorian fiction.[1]

Note

[1] I have discussed Conrad's work in *Poets of Reality: Six Twentieth-Century Writers* (Cambridge, Mass., 1965). In this essay I have adapted a few sentences from the Introduction to that book.

The Burning Bush: D. H. Lawrence as Religious Poet

by

Vivian de Sola Pinto

> I often think one ought to be able to pray, before one works.
> . . . I always feel as if I stood naked for the fire of Almighty God
> to go through me—and it's rather an awful feeling.[1]

> But primarily I am a passionately religious man, and my novels
> must be written from the depth of my religious experience.[2]

No ENGLISH NOVELIST EVER USED LANGUAGE LIKE THAT BEFORE D. H.
Lawrence did. We cannot imagine Fielding or Jane Austen or Scott or
Dickens, or even George Eliot or Thomas Hardy uttering such words.
They might, indeed, have been said by a few poets—by Blake, that
apocalyptic Christian, by Christina Rossetti, the pious Victorian Anglican, or by Gerard Manley Hopkins, the passionate Jesuit; but to find
them in the mouth of a writer who devoted most of his energies to prose
fiction is surely an event of great and revolutionary significance.

What exactly does Lawrence mean by the word "religious" in these
passages from his letters? He is certainly not using it in the sense in which
it is used by the ordinary man, in the sense of belonging to an organized
body of believers and of joining in its rituals and accepting its dogmas.
The starting point in an attempt to answer our question is provided by
T. S. Eliot at the end of his Foreword to Father Tiverton's Book *D. H.
Lawrence and Human Existence*, where he describes Lawrence as "a man
who, without being a Christian, was primarily and always religious."[3]

Lawrence's own remark to Earl Brewster is also relevant here: "We discussed the quality of *genius*. He assented that his genius was religious
because it was the search for truth that alone freed and vitalized him."[4]
The "search for truth" may perhaps be glossed here in existentialist terms
as the "search for transcendence," or in religious terms as the "search for
the divine."

Thomas L. Hanna, in his article "A Question: What Does One Mean
by 'Religious Literature'?"[5] after rejecting the category "either as a historical type" or as "an honorific gradation," concludes that "the most likely
approach . . . would be . . . if it [religious literature] exhibited the visible or invisible presence or potency of the divine." I would emphasize
Hanna's point that the term, if correctly used, is not "honorific." A good
illustration can be found in the treatment of the Hippolytus legend by
two great dramatists. The *Hippolytus* of Euripides is full of the presence
(sometimes visible and sometimes invisible) and potency of two goddesses, Artemis and Aphrodite. In the *Phèdre* of Racine, on the other
hand, although the gods are often mentioned, they constitute a mere convention or a striking metaphor, as in the famous line, "*C'est Vénus toute
entière a sa proie attachée*"; the drama is purely human and secular.

The earliest literature which has come down to us cannot be described as exclusively either religious or secular. All the elements of early
Greek religion are present in the *Iliad* and the *Odyssey*, and, at the same
time, these poems are incomparable pictures of the secular life of the
Greek heroic age. Longinus said that Homer made "gods of the men" in
the *Iliad* and "men of the gods"[6]: the divine and the human interpene-
trate each other so that it is impossible to say where one begins and the
other ends. The same can be said of the Old Testament sagas of the
patriarchs, Moses, the Judges, and the Kings, where the presence and
potency of Yahweh are inseparable from the human and quasi-historical
narrative. Lawrence described "the books of the Old Testament, Genesis,
Exodus, Samuel, Kings" as written "by authors whose purpose was so big,
it didn't quarrel with their passionate inspiration. The purpose and the
inspiration were almost one. Why, in the name of everything bad, the
two ever should have got separated is a mystery!"[7] The prophetic books
of the Old Testament, Job, and the Psalms are works of purely religious
inspiration, whereas the books of Ruth and Esther are secular stories—
almost what we should call historical novels. In Greece about the same
time we find the poetry of religious vision in Pindar, in Aeschylus, and in
Sophocles. They are followed by Euripides, who constantly humanizes
the old legends, while his attitude toward them is often strongly critical.
And after Euripides comes the New Comedy, where "realism" triumphs

and "the presence and potency" of the divine, still powerfully present in some plays of Euripides like the *Hippolytus* and the *Bacchae*, disappear altogether, and the gods are reduced to a mere literary device for the speaking of prologues.

The dichotomy between the religious and the secular in literature and art was enormously accentuated by the triumph of Christianity, an otherworldly religion with an uncompromising rejection of the world, the flesh, and the devil. One of the great difficulties encountered by early Christian writers was that in the view of the orthodox Christian all the best literature was pagan, the mouthpiece either of the world and the flesh, or, worse, of the devil in the shape of a false religion. The history of Western European culture for centuries is that of a series of attempts to escape from this problem by effecting a compromise between Christianity and the secular humanism of the pagan tradition. The first great attempt was made in the Middle Ages when Aristotle, Virgil, and even Ovid were Christianized; the result was the great flowering of medieval architecture, sculpture, painting, and poetry. The culmination in literature was Dante's *Divine Comedy*, but even here we can see that the compromise was uneasy. It is true that Dante allows a few good pagans to be saved and takes Virgil as his guide through Hell and Purgatory; but Virgil is excluded from Paradise, and even the best of pagan sages have to be content with a place in Limbo. Lawrence thought Dante "slightly dishonorable" for hiding the "vital dark fact" of his "cozy bifurcated wife and kids."[8] This criticism may seem grotesque, but there is a grain of truth in it, not of course with reference to the art of the *Divine Comedy*, but with regard to the extreme otherworldliness of medieval Catholicism, which excluded the flesh and blood of common humanity.

The breakdown of the medieval compromise is seen very clearly in the English poetry of the fourteenth century. One of the two major English poets of that period, William Langland, was decidedly a poet of the religious vision, whereas his contemporary, Geoffrey Chaucer, though a pious Catholic, was a poet of the secular eye, concerned almost entirely with human comedy, pathos, and romance. It is striking that at the end of his *Troilus and Criseyde* Chaucer shows himself to be deeply conscious of the split between his religious beliefs and his art: he regretfully describes his subject matter as nothing but "corsed olde rites" of the pagans and "thise wrecched worldes appetites."[9]

The next great attempt at a compromise between the Christian and the pagan visions is that which began with the Italian Renaissance of the fifteenth century, when the Platonists of the Florentine academy made their brave attempt to fuse the Christian tradition with what Chaucer had called the pagans' "corsed olde rites" and "thise wrecched worldes appetites."[10] The result in English literature is the poetry of Spenser, that amazing, crowded tapestry in which Christian knights, maidens, and hermits jostle with pagan gods, goddesses, nymphs, and satyrs, and Jehovah is cheerfully identified with Jove and Christ with Pan. The religious vision is present in Spenser, but it is heavily diluted with moral and political allegory and florid decoration.

As *The Divine Comedy* is the peak of the literature of the Middle Ages, so Shakespeare's plays are the peak of Renaissance literature; and Shakespeare's vision is as decidedly secular as Dante's is religious. The "bifurcated wife and kids" (not indeed very cozy) now have their revenge, and Juliet and her nurse, Portia and Desdemona and their husbands, and Cleopatra and her maids take the place of the remote Beatrice. Are "the presence and potency of the divine" to be found in Shakespeare? One school of modern criticism finds them, especially in the later plays, but the question is still open. Shaw's criticism of Shakespeare for lacking a philosophy and a religion[11] can be compared with Lawrence's of Dante; and again there is a grain of truth, not with regard to Shakespeare himself so much as to the civilization that lies behind his plays, a civilization that had failed to develop the Christian humanism of the Florentine Platonists.

In the seventeenth century we come to the great change in human consciousness of which the chief manifestation was the Enlightenment, when the theologico-metaphysical world-picture of the Middle Ages was replaced by the mechanico-materialist universe of Bacon, Descartes, Hobbes, Locke, and Newton. In the words of Blake, Heaven now became "a mighty circle turning and God a tyrant crown'd"; in other words, the cosmos was now thought of as a huge, soulless machine and God a remote, arbitrary monarch in an abstract Heaven. The Enlightenment did not kill orthodox Christianity, as some of its opponents feared that it might, but it infiltrated it and petrified it so that it became incapable of poetic vision. Strangely enough, in this century we can perceive a kind of abortive countermovement to the Enlightenment in certain writers, mostly connected with the Platonic tradition, who can be seen striving after a vision of "the presence and potency of the divine" not in the now outworn scheme of medieval theology but in the material world and the human mind.

This countermovement is well illustrated in the curious development of the last great English school of religious poetry, that of the Metaphysicals. The first two great Metaphysical poets, Donne and Herbert, are true poets of religious vision who find "the presence and potency of the divine" in the symbols of orthodox Christianity and the ritual of the Church; but this is no longer true of the two later Metaphysicals, Vaughan and Traherne. Both these poets undoubtedly thought of themselves as orthodox Anglicans, but, to adapt a saying of Lawrence's, we must believe the poetry rather than the poets. In their works the "presence and potency of the divine" tend to be envisioned not so much in the persons of Christ or God, but in the life of this world—in "nature," the human mind, and, especially in Traherne, childhood. There is a significant passage in Vaughan's poem "The Night," ostensibly a meditation on the passage in St. John's Gospel describing Christ's meeting with Nicodemus at night:

> No mercy-seat of gold,
> No dead and dusty *Cherub*, nor carv'd stone,
> But his own living works did my Lord hold
> And lodge alone.[12]

The tendency to find God in his "living works," and not in "dead and dusty" cherubs (the adjectives are significant) or in the "carv'd stone" of traditional theology, is carried still further in the prose and poetry of Thomas Traherne, who finds Heaven in the human mind and the material cosmos:

> Your enjoyment of the world is never right, till every morning you awake in Heaven; see yourself in your Father's Palace, and look upon the skies, the earth, and the air as Celestial Joys. . . . You never enjoy the World aright, till the Sea itself floweth in your veins, till you are clothed with the heavens and crowned with the stars. . . . And thus all ages are present in my soul, and all kingdoms, and God blessed for ever. . . . And thus all Angels and the Eternity and Infinity of God are in me for evermore.[13]

Beside this passage from Traherne's *Meditations* we can place the following by his contemporary, the rather heretical Puritan Platonist Peter Sterry:

> God, in the presence of his Glory, resides in every creature, as a Vail wrought with a figure of himself. Thus he constantly resides in every Creature, as the Root, and Being of its Being. . . . That which is seen in this Spirit of Immortality and Glory is an Immortal and

Glorious Spirit. This is the true multiplying, magnifying and Glori-
fying glass. Each dust is here known as the Bright Form of a Beautiful Star: each Star is discovered here to be a Heaven of Stars, a new
world of Glories.[14]

The line of thought represented by passages like these might have been
the basis of a new poetry of religious vision, but the "climate of opinion"
in the age of Hobbes, Locke, and Dryden was unfavorable to such a
development. Traherne and Sterry were isolated figures; the type of
thought represented in their works "went underground" in the eighteenth century, as Désirée Hirst has shown in her book *Hidden Riches*;[15]
it is to be found not in poets but in religious writers like William Law
and other, more obscure figures.

In the eighteenth century Christian poetry became, in the main,
limited to hymn-writing, the poetry of piety rather than that of religious
vision. There is genuine poetry in the hymns of Isaac Watts, the
Wesleys, and others, but it is poetry at a much lower temperature than
that of the Metaphysicals. The single exception is Christopher Smart, the
intensity of whose religious vision cut him off so completely from
communication with his contemporaries that he went mad. The main
stream of literature both in prose and in verse was decidedly secular, and
Dr. Johnson, the greatest critic of the age and a pious Christian, even
argued that religion was not a proper subject for poetry.[16] Nevertheless,
we can see a groping toward a non-Christian religious vision in the works
of certain poets, such as Thomson's pantheistic "Hymn" and Collins'
"Ode on the Poetical Character." In the last quarter of the century came
the great renovation of poetry that we call Romanticism, and this can be
seen, in one of its aspects, as a revival of the countermovement to the
Enlightenment, which had "gone underground" at the end of the
previous century.

William Blake was the first major poet of religious vision since the
seventeenth century, and more clearly than any of his contemporaries he
perceived what the nature of this vision in the post-Enlightenment world
must be. He called it the Fourfold or Divine Vision and described it very
precisely in a famous quatrain:

> To see a World in a Grain of Sand
> And a Heaven in a Wild Flower,
> Hold Infinity in the palm of your hand
> And Eternity in an hour.[17]

Equally relevant is the great aphorism in *The Marriage of Heaven and Hell:* "If the doors of perception were cleansed every thing would appear to man as it is, infinite."[18] Blake also enunciates the important principle that henceforth all myths must be regarded as psychological constructions within and not outside the human mind: "All deities reside in the human breast."[19]

The great Romantic poets—Blake, Wordsworth, Coleridge, Shelley, and Keats—were all gifted with what Blake called the Divine Vision. Unable to use the Christian symbolism, now petrified by the Enlightenment, they had difficulty in finding an "objective correlative" or myth to express their religious apprehension. Blake, the boldest spirit among them, constructed a new mythological scheme in which he incorporated certain Christian elements, but he was an isolated visionary whose work was ignored or misunderstood in his own time. Wordsworth, with a religious vision equal in intensity to Blake's, found his "objective correlative" in an impassioned contemplation of the divine in "Nature" at moments when "the doors of perception were cleansed," and, in his own words, he could "see into the life of things."[20]

Coleridge created one great myth in *The Ancient Mariner* and a fragment of a second in *Kubla Khan* before he sank into a mist of metaphysics and opium. Shelley and Keats continued Wordsworth's religious apprehension of Nature and also tried to revive the ancient Greek myths for their own purposes. When one looks from the distance of a century and a half at the achievement of the great Romantics, one has the impression of magnificence but incompleteness. In the words of A. O. Barfield, Romanticism never "came of age."[21] The Wordsworthian nature myth, Shelley's revival of Greek myth to express the idea of freedom, Keats' to express the idea of beauty—these could appeal to fine and cultivated minds with great aesthetic charm, but they could never have the penetrating reality, the vitalizing truth which the Christian myth had up until the mid-seventeenth century and the pagan myths had in the centuries before Christ. Blake's amazing construction symbolizing the disintegration of the faculties of the human mind under the form of the Four Zoas and their reintegration as the Whole Man has, indeed, something like this kind of truth, but it was too abstruse for his contemporaries to understand and is, perhaps, only beginning to have an impact in the present century.

At this point I propose to make a jump of about a hundred years to D. H. Lawrence, who, I believe, was the first major writer powerfully gifted with the religious vision after the great Romantic poets. When I say this I am not forgetting the very considerable achievements of Victorian literature, and I would again emphasize that the term "religious" is not being used in an honorific sense. The triumphs of English nineteenth-century writers after the great Romantics were not in the literature of religious vision, but in the secular art of the novel, in various forms of social and aesthetic criticism, and in certain kinds of poetry. Of course, there were exceptions. The great one was Gerard Manley Hopkins, who might be described as the Christopher Smart of the nineteenth century. The intensity of Smart's religious vision drove him into the madhouse; the intensity of Hopkins' drove him into the Jesuit order, almost the equivalent in the eyes of the Protestant upper middle class from which Hopkins sprang.

Between the Romantics and Lawrence lies the great development of the realistic novel in Western Europe: Jane Austen, Scott, Dickens, Balzac, Flaubert, Tolstoy, Dostoevsky, George Eliot, Thomas Hardy. When Lawrence began to write, the only literary forms of any vitality were the novel, the short story, the essay, and the short lyrical poem. Like Blake, but unlike Hopkins, Lawrence came from a working-class family and had to find a means of earning a living while developing his artistic genius. Blake solved the problem by mastering the artistic craft of engraving, which still had a market value in his day. For Lawrence, a miner's son, the only way of escape from the drudgery of the industrial machine was to become a teacher, and the only way of escape from the drudgery of teaching was to become a successful novelist. His genius had a threefold form. He had the qualities of a major novelist: profound psychological insight, wonderfully acute observation, the gift of narrative, and a strong pictorial sense (he was an able amateur painter). He also had the gift of a teacher or preacher: he was very successful in his short career as a schoolmaster, and he inherited a great tradition of preaching from the nonconformist religion in which he was brought up.[22] The third aspect of his genius was that of a poet of the religious vision in the sense already defined.

By "poet" I mean what the Germans call *Dichter*, a writer of imaginative works in prose or verse. It is with this aspect of his genius that this essay is concerned primarily. The early part of his career centered on the development of his gift as a novelist. As he wrote rather ruefully in an early letter, "I've got to earn my living by prose."[23] After two immature experiments and some good short stories, he produced a novel of major importance in *Sons and Lovers* (1913). This can be regarded as a work in the great English tradition of the autobiographical novel, a twentieth-century *David Copperfield* by a writer who has read

Freud and knows something about the new depth psychology. The title *Oedipus in Nottingham*,[24] that of a recent American study, sums up the aspect of the novel which has hitherto received the most attention. There is, however, another aspect which is less obvious, but for our purpose more important. The structure of the work is in the main secular and "realistic," but throughout it is possible to perceive overtones of the religious vision. These can be heard in the recurrent flower symbolism and in the development of Paul Morel's character and his relationship to Miriam. Louis Fraiberg describes these religious overtones in a perceptive passage: "*Sons and Lovers* . . . has the outer shape of a picaresque novel, the adventurous travels of the unformed soul among women. Its inner shape is that of the mirror image of a saint's life: it is the equivalent of a search for grace which can never be attained, though at times glimpsed and even touched."[25]

It has constantly been emphasized (and, of course, was emphasized by Lawrence himself) that Paul could not love Miriam as a man should love a woman because of his quasi-incestuous relationship with his mother, but there is another reason for the rejection of Miriam, which belongs to the "inner shape" of the novel. She is the representative of that "spiritual" religion, the otherworldly Christianity, which Lawrence believed to have become a pernicious abstraction in the twentieth century. Very significant is the following dialogue between Paul and Miriam:

> "It's not religious to be religious," he said. "I reckon a crow is religious when it sails across the sky. But it only does it because it feels itself carried to where it's going, not because it thinks it is being eternal."
>
> But Miriam knew that one should be religious in everything, have God, whatever God might be, present in everything.
>
> "I don't believe God knows such a lot about Himself," he cried. "God doesn't *know* things. He *is* things. And I'm sure He's not soulful."

The "soulful" God of the sentimental Christianity of the nineteenth century was to Lawrence what the "Nobodaddy" of eighteenth-century deism was to Blake. Lawrence was seeking a God Who would be vitally present in the flesh as well as in the spirit, the *eros* of the ancient Greeks, which the Christians had excluded from their theology. This is made clear in the curious quasi-biblical Foreword to *Sons and Lovers* which Lawrence sent to Edward Garnett but never published. There he proclaims a God "the Father, who is Flesh, forever unquestioned and unanswerable."[26] Immediately after he had finished work on Sons and Lovers, he passed on to a new and stupendous design: nothing less than the re-creation of the art of the novel, the transformation of this secular and prosaic form into a poetic vehicle for the religious vision.

The novel had been the creation of the materialist vision of the West European bourgeoisie, children of the Enlightenment with a sense of history as a continuous, unending succession of events in a spatio-temporal universe, which they regarded as the only reality. The novel reflected this historical sense. It is significant that Fielding, one of its founding fathers, called his novels "histories"; after Fielding, English novels were fictional "histories." Then Lawrence, the gifted novelist who had completely mastered this secular "historical" art, embarked on the great adventure of transfiguring it by giving it a new dimension to make it express his religious apprehension of a reality different from that of the spatio-temporal universe.

At first the work embodying this new art was to have been a single novel on a very large scale. There finally emerged two essentially poetical narratives, one of which has the structure of an epic, and the other, that of a tragedy. The underlying theme of both is the crisis of modern civilization, the clash between the traditional life of the community, based on myth and ritual, and the scientific and technological revolution. The Rainbow (1915) is an epic history of three generations of a yeoman family of the Midlands. The word "history," though, needs to be modified. It is not a fictional "history" as it would have been if the subject had been treated by George Eliot or by Thomas Hardy, but rather a "meta-history," the story of the evolution of the inner life of the Brangwens in the setting of an outer life portrayed with the consummate realistic art of the fully developed novelistic tradition.

This outer life, however, is interpenetrated and irradiated by the religious vision. The effect is produced partly by the use of the imagery of the English Bible, which still provided a living mythology for the Protestant community of the English Midlands at the end of the nineteenth century and the beginning of the twentieth. Certain biblical images recur, transfiguring the secular narrative and raising it from the plane of spatio-temporal "reality": God's covenant with Noah and the sign of the rainbow, the passage in Genesis about the love of the sons of God for the daughters of men, and the life-giving miracles in the Gospels, like the changing of water into wine at the marriage feast and the feeding of the five thousand. Beginning with the instinctive, almost animal life of the early Brangwens, we are led to the evolution of the modern consciousness in three generations: Tom Brangwen, who starts the emergence by his marriage to the Polish woman, Lydia Lensky; Will Brangwen, awakened to the aesthetic vision by Ruskin and the study of church architecture; his wife Anna, who rejects his church-Christianity; and finally their daughter Ursula, the representative of the fully awakened modern consciousness.

The center of the book is the great scene in Lincoln Cathedral in Chapter VII. This chapter is, in effect, a symbolic poem, an ode on the emergence of the modern spirit from the world of traditional myth and ritual. Will, the husband, is under the spell of the magnificence of the Christian tradition as embodied in the great building. Anna, too, is at first "overcome with wonder and awe," but then she reacts, resenting "his transports and ecstasies." While acknowledging "the great joy and verity" of the Cathedral, she "claimed another right": "The altar was barren, its lights gone out. God burned no more in that bush." This is the central point in the development of Lawrence's art, an affirmation, it may be noted, rather than a negation. He does not conclude, like Hardy and the nineteenth-century agnostics, that God has stopped burning. If not "in that bush," then somewhere else is the inference.

The latter part of the novel is the story of Ursula's painful quest for a bush where God does burn, the quest of the modern spirit for deliverance from the terror of a meaningless universe: "In everything she saw she grasped and groped to find the creation of the living God, instead of the old, hard, barren form of bygone living." This, undoubtedly, is an epitome of Lawrence's own quest, and part of his answer is certainly to be found in the memorable passage where Ursula rejects the claim of her teacher at Nottingham University College "that life consists in a complexity of physical and chemical activities." As she looks at "the unicellular shadow" under her microscope, "suddenly in her mind the world gleamed strangely, with an intense light. . . . Suddenly she had passed away into an intensely-gleaming light of knowledge. She could not understand what it all was. She only knew that it was not limited mechanical energy, nor mere purpose of self-preservation and self-assertion. It was a consummation, a being infinite. Self was a oneness with the infinite. To be oneself was a supreme, gleaming triumph of infinity." This is a record of a religious vision comparable to Blake's vision of the infinite in every thing when the doors of perception are cleansed.

But how can this vision of the divine in "the flesh," the mystery of life, above all in sex, be reconciled with the "terror of history," the condition of the modern world in all its "cold, stark, ashen sterility"? This was the agonizing question which was to obsess and torture Lawrence throughout the major part of his career. It is true that at the end of

The Rainbow there is the famous apocalyptic vision of hope, one of the great optimistic affirmations of modern literature, comparable to the conclusions of Blake's *Jerusalem* and Shelley's *Prometheus Unbound;* but this vision soon faded, and the epic of *The Rainbow* is succeeded by the tragedy of *Women in Love* (1920). Here Lawrence succeeds in creating tragic poetry out of the realistic material of the novelistic tradition. The tragedy is an epitome of the terrible bifurcation of the modern world in which imagination is divorced from power.

Rupert Birkin, obviously a projection of Lawrence's own personality, is the man of imagination, a poet and intellectual but unstable and rootless, and, like Lawrence himself, with a tendency toward sermonizing and degenerating into a *salvator mundi* and "Sunday school teacher." His friend and opponent Gerald Crich, the man of power, is one of Lawrence's most remarkable creations. He is a soldier, explorer, and captain of industry, with splendid physical and intellectual gifts, and he is a prince among lovers. Like Macbeth and Othello, he is a true tragic hero who destroys himself as a result of prostituting his magnificent potentiality to an unworthy cause. The cause of Gerald's downfall is his ruthless drive for mechanical efficiency, and it is obvious that Lawrence sees his fate as that of the England of his day. The central theme of the novel, in spite of its title, is the relationship between Rupert and Gerald. They are the two halves of a complete man which fail to come together. Rupert sees in Gerald "a sort of fatal halfness," but the same sort of "fatal halfness" can be discerned in Rupert himself. The wonderful wrestling scene in Chapter XX ("Gladiatorial") is profoundly symbolic: for a moment imagination and power are united, but it is only a moment of play, a piece of make-believe that cannot last.

Another aspect of the tragic bifurcation of the modern world is shown in the sexual life of the two men and the "women in love." Birkin, not without difficulty, achieves a true marriage with Ursula: "a new paradisal unit regained from duality"; and the description of their union has a religious dimension effectively suggested by the use of biblical imagery: "And now, behold, from the smitten rock of the man's body, from the strange marvellous flanks and thighs . . . came the floods of ineffable darkness and ineffable riches." But it should be noted that Rupert and Ursula achieve their "new paradisal unit" only by cutting themselves off from contemporary society, a process made easy by the fact that Rupert has a private income. Gerald, on the other hand, is incapable of a pure relationship like that of Rupert and Ursula. He is willing to marry Gudrun, but for him "marriage was not the committing of himself into a relation with Gudrun. It was committing himself to the acceptance of the established world." Gudrun is the female counterpart to Gerald, his "emanation," as Blake would have said. She is an artist, but a sort of luxury artist who creates charming little things. There are moments of tenderness in her relationship with Gerald, but for the most part it consists of an alternation of violent sexual ecstasy and equally frenzied repulsion, culminating in her flirtation with the gross Loerke and the terrible scene where Gerald nearly strangles her.

Gerald's agony and death on the snow-covered Tyrolese mountain-side and Rupert's meditation on his body form a sequence in which the art of the novel is transformed into tragic poetry of a quality that can be called only Shakespearean. It is important to notice, however, that Birkin (or perhaps we should say Birkin-Lawrence) finds consolation in his belief in "a vast creative non-human mystery . . . a God who can do without man." This God is "a fountain-head" that is "incorruptible and unsearchable." "To be man was as nothing compared to the possibilities of the creative mystery. To have one's pulse beating direct from the mystery, this was perfection, unalterable satisfaction." This was a faith that Lawrence even in his darkest moments never lost. It is comparable to Wordsworth's conviction that

> Should earth by inward throes be wrench'd throughout,
> Or fire be sent from far to wither all
> Her pleasant habitations, and dry up
> Old ocean in his bed left sing'd and bare,
> Yet would the living Presence still subsist
> Victorious. . . .[27]

Women in Love marks the end of the second phase of Lawrence's art. It was his great moment of tragic vision, and there is nothing more difficult for an artist than to pass beyond such a moment. Shakespeare had to pass through the agony of *Lear* and *Timon of Athens* before he could reach the vision of *The Winter's Tale* and *The Tempest*. The agony through which Lawrence had to pass was indeed terrible, and his greatness is seen in the fact that he finally emerged to something which can be described as an almost miraculous purification and spiritual regeneration. In the years immediately following World War I he suffered an overwhelming shock. Poverty, ill health, even persecution he might have endured, but these were now combined with a shattering of his faith in his countrymen and, indeed, in the whole of mankind, by what he regarded as the hideous crime of the Great War and the almost equally hideous condition of industrial society. He felt, as he wrote to

Lady Cynthia Asquith in November 1916,[28] literally "torn off from the body of mankind," and he was filled with a black fury against the contemporary world that recalls Shakespeare's Timon and Swift: "They are *canaille*, carrion-eating, filthy-mouthed *canaille*. . . . I wish to God I could kill them. I wish I had power to blight them, to slay them . . . in thousands and thousands. I wish to God I could kill them off, the masse of *canaille*. . . ."[29]

J. Middleton Murry is probably right in finding another cause for this terrible "disruption in the soul" in Lawrence's failure to achieve in his own sexual life that union of ideal and physical love, the "paradisal unit" which he imagined Ursula and Rupert to have attained in *Women in Love*. The outcome of this failure appears in the three novels that criticism has generally found to be unsatisfactory: *Aaron's Rod* (1922), *Kangaroo* (1923), and *The Plumed Serpent* (1926). Lawrence's conviction that the Christian doctrine of love was at the root of the diseased condition of modern society led him to what Murry calls "a willed lapse into mindlessness and a reversion to pre-Christian religion,"[30] the "dark gods" which dominate *Kangaroo* and *The Plumed Serpent*: "Sacrifice to the dark God, and to the men in whom the dark God is manifest. Sacrifice to the strong, not to the weak."[31] It is an attempt to deify power in all its manifestations, including hatred and cruelty.

This is the phase of Lawrence's work which has led some critics to see in him a precursor of fascism and Nazism, but this view is certainly mistaken. His attitude toward the idea of leadership was always ambivalent. He was saved by the earthy humor of the working-class Midlander, by his compassion, and by his Puritanism. Even in *The Plumed Serpent*, the most extravagant of his fantasies, he can make his heroine in a moment of sanity describe the revival of the "dark gods" of ancient Mexico as "high-flown bunk"; and in *Aaron's Rod*, where he makes his mouthpiece Lilly talk a lot of nonsense about submission to a heroic leader, he puts into the mouth of the same character words that express his horror at any sort of militarism or bullying: "I think every man is a sacred and holy individual, never to be violated. I think there is only one thing that I hate to the verge of madness and that is bullying." Eugene Goodheart is, however, certainly right when he declares that "Lawrence's conception of power is most deficient when he imagines it in its concrete political form."[32]

But the most important part of his work as a religious poet in the early 1920's is to be found not in his prose fiction but in his poetry, which has been commonly neglected or underrated. In *Birds, Beasts and Flowers* (1923) there is a truly religious apprehension of a power which is

not the dominating power of human politics but the creative power of
nature, combined with a sense of its nonhuman quality, its divine
"otherness," paralleled perhaps only in certain passages in Wordsworth's
Prelude. The magnificence of this kind of power is hymned in the vision
of the emergence of the Sicilian almond blossom from the "iron fastness"
of winter:

> . . . in a great and sacred forthcoming steps forth, steps
>   out in one stride
> A naked tree of blossom, like a bridegroom, bathing in dew,
>   divested of cover,
> Frail-naked, utterly uncovered
> To the green night-baying of the dog-star, Etna's snow-
>   edged wind
> And January's loud-seeming sun.
>
> Think of it from the iron fastness
> Suddenly to dare to come out naked, in perfection of blossom,
>   beyond the sword-rust.
> Think, to stand there in full-unfolded nudity, smiling,
> With all the snow-wind, and the sun-glare, and the dog-star
>   baying epithalamion.[33]

The same power is seen in the elemental grandeur of the snake at the
water-trough at Taormina in the most famous poem in the collection:

> He drank enough
> And lifted his head, dreamily, as one who has drunken,
> And flickered his tongue like a forked night in the air,
>   so black;
> Seeming to lick his lips,
> And looked around like a god, unseeing, into the air, . . .
>
> .   .   .   .
>
> For he seemed to me again like a king,
> Like a king in exile, uncrowned in the underworld,
> Now due to be crowned again.[34]

In the sequence of the tortoise poems the divine "otherness" is
contemplated with a mixture of humor, reverence, and compassion,
culminating in a passage where the agonizing paradox of sex, by which

Lawrence himself was tortured, is resolved and transcended by a vision of
the wholeness of the natural world:

> The cross,
> The wheel on which our silence first is broken,
> Sex, which breaks up our integrity, our single inviolability,
>   our deep silence,
> Tearing a cry from us.
>
> Sex, which breaks us into voice, sets us calling across the
>   deeps, calling, calling for the complement,
> Singing, and calling, and singing again, being answered,
>   having found.
>
> Torn to become whole again, after long seeking for what
>   is lost,
> The same cry from the tortoise as from Christ, the Osiris-
>   cry of abandonment,
> That which is whole, torn asunder,
> That which is in part, finding its whole again throughout
>   the universe.[35]

"In the destructive element immerse." No other writer has followed
that terrible precept of Conrad's more thoroughly than Lawrence, and no
other writer has achieved a more wonderful resurrection from the "destructive element" into a new vision and a new art than Lawrence did in
the last three years of his short life. In this last phase he seems like a man
awaking from a nightmare, the "Nightmare" of the famous chapter in
Kangaroo. In a letter written in March 1928, he explicitly rejects the
principle of leadership as "a back number" and asks for "a new relationship [which] will be some sort of tenderness, sensitive, between men and
men and men and women."[36] This, as Keith Sagar has pointed out,[37]
marks his final disavowal of the power principle which dominates the
three "unsatisfactory" novels. God, it was now clear to him, did not burn
in that bush. Lawrence's "tenderness" may seem near to the Christian
idea of love; he refused, however, to use the word "love" because he
believed that it was soiled by its association with "soulful" Christianity,
leading to what he calls the "faked love" produced by the impossible
command of Jesus to love our neighbor as ourselves.[38] His "tenderness"
has a sensuous and sexual connotation for which his word is "phallic,"
and, perhaps, it may be described as uniting the Christian agape with the

pagan eros. In another letter he speaks of restoring "the phallic consciousness, into our lives: because it is the source of all real beauty, and all real gentleness. And those are the two things, tenderness and beauty, which will save us from horrors."[39]

In his last years Lawrence found the burning bush in three visions or theophanies: the vision of the sacredness of sex and marriage, the vision of death as a majestic and healing power, and the vision of a resurrection into a world of joy, freedom, and beauty—the "flowering of life." The works that embody this new kind of awareness are three books of prose—*Lady Chatterley's Lover* (1928), with its important coda *A Propos of Lady Chatterley's Lover* (1930), *The Man Who Died* (1929), and *Etruscan Places* (1932)—and the poems published under the titles *Pansies* (1929) and *Last Poems* (1932). Of *Lady Chatterley's Lover* too much has already been written, and this is not the place to discuss either its merits as a novel or the degree of success attained by Lawrence in his bold attempt to use for serious purposes parts of the language which for centuries have been abandoned to ribaldry. The important element in the book for our purpose is its hymn to the divinity of the human body and to the holiness of true marriage, which, in Lawrence's words, has a rhythm akin to that of "the wheeling sun and the nodding earth . . . the staying of the planets and the magnificence of the fixed stars."[40] "The human body," he makes Lady Chatterley say in reply to her husband, who had called it "an incumbrance," "is only just coming to real life. With the Greeks it gave a lovely flicker, then Plato and Aristotle killed it, and Jesus finished it off. But now the body is really coming to life, really rising from the tomb. . . ." And the story ends with Mellors' faith in the "higher mystery," "the unnamed god" who shields the crocus and the pentecostal "forked flame" of true sexual union.

From such passages it is an easy transition to *The Man Who Died*, which Murry aptly described as "the angelic counterpart"[41] to *Lady Chatterley's Lover*. In this work Lawrence at last wrote a story in which he abandoned the realistic convention of the novelistic tradition. *The Man Who Died* is not a piece of historical fiction about Jesus, Whom, indeed, it never mentions by name. It is a symbolic poem in prose, and, like all symbolic works, has various layers of meaning. Part of its significance is certainly autobiographical: the Man Who Died is the Lawrence who had, indeed, risen from the tomb and finally given up his dream of being a great teacher and *salvator mundi*:

My triumph . . . is that I am not dead. I have outlived my mission, and know no more of it. It is my triumph. I have survived

the day and the death of my interference, and am still a man. . . .
The teacher and the saviour are dead in me. . . . How good it is to
have fulfilled my mission, and to be beyond it. Now I can be alone,
and leave all things to themselves. . . . What a pity I preached to
them! A sermon is so much more likely to cake into mud, and to
close the fountains, than is a psalm or a song. . . . Now I am risen
in my own aloneness, and inherit the earth, since I lay no claim on
it.

At a deeper level the story is a parable of a Christianity that might die
and be reborn, freed at last from the excessive spirituality of the churches
and regaining the pagan apprehension of the sacredness of the body and
the senses symbolized by the union of the Man Who Died with the
priestess of Isis.

The idea of The Man Who Died, or rather of the original form of
the story, called The Escaped Cock, came to Lawrence when he was
visiting the Etruscan tombs at Tarquinia with his friend Earl Brewster in
the spring of 1927.[42] There is certainly a close connection between the
story, the essays which grew out of his visit to Etruria, and the Last
Poems. They may be said to be all parts of the dying Lawrence's great
final apocalypse or vision of death and resurrection. He had been
interested in the Etruscans ever since he saw the remains of the Etruscan
walls at Fiesole in 1920 and had associated them in one of his poems with
the "sinuous flame-tall cypresses":

> The long-nosed, sensitive-footed, subtly-smiling Etruscans,
> Who made so little noise outside the cypress groves.[43]

This interest in the mysterious race of pre-Roman Italy led him to an
enthusiastic study of Etruscan art and finally to the visit to Tarquinia.
His exploration of the tombs was no mere piece of archaeological sight-
seeing but a sort of ritual act, an initiation into the experience of a death
which is also a resurrection into a world of wonder and beauty. Brewster
seems to have sensed this in his account of the excursion:

> How happy were our days at Tarquinia. . . . From the jewelled
> splendour of these dark tombs we came forth into the brightness of
> an April day and a blue sky, broken by hurrying white clouds: the
> fields through which we walked were gay with red poppies: our
> guide unlocked the door leading to another tomb, and we would
> descend again to behold the joyous scenes with which the Etrus-

cans, of such a distant world, chose to decorate the homes of their dead.[44]

Whatever truth may be in Lawrence's view of Etruscan civilization, there is no doubt that it provided him with a myth of deep religious significance. In the "sacred *patera*, or mundum," the round saucer with a raised knob in the center held by the figures in the tombs, he saw a symbol of "the plasm . . . the living cell, with its nucleus, which is the indivisible god of the beginning, and which remains alive and unbroken to the end, the eternal quick of all things, which yet divides and sub-divides, so that it becomes the sun of the firmament and the lotus of the waters under the earth, and the rose of all existence under the earth." The essays from which this passage is quoted, published after his death under the title *Etruscan Places*, have the form of a travel book, but everywhere they break into a poetry full of the vision of a free and happy life, the opposite of the robot existence of modern industrial society. It is a vision that might be called Lawrence's Paradise Regained:

> The natural flowering of life! It is not so easy for human beings as it sounds. Behind all the Etruscan liveliness was a religion of life. . . . Behind all the dancing was a vision, and even a science of life, a conception of the universe and man's place in the universe. . . . To the Etruscan all was alive; the whole universe lived; and the business of man was to live amid it all. He had to draw life into himself, out of the wandering huge vitalities of the world. The cosmos was alive, like a vast creature. . . . The whole thing was alive, and had a great soul, or *anima*: and in spite of one great soul, there were myriad roving, lesser souls; every man, every creature and tree and lake and mountain and stream, was animate, had its own peculiar consciousness.

The poetry which always seems to be bursting through the mold of these prose works finds its purest expression in the poems which Lawrence was writing in the last months of his life. Already, in the collection called *Pansies*, among the satires on the robot civilization of the modern world, there are poems full of the vision of a God Who is the ultimate truth at the root of human personality and the phenomena of nature:

> If you will go down into yourself, under your surface personality
> you will find you have a great desire to drink life direct
> from the source, not out of bottles and bottled personal vessels.

. . . .

> Communion with the Godhead, they used to say in the past.
> But even that is human-tainted now,
> tainted with the ego and the personality.
>
> To feel a fine, fine breeze blowing through the navel and the knees
> and have a cool sense of truth, inhuman truth at last
> softly fluttering the senses, in the exquisite orgasm of coition
> with the godhead of energy that cannot tell lies.
>
> The cool, cool truth of pure vitality
> pouring into the veins from the direct contact with the source.
> Uncontaminated by even the beginnings of a lie.[45]

The *Last Poems* are full of the presence and potency of a God Who is the great creative urge out of which comes the miracle of life:

> God is the great urge that has not yet found a body
> but urges towards incarnation with the great creative urge.
>
> And becomes at last a clove carnation: lo! that is god!
> and becomes at last Helen, or Ninon: any lovely and generous woman
> at her best and her most beautiful, being god, made manifest,
> any clear and fearless man being god, very god.[46]

For Lawrence, as for a Greek, belief in God was not inconsistent with a belief in the gods. "The Greeks, being sane, were pantheists and pluralists, and so am I," he had written in one of his essays,[47] and the one unknowable God is apprehended under the form of the old Mediterranean deities who come to life with astonishing freshness in these poems: the god Hermes shown as "a naked man, a stranger . . . with his cloak over his arm":

> God is older than the sun and the moon
> and the eye cannot behold him
> nor the voice describe him:
> and still, this is the God Hermes, sitting by my hearth,[48]

or Venus sporting among the fishes:

> and Venus among the fishes skips and is a she-dolphin
> she is a gay, delighted porpoise sporting with love and the sea

> she is the female tunny-fish, round and happy among the males
> and dense with happy blood, dark rainbow bliss in the sea.[49]

In his Preface to Harry Crosby's poems, Lawrence writes that "the essential quality of poetry is that it makes a new effort of attention, and 'discovers' a new world."[50] These words are particularly applicable to his own treatment of death in the *Last Poems*. The divine wonder, or "new world of glories," which in so many other places in his prose and verse he had discovered in the life of nature and man, he now with an extraordinary "new effort of attention" discovers in death itself, seen not as a destructive force but as a necessary complement to life, a liberation and a reconciliation. In "Bavarian Gentians," surely one of the greatest English poems of this century, the dark blue flowers become torches lighting the dying man down "the darker and darker stairs" to an underworld of majesty and splendor where the ancient myth of Persephone becomes the living symbol of the union of the soul with a divine bridegroom:

> . . . darkness invisible enfolded in the deeper dark
> of the arms Plutonic, and pierced with the passion of dense gloom,
> among the splendour of torches of darkness, shedding
>   darkness on the lost bride and her groom.[51]

There is indeed a hell of disintegration and horror for Lawrence; it is not, however, to be found in death but in falling out of the hands of the living God through godless self-knowledge:

> It is not easy to fall out of the hands of the living God:
> They are so large, and they cradle so much of a man.
>
> .   .   .   .
>
> And still through knowledge and will, he can break away,
> man can break away, and fall from the hands of God
> into himself alone, down the godless plunge of the abyss,
> a god-lost creature turning upon himself.[52]

At the very end of his life he was at work on a draft of what Richard Aldington believes he intended to be a long poem,[53] but it survives as only a series of fragments. In this poem death is seen as a healing oblivion and as a peace which is a necessary stage before resurrection into a new life. The "unhappy dead" are those who cannot truly die but cling to their little human "selves" or personalities; these are the dead who

> moan and beat
> against the silvery adamant walls of life's exclusive city.[54]

For those souls who are "willing to continue on the longest journey," death is "inward and lovely peace," "the sleep of God" where "the world is created afresh."[55] What was certainly to have been the core of the work is the wonderfully majestic and dignified fragment called "The Ship of Death," in which the ancient myth of death as a voyage through unknown seas, suggested to Lawrence by a little votive ship in one of the Etruscan tombs, is used with extraordinary vividness to express the mystery of the passing of the human soul beyond the world of time and space:

> Now launch the small ship, now as the body dies
> and life departs, launch out the fragile soul
> in the fragile ship of courage, the ark of faith
> with its store of food and little cooking pans
> and change of clothes,
> upon the flood's black waste
> upon the waters of the end
> upon the sea of death, where still we sail
> darkly, for we cannot steer, and have no port.

It is significant that the fragment ends with a vision of the little ship passing at last into a new dawn:

> Wait, wait, the little ship
> drifting, beneath the deathly ashy grey
> of a flood-dawn.
> Wait, wait! even so, a flush of yellow
> and strangely, O chilled wan soul, a flush of rose.[56]

"The ancients," Lawrence writes in *Etruscan Places*, "saw consciously, as children now see unconsciously, the everlasting wonder in things." His own gift at the end of his life was to be able to reveal the "everlasting wonder" of death and that "intimation of immortality" which is inseparable from it in the religious vision.

Karl Jaspers has written, "To-day, as always, art must, willy nilly, make Transcendence perceptible, doing so at all times in the form which arouses contemporary faith. It may well be that the moment draws near when art will once again tell Man what his God is and what he himself is."[57] Lawrence is a major artist whose work can be rightly termed "religious" because we can see in it a continual striving toward that moment. In the writings to which he devoted most of his energy, he had to use the form which "arouses contemporary faith," that is, the realistic novel. By an amazing effort of creative innovation in his early maturity, he almost succeeded—indeed in *The Rainbow* perhaps momentarily he did succeed —in transforming the novel, which was originally designed for entertainment and moral edification, into a form adequate for the religious purpose of telling "man what his God is and what he himself is." But the novel was not really a suitable form for this purpose, and the transformation could not be sustained. In the last phase of his work, where his religious vision is at its purest and most intense, we can see it finding its natural form in a kind of poetry, which, to use his own description, is "neither star nor pearl, but instantaneous like plasm."[58] At his death he seemed to be on the point of producing for the first time in England since Blake and Wordsworth a poetry of religious vision on a grand scale, in which Romanticism would indeed have "come of age."

Notes

[1] *The Collected Letters of D. H. Lawrence*, ed. Harry T. Moore (London, 1962), I, 189.

[2] *Ibid.*, I, 273.

[3] Father William Tiverton (The Rev. Martin Jarrett-Kerr), *D. H. Lawrence and Human Existence* (London, 1951), p. viii.

[4] Earl and Achsah Brewster, *D. H. Lawrence: Reminiscences and Correspondence* (London, 1934), p. 275.

[5] Thomas L. Hanna, "What Does One Mean by 'Religious Literature'?" *Comparative Literature Studies*, II (1965), 380.

[6] *Longinus on the Sublime*, ed. W. Rhys Roberts (Cambridge, England, 1907), p. 63.

[7] D. H. Lawrence, *Reflections on the Death of a Porcupine* (Philadelphia, 1925), p. 108.

[8] *Ibid.*, p. 115.

[9] Chaucer, *Troilus and Criseyde*, II. 1849–1851.

[10] See Edgar Wind, *Pagan Mysteries in the Renaissance* (London, 1958).

[11] Bernard Shaw, *Prefaces* (London, 1938), p. 522.

[12] *The Works of Henry Vaughan*, ed. L. C. Martin (Oxford, 1914), II, 522.

[13] Thomas Traherne, *Centuries of Meditations*, ed. B. Dobell (London, 1908), pp. 20, 78.

[14] V. de S. Pinto, *Peter Sterry, Puritan and Platonist* (Cambridge, England, 1934), pp. 149, 196.

[15] Désirée Hirst, *Hidden Riches* (London, 1964), pp. 162–266.

[16] See "Life of Waller" in *Lives of the Poets.*

[17] *The Complete Writings of William Blake*, ed. Geoffrey Keynes (London, 1957), p. 431.

[18] *Ibid.*, p. 155.

[19] *Ibid.*, p. 153.

[20] "Lines Composed Above Tintern Abbey," 1. 49.

[21] See A. Owen Barfield, *Romanticism Comes of Age* (London, 1944).

[22] See the interesting comments on this aspect of his genius by George A. Panichas, *Adventure in Consciousness* (The Hague, 1964), pp. 49–53.

[23] *Collected Letters*, I, 231.

[24] Daniel A. Weiss, *Oedipus in Nottingham* (Seattle, 1962).

[25] Louis Fraiberg, "The Unattainable Self," *D. H. Lawrence and Sons and Lovers: Sources and Criticism*, ed. E. W. Tedlock, Jr. (New York, 1965), p. 223.

[26] *The Letters of D. H. Lawrence*, ed. Aldous Huxley (New York, 1932), p. 98.

[27] *The Prelude*, Book V, 11. 29–34.

[28] *Letters*, ed. Huxley, p. 383.

[29] "The Nightmare" (Chapter XII), *Kangaroo* (New York, 1960), p. 255.

[30] See J. Middleton Murry, *Love, Freedom and Society* (London, 1957), p. 67.

[31] Chapter XIV, *Kangaroo*, p. 289.

[32] Eugene Goodheart, *The Utopian Vision of D. H. Lawrence* (Chicago, 1963), p. 142.

[33] *The Complete Poems of D. H. Lawrence*, ed. V. de S. Pinto and Warren Roberts (London, 1964), I, 306.

[34] *Ibid.*, 350–351.

[35] *Ibid.*, 366–367.

[36] *Collected Letters*, II, 1045.

[37] Keith Sagar, *The Art of D. H. Lawrence* (Cambridge, England, 1966), p. 225.

[38] See *Complete Poems*, II, 654:
When Jesus commanded us to love our neighbour
he forced us to live a great lie, or to disobey:
for we can't love anybody, neighbour or no neighbour to order,
and faked love has rotted our marrow.

[39] *Collected Letters*, II, 1046–1047.

[40] *A Propos of Lady Chatterley's Lover* (London, 1930), pp. 40–41.

[41] Murry, p. 78.

[42] Brewster, p. 123.

[43] *Complete Poems*, I, 296.

[44] Brewster, p. 123.

[45] *Complete Poems*, I, 481.

[46] *Ibid.*, II, 691.

[47] Porcupine, p. 135.

[48] *Complete Poems*, II, 692.

[49] *Ibid.*, II, 695.

[50] *Phoenix: The Posthumous Papers of D. H. Lawrence*, ed. E. D. McDonald (London, 1936), p. 255.

[51] *Complete Poems*, II, 697.

[52] *Ibid.*, II, 700.

[53] *Ibid.*, II, 597–598.

[54] *Ibid.*, II, 722.

[55] *Ibid.*, II, 725.

[56] *Ibid.*, II, 719–720.

[57] Karl Jaspers, *Man in the Modern Age* (New York, 1957), p. 141.

[58] *Complete Poems*, I, 185.

Aldous Huxley's Quest for Values:
A Study in Religious Syncretism

by

Milton Birnbaum

Given the nature of spiders, webs are inevitable. And given the nature of human beings, so are religions. Spiders can't help making flytraps, and men can't help making symbols. That's what the human brain is there for—to turn the chaos of given experience into a set of fairly manageable symbols. Sometimes the symbols correspond fairly closely to some of the aspects of the external reality behind our experience; then you have science and common sense. Sometimes, on the contrary, the symbols have almost no connection with external reality; then you have paranoia and delirium. More often there's a mixture, part realistic and part fantastic; that's religion. Good religion or bad religion—it depends on the blending of the cocktail.

—Aldous Huxley, *Island*

ALDOUS HUXLEY'S FIRST COMMENTS ON RELIGION INDICATE THAT HE BEGAN as a sardonic skeptic. In one of his earliest novels, for example, we find a character comment on God as follows:

I am that I am. . . . But I have with me . . . a physiologue, a pedagogue and a priapagogue; for I leave out of account mere artists and journalists whose titles do not end with the magic syllable. And

finally . . . plain Dog, which being interpreted kabalistically backwards signifies God. All at your service.[1]

In *Jesting Pilate*, published in 1926, he writes that it may be true
that "religion is a device employed by the Life Force for the promotion of
its evolutionary designs. But they would be justified in adding that
religion is also a device employed by the Devil for the dissemination of
idiocy, intolerance, and servile abjection."[2] In his essay "One and Many,"
found in *Do What You Will*, published in 1929, he declares himself
"officially an agnostic." He develops the theory that God is simply a
projection of the human personality: ". . . men make Gods in their own
likeness. To talk about religion except in terms of human psychology is an
irrelevance."[3] He ridicules the anthropomorphic conception of God
because it reflects the weaknesses and aspirations of the society in which a
particular god is worshiped. Using himself as an example, he writes that
when he is enjoying good health and when the weather is propitious, then
he can well believe that "God's in his heaven and all's right with the
world." "On other occasions, skies and destiny being inclement, I am no
less immediately certain of the malignant impersonality of an uncaring
universe."[4] In a poem he wrote in 1925 called "Philosophy," he says that
it is difficult to hear what God is saying because "God stutters." He
would prefer to believe in the sanctity of what he calls the "Human
Personality" than in the "myth" of God. "We do at least know something of Human Personality, whereas of God we know nothing and,
knowing nothing, are at liberty to invent as freely as we like."[5] The
reason that people believe in this "theological game" is that they find it
much more psychologically satisfying to conform to habit than to be
subjected to the discomfort of rebellious skepticism.

The vacuum created by Huxley's rejection of an anthropomorphic
conception of religion was filled in the 1920's by his espousal of the
Lawrentian doctrine of the instinctive life. Man should not favor what is
felt to be a false spirituality but should live passionately and instinctively.
In *Point Counter Point* Mark Rampion (who is supposed to represent
D. H. Lawrence) speaks of the three diseases plaguing mankind: "Jesus'
and Newton's and Henry Ford's disease." All three "diseases" could be
eliminated, both Lawrence and Huxley felt, by the rejection of science,
technology, and traditional Christianity. In *Do What You Will*, published the same year as *Point Counter Point*, Huxley makes the same
points. He writes that the world is faced with three dangers: (1)
monotheism and the menace of the "super-humanist" ideal; (2) "the
worship of success and efficiency"; (3) "the machine." Monotheism and

the "super-humanist" ideal constitute a danger because they are not based on any foundation in reality and thus do not allow the living of the fully instinctive life. "The worship of success and efficiency constitutes another menace to our world. What our ancestors sacrificed on the altars of Spirituality, we sacrificed on those of the Bitch Goddess and Taylorism."[6] "The machine" is a menace because it robs man of his creativity and makes him merely a passively efficient robot. These three menaces have killed people's instinctive love of the fully integrated life, and "the result is that they lose their sense of values, their taste and judgment become corrupted, and they have an irresistible tendency to love the lowest when they see it."[7]

When we analyze Huxley's comments on Judaism and Christianity, we can readily appreciate why the Nazi propagandists used some of his statements in their attacks on Western democracies.[8] In 1929, for example, he made the following attack on Jews:

> Their mission, in a word, was to infect the rest of humanity with a belief which . . . prevented them from having any art, any philosophy, any political life, any breadth or diversity of vision, any progress. We may be pardoned for wishing that the Jews had remained, not forty, but four thousand years in their repulsive wilderness.[9]

Similarly, in *Along the Road* he sympathizes with those who have to work "eight hours a day in an office for the greater enrichment of the Jews." In *Antic Hay* a stranger whom Gumbril meets on the train complains: "Hideous red cities pullulating with Jews, sir. Pullulating with prosperous Jews. Am I right in being indignant, sir?"[10] He blames the monotheistic religion of the Jews for the emphasis given by other peoples to wealth and materialism, for the sentimentality current in music, and for the inculcation of other false values in our civilization. It should be pointed out, however, that Huxley's blatant anti-Semitism disappeared after the advent of Hitler. In his later books he deprecates the savagery of the Nazis; in one of his novels, *After Many a Summer*, one of the minor characters is a sympathetic Jew who falls victim to the ruthless business cunning of Jo Stoyte, a non-Jew.

The kind of misfired generalization that characterizes his attack on the Jews also characterizes his castigation of what, at different times, he calls "Christianity," "Puritanism," "Calvinism," and "organized religion." His objections to "Christianity" are several: first of all, he attacks the cruel persecutions by the more fanatical Christians. Although in the following excerpt he is singling out the Puritans, he makes similar attacks on other Christian groups in many of his other works as well:

> The puritan was free to range the world, blighting and persecuting as he went, free to make life poisonous, not only for himself, but for all who came near him. The puritan was and is a social danger, a public and private nuisance of the most odious kind. Baudelaire was a puritan inside out. Instead of asceticism and respectability he practised debauchery. The means he used were the opposite of those employed by the puritans; but his motives and theirs, the ends that he and they achieved, were the same. He hated life as much as they did, and was as successful in destroying it.[11]

The cruelty which Huxley finds so distasteful in the Puritans is like the cruelty which he discovers among the Catholics in the centuries during the Inquisition. "In medieval and early modern Christendom the situation of sorcerers and their clients was almost precisely analogous to that of Jews under Hitler, capitalists under Stalin, Communists and fellow travelers in the United States. . . ."[12] In *The Devils of Loudun* he describes the brutality of the Roman Catholic hierarchy toward one of their own priests who refused to admit that he was inhabited by a devil. Their cruelty did not stem from their alleged hatred of heresy alone; it arose, according to Huxley, because their entire religion was motivated by hatred:

> Ecclesiastical history exhibits a hierarchy of hatreds, descending by orderly degrees from the Church's official and ecumenical hatred of heretics and infidels to the particular hatreds of Order for Order, school for school, province for province and theologian for theologian.[13]

In addition to attacking the extreme cruelty of both the Puritans and the Catholics, Huxley also blames them for making people believe that this world is but a gloomy interlude between earthly pain and celestial euphoria. "Christianity has always found a certain difficulty in fitting the unfatigued, healthy and energetic person into its philosophical scheme."[14] If perchance Christianity does come upon a person who says that he is quite happy for the moment, then it reminds him that this state of well-being is but illusory and certainly temporary; every silver lining is but hiding an imminent cloudburst. The Greeks, Huxley avers, were far wiser in being realistically pessimistic and in using this pessimism to justify their epicurean and instinctive way of life. Huxley here seems either to be unaware of or else ignorant of the fact that the same society which gave rise to the Epicureans also gave rise to the Stoics.

There are other features which Huxley attacks in Christianity. He seems to take unusual delight in pointing out that often its priests themselves do not practice the austerity which they so unctuously preach. In *The Devils of Loudun* he points out that essentially there were two Urbain Grandiers: Grandier the sensualist and Grandier the sermonizing priest. He describes how between Grandier's weekly debaucheries he was preparing sermons filled with "what eloquence, what choice and profound learning, what subtle, but eminently sound theology!"[15] When Grandier hears the discomforting news from one of his female parishioners that he is the father of her unborn child, Huxley describes his hypocritical reaction as follows:

> Shifting his hand from the bosom to the bowed head and changing his tone, without any transition, from the bawdy to the clerical, the parson told her that she must learn to bear her cross with Christian resignation. Then, remembering the visit he had promised to pay to poor Mme. de Brou, who had a cancer of the womb and needed all the spiritual consolation he could give her, he took his leave.[16]

In his essay "Variations of a Philosopher," published in *Themes and Variations*, Huxley analyzes the term "shepherd" to demonstrate how, like sheep, people never stop to consider that "a shepherd is 'not in business for his health,' still less for the health of his sheep." If a shepherd takes good care of his flock, it is only to fatten them for the eventual slaughter. People should consider the meaning of the term "shepherd" before they proceed to talk sentimentally about their pastors:

> Applied to most of the States and Churches of the last two or three thousand years, this pastoral metaphor is seen to be exceedingly apt—so apt, indeed, that one wonders why the civil and ecclesiastical herders of men should ever have allowed it to gain currency. From the point of view of the individual lambs, rams and ewes there is, of course, no such thing as a *good* shepherd; their problem is to find means whereby they may enjoy the benefits of a well-ordered social life without being exposed to the shearings, milkings, geldings and butcheries which have always been associated with the pastoral office.[17]

There are still other serious faults that Huxley has found with "most of the States and Churches of the last two or three thousand years." He complains that "compared with that of the Taoists and Far Eastern Buddhists, the Christian attitude towards Nature has been curiously insensitive and often downright domineering and violent."[18] Encouraged by "an unfortunate remark in Genesis," Christians have treated animals as things to be exploited for their own benefits. Furthermore, Huxley is very bitter against the Church because it has not offered any kind of opposition to the waging of wars. In *Ape and Essence*, where his bitterness has perhaps reached its most intense pitch, he writes:

> The brass bands give place to the most glutinous of Wurlitzers, "Land of Hope and Glory" to "Onward, Christian Soldiers." Followed by his very Reverend Dean and Chapter, the Right Reverend, the Baboon-Bishop of the Bronx advances majestic, his crozier in his jeweled paw, to pronounce benediction upon the two Field Marshalissimos and their patriotic proceedings.[19]

If we look at the ministers in Huxley's novels, we find that they are all satirically drawn. In *Crome Yellow* we have the Reverend Bodinham, who is much disturbed because his prediction of the coming of the Lord ("He'll sneak around like a thief") has not been realized. In *Antic Hay* we have the Reverend Pelvey, whose ineffectiveness as a preacher is satirically demonstrated: while the Reverend Pelvey is preaching, one of the audience to whom his religious message is directed is thinking of "trousers with pneumatic seats." In *Eyeless in Gaza* Mr. Thursley, a minister, is successful in his sermons and in the publication of his articles in the *Guardian*, but he becomes uncontrollably angry when his wife fails to fill up his inkwell. In *Time Must Have a Stop* Huxley pictures the minister-father of Mrs. Thwale as a completely futile man: while the minister is trying to reform the world, he does not realize that his daughter is becoming bitterly opposed to religion; ironically enough, it is the minister's daughter who worships material comfort and commits adultery.[20]

Of all the Christian faiths, Huxley seems to have the greatest respect for Catholicism and the greatest admiration for Quakerism and those early Christians in whom he found mystic strains. The Quakers he admires for their opposition to war and for their contributions in alleviating some of the world's ecological problems. As for his attitude toward Catholicism, he writes:

Catholicism is probably the most realistic of all Western religions. Its practice is based on a profound knowledge of human nature in all its varieties and gradations. From the fetish-worshipper to the metaphysician, from the tired business man to the mystic, from the sentimentalist and the sensualist to the intellectual, every type of human being can find in Catholicism the spiritual nourishment which he or she requires. For the sociable, unspiritual man Catholicism is duly sociable and unspiritual. For the solitary and the spiritual it provides a hermitage and the most exquisite, the profoundest models of religious meditation; it gives the silence of monasteries and the bareness of the Carthusian church; it offers the devotional introspection of À Kempis and St. Theresa, the subtleties of Pascal and Newman, the poetry of Crashaw and St. John of the Cross and a hundred others. The only people for whom it does not cater are those possessed by that rare, dangerous, and uneasy passion, the passion for liberty.[21]

Presumably it is Huxley's "passion for liberty" which constitutes one of the reasons for his objection to Catholicism. But there are other reasons. I have already spoken of his attacks on Christianity because of its failure to oppose wars and its encouragement of materialistic success even to the extent of treating animals as mere property; Huxley does not exculpate Catholicism from his generalized attack on Christianity. He also objects to Catholicism (at least to Catholicism as it is practiced in England) because it stresses the ritual at the expense of the more meaningful "mental prayer." In *Eyeless in Gaza* we note the following extract from the diary of Anthony Beavis: "For English Catholics, sacraments are the psychological equivalents of tractors in Russia."[22]

It is not the ritual in Catholicism alone to which he objects; he seems to find little value in the ritual of any religion. In *Eyeless in Gaza* he describes a funeral in which he satirizes the significance of the accompanying ritual. After describing the playing of the organ, the "little procession of surplices," the flowers, the singing, and the intoning of the funeral prayer, he points out the ineffectiveness of all this ritual on Anthony Beavis: "But Anthony hardly heard, because he could think of nothing except those germs that were still there in spite of the smell of the flowers, and of the spittle that kept flowing into his mouth. . . ."[23] Similarly, in *Ape and Essence* he describes the procession in honor of Belial and refers to "the collective imbecility" which is one of the products of ceremonial religion.

Having found little cause for admiration in either Judaism or

Christianity, Huxley turned to the East to find the answer to his religious quest.[24] It should be emphasized at this point that Huxley's apparent rejection of the Judeo-Christian tradition did not mean his denial of either the worth of religion or of the existence of God. As early as 1926 we find him writing: "The fact that men have had stupid and obviously incorrect ideas about God does not justify us in trying to eliminate God from out of the universe. Men have had stupid and incorrect ideas on almost every subject that can be thought about."[25]

Whenever Huxley found elements of mysticism, as he did in the Book of Ecclesiastes; in the writings of such mystic Christians as St. Augustine, St. Bernard of Clairvaux, Meister Eckhart, Walter Hilton, William Law, St. François de Sales, Thomas Traherne, and others; and in the Sufi books of Islam, he accepted their teachings of contemplation, renunciation of worldly preoccupation, and the practice of love. It is, therefore, not so much religion itself that he was rejecting but what he felt was the perversion of the religious essence.

Mysticism is not an easy concept to define. As Huxley himself wrote, there are elements of mysticism common to nearly all religions. Inasmuch as he embraced not the mysticism of any particular religion (although he leaned more toward Buddhism than to any other) but rather mysticism itself as a kind of philosophical concept, perhaps the definition given by Evelyn Underhill, two of whose books he includes in the bibliography in The Perennial Philosophy, most clearly explains mysticism in the sense in which Huxley uses it: "I . . . understand it to be the expression of the innate tendency of the human spirit towards complete harmony with the transcendental order, whatever be the theological formula under which that order is understood."[26] It is significant that the one book of Huxley's entirely devoted to a survey of mysticism as it has appeared in all religions in all ages is called The Perennial Philosophy, not The Perennial Religion. Huxley himself declares both his incompetence and his lack of desire to note the differences among the various modes of mysticism as manifested in the different religions. He says, for example, "I am not competent, nor is this the place to discuss the doctrinal differences between Buddhism and Hinduism."[27] Although The Perennial Philosophy is his only book devoted entirely to a critical interpretation of selections from mystical writings, his comments on this subject go back much further.

Huxley's first comments on mysticism were hostile. In 1929 he was writing: ". . . the mystics are never tired of affirming that their direct perceptions of unity are intenser, of finer quality and intrinsically more convincing, more self-evident, than their direct perceptions of diversity.

But they can only speak for themselves. Other people's direct intuitions of diverse 'appearances' may be just as intensely self-evident as *their* intuition of unique 'reality.' "[28] But in another essay of the book from which the previous quotation is taken, he admits that "it is also true that, in certain circumstances, we can actually *feel*, as a direct intuition, the existence of the all-comprehending unity, can intimately realize in a single flash of insight the illusoriness of the quotidian world of distinctions and relations."[29] Even in his earlier novels we detect some elements of mysticism—the urge for a contemplative life, the distrust of a life of action. Thus in *Those Barren Leaves*, Calamy (who at the end retires to the hills to start a life of pure contemplation) says: "The mind must be open, unperturbed, empty of irrelevant things, quiet. There's no room for thoughts in a half-shut, cluttered mind."[30] Later he comes out even more strongly for the contemplative life:

> No, it's not fools who turn mystics. It takes a certain amount of intelligence and imagination to realize the extra-ordinary queerness and mysteriousness of the world in which we live. The fools, the innumerable fools, take it all for granted, skate about cheerfully on the surface and never think of inquiring what's underneath. They're content with appearances, such as your Harrow Road or Café de la Rotonde, call them realities and proceed to abuse any one who takes an interest in what lies underneath these superficial symbols, as a romantic imbecile.[31]

It should not be assumed that Huxley completely believed in mysticism back in the 1920's; but even when he denies the claim of the mystics that they achieve a unity with God, he qualifies this denial by writing that "That does not in any way detract from the value of mysticism as a way to perfect health."[32] Similarly, in *Brave New World*, published in 1932, he is more against the tendency of the world to drift into a technological "utopia" than he is for mysticism; but in this book, also, we detect unmistakable signs of his eventual conversion to mysticism. Thus, as Mustapha Mond is signing the papers banning a work on "A New Theory of Biology," one of the reasons for his proscription of the book is that people might begin to think that "the goal was somewhere beyond, somewhere outside the present human sphere; that the purpose of life was not maintenance of well-being, but some intensification and refining of consciousness, some enlargement of knowledge."[33]

Eyeless in Gaza, published in 1936, contains Huxley's first complete endorsement of mysticism. In it he outlines the details of his mysticism which he was to elaborate in his subsequent works. It is in this book that he first advocates the achievement of a union with God. Evil is that which separates man from man; manifestations of evil, such as hatred, greed, and lust, should be avoided. Good is that which unites; love, compassion, and understanding are demonstrations of unity. Huxley admits that this unity is difficult to achieve, but man should at least attempt to achieve it through meditation and inner serenity. Through the attainment of inner peace, he will be better able to withstand the external evil which is the condition of the world. From the notebook of Anthony Beavis we take the following expression of Huxley's mysticism at this time:

Empirical facts:

One. We are all capable of love for other human beings.

Two. We impose limitations on that love.

Three. We can transcend all these limitations—*if we choose to*. (It is a matter of observation that anyone who so desires can overcome personal dislike, class feeling, national hatred, colour prejudice. Not easy; but it can be done, if we have the will and know how to carry out our good intentions.)

Four. Love expressing itself in good treatment breeds love. Hate expressing itself in bad treatment breeds hate.

In the light of these facts, it's obvious what inter-personal, inter-class and inter-national policies should be. But, again, knowledge cuts little ice. We all know; we almost all fail to do. It is a question, as usual, of the best methods of implementing intentions. Among other things, peace propaganda must be a set of instructions in the art of modifying character.[34]

In *Ends and Means* Huxley repeats some of the thoughts concerning mysticism which he expressed in *Eyeless in Gaza*, but he adds some new features. Thus he again writes that "Meditation . . . is the technique of mysticism."[35] But he emphasizes the necessity of intuition in attaining this detachment from the world of animality. He again stresses the importance of will power in helping the individual to achieve the intuitive experience which will bring him into the mystical state: "What we perceive and understand depends upon what we are; and what we are depends partly on circumstances, partly, and more profoundly, on the nature of the efforts we have made to realize our ideal and the nature of the ideal we have tried to realize."[36] Since the will is so important in achieving the mystical experience, Huxley particularly urges the reader to remember Irving Babbitt's statement that meditation produces a "super-rational concentration of will." Huxley concedes that all of us have animal instincts which cannot be ignored, but he does not want us to devote our entire attention to the satisfaction of these instincts. "Goodness is the method by which we divert our attention from this singularly wearisome topic of our animality and our individual separateness."[37] This loss of preoccupation with bodily needs may cause some physical suffering, but it is more than adequately compensated by the knowledge and the inner serenity which accompany the mystical experience. The nonattachment of mysticism is infinitely preferable to the attachment of the individual to the pursuit of the life of meaningless action.

In his next novel, *After Many a Summer*, Huxley further elaborates his theories of mysticism. His espousal of the life of self-transcendence is thus expressed in the answer which Mr. Propter gives to Pete's question as to what good is and where it is to be found:

On the level below the human and on the level above. On the animal level and on the level . . . well, you can take your choice of names: the level of eternity; the level, if you don't object, of God; the level of the spirit—only that happens to be about the most ambiguous word in the language. On the lower level, good exists as the proper functioning of the organism in accordance with the laws of its own being. On the higher level, it exists in the form of a knowledge of the world without desire or aversion; it exists as the experience of eternity, as the transcendence of personality, the extension of consciousness beyond the limits imposed by the ego. Strictly human activities are the activities that prevent the manifestations of good on the other two levels. . . . Directly or indirectly, most of our physical ailments and disabilities are due to worry and craving. We worry and crave ourselves into high blood pressure, heart disease, tuberculosis, peptic ulcer, low resistance to infection, neurasthenia, sexual aberrations, insanity, suicide. Not to mention all the rest.[38]

In addition to craving liberation from the fetters of the ego, Mr. Propter wants liberation from time, which he describes as "a pretty

bothersome thing." Furthermore, the cultivation of virtues is not sufficient; it must be the cultivation of the right virtues—specifically, understanding and compassion. The possession of the other virtues is no
guarantee of virtuous conduct: "Indeed, you can't be really bad unless
you do have most of the virtues. Look at Milton's Satan for example.
Brave, strong, generous, loyal, prudent, temperate, self-sacrificing."[39] But
because Milton's Satan lacked the qualities of understanding and compassion, he could not be a virtuous leader.

In *Grey Eminence*, published in 1941, Huxley gives two additional
suggestions to those who would embrace mysticism: First, the good
achieved by a practice of mysticism "is a product of the ethical and
spiritual artistry of individuals; it cannot be mass-produced."[40] Secondly,
people should beware of "only false, ersatz mysticisms—the nature-
mysticism of Wordsworth; the sublimated sexual mysticism of Whitman;
the nationality-mysticisms of all the patriotic poets and philosophers of
every race and culture, from Fichte at the beginning of the period [the
nineteenth century] to Kipling and Barrès at the end."[41] The only valid
manifestation of mysticism is the intuitive knowledge and love of God.

It is in *The Perennial Philosophy* that Huxley gives the fullest
expression to his espousal of mysticism. Technically it is an anthology of
selections from the utterances of many of the religious writers from
previous centuries who have espoused mysticism, or what he calls the
"Perennial Philosophy": "This book . . . is an anthology of the Perennial Philosophy; but, though an anthology, it contans [sic] but few
extracts from the writings of professional men of letters and, though
illustrating a philosophy, hardly anything from the professional philosophers."[42] Only those who have made themselves "loving, pure in heart,
and poor in spirit" are capable of apprehending the nature of this
perennial philosophy, which, he says, "is primarily concerned with the
one, divine Reality substantial to the manifold world of things and lives
and minds."[43] The book is divided into twenty-seven chapters dealing
with various aspects of human and divine experience. The importance of
the book, however, lies not in the selection of excerpts from the writings
of others (excellent though they may be) but rather in the ample
comments which Huxley makes on these excerpts. His views can be
summarized as follows: every phase of human activity must be judged in
terms of its hindering or facilitating the achievement of the ultimate
purpose of life: "In all the historic formulations of the Perennial Philosophy it is axiomatic that the end of human life is contemplation, or the
direct and intuitive awareness of God."[44] That society is good which
does not emphasize technological advances but makes possible and

desirable the pursuit of contemplation. The love which is released by the exercise of this intuitive contemplation will cure many of the evils that are plaguing mankind. Thus this love will lead to the treating of nature kindly: the earth's resources will no longer be ravaged by people motivated only by self-interest. Similarly, this love will restore man's creativity in work so that he will no longer be a slave to the machine. This love will also make it impossible for political rulers to oppress their peoples. Above all, it will release the individual from bondage to selfhood and from the fetters of time and sensual demands. The liberation from these fetters will even rid us of the ailments of "most of the degenerative diseases": our heart, kidneys, pancreas, intestines, and arteries are now subject to deterioration because we do not live in harmony with "the divine Nature of Things." Self-denial will not only bring us into union with the essence of the Godhead, but will, in so doing, relieve us of all our physical pain.

Man should not be troubled by such problems as the origin of the Divine Ground or the seeming injustice of seeing evil people prosperous and good people impoverished. God *is* because He *is:* "Only when the individual also 'simply is,' by reason of his union through love-knowledge with the Ground, can there be any question of complete and eternal liberation."[45] As for the seeming injustice of the "bad" man enjoying prosperity and the "good" man afflicted with poverty, Huxley offers the following explanation: "The bad man in prosperity may, all unknown to himself, be darkened and corroded with inward rust, while the good man under afflictions may be in the rewarding process of spiritual growth."[46]

Until the Perennial Philosophy is adopted and recognized as "the highest factor common to all the world religions," until the worshipers of every religion renounce their egocentric, time-based, and false idolatries, then "no amount of political planning, no economic blue-prints however ingeniously drawn, can prevent the recrudescence of war and revolution."[47] What is the way to achieve this ideal state? To answer this question, Huxley recommends Buddha's "Eight-fold Path":

Complete deliverance is conditional on the following: first, Right Belief in the all too obvious truth that the cause of pain and evil is craving for separative, egocentred existence, with its corollary that there can be no deliverance from evil, whether personal or collective, except by getting rid of such craving and the obsession of "I," "me," "mine"; second, Right Will, the will to deliver oneself and others; third, Right Speech, directed by compassion and charity towards all sentient beings; fourth, Right Action, with the aim of creating and maintaining peace and good will; fifth, Right Means of Livelihood, or the choice only of such professions as are not harmful, in their exercise, to any human being or, if possible, any living creature; sixth, Right Effort towards Self-control; seventh, Right Attention or Recollectedness, to be practised in all the circumstances of life, so that we may never do evil by mere thoughtlessness, because "we know not what we do"; and, eighth, Right Contemplation, the unitive knowledge of the Ground, to which recollectedness and the ethical self-naughting prescribed in the first six branches of the Path give access. Such then are the means which it is within the power of the human being to employ in order to achieve man's final end and be "saved."[48]

Huxley is not excessively optimistic that these prescriptions will be followed by most people. "But then no saint or founder of a religion, no exponent of the Perennial Philosophy, has ever been optimistic."[49]

It would seem that Huxley's search for the "ideal" religion would end in the place where religion began—in the East. Huxley's insatiable intellectual thirst, however, refused to be permanently quenched. It should be remembered that Huxley was the grandson of Thomas Henry Huxley, the scientist, and the grandnephew of Matthew Arnold. Huxley's soul was always the battleground between the challenging barks of "Darwin's bulldog" (Thomas Henry Huxley's sobriquet) and the melancholy promptings for withdrawal of his maternal granduncle. The urgings for self-transcendence gave way to a continued scientific probing. And so in his essay entitled "The Double Crisis," published in Themes and Variations in 1950, Huxley again calls upon technological science to help solve the world's problems. It is somewhat difficult to reconcile the advocacy of self-mortification found in The Perennial Philosophy with the advice given in the following excerpt:

Man cannot live by bread alone; but still less can he live exclusively by idealism. To talk about the Rights of Man and the Four Freedoms in connection, for example, with India is merely a cruel joke. In a country where two thirds of the people succumb to the consequences of malnutrition before they reach the age of thirty, but where, nonetheless, the population increases by fifty millions every decade, most men possess neither rights nor any kind of freedom. The "giant misery of the world" is only aggravated by mass violence and cannot be mitigated by inspirational twaddle.

Misery will yield only to an intelligent attack upon the causes of misery.[50]

In the last ten years of his life Huxley continued to turn to science, both to help solve the world's problems of feeding its excessive population and settling its economic difficulties and to provide the means to increase his own aesthetic and religious perceptions. All the books published in his last decade—*The Doors of Perception, Heaven and Hell, Tomorrow and Tomorrow and Tomorrow, Brave New World Revisited, Island*, and, finally, *Literature and Science*—indicate Huxley's return to his first love—science. He himself experimented with several drugs—mescalin, LSD (lysergic acid diethylamide), etc.—to help increase his aesthetic and spiritual awareness. His intention was to utilize science to facilitate the achievement of a beatific union with the Godhead, but one wonders whether in his metaphysical edifice the temple did not become the waiting room to the laboratory.

In his last published novel, *Island* (1962), Huxley no longer offers man the choice he offered him in *Brave New World* (1932)—the meaningless diversions of a mechanized Utopia or the almost equally barren existence of the primitive. In his last Utopia Huxley attempts to make the best of both worlds. He had always realized—his attacks on the Judeo-Christian tradition notwithstanding—that "the ethical doctrines taught in the Tao Te Ching, by Gotama Buddha and his followers of the Lesser and above all the Greater Vehicle, in the Sermon on the Mount and by the best of the Christian saints, are not dissimilar."[51] What Huxley actually wanted was a kind of fusion of the mystical contributions of the East with the technological improvements of the West. What had happened, unfortunately, was that East and West had borrowed not the best but the worst features of each other's cultures; in *Ape and Essence* he comments on how Belial "persuaded each side to take only the worst the other had to offer. So the East takes Western nationalism, Western armaments, Western movies and Western Marxism; the West takes Eastern despotism, Eastern superstitions and Eastern indifference to individual life. In a word, He [Belial] saw to it that mankind should make the worst of both worlds."[52] In *Island* Huxley found the perfect solution: "Our recipe is rather different: Take twenty sexually satisfied couples and their offsprings; add science, intuition and humor in equal quantities; steep in Tantrik Buddhism and simmer indefinitely in an open pan in the open air over a brisk flame of affection."[53] The marriage of science and religion does not seem to work very well in his fictional island of Pala, for at the end of the book the greedy and the vulgar are about to smash the moksha-induced beatitudes of the fortunate ones. The insects at the end of the book are still vulgarly copulating—to the background music of Bach's "Fourth Brandenburg Concerto"—and the female insect still devours the male after the sexual consummation. It is quite true that Will Farnaby, the central character, has learned karuma (compassion) and has achieved an inner strength to help him withstand the inevitable onrush of idiocy, materialism, and war. But one wonders whether this inner illumination is the result of wisdom and free will or of the moksha-medicine, "the reality revealer, the truth-and-beauty pill." Curiously enough, moksha, as the Indian scholar Nagarajan relates,[54] means "freedom for evermore." A freedom induced by a mushroom-produced drug seems hardly different from the euphoria resulting from the taking of soma in Brave New World.

Essentially, then, Huxley's religious quest was a paradoxically tortuous one. He began by mocking and rejecting the Judeo-Christian tradition (though accepting its occasional manifestations of mysticism), flirted temporarily with the Lawrentian doctrine of instinctive living and "blood consciousness," changed to contemplative investigation, turned to the East for further illumination, and died in the West trying to balance in an uneasy syncretism the Caliban of Western science with the Ariel of Buddhist mysticism. One speculates whether it was a consummation devoutly to be wished. The religious syncretism turned out to be a synthetic product; the metaphysical quest ended with a pharmacological solution.

Notes

[1] *Antic Hay* (New York, 1923), p. 79.

[2] *Jesting Pilate: An Intellectual Holiday* (New York, 1926), p. 58.

[3] *Do What You Will: Essays* (New York, 1931), p. 1.

[4] *Ibid.*, p. 2.

[5] *Ibid.*, p. 141 ("Fashions in Love").

[6] *Ibid.*, p. 83 ("Spinoza's Worm").

[7] *Ibid.*, p. 88.

[8] See, for example, Wilhelm Poschmann, *Das Kritische Weltbild bei Aldous Huxley: Eine Untersuchung über Bedeutung, Grenzen und Mittel Seiner Kritik*, Doctoral Dissertation (Bonn, 1937). See especially pp. 39–40, 42–48, 60–63.

[9] *Do What You Will*, p. 18.

[10] *Antic Hay*, p. 263.

[11] *Do What You Will*, pp. 192–193.

[12] *The Devils of Loudun* (New York, 1952), p. 122.

[13] *Ibid.*, pp. 19–20.

[14] *Texts & Pretexts: An Anthology with Commentaries* (New York, 1933), p. 287.

[15] *The Devils of Loudun*, pp. 26–27.

[16] *Ibid.*, p. 35.

[17] *Themes and Variations* (New York, 1950), p. 57.

[18] *The Perennial Philosophy* (New York, 1945), p. 77.

[19] *Ape and Essence* (New York, 1948), pp. 45–46.

[20] The satire of ministers is not confined to the novels. In his essays he also minimizes the effectiveness of churchmen when they attempt to practice their "Christian ideals":

> In the lounge, waiting for the coffee, we got into conversation with the clergyman. Or rather, he got into conversation with us. He felt it his duty, I suppose, as a Christian, as a temporary chaplain in the Anglican diocese of Southern Europe, to welcome the newcomers, to put them at their ease. "Beautiful evening," he said, in his too richly cultured voice. (But I loved him for his trousers.) "Beautiful," we agreed, and that the place was charming. "Staying long?" he asked. We looked at one another, then round the crowded hall, then again at one another. I shook my head. "Tomorrow," I said, "we have to make a very early start." (*Do What You Will*, pp. 111–112 ["Paradise"]).

[21] *Proper Studies* (London, 1927), pp. 186–187 ("The Essence of Religion").

[22] *Eyeless in Gaza* (New York, 1954; copyright 1936), p. 386.

[23] *Ibid.*, p. 25.

[24] It should be pointed out that his few references to Mohammedanism indicate a dislike for that religion also. In "In a Tunisian Oasis," published in *The Olive Tree* in 1937, he writes that "Too much insistence on the fatalism inherent in their [Arabs'] religion has reduced them to the condition of static lethargy and supine incuriousness in which they now find themselves." He blames the Arabs' religion for the fact that "half their babies die, and that, politically, they are not their own masters." This "static lethargy and supine incuriousness" which he attributes to the Mohammedan religion sounds rather incongruous when juxtaposed with the comment he made about Mohammedanism some eight years later in *The Perennial Philosophy* (p. 158): "And in Mohammedanism we find a system which incorporates strongly somatotonic elements. Hence Islam's black record of holy wars and persecutions—a record comparable to that of later Christianity, after that religion had so far compromised with unregenerate somatotonia as to call its ecclesiastical organization 'the Church Militant.' "

[25] *Jesting Pilate*, p. 219.

[26] *Mysticism: A Study in the Nature and Development of Man's Spiritual Consciousness* (New York, 1911), p. x. Christopher Isherwood, who espouses the Vedanta type of mysticism, writes: "Vedanta also teaches the practice of mysticism; it claims, that is to say, that man may directly know and be united with his eternal Nature, the Atman, through meditation and spiritual discipline, without the aid of any church or delegated minister." This quotation is taken from pp. xii–xiii of the Introduction to *Vedanta for Modern Man* (New York, 1951), a collection of various writings on Vedanta, edited by Isherwood. To this anthology Huxley contributed several essays. To Huxley mysticism is one of the two branches of spirituality: "Spirituality is—asceticism and mysticism, the mortification of the self and ultimate Reality." See his "Readings in Mysticism," *Vedanta for the Western World*, ed. Christopher Isherwood (Hollywood, 1945), pp. 376–382. It should be noted, however, that Huxley elsewhere speaks out against the "mortification of the self."

[27] *The Perennial Philosophy*, p. 9.

[28] *Do What You Will*, p. 38 ("One and Many").

[29] *Ibid.*, p. 63 ("Spinoza's Worm").

[30] *Those Barren Leaves* (London, 1925), p. 347.

[31] *Ibid.*, p. 370.

[32] *Jesting Pilate*, pp. 217–218.

[33] *Brave New World* (New York, 1950; copyright 1932), p. 211.

[34] *Eyeless in Gaza*, p. 156.

[35] *Ends and Means: An Inquiry into the Nature of Ideas and into the Methods Employed for Their Realization* (New York, 1937), p. 332 ("Beliefs").

[36] *Ibid.*, p. 333.

[37] *Ibid.*, p. 346.

[38] *After Many a Summer Dies the Swan* (New York, 1954; copyright 1939), pp. 99–100.

[39] *Ibid.*, p. 95.

[40] *Grey Eminence: A Study in Religion and Politics* (New York, 1937), p. 303.

[41] *Ibid.*, p. 77.

[42] *The Perennial Philosophy*, p. viii.

[43] *Ibid.*

[44] *Ibid.*, p. 294.

[45] *Ibid.*, p. 238. (See also his essays "Seven Meditations" and "Reflections on the Lord's Prayer," *Vedanta for the Western World*, pp. 163–170 and 298–312.)

[46] *Ibid.*, p. 239.

[47] *Ibid.*, p. 200.

[48] *Ibid.*, pp. 202–203.

[49] *Ibid.*, p. 211.

[50] *Themes and Variations*, p. 257 ("The Double Crisis").

[51] *Ends and Means*, p. 327 ("Beliefs").

[52] *Ape and Essence*, p. 184.

[53] *Island* (New York, 1962), p. 103.

[54] See S. Nagarajan's article "Religion in Three Recent Novels of Aldous Huxley," *Modern Fiction Studies*, V (Summer 1959), 153–165.

Masefield and Spiritualism

by

G. Wilson Knight

The dead don't die. They look on and help.
—D. H. Lawrence in a letter to J. Middleton Murry (2 Feb. 1923)

In this essay I append the original date of English publication as given in Geoffrey Handley-Taylor's indispensable bibliography *John Masefield, O.M.* (London, 1960), at a book's first mention and again at a main entry. For the prose I give chapter numerals when available.

THE POET LAUREATE'S SIXTY YEARS OF CREATIVE WRITING HAS QUALITIES of epic and spiritual significance elsewhere unmatched. His style, preferring direct narrative to "discussion of states of mind and soul" (*So Long to Learn* [1952], p. 103), is lucid: what cannot be said simply will not be said at all. Even in literary criticism, his *William Shakespeare* (1911; new version, 1954) and *Chaucer* (1931), he illustrates Arthur Quiller-Couch's ideal of the concrete noun and the active verb. Though his life's survey covers the most awful problems of human destiny, he has written little that cannot be followed by a boy.

Though his early *Multitude and Solitude* (1909, VI, p. 139; VII, p. 170) asserted the importance of a moral purpose, Masefield's social novels lack fire. *The Hawbucks* (1929) is an indecisive study of country gentlefolk, perhaps saved only by a hunt and a blizzard. *Eggs and Baker* (1936) is a strong indictment of social injustice, rising to an exciting murder trial in which two men are convicted, one unjustly. In *The*

Square Peg (1937) an armaments manufacturer who loathes the cruelties and crudities of a fox-hunting society creates a garden city and an art-center. Of these the second has its claims: no one else has written more strongly on the horrors of the death penalty; but the coloring of all three is dull. It seems that the novel of moral engagement proved for Masefield a blind alley.

His strength is in action. Games and sports, honored by classical epic, and today—in their bridging of combat and friendliness—perhaps our best hope on the international scene, are given their poetry: hunting in *Reynard the Fox* (1919), racing in *Right Royal* (1920), cricket in "Eighty-Five to Win" (*The Bluebells and Other Verse* [1961]), and boxing in *The Everlasting Mercy* (1911) and "A Tale of Country Things" (*On the Hill* [1949]). In *Multitude and Solitude* (VI, p. 139; VII, p. 170) literature is contrasted with action; and so in *Dauber* (1913) is painting. Art is best when it is itself action, as in the combination of artistry and athletics in the circus (*King Cole* [1921] and *The Country Scene* [1937]); in ballet (*The Square Peg and Tribute to Ballet* [1938]); in spoken verse (*With the Living Voice* [1925] and *So Long to Learn*, pp. 195–217); and in drama, especially, as in *A Macbeth Production* (1945), if homemade. Art must honor its basis: "All art comes from the power that does rough work and the pride and joy of doing that rough work well" (*The Square Peg*, p. 52). Masefield asks for a new totality of "supreme art" (*So Long to Learn*, p. 183) both communal and inclusive, "exquisite to hear" and "beautiful to watch" (*I Want! I Want!* [1944], p. 18).

His outlook is youthful. In the visionary "Ossian," III (*The Bluebells and Other Verse*), supernal experience is set in "the land of youth." From the small boy Kay Harker in the child-fantasies *The Midnight Folk* (1927) and *The Box of Delights* (1935) to the youths of the adventure stories, his heroes are young. In *A Book of Discoveries* (1910) a man of active experience initiates two boys into the wonders of woodlore and the skills of scoutcraft. Boys should learn to enter "other lives than their own . . . they should know what the red thing in the pond eats, how the weasel hunts, how the partridge calls at twilight. There is no greater delight on earth than to enter another brain by an act of the imagination." Life, "always miraculous," is "the only lesson worth learning" (p. 206). Again, all "wisdom" and "progress" come from "looking so closely at a thing" that one sees "its meaning as well as its appearance" (p. 311).

Nature is to be both learned and fought. In narrative after narrative we are shown the terrifying antagonists of ocean and jungle and how to master them; by skill and with the help of spirits. Masefield's keen sense of spirit-powers is one with his poetic ability to realize *action* in animal and man, for action and spirit-powers are close. In his world, spirits intervene, like the deities in Homer and Virgil.

To Homer, Masefield was devoted (*So Long to Learn*, p. 213), and in his own narratives of contest and exploration he is Homeric. He has Homer's admiration of beautiful and efficient crafts, as when he sees "strength and beauty" in a reef-knot (*Jim Davis* [1911], IV, p. 48), or writes at length of his experiences in a carpet factory in *In the Mill* (1941). He has also Homer's acceptance of terrible deeds, as uninhibited as those of the children in *The Box of Delights* (III, p. 82) playing at pirates: "And you'll be captured and tortured, and then you'll have to walk the plank." In his accounts of sixteenth- and seventeenth-century buccaneering in *On the Spanish Main* (1906) he records massacres and tortures with an unruffled calm. In *Lost Endeavour* (1910; 1; X, p. 84) we have:

> "A lad of tender heart," said one of the Spaniards.
> "Bueno," said the others, when my remarks had been trans-
> lated to them. "Bueno joven." They looked at me as if I were some
> rare bird, as if goodness were stuck about me like feathers.

We must not look for sensitivity where it does not exist. Brave men, however rough, win respect.

Spanish America holds for Masefield a fascination which gives *On the Spanish Main* and his poetic drama *Philip the King* (1914) a luster not quite enjoyed by his other historical books: *Sea Life in Nelson's Time* (1905), grimly detailing the horrors of naval service; *The Tragedy of Pompey the Great* (1910); the novel *Badon Parchments* (1947), on Arthurian Britain; the Byzantine stories *Basilissa* (1940) and *Conquer* (1941); and *Martin Hyde* (1910), notable for its description of the Battle of Sedgemoor, on Monmouth's rebellion. Masefield's knowledge of the logistics and technicalities of ancient and modern warfare appears inexhaustible.

Writing on the two World Wars (*Gallipoli* [1916], *The Old Front Line* [1917], *The Battle of the Somme* [1919], and *The Nine Days Wonder* [1941]), Masefield makes heroism burn from a straight description of what was done and of the techniques and courage that did it. Even in propaganda lectures for America, while attributing the war to the evils of an autocracy, he is characteristically reluctant to "abuse our present enemies" ("The War and the Future," in *St. George and the*

Dragon [1919], pp. 65–69). His instincts tend toward the dramatic impersonality of Sherriff's *Journey's End.*

His views on fox-hunting are significantly ambivalent. *Reynard the Fox* is written from an exact identification with the activating instincts of fox, hounds, and huntsmen in turn and without favoritism. The fox, gracious in movement "above all English animals" (*Martin Hyde,* XXIII, p. 283), he loves; and yet he can in his essay "Fox-Hunting" (*Recent Prose* [1924], p. 160) regard a hunt as "the most beautiful and the most stirring sight to be seen in England," the thrill of horn and hounds in cry "ringing into" the "soul" and awaking racial and animal memories "of when one hunted with the pack, or was hunted." But again, the whole novel *The Square Peg* turns on a withering indictment of the brutality and stupidity of hunting. These uncanny balances recall the balance of sensitivity and admiration in Byron's descriptions of a bullfight and the Battle of Waterloo in *Childe Harold* (I; III). When in *Eggs and Baker* two boys engage a bull for fun, they feel that "for the first time, they were really living" (p. 60).

Masefield writes from the heart of human and animal creation. Knowing man's animal instincts and stern destiny, he can forgive much, as in this from *Live and Kicking Ned* (1939, p. 81): "Mind, he was a cruel, terrible savage who had murdered two men, one of them in cold blood. I didn't care about that. I know that I would have given my life to save him. There was something about that fearful creature that I could love and pity." In *The Midnight Folk* (1927; illus. edn. 1931, 135) we hear that "courageous energy is always valued" and criminals accordingly remembered. A corresponding sympathy is accorded all victims of the "unjust cruelty" of "criminal law" (*Martin Hyde,* XXI, p. 263). Where, however, evil is undiluted and sophisticated, the answer is immediate. In *Sard Harker* (1924, p. 318) a declared apostle of evil who scorns rough seamen as brainless slaves is told: "Their religion is to risk their lives and mortify their flesh in order to bring bread to their fellows. . . . In doing that, they make iron swim and dead-weight skim and the dead thing to be beautiful. Show me a finer religion, you who are already carrion for the want of one." Masefield has left little social propaganda, and he prefers insight to morals. Nevertheless, his admiration for the bravery of simple men and his identification with their lot do them honors unknown to propaganda.

His central valuations are imaginative. From *Salt Water Ballads* (1902) onward he is fascinated by ships and navigation. He has written of actual ships in *The Conway* (1933) and *New Chum* (1944)—both on the *Conway*—and in *The Wanderer of Liverpool* (1930). Of these he lists, knows, and loves every detail. Ships, often regarded as living creatures, have the grace and beauty men usually attribute to women (*The Bird of Dawning*, 1933, p. 23), whose place they fill in Masefield's narratives, where his feminine characterizations are slight, the boy-girl Aurelia in *Martin Hyde* being perhaps his best; but in drama his women are strong.

Ships take us to South America, where nature is terrifying, but where there is color, gold to be won, and an atmosphere, as in *Lost Endeavour*, wherein ancient spirit-wisdom survives. The treasure may, as in *On the Spanish Main* (XII, p. 161; XIV, p. 198) and *The Midnight Folk* (as above, illustrated, pp. 6, 274–275), be ecclesiastical treasure. More widely, all gold-quests reflect that gold written into the lyrics "The Golden City of St. Mary" (1902) and "The Seekers (1903?)," with its quest for a "Holy City" beyond the horizon. So the Frenchman of "El Dorado," in *A Tarpaulin Muster* (1907; 50), risking his life for Inca gold, is "a pilgrim, a poet, a person to reverence."

Though seldom a moralist, Masefield has what might be called a "super-morality" and a "super-sociology" concerned with what is basic, elemental, and universal. His evil is the chaos to be mastered by man on every level of craft and art. His wisdom-bearers are outsider types: the anarchic hero of *The Everlasting Mercy*, the half-mad Gaffer of *The Tragedy of Nan* (1909), and the Madman of *Good Friday* (1916), as well as King Cole in *King Cole*. These challenge no particular society; their "wild souls," as the Madman has it, exist as a challenge to society in general, even to life itself.

There is for Masefield "some soul of goodness," to adopt Shakespeare's phrase, in things wild. In the poem "Fire" in *On the Hill* a young Hunter rejects marriage for the powers of nature's vastness:

> I shall ask no more of the world, for the world is here,
> A power so great, it is past man's power to speak;
> Beauty and truth more bright and keen than a spear,
> Joy for the sorrowing man and strength for the weak.
> I fear no horror that death and the world may wreak,
> I am a thing the Fire that burned me bought,
> I am the Fire's now and Fire I seek,
> I have been aware of the wilds and living is nought.

There is much of Shakespeare's Timon in Masefield: the elements, whether as comrades or contestants, are his soulmates. Nevertheless, like Shakespeare, he respects society, for he believes in civilization and order;

but somewhere in what is *wild* lie a beauty and a truth which they lack. This he knows because he is an artist and because he is aware of spirits. The concepts "Beauty" and "Truth," or "Wisdom," recur almost as a theology, but not "Goodness," for ethical terms are soiled. His hope is rather to draw men "to thoughts like planets and to acts like flowers" (*King Cole*).

II

The artist hero of *Dauber* (1913) qualifies painfully as a seaman, battling mast-high in a storm of "devilish" malice (VI). Later he has a fatal accident and dies with the words: "It will go on." So it does, for the great ship comes safe to port: "onwards she thundered, on," "the new-come beauty stately from the sea," moving "like a queen" (VII). The implications are pure Masefield. The word "devilish" is important. Man's conflict with the elements on the material plane of skill and science is part of a wider elemental conflict of demonic and angelic powers. At moments of crisis those greater powers may be sensed.

Two of the best prose narratives, *The Bird of Dawning* (1933) and *Victorious Troy: Or, The Hurrying Angel* (1935), make contact with these powers. In the first a ship engaged in the homeward race of the China traders meets disaster and sinks; and we are with sixteen men in a small boat commanded by the young second mate, Cyril Trewsbury. We follow their fears, angers, hunger, thirst, and thwarted hopes, all demanding of the hero every resource of leadership. The situation is new: "In all his previous sea-service the wrestle had been with the wind, to use it and master it"; now it is only the "appalling water so close at hand" (p. 93). The ocean assumes an evil quality: its waters are "devils," a great wave crests "like the Judgment Day," sharks draw near foreshadowing death (pp. 93–94, 128, 179–180). Against these antagonists stands man's will (p. 122).

In half-sleep the men are "haunted" by evil "shapes" (pp. 172–173); but to Trewsbury on his waking the stars promise a greater power, and he has a conviction of "someone much greater than a human being" who is "trying to convince him that all would be well," a guardian "spirit of blessing," maternal, saintly, and loving (pp. 173–174). Then they find the newly deserted *Bird of Dawning*, man her, and win the race home. The relation of the two parts is loose, but in Masefield's world meaningful: disaster, endurance in a small boat, spirit-help, and the winning through to victory. The elemental antagonist is regarded as evil.

Yet more powerful is *Victorious Troy*. The ship *Hurrying Angel* is commanded by an experienced but tyrannical captain given to drink who runs improper risks to make better time. A cyclone approaches. Through the mind of our eighteen-year-old apprentice hero, Dick Pomfret, we have a succession of sickly atmospheric experiences leading to associations of "The Enemy," "hell," and devils (p. 49). The ship seems to be "suffering" and "crying" for help (p. 48). Impressions of horror accumulate. The water is "malevolent" (p. 133) and the air devilish (p. 193). There is a fiendish quality about it all: "like a revolution or a war, it had drawn into its madness all the sanity near it" (p. 203). There is no sensation of "majesty" or "power," no "big, determined evil, but limitless hordes of selfish evils . . . determined each to rend his neighbour, even if it rent himself" (p. 209). We are told that men have been known to go mad "from the sight of a cyclone sea" (p. 211).

The descriptions attain amazing feats of startling, fantastic, lurid light and color: "a flash of bluish, searing fire" leaps down the mast into the sea, burning, as it seems, "a hole" in it:

> Instead of collapsing, the mizen-mast shone out conspicuously with balls or fuzzes of luminousness, which crowned the snapped cap, went down the lifts to the yardarms, and stuck like globes there. . . . One greenish globe flopped across the poop close to Dick: it was like a fish that he had caught in a night of phosphorescence (p. 204).

Pressure and suspense are maintained by a descriptive coloring the more cogent for its entanglement with every relevant detail of ship and navigation and the psychology of men in peril. When a vast wave threatens destruction, one is not "scared" but just "interested" (p. 83).

The cyclone is a living entity: "it *is* dogs; nothing else could make that noise" (p. 80); or "guns" (pp. 46, 192). Its appalling abnormality is driven home: "This noise could not be wind. This was some new, untested, unknown force coming into the world for the first time" (p. 96). It is alive and it is evil. Its intended victim, the ship, is also alive, "like an animal cruelly hurt, kicking in death" (p. 193).

As in *The Bird of Dawning*, there is help from beyond. The hero, Dick, late from college, has to assume control and, when exhausted, dreams that he is being questioned by an ironically contemptuous Examiner as to the correct procedures to be followed in such a crisis (pp. 184–189). Dick answers as best he may. During the interrogation the Examiner gives advice which is eventually followed. It is more than a dream: "Dick was in a state between sleep and stupor. In that state the

figure of the Examiner seemed present just in front of him" (p. 189).
The spirit-powers use Dick's college memories to get a message through.

The ship loses two of her three masts; she is a hopeless derelict,
foundering. The officers are overboard or out of action. Dick finds the
Captain, grievously hurt. Hitherto he has been unreasonable and brutal,
but he is a fine sailor and a man of authority. He at first curses Dick, but
later softens and ratifies his position in command. The first sign of his
softening comes at the moment when, the cyclone's center being cleared,
the danger is passing. The elemental drama is for an instant reflected into
the human soul. The stars, now again clear, herald salvation, as "Sons of
God" (p. 207). The *Hurrying Angel* is saved, the hero acclaimed, and his
professional future assured. Never was a happy ending more convincingly
won.

In these two narratives elemental evil is mastered by human will,
courage and efficiency, with the aid of spirit-powers greater than the
antagonist. Calamity is not always so averted: the title *Victorious Troy*
refers to the book's sonnet epilogue on the contrasted sufferings of
ancient Troy.

The elemental antagonist may be either sea or land. *Sard Harker*
(1924) and *Odtaa* (1926) are adventure stories set in tropical America
within a surrounding action of imaginary politics, but our main interest
is again in man's contest with nature, with evil through nature, and in
spirits of help.

The sailor Sard, guided by a recurring dream, gets into trouble on
land preventing his return to his ship, the *Pathfinder*. Nature is horrible. Once he has to fight through vegetation "sickly with the forms
and the smell of death," "evil" in its "over-abundant life"; among
poisonous plants and swarming insects; and through a sucking bog which
"chuckles" in triumph (pp. 119, 121, 127). Later, after escaping from a
prison, Sard comes on a house among foothills which radiates goodness.
Good people must once have lived there. He calls but gets no answer, and
yet "he felt quite certain that the thicket was full of people looking at
him" (p. 204). He finds a ruined chapel with faded painted heads in
fresco. For Masefield childhood is a strong power; and in his sleep Sard
hears and sees a boy friend, who had died eleven years before, calling as
from a vast "distance." Above the altar stand blessed figures and a
trumpeter, pointing and urging him to be gone:

> "What is it, Peter? What is it, you great spirits?"
> But the women faded from him, Peter faded from him into the
> wall, but he could still see the shining trumpet and notes like flakes

of fire falling all around him. The trumpet dwindled slowly and resolved itself into the blossoming branch that had grown through a crack in the wall (pp. 207–208).

As he wakes, the figures are again the old frescoes. A smell of burning mingles with his memory of the command to be gone. Warned in time, he escapes a bush fire.

Later, lost among mountains, he sees in "dream or fever" a female figure like the "spirit" of his ship, the *Pathfinder*, "fierce, hard and of great beauty." It says: "I am the *Pathfinder*. I can find a path for you." He is directed to safety. Afterward "it was in his mind all blurred, like the events of a fever, sometimes it seemed the only reality among things dreamed" (pp. 243–244). In such events Masefield works on the borderline of sleep and waking.

In *Odtaa* the eighteen-year-old hero, Highworth Ridden, is plunged into a succession of appalling jungle experiences, again in South America. Alone with his horse he comes up against a horrible bog and a pool of reddened water like "stagnant blood," with hundreds of dead trees standing in it (XII, p. 203). He is starving, blistered, nearly blind (XIV, p. 233).

Once earlier he had awakened by night in mid-jungle: an impulse "from the heart of things was calling him to rise." His horse is staring at something he himself cannot see, and "a wave of fear" passes from animal to man. Whether the enemy is beast or ghost he cannot tell. The tension lessens, and the horse's eyes follow the enemy as it moves slowly round. It again returns: "When it deliberated, its will hardened against them, the horse knew it, and Hi knew it from the horse" (XII, pp. 198–199). There is in or behind nature a more than natural evil, compared with which nature's normal evils are a relief:

Then the night, which for some minutes had seemed to hold her breath, began again to speak with her myriad voices out of the darkness of her cruelty. The whisper and the droning of the forest sharpened into the rustlings of snakes, the wails of victims, the cry of the bats after the moths, and the moan of the million insects seeking blood (XII, pp. 119–120).

Dawn brings the brighter energies of daylight nature. Meanwhile, Hi "had never understood what night was, now he knew" (XII, p. 201; for another account of a ghostly night, see "Ryemeadows" in *Old Raiger and Other Verse* [1964]).

There are good spirit powers also. Hi hears voices advising him, as from a flock of invisible birds (XIV, pp. 228–229). He wins through to comparative safety. In a hut with a stranger, Anselmo, he senses the spirit of a former occupant, Dudley Wigmore (XV, pp. 244–245, 249, 257) and in the "fiery mist" (XV, p. 250) of sleep is aware of its distress. Later in a dream and also *after waking* Hi sees him "distinctly," and, as he fades, the wall too, through him (XVI, p. 263). Wigmore, who had been murdered by Anselmo, urges Hi to escape. Words come immediately without sound: "a sentence floated into his mind as clearly as though a voice had spoken in his ear" (XVI, pp. 263–264). On the way to his escape, Hi sees Dudley Wigmore clearly, by day, and under his direction eludes Anselmo (XVI, pp. 269, 276–277).

Afterward, again in dire straits, Hi is visited in sleep by a figure known in his *childhood* dreams: "all peace, courage, goodness and happiness were in her face" and "hope so bright" that danger pales. As on other such occasions, but even more powerfully, the spirit-reality is not confined to sleep. She helps him to rise, leads and accompanies him, gives him medicaments, and empowers him with a song. "What happened to him in these hours he never knew, save that he was miraculously helped"; "they were among the intensest hours of his life" (XVII, pp. 287–290).

Other novels show similar tendencies. In *The Hawbucks* (pp. 256–257, 261) the hero, battling by night against snow, senses, as in *Odtaa*, his horse's fear and then hears a cry which later turns out to have come either from a girl then dying at a distance or from an intuition of that death received by a woman within call; and in *Eggs and Baker* and *The Square Peg* tragedy is averted by conclusions of spiritualistic tone. In *Martin Hyde* the boy-hero is encouraged by a sense of the presence of his dead father, who had believed in the rightness of Monmouth's cause (XVIII, p. 228; XXIV, p. 293). In *Conquer* an inspiration from some "spirit" (p. 117) enables Origen to save Byzantium.

In our four adventure narratives we have watched heroes faced by hostile nature, together with an evil coming from or from behind nature, and the advent of help from spirit-powers. The conditions of their breaking through are in Masefield's valuations the hero's will and hope; he does not use the word "faith." In the sonnet epilogue to *Victorious Troy* we read of "Hope the living Key unlocking prison"; and "Helpers" are grouped with "Hopes" in the Epilogue to *Grace before Ploughing* (1966).

That such powers attend human adventure is witnessed by Homer, Virgil, and the Old Testament. There are other and recent evidences. In *My Early Life* (1930 and reprints, XXI) Winston Churchill tells us how, when at a loss during his escape from a prison camp in South Africa, he was "led" by an "unconscious or sub-conscious" power, which recalled the power he had known when writing with a "Planchette pencil," to an Englishman's house, and safety. Another interesting experience is recorded in Charles Lindbergh's account of his world-famed Atlantic flight in *The Spirit of St. Louis* (1953; VI, Twenty-Second Hour, pp. 389–90). Troubled by drowsiness and uncertain of his navigation, he became aware of spirits around him—just like the spirits in *Odtaa*—speaking with human voices, "conversing and advising on my flight, discussing problems of my navigation, reassuring me, giving me messages of importance unattainable in ordinary life" (p. 389). He was "on the border-line of life and a greater realm beyond," and death was known as an entry to a greater freedom (p. 390). In Harold Owen's *Journey from Obscurity* (1965) there is a comparable account of ancestral spirits functioning as saviors from an "incalculable distance" (as in *Sard Harker*) during the author's nightmare experience when alone on an evil-impregnated hulk in the south seas. Since then he has been convinced of a reality transcending "all earthly happenings" (Vol. III, 1, pp. 9–10; II, pp. 28–33, 37). Even more impressive is his account of how, on entering his cabin in South Africa, he learned of Wilfred Owen's death, finding his poet brother seated there with soft eyes "trying to make me understand" (XIV, pp. 198–201).

Masefield had himself had a major experience of the paranormal. In *So Long to Learn* (pp. 185–187) he describes how, when his work was not progressing, he heard a male voice say, "The spring is beginning." Soon after, while crossing a fence separating a wood from open ground, the spirit helpers apparently using that action for their purpose, he knew that he was to write "a poem about a blackguard who becomes converted"; the poem appeared "in its complete form, with every detail distinct," and he started writing it down at once. That night, alone in a country house, he continued hour after hour until the door of his room "flung itself noisily wide open." He took the warning and went to bed. *The Everlasting Mercy* (1911) proved the turning point of his literary career.

Such help is perhaps most usually, and certainly most strikingly, experienced by men of action who risk death. Will, courage, hope, and perhaps loneliness and the dark, appear to be favorable conditions. It may happen to a whole community in wartime. When in *St. George and the Dragon* (pp. 5, 17) Masefield writes of "the dead" creating a nation's "great soul," able to guide it in "trouble" and "calamity," or calls the victory at the Marne a "miracle," the phrases are more than decoration. In *The Nine Days Wonder* (54), on the sea rescue at Dunkerque, after observing the "will to help from the whole marine population of these islands," he continues:

> It is hard to think of those dark formations on the sand, waiting in the rain of death, without the knowledge that Hope and Help are stronger things than death. Hope and Help came together in their power into the minds of thousands of simple men, who went out in the Operation Dynamo and plucked them from ruin.

On a national scale the event was of similar quality to those which we have been discussing. The belief in the Angels of Mons arose from a similar recognition.

III

In treating of these events of spiritualistic perception, Masefield handles, with a precision probably finer and more enlightened than that of any of his predecessors, truths that have saturated imaginative literature from the Bible and Homer to Blake, Byron, Ibsen, and the spiritualistic dramas, studied in my book *The Golden Labyrinth*, of the last hundred years. Among our leading contemporary poets, Yeats, Eliot, D. H. Lawrence ("The Ship of Death"; see George A. Panichas, *Adventure in Consciousness* [1964]), Auden ("The Cave of Making," in *About the House*), and Francis Berry (*Ghosts of Greenland*) make poetry from spirit survival and spirit communion; and on all occult matters John Cowper Powys writes as an adept.

His uncanny genius for experienced fact unclouded by theory empowers Masefield's uninhibited treatment of the supernormal. As a boy he came to the *Conway* with a store of ghost stories (*New Chum*, pp. 28–29, 109–110, 117). The short pieces of *A Tarpaulin Muster* are rich in hauntings and fairy lore ("The Pirates of Santa Anna," "Ghosts," etc.); and water spirits are vivid in "Sea Superstitions," in *A Mainsail Haul* (1905; enlarged 1913). In *Sea Life in Nelson's Time* (Epilogue, pp. 216–218) the spirits of long-dead sailors are imagined as watching the good which their sufferings have won for later generations. *In the Mill* (p. 118) recalls an experience by Masefield himself, in a dream, of precognition. Many late poems handle events of an uncanny nature. In the volume *On the Hill* we are in "Jouncer's Tump" fascinated—"it staggers me"—by an old man's unaccountably knowing the contents of an ancient tomb; in "Cry Baby Cottage" by the weepings of a murdered child leading to the discovery of its bones; and in "Blown Hilcote Manor" by an old house filled with "happy folk" from its past. In *The Bluebells and Other Verse*

"John Grimaldi" tells of the well-established yet brief return of a lost sailor which seems to have been caused by his longing for home when he was dying at sea. The narrative poem *Old Raiger* (1964) turns on an act of purposeful soul-projection. In the poem of childhood reminiscences, *Wonderings* (1943), Masefield tells us how as a child he saw "three immense floating giants . . . linked as one." It is presumably these who are recalled in *Grace before Ploughing* (1966; XI, "The Angel") as two linked figures like and yet unlike an angel, of "enormous power."

A too exclusive concentration on spirit-reality, or on mysticism or religious dogma, will no more make great literature than will an exclusive reliance on an earth-plane realism. Imaginative literature arises from the impact of the one category on the other; its central aim is to involve us in the entanglement and interaction. Nor is it enough to state this, however exquisitely, as Eliot states it in his *Four Quartets*: men and spirits are dynamic beings, and only through the literature of action in narrative or drama can their *interaction* be effectively established.

Masefield's balance of animal and spiritual powers may be illustrated by a comparison of *Reynard the Fox* (1919) and *Right Royal* (1920). In the first, emphasis falls on human and animal instinct: the Huntsmen's excitement, the "hot gulps" of scent giving the hounds "agonies of joy," and the Fox's strength failing as he hears "the thud in the blood of his body deeper." The poet is inside each in turn; but this power of "being inside" is itself an agile telepathy beyond sense-perception; like the Fox's own alertness in sleep coming from "the self who needs neither eyes nor ears."

In *Right Royal* the emphasis falls on spirit. The very "Force" of the horse Right Royal is capitalized as almost a spirit-being; we are told that "a Spirit gives some" of his "Power"; and at a crisis his "soul" "thrilled up through each hand" of his rider. The thoughts and desires of people watching the race are like "floatings of fire" affecting the contestants for good or ill. The spirit "Helpers" of those concerned may, like the assisting deities in Homer and Virgil, be invoked. They are powerless to aid the "despairing," but otherwise able from their "glittering" world to assist, when things are difficult, by cunning, indirect, telepathic ways:

> As the white, gleaming gannet eyes fish in the sea,
> So the Thought sought a mortal to bring this to be.

This "thought from the Helper" duly fixes in the mind of a friendly racer who during the race hands it on to the rider of Right Royal, and confidence returns not only to the rider but to the horse also:

All his blood was in glory, all his soul was blown bare,
They were one, blood and purpose, they strode through the air.

"Blood" and spirit-realities, animal and man are intermixed. The action is tangled in recognition of "a world beyond sense," where "man" and "beast," "spirit" and "soul" are in direct communion: "the World as it Is," whence come "Beauty" and "Wisdom," countering the "Fate" which rules existence. Given the psychological conditions, Fate's barrier may be broken and the Helpers act.

The prose narratives already discussed have shown spirit-realities breaking into human existence. Two earlier stories, *Multitude and Solitude* (1909) and *Lost Endeavour* (1910), were written more wholly around this relationship. Masefield established his main axes of reference early.

In the first story a writer, after the death of his idealized love, Ottalie, is led by a series of coincidences to believe that she is impressing him, "using the torn page, the magazine, and the naval officer, as her messengers" (VI, p. 123), to a scientific exploration in Africa to find a cure for sleeping sickness. In Africa the hero and a companion come on a kraal of natives dying from the disease near ancient ruins left by Phoenician goldtraders. They are deserted by their servants and fall ill themselves. A fearful storm, in Masefield's magnificent style, unlooses its terrors; and by night, in this community of dead and dying, his companion unconscious, the lonely hero, himself sick almost to death, endures a sense, as did the other heroes, of a supernatural evil, here associated with the pagan ruins (XI, pp. 266–268). Ottali's "presence is" felt, and he calls for help in his experiment: it was "as though an older, unearthly sister walked with him, half friend, half guide" (XI, pp. 271, 274). Now at last his experiment succeeds, and the two men are saved, though on their return they learn that their discovery has been forestalled.

The medical matters are handled in scientific detail. To science, nature is an enemy: "we are out to fight her wherever we can find her" (X, p. 237). Against nature stand man's courage and will, wresting victory, inspired and aided by the dead. The key thought is: "Perhaps the dead look on the living souls as notes in a music, and play upon them, making harmony or discord, according to the power of their wills and the quality of their nature" (II, p. 31).

Within a surrounding action of seventeenth-century slavery and buccaneering in Central America, *Lost Endeavour* concentrates on the finding of a community living near the ruins of an ancient civilization, preserving its traditions and faith and expecting the advent of a young

leader and the return of the old gods. This community practices a magic
such as would be condemned by the Christian Church (2; X, pp. 205–
208). There is a temple with hieroglyphs in Egyptian style and walls
ablaze with color.

Masefield's historical imagination is fascinated by ancient ruins: at
home, the hill camp and fortifications of *A Book of Discoveries*; in Africa,
the Phoenician ruins of *Multitude and Solitude* and the mysterious white
civilization in *Live and Kicking Ned* (1939); in the East, the carved
memorials of a golden age in the poem "Pavilastukay" (*Natalie Maisie
and Pavilastukay* [1942]). In America there is the chapel of *Sard Harker*
and an ancient Sun Temple in *Odtaa* (XVI). In *Lost Endeavour* the
theme is exploited in direct relation to Masefield's spiritualistic insights,
which are here given their philosophy. There is a higher wisdom and
magic than that of the Indian community, "preserved at a college of
priests" on an adjacent island (2; X, p. 210) and to be related to that "immortal nature" of which our world of color and odor is a mere shadow
and which itself is "shadow" of a yet "higher spirit" (2; XI, p. 211).

One of our two heroes fights towards this island college through a
"nightmare" jungle of "pulpy" vegetation, poison-weeds and spikes like
"skeleton fingers," where "a low kind of life festered and wallowed." The
question is "which should win"—it or man with his wits and machete
(2; XI, pp. 220–222). There is a smell "as of death," such as is always
found "where nature is left alone to her luxury and waste." When the man
is near exhaustion, the forest is full of "fiendish glee"; but he recovers. A
strange sound turns out to be a "war-whistle" made from a stream filling
an artificial receptacle with holes (2; XII, pp. 224, 228; XIII, p. 233).

He climbs to a sea view, with now "a salt clean tang" in the air (2;
XIII, p. 236). From this height at sunset the woods below, no longer hideous, flame out scarlet, crimson, and gold. His "guardian spirit" offers him
shelter in an ancient cave cell with an altar and mosaics, wherein are
remains of a long-dead priestess "of some higher race than the Indians"
(2; XIV, p. 238). Here he has a dream:

My dream was not like common dreaming, in which the dream
dominates the personality; but wonderful and kingly, my own self,
awake and strong, directing my own actions. When I say that I
dreamed I express myself badly. I should say that I woke up into a
new and vivid life, more splendid than this, a life of intenser colour
and finer ecstasy, in a world conducted by another intelligence and
governed by other laws. It was, as I suppose, the real world, of
which this world is nothing but the passing shadow. I woke up,

then, in the cave where I had fallen asleep, but I woke up into its
reality. The walls of hewn stone were changed to opal in which fire
burned. The fire on the hearth was like visible music. I cannot
describe the beauty of the flame in any other way. The trees outside
stood like an array of knights in mail. Their fruits were like lamps,
their leaves like jewels (2; XV, pp. 243).

Old plaques take on color and life. Two great serpents hiss and sway to
a sound of drums. He is somehow "aloft," looking down on his own
body. There is music:

Then, in the middle of the music, the inner wall parted with a
crash, and I was within, touching the altar, which glowed red like a
great pulsing ember. It was like a heart, contracting and expanding.
It was an ecstasy to touch it; for it was no longer a slab of rock for
sacrifice. It was the very heart of the goddess which received the
sacrifice (2; XV, p. 244).

The "withered" remains of the long-dead priestess become alive: "The
figure rose slowly, full of life and power; glowing with life that was like an
internal fire, visible and tangible to me" (2; XV, p. 245). Throughout,
sensory perception is strong. Senses ("visible music") mix, dissolved into
a direct perception including all senses but dependent on none.

Suddenly he is standing outside the cave cell, on a hill, seeing the
island as a map and the Temple of Wisdom. Then he is back in the cave.
Relics and dust are as before. The grand snakes are mosaics; the priestess
is a shriveled figure beneath a cloth. He finds the Temple, massively
loaded with "golden carvings," "the worth of a kingdom" (2; XVI, p. 254),
but for the rest, there are only skeletons. The inhabitants had died from a
pestilence, unknown to the Indians on the mainland.

The story is saturated with spirit-properties. Again and again the
mind receives "something like a word spoken inside my brain," which
some would call "an intuition or some other absurd name, such as the
English delight to make for things which they do not understand" (2; X, p.
198). "The Occult Way" is said to be "for the enlargement of Human
Knowledge, which must ever be the aim of a Rational Man" (2; VII,
p. 183). The book's crammed sensory effects are one with the occult sig-
nificances: "I felt that those lands and islands, where the moon is glorious
and the air is heavy with spice as though incense was always being crushed,
were full of all manner of presences" (2; VII, p. 187). The natives are
attuned to what lies beyond: "It needs the Indian life to make it all that—
fireflies, and the moon coming, and the incense smouldering on the

copper; but if I had an Indian drum here, and could beat long enough, as the Indians beat, I would take you out of your personal lives into the life into which all life ebbs at death" (2; XII, p. 229). Masefield's imaginative obsession with tropical America in all its natural threat and golden promise is explained. Gold may be either treasure to loot or a spiritual symbol; in *Lost Endeavour* the Temple's gold is finally looted by unprincipled men, to the distress of the two heroes, who try to prevent the sacrilege.

Multitude and Solitude and *Lost Endeavour* are patterned on man's will to control nature by, in the one, a spirit-guided science and, in the other, magic. Magic, as in Shakespeare's *The Tempest*, has a poetic authority not readily present in theology or metaphysics; it is more dramatic, and it is dramatic because it concerns human activity within an environment to be mastered.

Lost Endeavour turns on "some secret, long forgotten by the white races," which is able to establish direct "communion" with supernal powers: "And why, in that great strange land, overgrown with forests, in which mysterious peoples had built and vanished, should there not be a record of wisdom, wilder and stranger than any wisdom preserved by us?" "Wilder": this is a key thought (3; XIV, p. 352). Here, as in *Pavilastukay*, Masefield's emphasis corresponds to John Cowper Powys' intuitions, studied in my book *The Saturnian Quest*, of a lost, golden life-way hard to recover.

We today probably find magic easier to accept when mediated through childhood fantasy. *The Midnight Folk* (1927) and *The Box of Delights* (1935) handle lightly and often with a delightful humor substances elsewhere within Masefield's serious concern: woodlore and animals, hunting, piratical adventures. Many of the more amazing events, such as the adventures into the mythological or historical past, have imaginative validity. The philosophic and the absurd join forces. In *The Box of Delights* the metaphysics of Time make brilliant fun in Arnold of Todi's song (X), and the melodramatic villain Abner's argument on the good done by his multifarious villainies offers a fascinating insight into the moral paradoxes of life and letters (XI). When in *The Midnight Folk* (illus. ed., 1931; pp. 157, 275, 279) the image of "the lovely golden lad," St. George, is missing from the salvaged ecclesiastical treasure, being still with the Mermaids, we have a symbolic gem inviting depth on depth of interpretation.

Magical paradises of sea depths or woodland have visionary impact. The boy-hero's many flights in sleep are of the kind known as "astral projection" and may be related to a remarkable passage on crashing death followed by release and thoughts of ascending flight in *A Book of Discoveries* (pp. 155–156). On one of these flights, in *The Midnight Folk* (p. 200), he enjoys clairvoyant insight of the townspeople as they sleep: "There they all were, and floating about them as they slept were the loveliest people Kay had ever seen; they were like people made of light and of rainbows, and with exquisite faces and hands." Both stories work on the interplay of sleep and waking life in such a way as to jostle the spiritualistic and the normal. When halfway through *The Midnight Folk* the dream events unexpectedly become part of daylight reality, the shock is purposeful: it happened like that in *Lost Endeavour* and *Odtaa*. Similarly, when pictures come alive we are reminded of *Lost Endeavour*, *Sard Harker*, *Melloney Holtspur* (1922), and *The Dream* (1922). Masefield's two child-fantasies may be read as introductions to his world.

Cole Haulings, in *The Box of Delights*, the Punch and Judy wizard at home in all ages of history, is a relative, or more, of the central figure of what is probably Masefield's most important poetic narrative, *King Cole* (1921). A disgruntled traveling circus in bad luck and ill humor is confronted by King Cole, who since death has returned as "an old, poor, wandering man with glittering eyes" to help those in distress. His dialogue with the Showman is a fine example of unforced stychomythia:

SHOWMAN: What trade are you?
KING COLE: I am a wandering man.
SHOWMAN: You mean, a tramp who flutes for bread and pence?
KING COLE: I come, and flute, and then I wander thence.
SHOWMAN: Quicksilver Tom who couldn't keep his place.
KING COLE: My race being run, I love to watch the race.
SHOWMAN: You ought to seek your rest.
KING COLE: My rest is this,
The world of men, wherever trouble is.

Fluting, he leads the mud-bedraggled circus through the town. As his "soul" enters his fluting, "the spirits that inhabit dream" gather round him. The circus takes on glory: "they shone like embers as they trod the road." Then:

And round the tired horses came the Powers
That stir men's spirits, waking or asleep,
To thoughts like planets and to acts like flowers,

> Out of the inner wisdom's beauty deep:
> These led the horses, and, as marshalled sheep
> Fronting a dog, in line, the people stared
> At those bright wagons led by the bright-haired.
>
> And, as they marched, the spirits sang, and all
> The horses crested to the tune and stept
> Like centaurs to a passionate festival
> With shining throats that mantling criniers swept
> And all the hearts of all the watchers leapt
> To see those horses passing and to hear
> That song that came like blessing to the ear.
>
> And, to the crowd the circus artists seemed
> Splendid, because the while that singing quired
> Each artist was the part that he had dreamed
> And glittered with the Power he desired,
> Women and men, no longer wet or tired
> From long despair, now shone like queens and kings,
> There they were crowned with their imaginings.

King Cole's spirit-magic is bedded in human psychology; the glorified circus is an externalization of a "Power" already humanly conceived, and so existent. It is also embedded in earth-nature. Masefield's favorite country animals are present: foxes, hares, rabbits, stoats, mice; birds who "bring delight and understanding" to man; and flowers. They remind the Prince, who is visiting the town, of his childhood:

> Once in my childhood, in my seventh year,
> I saw them come, and now they have returned,
> Those strangers, riding upon cars that burned,
> Or seemed to burn, with gold, while music thrilled . . .

The circus artists bring "Beauty and Wisdom." They are later called "the Bringers Down of Beauty from the stars." They are honored both for their athletic "skill" and also for "wisdom." Their circus rises beyond the daily "coil" of existence; its art is "lived" within "eternity" beyond worldly miseries, in "speed," "colour," and "beauty." It is an ordinary circus, no more. Its glory was simply the artists and their art seen as by a spiritual X-ray, like Kay Harker's clairvoyance.

The performance is successful. The tent is struck, the circus gone, King Cole alone as night falls, piping of man's troubled life, until he fades. What he has revealed is what all of us, at times, may know:

> But where the juggler trudged beside his love
> Each felt a touching from beyond our ken,
> From that bright kingdom where the souls who strove
> Live now for ever, helping living men.
> And as they kissed each other; even then
> Their brows seemed blessed, as though a hand unseen
> Had crowned their loves with never-withering green.

Love, art, and spirit-communion, all are as one, from the one "kingdom."

The poem is warmly realized. Its Berkshire terrain is exactly located, and King Cole a legendary figure known in carols. It is beautifully patterned on the inter-shifting planes of sordid exterior and inward glory.

The natural medium for occult projection is drama, and Masefield's dramatic achievements are powerful. In *Philip the King* (1914), a poetic drama recalling Aeschylus' *Persae*, Philip awaits news of the Armada. His imperial pride is countered by avenging spirit voices from those whom he or his nation has wronged, at home and abroad. Receiving news of the outcome from ghosts of his lost sailors and a messenger, he accepts disaster with a noble, and religious, equanimity. His imperialism is one with his religious faith, and there is no dramatic condemnation, except, following *The Persae*, against his pride. Fate rules:

> We are pieces played,
> Not moving as we will, but as we are made.

Chastened, he plans another Armada. Throughout, historic insight combines with numinous perception.

The Tragedy of Nan (prod. 1908; pub. 1909) and *Melloney Holt-spur* (1922) are major works. In the first the emphasis is on the earth-plane, and in the second on spirit life; but both dramatize the interplay. Both have powerful, wronged, heroines.

Nan, a drama in the Gloucestershire dialect of rustic life and sordid deeds by the Severn, is close to earth and country ways, to farm life and woodland and the great river whose flood dominates the conclusion. From these flower its glory. The girl Nan is probably Masefield's best feminine creation. Her father had been unjustly hanged for stealing, and she is herself further wronged on all sides by human baseness. She murders her unworthy lover and, inspired by broken phrases from the wandering yet half-purposeful mind of the old Gaffer, goes garlanded for death to drown herself in the flood, our sense of tragic exaltation being echoed by the Gaffer's cry accompanying, in morality's despite, Nan's crime: "O Love, you be a King. A King."

The driving force, as in Shakespeare's *Timon of Athens*, is that great Love which for Nan has been desecrated and for which she dies. The drama raises tragedy to glory, but the glory is earth-based and redolent of earthly experience, including Nan's ghastly, yet applauded, deed.

Symbols flower from actual events. The horn of a coach becomes in the Gaffer's mind a horn calling Nan, hoofbeats correspond to heartbeats: "The horn. The horn. Gold hoofs beating on the road. They beat like the ticking of a 'eart. Soon. Very soon. The golden trump." A Gold Rider assumes presence, slaying ghosts, slaying death-as-death: "Angels. Gold Angels. The devil walks the dark at twelve. Ghosts. Ghosts. Behind the white 'edstones. Smite 'em, Gold Rider. Smite 'em with thy bright sharp spear" (III). "Gold Angels" both suggest the St. George–figured coins paid to Nan by the Government in recompense for her father's unjust execution and blend into the Gold Rider, a St. George figure whose horse's hoofbeats are also those of the coach in which the Government officials are to return. The Severn Bore is a natural event, but is here also a summoning as from a dimension beyond death. The interlockings awake intimations that what on one level are chance events may on another shadow purposes unguessed. As Pope tells us in his *Essay on Man* (I, 57–60):

> So Man, who here seems principal alone,
> Perhaps acts second to some sphere unknown,
> Touches some wheel, or verges to some goal;
> 'Tis but a part we see, and not a whole.

In *Multitude and Solitude* the hero was led to his destiny by a series of spirit-impelled "chances."

In *Melloney Holtspur* Melloney has been deeply wronged by her artist lover, Lonny Copshrews, and after the death of both impresses a person on earth to reveal his deeds to the mother of his daughter's lover in order to obstruct the girl's marriage. The action, involving two generations and two types of existence, is complicated for the reader but would be clear in performance. Lonny wants the "old stain washed away" (II) by the new generation, but Melloney and the Man in Armor, a figure in the old house serving as the voice of cosmic law, demand his suffering.

There are three orders of dramatic conflict: that on earth; that of Melloney and Lonny as earth-bound spirits in mutual opposition; and that of the one drama with the other. The influence of spirits on human beings is accepted as normal: "This life is a mysterious game, and we only play half our game ourselves" (I). There are three children of brilliantly characterized talk, one of whom enjoys a direct sight of Melloney's spirit such as the other two cannot because "they have not the power" (III).

Dramas of spirit vengeance and evil descending from one generation to the next date back to the Greeks; and when Lonny denounces the law refusing to let evil dissolve, we are in the world of Aeschylus' *Oresteia*. *Melloney Holtspur* brings to the Aeschylean and Shakespearean tradition insights learned from the spiritualistic advances of our century. Never was the hell of self-recognition and self-judgment, adumbrated by the tragic heroes of Shakespeare and by Byron's Manfred and asserted by Spiritualism, more fearfully convincing than in Lonny Copshrew's agony as he watches his past actions maturing through the revengeful Melloney to hurt his daughter. Melloney is no angel. She is in her own hell of earth-bound vengeance. The only ultimate authority here is the Man in Armor, who insists on "atonement" (IV). What exactly that means and how it eventually comes is not quite clear, but come it does: Melloney forgives, she and Lonny are freed from their torment, and the young are made happy.

The agonizing results of wrong-doing are before us, but we also hear that Lonny, being a great artist, had, whatever his sins, "greatness of soul" (III). Masefield's own valuations are regularly more aesthetic than ethical. What he here dramatizes is less a judgment than the inevitable sequence, which Spiritualism teaches, of cause and effect: "You set the wheel of the law moving. It has to go on to fulfillment" (IV). This is probably the most authoritative spiritualistic drama yet composed. Asked what is Reality, the Man in Armor, blending the creeds of Nietzsche and of Spiritualism, answers: "The godhead of man. The brotherhood of man. The communion of spirits" (II).

IV

We have considered works entangling the spiritualistic and the earthly. Christianity, dramatizing the Incarnation, is our supreme imaginative expression of this entanglement. We often do well to regard the Christian myth as symbolic of general truths. All men are spirits mysteriously incarnated into earthly life; all are potentially sons of God; and all pass through suffering and death to a new state, or resurrection, of a plenitude no less than physical. Were the Christian dogmas not widely relevant, humanity would not have responded. So also the Christian's belief in Christ's presence is as a universalization of the experience of all ages and races, culminating in modern Spiritualism, that those who have died exist as powers. It follows that a poet by nature or experience spiritualistically attuned will be the better qualified to handle the Christian myth. I use the term "myth" advisedly, since I am regarding the Christian story, including all its miracles and marvels, in terms rather of imaginative authenticity than of ecclesiastical command.

If indeed his Helpers guided Masefield when in literary difficulties to compose, as he tells us, a narrative poem on the theme of Christian conversion, they chose wisely: for nothing could hold better promise of both poetic power and popular response.

The Everlasting Mercy (1911) presents an anarchic young man—poacher, fighter, and drinker—whose violences culminate in a denunciation of society and his charging by night through the town naked, ringing the fire bell, banging on doors, and shouting that hell is let loose. Like Shakespeare's Timon, Saul Kane denounces society as a "sanctimonious crowd" of petty vices, and condemns the Parson and his Church as time-serving descendants of Caiaphas helping to crush the poor while supporting privilege in the name of God. The Parson has his defence. The existing order has come about through centuries of laborious growth, and it does, in fact, work, however imperfectly:

> We're neither saints nor Philip Sidneys,
> But mortal men with mortal kidneys.

The balance is held. Even so, this couplet acts as a reminder of superlative human excellences, in church and state; and the poem's power is lodged not in the Parson but in the hero who, though an unbeliever, claims kinship to those "sons of light" preferred by Christ to the "trained" mind that merely "talks" of light while remaining skeptical of any genuine experience.

Christian feeling, intermittent throughout, rises to a climax at the hero's conversion:

> And in my heart the drink unpriced,
> The burning cataracts of Christ.

The crashing power of this needs no advertisement, but its exact nature may be missed. Official Christianity is respected, but what the poem's *action* offers is at once more Pauline and more Nietzschean. Saul Kane's violences, like Paul's (or Saul's) first "threatenings and slaughters" (Acts IX, 1), rise from a directionless power subsequently directed, from negative to positive; but it is all one power. As Pope tells us in his *Essay on Man* (II, 183–184):

> The surest Virtues thus from Passions shoot,
> Wild Nature's vigor working at the root.

The names "Kane" and "Saul" define the transition.

It is possible over a number of years to recognize this and to recognize the compacted force of the "cataracts" couplet, without recognizing that the two recognitions are the same. "All convincing imagery," writes John Davidson, "is scientific truth" (*The Triumph of Mammon* [1907], Epilogue, p. 160). The couplet could be suggesting a new, more fiery "drink" for the "heart," in place of Kane's former intoxicants; but there is more to it than that. During his period of intransigency he had compared himself to the "sons of light," and his conversion is now given the line "O glory of the lighted mind." The "burning cataracts," soft syllables supervening on harsh, are *the powers of Niagara transmuted to electricity, torrential water to light, passion to spirit.* In pursuance of his habitual insights into the elemental powers, Masefield has composed a couplet that rings supreme in the poetry of conversion. Thereafter in the poem the word "Christ," so often feared, is daringly reiterated. The poet has won this freedom.

Good Friday (1916) stands supreme among British dramas of Christ. The Trial and Crucifixion are approached through an exact respect to historical detail. Jesus himself does not appear, but his presence is felt, and the nature of his challenge is defined by the aged Madman, personifying martyrdom; once rich, but now, for having seen "truth like a perfect crystal, life its flaw," blinded and a beggar. His central speech is synchronized with, and enacts for us, the Crucifixion.

Wild birds have their flight, but whenever the "wild souls of men"—men with the wildness and vision of Saul Kane and the Hunter of *Fire*—step beyond their companions' blindness to "where the skies unclose," they are met by "the spitting mob" like a "bull gone mad." (Masefield's poem of reminiscences, *Wonderings*, records what terror a bull could be to him in childhood.)

Like those earlier visionaries, Jesus is now himself suffering. He is regarded not as unique, but as one of many:

> Beauty and peace have made,
> No peace, no still retreat,
> No solace, none.
> Only the unafraid
> Before life's roaring street
> Touch Beauty's feet,
> Know Truth, do as God bade,
> Become God's son.

Only he with the courage for it becomes, like Jesus, "God's son"; but the way is open to all. There is a pause. Then, with yet another emphasis on courage:

> Darkness, come down, cover a brave man's pain,
> Let the bright soul go back to God again.
> Cover that tortured flesh, it only serves
> To hold that thing which other power nerves.
> Darkness, come down, let it be midnight here,
> In the dark night the untroubled soul sings clear.

> [*It darkens*]

> I have been scourged, blinded and crucified,
> My blood burns on the stones of every street
> In every town; wherever people meet
> I have been hounded down, in anguish died.

> [*It darkens*]

> The creaking door of flesh rolls slowly back;
> Nerve by red nerve the links of living crack,
> Loosing the soul to tread another track.

The voice should pause, and its tone change for "another track."

After the agony comes release, and to the understanding of it we must bring full knowledge of Masefield's spiritualistic insights:

> Beyond the pain, beyond the broken clay,
> A glimmering country lies
> Where life is being wise,

All of the beauty seen by truthful eyes
Are lilies there, growing beside the way.
Those golden ones will loose the torted hands,
Smooth the scarred brow, gather the breaking soul,
Whose earthly moments drop like falling sands
To leave the spirit whole.
Now darkness is upon the face of the earth.

The lines are to be read as widely applicable for all such men of suffering
and courage. The "Golden Ones" are spirit guardians waiting to welcome
the new arrival, as when in A Play of St. George (1948) Spirits guide
the martyred hero beyond death, asking him to listen for the music,
saying, "That is the language here."

The Madman's central speech is in itself a compacted drama.
Masefield has a Shakespearean power of rising to a supreme occasion,
though Shakespeare never handled such an occasion as this. The Crucifixion lines have a dramatic force scarcely equaled, certainly never sur-
passed, in English; and the conclusion holds a spirit gospel whose every
phrase demands an exact reading.

Good Friday is not doctrinally governed; it handles the living facts
on which doctrine was subsequently based. Masefield himself moves
cautiously in that direction. The less vivid prose-drama The Trial of Jesus
(1925) develops more fully Jesus' Messianic claim to divine sonship. In
The Coming of Christ (1928) various Spirits discuss with Anima Christi,
"the Soul of Christ," his coming Incarnation; and though he is called the
"Divine One," there is also fear of the Incarnation inspiring "some future
creed" for "the apathy about Man's brutal heart." When one of the
Shepherds bases his belief in God on certain saving experiences he has
known like those recurring in Masefield's prose stories, we have an interesting link. Easter (1929) dramatizes not the physical resurrection of a
man but the appearance from the tomb of the "Anima Christi" which
Mary Magdalene, thinking of the man, calls "His quickened spirit."

In these later, small dramas Masefield is trying so far as may be to
develop his visionary Christianity, as the life of Jesus was developed by
the Church, to include the philosophical and the doctrinal. He does not
so much follow doctrine as identify himself with the process of its
making. He is still writing from his own imaginative center.

Masefield's beliefs never range far from the humanistic and the
spiritualistic. The creed of Melloney Holtspur includes "the godhead of
man," and any man brave enough may, in the Madman's words, become
"God's son." In Pavilastukay the hero finds ruins of a golden age:

> Slowly, still marvelling, he crossed the grass
> Towards the Palace, thinking "This was wrought
> By men who never let Life's minute pass
> But stretched their eager hands to it, and caught,
> And pressed this glory from it, strength and thought
> Working as one, to this undying thing
> In praise of Man, Earth's only god and king."

That, though not to be read as a final or inclusive statement, is part of Masefield's poetic world, in alliance with other apprehensions.

V

Masefield's strength is one with the sternness of his outlook. His *Collected Poems* (1923) opens with "A Consecration," promising to write of the abandoned and unhonored; and from buccaneer to prophet, he has done so. Fearful, mostly unjust, hangings, as in *The Camden Wonder* (1909), *Nan, The Widow in the Bye Street* (1912), *Eggs and Baker, Dead Ned* (1938), and presumably *The Condemned Cell* (1927?, not published), are an obsession. Never were Christ's physical sufferings more unflinchingly described than in *The Trial of Jesus*. *Sea Life in Nelson's Time* is a cold and cauterizing account of how our "naval glory" was built by the agonies of "barbarously maltreated men" (p. 123). Modern war is presented in stark, factual outline. Nowhere in literature is elemental nature more fearful.

In *Pavilastukay*—on the lost golden age—we are told that contemporary man "gives his brief gasp to cut his brother's throat"; that, though nature is pitiless, "Man is not Nature but a something gained," gained at "great cost" and now in peril. Splendour once existed:

> Pray not to any god for it, but plan,
> Imagine, work, determine, struggle still
> That out of modern man there may come MAN.

Despite
>   any devilry devised
> By things called soldiers serving things called states,

the thought of Pavilastukay remains a "star." What has been, can be, though "man's paces as a spirit are not swift" (*The Wanderer of Liverpool*, p. 80).

The seventy pieces, most of them sonnets, of *Lollingdon Downs*

(1917) probe the copresence in man of physical brittleness and spiritual power; nothing of skepticism is shirked, nor its countering by deathless intimations. In "The Night of Kings" (*The Bluebells and Other Verse*) a balance of spirit evidence and skepticism is subtly related to the birth of Christ. "A Creed" (1910?; in *Ballads and Poems*) is a memorable statement on reincarnation. Such poems go as far as static enquiry can, but Masefield's greater contribution is in the dynamics of narrative and drama, since beauty only "lives in the attempt to make it ours" (*The Wanderer of Liverpool*).

We are not alone. However dark the hour, there is always some "muttering from beyond the veils of Death" ("August, 1914"). In *King Cole* we learn that "up on the bitter iron there is peace" and that "there is a help that the abandoned know." In *Grace before Ploughing* ("Early Reading") Masefield records his early certainty of pre-existence, survival, and "spiritual powers" ready to help "bright human endeavour." His life has been given to the defining of this help. It depends on man; it is born of his hope, awakes his courage, and makes him godlike. The heroic, though seldom colored except through the actions concerned, is once finely enphrased when the troops at Gallipoli are seen as "bronze"-bodied "gods," more "grand" in their "half-nakedness" than "clad men" (*Gallipoli*, p. 165). Courage is spirit-prompted. In "The Hounds of Hell" (*Enslaved and Other Poems* [1920]) St. Withiel twice fails in courage before a pack of devil-hounds ravaging the land. The third time he is encouraged by caroling bird-spirits whose task it is, we are told, to reveal to man *his* own resources, which he cannot know "unless we give the clue." Then brave, he faces the pack, and at once the horror shrivels.

Birds may be spirits, and so, with their "steeple"-pointing masts (*Sard Harker*, p. 25), driven by the upper airs to plunge through ocean, may ships. The names *Bird of Dawning*, *Hurrying Angel* (in *Victorious Troy*), and *Pathfinder* (in *Sard Harker*) are significant: the *Pathfinder* actually appears as a spirit. The experience can touch ecstasy, as in this passage from "Being Ashore," in *A Tarpaulin Muster* (1907), on voyaging off the River Plate:

We were tearing along across a splendour of sea that made you sing. Far as one could see there was the water shining and shaking. Blue it was, and green it was, and of a dazzling brilliance in the sun. It rose up in hills and in ridges. It smashed into foam and roared. It towered up again and toppled. It mounted and shook in a rhythm, in a tune, in a music. One could have flung one's body to it as a sacrifice. One longed to be in it, to be a part of it, to be beaten and banged by it. It was a wonder and a glory and a terror. It was a triumph, it was royal, to see that beauty.

And later, after a day of it, as we sat below, we felt our mad ship taking yet wilder leaps, bounding over yet more boisterous hollows, and shivering and exulting in every inch of her. She seemed filled with a fiery, unquiet life. She seemed inhuman, glorious, spiritual. One forgot that she was man's work. We forgot that we were men. She was alive, immortal, furious. We were her minions and servants. We were the star-dust whirled in the train of the comet. We banged our plates with the joy we had in her. We sang and shouted, and called her the glory of the seas.

Against "the base ones of the spiritual world," for there are bad spirits enough, a fine ship is "guarded by a presence erect, winged, fiery" from the "intellectual kingdom," strong and "mailed" ("Ghosts," in *A Tarpaulin Muster*).

But it is only because Masefield knows and loves every fact and artifact of their constitution, every spar, bolt, and rope and the exact stresses on each at any moment of good or evil fortune, and what to do about it, that he has the right, of a kind perhaps which no comparable writer has ever had, to know ships as spiritual entities. There is no sentimentalizing. Ships are life itself, in its danger, its suffering, and its perfection. Within a ship there may be "a hell": "men mutinous, officers overdriven, boys in misery, the captain drunk"; yet from without she is an "image of wonder," and "one should not question beauty" (*Captain Margaret* [1908], p. 274).

The Wanderer of Liverpool (1930) is an account in prose and poetry, with name lists, dates, statistics, technical descriptions, and pictures, of the various voyages of Masefield's favorite, ill-fated ship. It is a love relationship and has a notable farewell entitled "Wanderer and Wonderer":

> We two were subtlier linked than most
> By thrilling atoms of the ghost
>
> And shall perhaps be, still, anon,
> In wondering and wandering on,
>
> From whence none knows, to where none knows,
> Save from the gas-whirl to the rose,

And from the rose to man, and thence
To spirit that has beaten sense.

To that that can annihilate,
To Heat, all Death, to Light, all Fate,

And is all spirit, spark and spur,
Magnificence and minister,
To Wonderer and Wanderer.

So he parts, for a while, from his "sea-wandering bird" (p. 119).

We today study and use physical creation without recognition of the spirit-powers lending it life, form, and grace. Our art is consequently chaotic, ugly, and inert. In place of intellectual obscurity and psychological disease Masefield offers lucidity and health; in place of inertia, action. This he can do because he knows both the worst terrors of terrestrial existence and the sources of help.

In his *Shakespeare and Spiritual Life* (1924), on Shakespeare's entangling of supernatural phenomena with human drama, he has left us a valuable comment on *The Tempest:* "The attainment of intellectual power, being a life-work in itself, takes the man who should be the ruler from his government: he is thereupon deposed by the knavish and the greedy, and cast out among the brutish: unless he can bend spirits to his aid, this world will be no safe place for his daughter." The word "bend," following the beliefs of Shakespeare's play, is misleading. Elsewhere, in accord with the teachings and experiences of modern Spiritualism, Masefield knows that no such "bending" is in question. The Helpers are waiting, and it is for us to make possible their entry.

God in Modern Poetry

by

Derek Stanford

I

MY OPENING THEME IN THIS ARTICLE IS POETRY AND REVELATION SEEN AS part of a wider scheme—God in contemporary poetry. This means that the kind of revelation with which we are concerned is revelation of God; that the field in which we are going to observe it is the field of poetry; and that we will fix our attention on the twentieth century. But before we proceed to examine specific instances, we should first consider the nature of revelation in general.

I want in this essay, as far as I can, to avoid the temptation of the highfalutin. I want to suggest that poetry (in whatever high region its branches may spread) has its roots in the soil and the stress of daily living. Agreeing, then, to be as down-to-earth as possible, let us ask ourselves what we mean when we use that common turn of speech, "it came as a revelation to me." Clearly we do not keep this idiom solely for matters of an exalted nature. We apply it on a hundred different occasions: to the sudden understanding of a friend's action, to the dawning appreciation of a problem that had previously baffled our intelligence, to anything that rapidly shows itself in a new, unusual, or unexpected light. And here, perhaps, we can pause a moment, for I think we have sufficiently arrived at a clue to the nature of revelation: it is a showing, a spontaneous unveiling, and it is always firsthand and fresh. What it is not (though there is no reason why it should run counter to these things) is explanation or accepted knowledge. It clears the steps of logic at one leap, and it adds to, rather than repeats, what we possess.

But I do not want to claim too much for my subject. What we are especially to study here is not what we know as divine revelation. Poetic revelation carries with it no sanction or authority of Bible, Church, or Creed. Its only credential is that of, its only appeal that to, the imagination. But the way in which this faculty, whether of believer or of unbeliever, frames an image or notion of God is obviously a matter of interest to Christians. It tells us, among other things, a little of what the subconscious mind of our time is thinking and of how the object of its thought is being treated.

In a fashion, of course, all revelation is revelation of God, the ground of our being. In this sense all revelation refers to the First Mover by telling us about ourselves as His creation or about the universe which He set in motion. But what to the mystic's inner eye may appear as continuous affirmation of God's being, to the world as a whole wears a more motley dress. I should like, then, to make a preliminary distinction between that poetry in which the revelation speaks in positive terms of God and that in which it expresses itself negatively in terms of deprivation. Since so much of the poetry of our day is poetry of *negative revelation*, I will begin with this.

When Nietzsche, in the eighties of the last century, proclaimed the death of God, his statement helped to change the Western world. Naturally enough, it did not change God, but it played its part in changing man's awareness of Him. It helped, as do all negative expressions, to injure and impede the means by which we find access to what is positive. In other words, the declaration of God's death assisted in a very real sense toward the decay and the decrease of vision.

The consequence of this—for those who accepted Nietzsche's statement—was that the world too seemed to be dying. In this essay I am concerned with contemporary poetry, with verse that has been written in our lifetime. But if we go back to Nietzsche's day, we find his *Gotterdämmerung* restated in a conscious deathward movement in the arts. This movement, which was self-styled the Decadence, continued, sometimes underground and sometimes in the open, until it culminated in the poetry of the 1920's—the peak period of disintegration.

Here, in poem after poem, the body of the world is mirrored for us flawed, breaking, or already fragmented. One poet, Edgell Rickwood, with a kind of magniloquent pessimism, entitled a certain piece of his "For the Passing of the Entire Scheme of Things." William Butler Yeats, in "The

Second Coming," presented an apocalyptic picture of a humanity with its hub or axle removed:

> Things fall apart; the centre cannot hold;
> Mere anarchy is loosed upon the world,
> The blood-dimmed tide is loosed, and everywhere
> The ceremony of innocence is drowned;
> The best lack all conviction, while the worst
> Are full of passionate intensity.

Significantly the next three lines take us to the heart of our subject. "Surely some revelation is at hand," writes the poet. "Surely the Second Coming is at hand." But this "revelation," this "Second Coming" is not of Christ but of the Anti-Christ. Among other readings of this poem, we may take it as a terrible prophetic image—

> A shape with lion body and the head of a man,
> A gaze blank and pitiless as the sun—

of the harsh totalitarianisms which in the twenties, when the poem was written, were still in embryonic state.

But in the poetry of negative revelation, this piece by Yeats is something of an exception. For the poets who assented to Nietzsche's statement that the age was distinguished by "the death of God," the result was commonly a poetry of inanimism, a poetry of deadened nature. "I have nothing but the embittered sun," writes Yeats in this mood in another poem.

It was as if, with the disappearance of the image of God from man's mind, an invisible warming pulse, which had fed the bloodstream of the air, stopped. Imaginatively speaking, the earth seemed to be preparing for a new petrifaction, a second Ice Age. And for poetry, which looks inward upon man as much as it looks outward on the world, the springs of emotion appeared to be drying. From the wells of faith, hope, and charity there came a hollow, unwatered sound. To illustrate this intuition of a dying solar system, I should like to quote part of a little-known poem by a little-known but interesting poet—"The Dry Heart," by Allan Porter:

> When the sun passed, who poured around
> Comfort over the barren ground,
> At whose divine and peaceable gaze
> Earth flowered in beauty and shone with praise,

> When death had stolen the brave sun
> The earth was bitterly alone.

The passing away of the sun is followed by the reign of the moon; and the last section of the poem speaks of the withering of all things beneath it:

> The round and miserable disc,
> The empty moon, is the sun's ghost:
> The sun is dead.
> I see it like a heart grown dry.
> The sun is dead.
> If it is cold in this grey land
> And if the moon above is cold,
> If all the arctic of the sky
> Looks down on the Antarctic earth,
> I know the sun himself is dead
> And nothing of the ancient warmth
> Stirs in the dying universe.

This is why I said that Yeats' poem "The Second Coming" is something of an exception in the poetry of negative revelation. For whereas most of the poets of the day, who were trying to shape an imaginative complement to Nietzsche's statement on the death of God, saw the universe as deprived of spirit, as emptied of supernatural content, Yeats went beyond this state, coming out, so to speak, on the far side of it, to find the return of the supernatural not in the Incarnation of Good but in the total embodiment of Evil:

> And what rough beast, its hour come round at last,
> Slouches towards Bethlehem to be born?

In the poetry of revelation, I think we can speak of this poem as expressing a sort of double-negative vision. It is not a common quality in contemporary poetry, though lesser degrees of it can be discovered.

Martin Heidegger has described the consciousness of our time as one in which a sense of "God's self-withholding" conditions our thoughts. "It is the time," he writes, expanding and explaining this paradox, "of the gods that have fled *and* of the god that is coming. It is the time of *need*, because it lies under a double lack and a double Not: the No-more of the gods that have fled and the Not-yet of the god that is coming."

What Heidegger is doing here is projecting a state of consciousness on to the world at large. He is coloring the universe with pigments out of his own mind; but the idea he holds of this interim epoch is of general consequence insofar as it is symptomatic of the age. For poets whose response to the world is akin to that of Heidegger, it is not the non-existence or the existence of God which they sometimes seek to express. What teases and haunts them is the dim sense of a God who cannot be located; a God, as it were, beyond the mind's horizon; a God sought for but undiscovered. "Reality," writes the French poet Rimbaud, "is else-where"; and for those tormented by an inkling of deity which fails to crystallize into an image, reality is indeed somewhere else. For them the world is alien and unreal—

> Jerusalem Athens Alexandria
> Vienna London
> Unreal

writes T. S. Eliot in *The Waste Land*. For such poets a mood of un-diagnosed homesickness is the emotion they are most aware of. In part perhaps we can lay this emotion at the door of a disappointed idealism. The simple belief in social utopias has been waning since the turn of the century; and as a result the perfectionist urge of many people, balked of previous outlets, has attached itself to the goal of all goals, which is God. But this attachment has been subconscious, the poet has been disturbed and made uneasy, filled with profound nostalgia for an object remaining in the dark.

In David Gascoyne's poetry there are many distinctions, many grades of this negative revelation. It is a property which we detect more by tone than by statement, more by a certain pathetic vibration than by an open confession. Sometimes we sense it (this dark, starved fumbling for God) in a poem ostensibly secular. So in David Gascoyne's "Eros Absconditus" the sought-for, finite relationship can be read in the light of the Forty-second Psalm: "Like as the hart desireth the water-brooks, so longeth my soul after thee, O God."

> Not in my lifetime, the love I envisage:
> Not in this century, it may be.
>   Nevertheless inevitable.
> Having experienced a foretaste of its burning
> And of its consolation, although locked in my aloneness
> Still, although I know it cannot come to be

Except in reciprocity, I know
That true love is gratuitous. . . .

Other poems by David Gascoyne express an intermittent revelation, a positive insight lapsing into an unformulated but still excited spiritual twilight. There are hints of glory, of God around the corner, momentarily glimpsed or missed by a hair's breadth in a number of his pieces; but in two poems particularly, "The Gravel-Pit Field" and "Sanctus," revelation grows and is sustained, or its sudden lapsing is explained in terms which do not contradict. I quote "Sanctus" as being shorter:

Incomprehensible—
O Master—fate and mystery
And message and long-promised
Revelation! Murmur of the leaves
Of life's prolific tree in the dark haze
Of midsummer: and inspiration of the blood
In the ecstatic secret bed: and bare
Inscription on a prison wall, "For thou shalt persevere
In thine identity . . .": a momentary glimpsed
Escape into the golden dance of dust
Beyond the window. These are all.

Uncomprehending. But to understand
Is to endure, withstand the withering blight
Of winter night's long desperation, war,
Confusion, till at the dense core
Of this existence all the spirit's force
Becomes acceptance of blind eyes
To see no more. Then they may see at last;
And all they see their vision sanctifies.

Here it is interesting to note that whereas the second verse-paragraph, dealing with the lapse of vision, is discursive and coherent, the first, conveying the vision itself, is ejaculatory and disjointed—no more than a sort of inspired shorthand. The reason for this must, I think, be sought first in the unpreparedness of the secular mind to receive the stuff of vision. The mental regimen of the saints helped them to hold the clear outline of their vision, but the modern mind—not subject to *ascesis*—is rendered confused by a like experience.

As T. S. Eliot says in his monograph on Dante, "We have nothing but dreams; and we have forgotten that seeing visions was once a more significant, interesting, and disciplined kind of dreaming." A secondary cause in the comparative unroundness of vision in this poem is, perhaps, the poet's lack of poetic theology. "The murmur of leaves," the "inspiration of the blood," the writing on the wall, and the "golden dance of dust" outside the window—all of which are burdened inexplicably with meaning—are so many separate visionary symbols. Together they constitute the jigsaw fragments of a larger meaning which we cannot quite assemble.

This is one of the disadvantages which a poet moving toward a Christian viewpoint in a largely secular culture must probably accept. To ask him first to get his theology right, and then to square his poetic perception with his fledgling sense of theology, may well be to upset his creative balance. There is, too, a further question involved in the fact that revelation always, in a manner, supersedes doctrine or at least appears to do so. Between doctrine and revelation there is often some measure of disharmony or tension. Ideally it might be desirable for poetic revelation to submit itself to the clarification and censorship of doctrine; but for the so frequently uncatechized poet, in a partly materialistic culture, the important thing is to catch hold of God wherever and however he can. This means that the poet's arrest of the divine will sometimes appears as irregular, distorting. It means also that the poet must give first place to such revelation as he receives, and place his trust, poetically, in it.

Naturally this method of working is not to be followed by Christian poets who have long possessed the properties of faith. From them we may expect a more normal balance between doctrine and revelation. My remarks refer to convert poets or to those at a preconversion stage (to semi-gnostics and yielding agnostics), in the belief that what I have said corresponds to the natural workings of their minds at that phase of their development and that what is natural is, in such cases, best.

Another feature requiring explanation to the Christian reader of contemporary poetry is that a poet may write at one moment as if his revelation had made him a believer and at another moment as if a second revelation had quite reversed this process for him. Then, in addition, there will be revelations that cause the poet to occupy varying positions along the line between faith and disbelief. Contrasted with the less mobile behavior of the theological sense, the Christian reader may find these giddy flights a sign of the soul's disappointing fickleness. What he is confronted with here is what Marcel Proust called "the intermittences of the heart": the unconscious movements of an inward sense which sporadically rise to conscious expression and startle through their apparent discrepancy.

Of course, if the Christian reader is acquainted with the spiritual motions recorded in the lives of the saints and mystics—the swinging of the compass of their feelings between the points of privation and bliss—he has at hand some sort of analogy by which to understand the mind of the modern poet. But whereas these "intermittences of the heart" take place in the saint against a constant background of faith, in the poet they are recorded against an unstable flickering screen—a screen scrawled over with denial, doubt, and faith.

So far I have been referring to the poet's negative revelation of God; and I must now burden the reader with a third confusing notion: the idea of a partial poetic revelation. By the term "partial revelation," I mean a positive revelation of God through the poetic medium, but one where the partiality of vision serves to distort, by accentuating only one side or aspect of deity.

In the first section of David Gascoyne's religious sequence *Miserere*, we have an outstanding example of this. Briefly, the poem's imaginative concentration lies in the thought of the crucified as opposed to the risen Christ. By this I do not wish to imply that David Gascoyne does not subscribe to a belief in the Resurrection. As a person he may or may not. But as a poet, in the pieces which form the sequence *Miserere*, the accent falls on the agony of Christ—his betrayal, torture, and death on the Cross. This emphasis on the figure of the unrisen Christ is one we encounter in much modern art. Ours is ostensibly a tragic age in that the consciousness of our defects, the diagnosis of our ills, is far in advance of our reconstructive will: our intelligence transcends our spirit and our heart.

This being so, it is not unnatural that to many the darker elements in the Christian story—the Fall and the Crucifixion—should seem more telling and more significant than the causes for final optimism and praise. Paul Tillich has commented that in contemporary religious art the Cross or its equivalent is the most expressive symbol. Symbols "such as resurrection," he observes, "have not yet found adequate artistic representation," and so it would often seem to be with other traditional "symbols of glory."

Nor is this greater accessibility of Christian images of sin and pain limited to the imagination of unbelievers. In the work of the powerful French painter Georges Rouault, for example, we have proof of how the torment and horror of Christ's dying hours upon the Cross have obsessed a Roman Catholic imagination to the exclusion of other elements in the divine tale. Again it is not a question of disbelief in the Resurrection. It is merely that the martyred, atoning God, assuming man's own helplessness, speaks more directly to many minds today than does the image of a risen Lord. Oppressed and persecuted as we are by largely impersonal forces of history, the scapegoat God who was sacrificed to powerful interests provides a parallel to many, irrespective of faith and creed.

As Jacques Maritain says of Rouault, he paints "the wound of Sin" with a "purity—almost Jansenist." There is something of this about David Gascoyne, who portrays the Crucifixion in an exclusive light of sin and fallen nature.

II

In any discussion of God in modern poetry, T. S. Eliot must prove the central figure. His work in drama, verse, and criticism occupies a canonical position because it embodies in its course both *negative* and *positive* revelation. Emotionally and spiritually, he traveled through desolation to a firm and conclusive love of God and man. Almost alone of modern poets, Eliot has succeeded in representing the poles of denial and belief, expressing both of them memorably. Then, again, he is one of the few verse-writers whose language and style have not suffered under the discipline and weight of orthodoxy. Complete traditionalism, no less than total skepticism (apparent in Eliot's early work), have implicated equally the *poet* and the *man*. In his work we observe the full union first of the intelligence of disbelief, then of belief, with the poetic imagination. In my following remarks on this writer, I will attempt to indicate these main combinations of disbelief and belief with imagination.

It would probably be true to say that T. S. Eliot is the most uncomfortable of important contemporary poets. Indeed, it might be said that he was one of the inventors of poetic uncomfortableness: I speak, of course, of his verse, not his person. Two hundred years ago this statement would have sounded a singular recommendation; but ours is a strangely uncomfortable age and stands in need of a strong disturbed mind through which to get itself expressed.

Those who saw Eliot's play *The Confidential Clerk* must have wondered at the change of tone apparent in it. Regarding each of the difficult and frightening characters, the old clerk Eggerson affirms that he or she has "a good heart," "a heart of gold." As Colby, his young successor, remarks, "everybody seems to be kind-hearted"—a novel discovery or admission for one of Eliot's characters to make. But then, indeed, *The Confidential Clerk* marks the true emergence of this poet from the waste land: from both the dust bowl of materialistic living and from the lonely nighttime of the soul. "A cold coming we had of it. . . . A hard time we had of it," say the three kings recalling their travels to see the infant Jesus in "Journey of the Magi."

Without this uneasy beginning, the reconciliation with human living, which springs up in *The Cocktail Party* and finally flowers in *The Confidential Clerk* and *The Elder Statesman*, might seem too simple or unmerited—the naïve well-wishing of an inexperienced fancy. But likewise, without this blossoming forgiveness, this late and loving justice to humdrum human cares, the poet's years in the wilderness, in the arid desert between two worlds, or in the dry, rarefied ether of supernatural concerns, we might well feel—in his own language—to have been "twenty years largely wasted." As it is, the price has been paid and the pearl of rare merit purchased.

The poet's progress has followed three stages: first, a detachment from faulty affections; secondly, a single-minded striving after God; and thirdly, a generous re-acceptance of the human. "This is His commandment," writes St. John the Apostle, "that we should believe on the name of His Son Jesus Christ, and love one another." And it is by this power to look with charity on all men that St. John measures the validity of conversion. "We know," he says, "that we have passed from death unto life, because we love the brethren. He that loveth not his brother abideth in death."

But this is to anticipate the whole tenor of Eliot's career. Let us return to his early phase: the first phase of his pioneering in poetic uncomfortableness, as I have called it. Randall Jarrell has spoken of the poet's temperamental isolation; and this aloneness is everywhere evident in Eliot's early work up to the time of *Ash Wednesday*. Answerable for many of the troubled notes that go to make up our impression of these poems, the problem of communication must be reckoned prominently. As Sweeney complains in "Sweeney Agonistes":

> I gotta use words when I talk to you
> But if you understand or if you don't
> That's nothing to me and nothing to you.

This problem of communication, in its turn, arises from the lack of a common spiritual language whose usage is still widely current. These poems, which almost despair of making the reader grasp their drift, were written before Eliot had discovered the speech of Christianity and the

Church existing like a separate patois in the language of a largely non-Christian society.

There were also, I would venture, psychological factors which make the question of establishing contact a terrible issue. Themes of misunderstanding and the absence of sympathy are encountered freely in the early poems. In "The Love Song of J. Alfred Prufrock" the young middle-aged man asks, "And would it have been worth it?"

> To say: "I am Lazarus, come from the dead,
> Come back to tell you all, I shall tell you all"—
> If one, settling a pillow by her head,
>   Should say: "That is not what I meant at all.
>   That is not it, at all."

Would it, in other words, have been worth the young middle-aged man's trouble to describe, at great effort to himself, some spiritual intuition he had had, only to find his meaning misunderstood, his soul laid bare in cross-purpose conversation?

Contrary to what has been generally believed, "The Love Song of J. Alfred Prufrock" and *The Waste Land* are both concerned with spiritual rebirth. But the dilemma facing the poet was how to express such intimations for those without a spiritual vocabulary, those whose points of reference on all occasions seemed limited to the materialistic.

As a result of this failure of exchange, the poet feels locked in on himself. "My external sensations," writes F. H. Bradley, whom Eliot quotes in his notes to *The Waste Land*, "are no less private to myself than are my thoughts or my feelings. In either case my experience falls within my own circle, a circle closed on the outside." Here is Eliot's poetic version of this segregated condition of mind:

> I have heard the key
> Turn in the door once and turn once only
> We think of the key, each in his own prison
> Thinking of the key, each confirms a prison.

Eliot's preconversion poetry mirrors the discomforts, discontents, and perdition of living today on a material level; the poetry following upon his conversion speaks of the difficulties and the dangers of living improperly on a religious plane. In *Murder in the Cathedral*, Thomas à Becket asks himself, in agony of mind:

> Is there no way, in my soul's sickness,
> Does not lead to damnation in pride?
>
> .   .   .   .
>
> Can sinful pride be driven out
> Only by more sinful? Can I neither act nor suffer
> Without perdition?

And later his self-catechism reveals the following disturbing truths:

> Ambition comes when early force is spent
> And when we find no longer all things possible.
>
> .   .   .   .
>
> Sin grows with doing good.
>
> .   .   .   .
>
> Servant of God has chance of greater sin
> And sorrow, than the man who serves a king.
> For those who serve the greater cause
> May make the cause serve them.

In this play the "lower" and the "higher" sins (of those who live respectively at the natural or the supernatural level) are expounded to the audience. Of the latter, we have the examples just given. Of the former, we find superlative expression in the Chorus of the Women of Canterbury immediately before the murder of Thomas. What we have here is a critique of pantheism. (Spinoza was not placed on the Index for nothing!)

To put it less philosophically, what the following passage offers is an exposition of living on the natural level carried to perverse and extreme limits. And the perversity consists in that, while the flesh assents to the natural order, the spirit has transcended it, even though it cannot veto the action and the affirmation of the flesh:

> Nothing is possible but the shamed swoon
> Of those consenting to the last humiliation.
> I have consented, Lord Archbishop, have consented,
> Am torn away, subdued, violated,
> United to the spiritual flesh of nature,
> Mastered by the animal powers of spirit,
> Dominated by the lust of self-demolition,
> By the final utter uttermost death of spirit,
> By the final ecstasy of waste and shame.

The assent of the Women of Canterbury to the forces of expediency which kill the Archbishop puts them back on a purely animal plane. In rejecting the human privilege of decision, they reject the order of good and evil. But the animal level is a level unsatisfactory for human living. To try to live "before good and evil," just as much as to live beyond them, is at length repulsive to the human spirit. One cannot live in the world of the Fall as though it were the Garden of Eden: spirit and conscience are wronged by the effort.

The images which precede this self-analytical passage are images descriptive of natural perversity. They are signs of a moral back-to-frontedness:

> I have smelt
> Corruption in the dish, incense in
> the latrine, the sewer in the incense,
> the smell of sweet soap in the woodpath.

But we must not see in this critique of man's immersion in nature a deprecation of the natural order itself. It is only the wrong subordination of the human to its base, the physical, which the poet criticizes here. Indeed, after the murder of Thomas is seen by the Chorus in its right perspective—as a sacrifice after the manner of Christ's, by which man is shown a pattern of redemption from the mirage of a pseudo-animal existence—the whole world of nature is revealed in all its sacramental rightness:

> We praise Thee, O God, for Thy
> glory displayed in all the
> creatures of the earth,
> In the snow, in the rain, in the
> wind, in the storm; in all of
> Thy creatures, both the hunters
> and the hunted.
> For all things exist only as seen
> by Thee, only as known by Thee,
> all things exist.
>
> . . . .
>
> They affirm Thee in living; all
> things affirm Thee in living;
> the bird in the air, both the
> hawk and the finch;

> the beast on the earth, both the
>   wolf and the lamb;
> the worm in the soil; and the
> worm in the belly.

From the middle of his career onward, there do exist moments of positive revelation in Eliot's verse. As early as *Ash Wednesday* we have glimpses of the beatific vision, imparted largely in the terms of Beatrician vision in Dante. There is also in this poem the beautiful address to Mary—

> Lady of silences
> Calm and distressed—

based on St. Bernard's hymn to Our Lady in Canto Thirty of the *Paradise*.

The greatest source of positive revelation in Eliot's poetry is his *Four Quartets*. Here the spirit's apprehension of God is chiefly associated with the idea of timelessness. But of these moments we may say, as Eliot says in "Little Gidding,"

> There is no earth smell
> Or smell of living thing. This is the springtime
> But not in time's covenant.

Putting it another way, I could remark that these moments seem to be the regard of the specialist in contemplation. Or, again, we may be happy enough to know such moments, but we come or choose to understand them in another sense than Eliot's. When he speaks of privation, of self-doubt, of futility, or of despair, his words articulate the feelings of many. When, in contrast, he speaks of bliss, of the hard-won spiritual token of the ascetic, there are few persons who can share with him in his lonely joy. He is far ahead of most of us; and, laggard-like, we are the losers.

Eliot has reconciled himself to a wise, forgiving affection for the human. We are none of us continuously, if ever, lovable; yet Christ taught us how to love what our egoism would otherwise reject. It is a happy thought that, after a lifetime's spiritual endeavor, Eliot should have learnt to express this truth in his own way so finely.

III

When a traditional culture pattern breaks up, men seldom jettison it *in toto*, but rather they preserve it in its fragments, eclectically combining certain of its aspects with those of other attitudes alien to it. This, for something like half of the West, is what has happened to the Christian world-picture. If few retain it completely, like an uncracked mirror in the mind, still fewer do not possess a sliver or two of it among their moral-intellectual convictions. The mirror may appear to be shattered; but the pieces lie around, and many of them get pocketed.

Such was the case with Dylan Thomas—a poet who preserved a notion of God inherited from his Welsh chapel environment, even though it had to be fitted into the ethos of his family background as represented by his atheistic father. With one part of his nature, when young, he wished to be free of the Christian inheritance:

> I have longed to move away but am afraid;
> Some life, yet unspent, might explode
> Out of the old lie burning on the ground,
> And, crackling in the air, leave me half-blind.

Here it was the punitive aspect of deity—"the wrath-side of God" as Jung calls it—which frightened the break-away Thomas, heavy with a sense of disobedience and guilt.

This was only one of Thomas' reactions, for with another side of himself he accepted the idea of God as part of the casual furniture of nature. This acceptance carried no theological commitment and was primarily an imaginative affair. It was very much a part, however, of Thomas' poetic world: nothing is stranger than this non-Christian poet's familiarity with God. This comes out in a note which he wrote to his *Collected Poems*, a jaunty, casual, sincere expression of faith. "I read somewhere," Dylan Thomas says, "of a shepherd who, when asked why he made, from within fairy rings, ritual observances to the moon to protect his flocks, replied: 'I'd be a damn' fool if I didn't!' These poems, with all their crudities, doubts, and confusions, are written for the love of Man and in praise of God, and I'd be a damn' fool if they weren't."

However I think we can extract from the next passage some further indications of the poet's notion of deity. "O God, Thou art everywhere all the time," cousin Gwilym begins his sermon in one of Thomas' short stories, "in the dew of the morning, in the frost of the evening, in the field and the town." This is as clear a statement of immanence as one could desire.

Now the philosophical equivalent of the idea of immanence, expressed in non-Christian terms, is pantheism, a belief which—in Bertrand Russell's definition—"holds that God and the world are not distinct and that everything in the world is part of God." There is no need for me to emphasize here the likeness and the difference between immanence and pantheism. The main distinction for Christians consists in that pantheism recognizes a constant multiple incarnation of God through every form in nature, but immanence holds that God was incarnate only once, in His Son Jesus Christ.

Generally, we think of pantheistic poetry as bearing good tidings: as confirming us, imaginatively at least, in our dim sense of kinship and union, by means of which we partake the more of God. This is the simple, undifferentiated, sacramental notion of pantheistic thought; and it is one which we can trace in many religions of the world: in the Dionysiac cults of Greece, in the recurrent worship of mother-goddesses, and in the animal deities of Egypt. Central to this pantheistic faith is the feeling that matter is creative: that the emergent principle of spirit works directly and inwardly through it.

But in Thomas' poems the pantheistic notion is often presented as a cause for grief. Matter is seen as being informed by a spirit of self-destruction, by a spirit of final inanition and waste. The following oft-quoted passage illustrates this expenditure without renewal in metaphorical terms:

> The force that through the green fuse drives the flower
> Drives my green age; that blasts the root of trees
> Is my destroyer.
> And I am dumb to tell the crooked rose

> My youth is bent by the same wintry fever.

> The force that drives the water through the rocks
> Drives my red blood; that dries the mounting streams
> Turns mine to wax.
> And I am dumb to mouth unto my veins
> How at the mountain spring the same mouth sucks.

What Thomas pictures here is something opposed to all those ideas of recurrence, evolution, or redemption which men have entertained of the future. In this poem his attitude has much in common with that of those nineteenth-century scientists who thought of the universe as a clock which was running down or as a pot of boiling water which was losing its heat and freezing.

This flaw in Thomas' pantheism, I think, we can trace to the earlier quotation "O God, Thou art everywhere," preached by young Gwilym. But over and against this motive of God's omnipresence, we have the further one of his omniscience, of his all-seeingness; and this is not without its disturbing side: "Thou canst see everything we do, in the night and day, in the day and the night, everything, everything." In this conclusion of Gwilym's sermon there is a note of exasperation that one cannot get away from God, that always, without let-up, His eye is upon us; and this, for the sinner, implies a sense of guilt.

The point which Thomas is making differs from both the Christian position and that of the man who feels himself a virtuous being in a hostile universe. The Christian says, "Yes, mine is the sin. If man had not chosen evil in Eden, there would have been no Fall. The universe itself was well enough designed." In contrast we have the person who says, "Humanity is all right. It is only its fight against a cruel nature which makes man appear sinful. It is really the universe which planned itself wrongly or was molded indifferent to man's existence." This is the position which we encounter in the poetry of Alex Comfort; and it is one which informs the writings of Jean-Paul Sartre and of Albert Camus.

But Thomas' attitude is distinct from theirs:

> The force that through the green fuse drives the flower
>
> .   .   .   .
>
> Is my destroyer.

Man, as Thomas regards him, is just a part of the universe. He is not a being distinguishable from it. Man and flower share the same life-force, and flower and man suffer the same fate. Both man and his cosmos are subject to this flaw, to this flowering followed by exhaustion and death. The law of diminishing returns conditions the life of them both. All this, quite naturally, is admitted by the Christian; but whereas the latter goes on from this point of bodily destruction to place his faith in the future of the soul, Thomas stops at the stage of death. Spirit and body are to be identified, and the end of one is the end of the other. This is, sketchily, what I mean when I talk of Thomas' "guilty" pantheism.

Perhaps I can make my distinction more vivid by referring to a book published some years ago by Gerald Heard, *God in History*. Not only does it deny the Hellenic idea of a primitive Golden Age and the Christian idea of the Garden of Eden, but, according to Heard, prehistoric records suggest that long before man was on earth, a tragic flaw and an aberration marked the earliest animal life. To substantiate his theory of a fallen creation in which all things were involved, Heard advances some interesting evidence. Natural historians once mostly supposed that malignant growths were evils from which animal life, in its first phases, was happily exempted. They assumed that these were troubles unknown to prehistoric beasts, whose end generally came from conflict with rivals or from the feebleness of old age which prevented them from seeking food. However, the recent reassemblage of the bone structures of certain of these beasts shows that many of them died ravaged by terrible chronic cancers.

In his *Apologia* John Henry Newman speaks of the sense of some vast aboriginal calamity, by which one might explain the suffering in the world and the long history of that suffering, even if one did not accept the Christian story. This was a feeling which Thomas could not evade in his poetry. He wrote, he says, "for the love of Man," but man, like the universe, was born with a flaw. In his poem "Before I Knocked" an unconceived child speaks of its premonition of fate and pain in its life to come:

> As yet ungotten, I did suffer;
> The rack of dreams my lily bones
> Did twist into a living cipher,
> And flesh was snipped to cross the lines
> Of gallow crosses on the liver
> And brambles in the wringing brains.

Thomas' "guilty" pantheism is clearly of tragic order.

That the poet in his pantheism should not have been able to forget the Old Testament God of judgment may appear to Christians as a good thing. Man, as the pantheist insists, is certainly one with the body of nature. At the same time man must never forget that he is the head of that natural body, the apex-member of that living hierarchy. To vacate this commanding and responsible position is to slip back into the stream of sensation without judgment, of vitality without values, which only the animal world can know. The image of Jehovah preached in the Welsh chapel was always at the back of Thomas' mind, stopping him from taking the last plunge. Guilt, however vague, however vicariously expressed, was the Christian lifeline in his case.

In Thomas' "Poem on His Birthday," a self-elegy of one who sails "out to die," we have what the Wesley hymn refers to as "a closer walk with God." This is a poem which may well baffle the systematic intelligence, because in it God is both affirmed and denied. In the following passage the poet speaks of the despair and grief left for him on earth in his own self-ruined life. Eagerly he looks toward death to free him:

> Terror will rage apart
> Before chains break to a hammer flame
> And love unbolts the dark.
>
> And freely he goes lost
> In the unknown, famous light of great
> And fabulous, dear God.
> Dark is a way and light is a place,
> Heaven that never was
> Nor will be ever is always true,
> And, in that brambled void,
> Plenty as blackberries in the woods
> The dead grow for His joy.
>
> There he might wander bare
> With the spirits of the horseshoe bay
> Or the stars' seashore dead,
> Marrow of eagles, the roots of whales
> And wishbones of wild geese,
> With blessed, unborn God and His Ghost,
> And every soul His priest.

In this poem Thomas thinks of God as "dear," yet somehow "fabulous" and "unborn," and Heaven as a place "that never was/Nor will be ever," yet "always true." What can we make of these paradoxes? Are they anything more than self-contradictions? Let us reflect on some of his terms. Perhaps when Thomas speaks of God as "dear," he is thinking of the desirability of the notion of God. But I think the word is used more instinctively here to refer to the soul's longing for its creator. "Dear" always carries with it the sense of intimacy, of someone emotionally near at hand. When we pass on to the term "fabulous," all the affirmative vibrations of the first word may seem to be lost. But "fabulous" need not be taken as synonymous with "unbelievable." Its suggestion here may be rather "that which appears as highly strange, as fantastic, even, to the rational mind." A third connotation is "that which belongs to the nature of the fable rather than to the more prosaic narrative."

So far, we see, there is no real contradiction. Nor need the term "unborn" disturb us. God is spoken of as unborn possibly because a faith in him, a feeling of certitude concerning his existence, has not yet been born in the poet. If this is so, the term is subjective and in no way denies God's objective being.

Heaven "that never was/Nor will be ever" and yet is "always true" presents, at first glance, a harder problem. One reading of the sense, however, may be that heaven, whose reality has always existed, bears no resemblance to what man has believed, or now believes, its nature to be. The truth of its existence must be taken in conjunction with the false-hood of all our notions of it.

This is one way, a pan-Christian way, of interpreting this poetic puzzle; but to me the statements Thomas makes here seem rather to invite comparison with the celebrated *mot* which parodies yet serves to summarize the thinking of Santayana: "There is no God, and Mary is His Mother." I mention Santayana's name on purpose. In his *Animal Skepticism and Faith* he describes himself as "an ignorant man, almost a poet." When a philosopher, however ironically, can humble himself in this fashion, his words may assist us in understanding the self-subsistent undefining images of art.

A passage from Santayana's Preface may help us to view the enigma of Thomas in an unusually fruitful fashion:

> I lay siege to truth only as animal exploration and fancy may do so, first from one quarter and then from another, expecting the reality to be not simpler than my experience of it, but far more extensive and complex. I stand in philosophy exactly where I stand in daily life; I should not be honest otherwise. I accept the same miscellaneous witnesses, bow to the same obvious facts, make conjectures no less instinctively, and admit the same encircling ignorance.

Santayana is saying that his philosophy is not all of one piece in the sense, for example, of a straight length of string. The thoughts that feed it do not come blowing single-mindedly from one direction. Instead, the "miscellaneous witnesses," which go to make up his picture of things, are met with first in one quarter and then in another. Nor does he pretend that his self-patterned world has the validity of a cosmic blueprint or of a map metaphysically to scale. "My system," he frankly admits, "is no system of the universe."

Santayana likewise provides a useful lead-in to Thomas when he draws a distinction between moral and animal faith. The latter he describes as "a sort of expectation or openmouthedness"; whereas "when a man believes in another man's thoughts and feelings, his faith is moral, not animal." It would be interesting to compare this distinction between moral and animal faith with that which the Roman Catholic Church establishes between acquired and infused knowledge: acquired knowledge being that which the Church teaches, infused knowledge that which God implants in us. Now those of the Christian faith have generally expressed their sense of infused knowledge, at least partly, in terms of knowledge acquired. But if we say that Thomas' poetic intuition represents a kind of infused knowledge, then this is just what he does not do. His faith being of an animal order, he does not believe that he should express it in terms of "another man's thoughts and feelings." And because, as Santayana tells us, animal faith is "a sort of . . . openmouthedness," Thomas expresses both negative and positive reactions to the thought of deity and after-existence: "blessed, unborn God and His Ghost," "fabulous, dear God," "Heaven that never was/Nor will be ever is always true."

We have become accustomed to hearing poetry spoken of as the language of paradox. Thomas is not a metaphysical poet in the sense we allow to Donne or to Eliot. Intellectual curiosity, a mental passion in dealing with ideas, plays little part in his poetry. But what we *do* have in it are the warring sentiments at play within us. God, though *felt* to be unbelievable ("fabulous"), is nonetheless "dear." Then *sentiment* of a *belief* remains after the disappearance of intellectual, dogmatic conviction. Similarly, though no show is made of establishing the truth of denial, the sentiment of doubt is expressed. And these two feelings fuse in a poetic clinch which makes for paradox.

Thomas was a poet of religious temperament, nourished in a literary culture of doubt. Certitude, proof, or commitment had no part in his thinking. He was an agnostic who retained a naturally religious imagination.

IV

In poetry which touches on religious themes today, we observe paradox upon paradox. What, for example, is the orthodox believer to make of D. H. Lawrence's "Lord's Prayer"—a religious poem by a non-Christian which draws its basic diction and thought from the great petition Christ taught his disciples? With superb certitude Lawrence uses

the language of a faith which is not his own. Never for one moment can
we doubt the feelings of reverence and conviction in his address. At the
same time his divergence from the Christian point of departure of the
poem is so immense that only the poet's obvious sincerity prevents us
from taking the notion (particularly in the ninth line) as a deliberate
parody:

> For thine is the kingdom
> the power, and the glory.
>
> Hallowed be thy name, then
> Thou who art nameless—
>
> Give me, Oh give me
> besides my daily bread
> my kingdom, my power, and my glory.
>
> All things that turn to thee
> have their kingdom, their power, and their glory.
>
> Like the kingdom of the nightingale at twilight
> whose power and glory I have often heard and felt.
>
> Like the kingdom of the fox in the dark
> yapping in his power and his glory
> which is death to the goose.
>
> Like the power and the glory of the goose in the mist
> honking over the lake.
>
> And I, a naked man, calling
> calling to thee for my mana,
> my kingdom, my power, and my glory.

At first it appears as if Lawrence had superimposed an anthropocentric interpretation upon a theocentric formulary. This, however, is to
oversimplify the complex, subtle currents of thought and feeling which
are changing the traditional speech of the prayer. For example, the
dependence of man's fulfillment upon God's existence is made apparent
in the phrase "turn to thee":

>All things that turn to thee
>have their kingdom, their power, and their glory.

What we have in this poem is a *sense of man's existence* in which the theocentric and the anthropocentric are juxtaposed and sustained in balance, so that they do not cancel one another out.

As surprising, perhaps, is the paradox with which Philip Larkin's "Church Going" concludes—a sadly ironic poem by an agnostic. (It is important to remark that the irony is as much at the expense of the nonbelieving poet as of the churchgoer, "ruin-bibber," or "Christmas-addict.")

>A serious house on serious earth it is,
>In whose blent air all our compulsions meet,
>Are recognized, and robed as destinies.
>And that much never can be obsolete,
>Since someone will forever be surprising
>A hunger in himself to be more serious,
>And gravitating with it to this ground,
>Which, he once heard, was proper to grow wise in,
>If only that so many dead lie round.

We may sense that there is more in this passage than the humanist's homage to the Church as the engenderer and grand repository of seriousness. It is, possibly, in the last three lines (which outwardly seem the most ironical) that the poem becomes clearly positive. What may appear as an ironical comment on the community of the faithful departed can also be taken as an affirmation of continuity—the spiritual solidarity of the quick and the dead.

One of the causes of paradox in modern verse dealing with religious themes is the frequent dissociation of the *theological imagination* from the poet's *sense of the numinous*. Even in Eliot's poetry, the finest passages of which communicate a *sense of the numinous* (the first verse-paragraph of "Little Gidding," the first section of "Burnt Norton" from the tenth line onward) are not those in which the *theological imagination* is most explicit.

For the most part in this essay I have taken the image of God in modern poetry to reflect the break-up of a culture pattern conceived in traditional Christian terms. In this disintegrating situation, I believe that the poets have performed a preserving and commemorating function. Through their creative imaginations they have retained in eclectic fashion the parts, if not the whole, of the structure of faith. Poetry, as I see it, has helped to cut down the losses of religion.

This, admittedly, is but one way of regarding the position; and I should therefore like to end by summarizing a more positive argument, viz., that advanced by Paul Tillich. In an essay, "Belief-ful Realism," he envisages "a language without symbols." "Perhaps," he writes, "it is a sign of the maturity of our religious development that its prophetic word—so far as any such is used—grasps the transcendent without symbol, just as it is a sign of the genius of great poets that they have at their command words that are both unsymbolic and precise and nevertheless penetrate into the deepest levels of our existence."

As an example of this theologically unsymbolic poetry, Tillich instances the later verse of Rilke. The gist of his argument, however, is much more far-reaching, for he endorses the notion not only of a theologically unsymbolic poetry but also of *theologically unsymbolic religion*. "It might well be the highest aim of theology," he declares in an article entitled "The Religious Symbol," "to find the point where reality speaks simultaneously of itself and of the Unconditioned in an unsymbolic fashion, to find the point where the unsymbolic reality and symbol is suspended." "If this were possible," maintains Tillich, "the deepest demand of the religious consciousness would be fulfilled: religion would no longer be a separate thing."

Tillich attempts, at this point, to guard against the implication that he is handing over religion to the workings of aesthetic awareness. "This in no way signifies," he writes, "that religion should be reduced to an artistic or scientific approach to reality. It signifies rather an immediate concern with things in so far as they confront us unconditionally, that is, in so far as they stand in the transcendent." Tillich's proviso, warning off art from putting the halter round religion, is clearly necessary to his position. Yet behind the awareness of art and behind the moment of religious awareness, there operates (equally but distinctly) *intuition*. To reword Tillich's thought in terms of Croce's aesthetic (of art as intuition and intuition as the material of knowledge) would undoubtedly provide us with a fresh perspective of the image of God in modern poetry.

Albert Camus: Sainthood Without God

by

John Cruickshank

THERE EXISTS TODAY—AS I SUPPOSE THERE HAS EXISTED FOR CLOSE TO TWO thousand years—a type of Christian intellectual imperialism with which I have very little sympathy. Too often writers and thinkers of anti-Christian convictions have posthumously appeared, at the hands of certain critics, as fundamentally religious, or even orthodox. Sometimes this orthodoxy can be obtained only by reversing most of their stated arguments and attitudes or by saying, in effect, that the concept "white" can be defined and understood only by reference to the concept "black." Even where moral and intellectual somersaults are not resorted to, the work of many writers has been only partially presented to the reader, or the conception of Christianity invoked by the critic is so blurred and emasculated that any artist who has thought at all seriously about man's place in the scheme of things qualifies for canonization. At the outset, therefore, a distinction ought to be made between writers who are Christians and writers who pose interesting and important problems for the Christian reader. Not so very many great literary figures belong to the former category, but a large number of writers come into the latter one: Tolstoy, Melville, Pirandello, Hardy, Gide.

More recently, and not least where French literature is concerned, the religious relevance of many novelists and playwrights is a striking feature. Quite apart from Roman Catholic artists like Bernanos, Mauriac, Greene, or Marcel, many non-Christian writers from Malraux to Beckett have produced works which, as Gaëtan Picon puts it, have become "instrument[s] of metaphysical consciousness" and thus of concern to the Christian reader. It is not always easy to understand why this predominantly metaphysical literature has arisen so notably in our own day. It may be in part a reaction against the formalism and abstraction of a certain kind of academic philosophy. Or it may well have to do with some transcendental need to which a consciously secular age unconsciously responds. It can also be related to certain forms of philosophical opposition to idealism in Europe (e.g., phenomenology and existentialism) with a consequent convergence of literature (with its emphasis on individuality and particularity) and metaphysical speculation. Literature and philosophy have increasingly made common cause since the latter turned more and more from the contemplation of essences to the scrutiny of existence. The assumption behind this trend was put succinctly by Merleau-Ponty when he wrote in 1945: "True philosophy is re-learning to look at the world, and in this sense a simple story can present us with as much 'depth' and meaning as would a philosophical treatise." Finally, insofar as man's condition has been presented in dramatic or pessimistic terms in a world where "God is dead" and there is no transcendence, the analysis made differs little from that to be found in one traditional strand of Christian thought represented by the Book of Ecclesiastes, by Saint Augustine, by Pascal, by Kierkegaard, and by certain contemporary theologians. Anyone familiar with the theological doctrine of man's threefold estrangement—from the ground of his being, from other beings, and from himself—will quickly recognize the philosophical landscape in the worlds of Malraux, Camus, Sartre, and Beckett.

The writings of Albert Camus present their Christian readers with a challenge and a temptation. The challenge has to do with the fact that Camus outlined a noble and rigorous humanist position while stating categorically that he rejected the Christian premises and remained "outside Christianity." The temptation arises because of Camus' sense of the "appetite for divinity" in man and his clearly expressed opposition both to automatic anticlericalism and to what he called "vulgar and threadbare" antireligious attitudes. This position has prompted some commentators to present his writings as the work of a man who was a Christian in all but name—an animus naturaliter religiosa. I believe this interpretation to be wrong and hope to show, in accordance with the distinction made earlier, that Camus explores problems which the Christian cannot evade but that he is not un chrétien qui s'ignore. As regards the challenge, this is the chief point of interest where this essay is concerned, and much more will have to be said about it. Straight away, however, it is worth emphasizing that Camus offers a challenge not only to the Christian but, with equal force, to a prominent kind of atheistic humanist. In each case the reasons for his opposition take very similar form and much of his distinctness and freshness as a thinker lies in this dual position which his writings defined with increasing clarity and conviction. As Camus pondered on the nature and the problems of his age, he accepted that, in the last resort, only two really major attempts have been made to account for man's experience of the world—Christianity and Marxism. Much of the interest and the drama of his thought are to be found in the fact that he searched for an alternative that would explicitly reject both these dogmas. As one reads the vast amount of criticism of his ideas written during his own lifetime, one is struck by the fact that he was much more frequently attacked as a non-Marxist than as a non-Christian.

It is clear that Camus reached his celebrated doctrine of the absurd—his exposition of contemporary nihilism—without bringing to the question any deep familiarity with religious beliefs and attitudes. In his early years, largely because of his grandmother's influence, he fulfilled the outward observances which culminated in the rite of the *première communion* at the age of ten. His mother, however, had little patience with religion, and the Christianity which he saw practiced by his grandmother was that religion of desperation, a despairing attempt to soften the bitter reality of imminent death, which he describes in one of his earliest published essays in *L'Envers et l'endroit*. The old woman whose portrait he gives us in this volume, no doubt modeled on his grandmother, clings to her religion through fear and for prudential reasons, not from love of God. Later in life Camus was to be deeply impressed by several Christian friends, particularly the young poet René Leynaud, who was killed by the Germans in 1944. He also made contact with a very different kind of Christianity from that practiced by his grandmother in the writings of Simone Weil and of Jean Guitton. One can say that when he elaborated his account of the absurd, he had little sympathy with, and virtually no understanding of, Christian doctrine. Later, during and after World War II, as he began to define his theory of revolt in response to the inhumanity to which atheistic nihilism had given rise, he knew a good deal more about Christianity even while maintaining that something like the ancient Greek way of life, rather than the later Christian inheritance, provided the best—perhaps the only—hope for Europe.

The long philosophical essay *Le Mythe de Sisyphe*, the novel *L'Etranger*, and the plays *Caligula* and *Le Malentendu* are the main sources of our knowledge of what Camus meant by "the absurd." He used the expression primarily to describe the sense of bafflement which strikes us when we confront our own experience of the world and attempt to account for it in rational terms. The absurd is much of what we find inexplicable to human reason. It includes many things that defy rational explanation or seem to confound and controvert our sense of fair play in the scheme of things, our desire for happiness, and our need to find pattern and purpose in existence. In *Le Mythe de Sisyphe* Camus outlined such evidence of the absurd as a sudden, unbidden questioning of the purpose of existence and the meaning of the lives we lead; the sense that time is bearing us quickly and with "mathematical certainty" toward physical disintegration; the consciousness of our brief human lives in contrast to the endurance of inanimate nature; the "otherness" of other people and even of an element in ourselves; the waste of so much human potential in apparently arbitrary sudden death or protracted suffering through fire, flood, earthquake, famine, etc.

All this reminds one of certain biblical passages, Psalm 90, for example:

> Thou turnest man to destruction and sayest, Return, ye children of men. . . . For all our days are passed away in thy wrath: we spend our years as a tale that is told,

or again, in the Book of Ecclesiastes:

> Then I looked on all the works that my hands had wrought, and on the labour that I had laboured to do; and, behold, all was vanity and vexation of spirit, and there was no profit under the sun. . . . All go unto one place; all are of the dust and all turn to dust again.

There is, nevertheless, an important difference between the pictures of man's plight to be found in the Bible and in the writings of Camus. Camus, unlike the Christian, believed neither in God nor in redemption nor in the afterlife. Consequently, his conception of the absurd must be seen in relation to a universe without the presence of any omniscient or omnipotent power and in relation to a human life which ends with death in the same way as does the life of any other organic creature. What Camus and the Christian have in common is their acute sense of the disproportion they have found between the world as their intellects *expected* it to be and the world as their intellects *report* it to be. Now it is reasonable that the Christian, with his belief in a loving God, should expect a certain order and justice in the fabric of the universe; it is much less logical that the atheist should bring to life a similar expectation. Strictly speaking, for the atheist there should be no drama or tragedy in the fact that he thought the world was constituted in a particular way but now finds it to be constituted in another. There is no strong reason why a world, which he does not ascribe to the creative act of a loving and divinely shaping intelligence, should conform to the intellectual assumptions of a human mind. Admittedly there is a gap whose radical nature he did not fully grasp before, but such a gap was always a logical possibility and cannot reasonably be interpreted by the atheist as a tragic abyss. It is on the basis of such arguments that Robbe-Grillet has pointed out, in his criticism of Camus and Sartre, that man and the world are separated by differences which only masochism or a signal lack of logic can convert into tragic separation. On the other hand, the Christian expects a sharp lack of correspondence between infinite God and finite man. A God Who conformed entirely to the categories of human reason would be a God circumscribed by human limitations—i.e., not God at all. Indeed, what would really be absurd in this context would be the non-existence of the absurd. In a word, the absurd has meaning and importance within a theistic framework; it is tragic because of man's inadequacies, but the Christian has faith (Pascal's "wager" or Kierkegaard's "leap") that this tragedy can be removed by God's grace.

It is precisely because the absurd depends on theism for its significance that writers such as Camus and Sartre seem to give evidence of certain theistic vestiges in seeing man's situation in the world as a kind of human loss. Even Sartre, more rigorously philosophical than Camus in his writings, speaks of man as being *abandoned* or *condemned to be free*. Such dramatic and emotive language prompts the question: "Abandoned and condemned by whom?" In the case of Camus, what looks like a hint of possible nostalgia for God comes nearest to direct expression when he observes in *L'Homme révolté* that "nothing can discourage the appetite for divinity present in the human heart." I think it is also significant in this connection that Camus does not locate the absurd in the creation as such (a major point of difference from Sartre) but in the relationship between the individual and his own experience. He writes in *Le Mythe de Sisyphe*:

I said the world was absurd, but I was being too hasty. All one can say of the world is that it is not amenable to reason. The absurd, however, is the confrontation of this non-rational world with the desperate desire for clarity which is one of man's deepest needs. The absurd depends as much on man as on the world for its existence.

This passage allows a Vigny-like complaint about the silence or absence of God, as distinct from an affirmation of God's nonexistence. In fact, Camus sometimes seems to waver between straightforward agnosticism and a moral accusation of God's apparent indifference. The sequence through which accusation becomes disbelief is set out briefly in a sentence from L'Homme révolté: "But a longer contemplation of this injustice, a more bitter approach, transformed the 'even if you exist' into 'you do not deserve to exist,' therefore 'you do not exist.'" Earlier in the same book Camus writes: "As soon as a man submits God to a moral judgment he kills God in his own heart." One is reminded of Stendhal's characteristic remark that "God's only excuse is His non-existence." In his essays (as distinct from the novels and plays, where other characters speak) Camus does not write as positively as this but is certainly inclined to argue that, if God exists, He must be unjust. In L'Homme révolté again he expresses sympathy with Sade's view that God's existence would imply that He is "indifferent, wicked or cruel." Camus also points out, echoing Pascal, that not to wager on God's existence is to wager against it, and he insists on what he calls "the paradox of an all-powerful and malevolent, or benevolent and sterile, God."

These various quotations emphasize the fact that Camus' agnosticism ("I do not positively believe in God, but I am not an atheist nevertheless") was fed by the so-called problem of evil. I take it that one means by this problem the difficulties raised by two distinct questions: Why do men suffer unjustly? And why do men cause unmerited suffering to one another? The first question would arise in the case of a small child who not only dies of cancer of the throat but suffers atrociously in the process. How is this to be related to a coherent scheme of things and a God of love? The second question arises, with equal urgency, in the case of a small child sent to the gas chambers in a concentration camp. What are we to make of a human nature capable of this cruelty? The difficulties that beset the Christian position should not blind us to those that should similarly worry the humanist. In an interview with Emile Simon reprinted in Actuelles I Camus says: "There is the death of children which signifies divine cruelty, but there is also the murder of children which indicates human cruelty."

The first of these problems—that facing the Christian—is dramatized by Camus in his novel La Peste when the Jesuit priest, Father Paneloux, witnesses the agonized death by the plague of Judge Othon's son. The following conversation between Father Paneloux and the non-believing Dr. Rieux shows Camus' handling of the problem at its best and suggests his belief in the possibility and desirability of a Christian-agnostic dialogue:

"I understand," Paneloux said in a low voice. "That sort of thing is revolting because it passes our human understanding. But perhaps we should love what we cannot understand."

Rieux straightened up slowly. He gazed at Paneloux, summoning to his gaze all the strength and fervour he could muster against his weariness. Then he shook his head.

"No, Father. I've a very different idea of love. And until my dying day I shall refuse to love a scheme of things in which children are put to torture."

A shade of disquietude crossed the priest's face. He was silent for a moment. Then, "Ah, doctor," he said sadly, "I've just realized what is meant by 'grace.'"

Rieux had sunk back again on the bench. His lassitude had returned and from its depths he spoke, more gently.

"It's something I haven't got; that I know. But I'd rather not discuss that with you. We're working side by side for something that unites us—beyond blasphemy and prayers. And it's the only thing that matters."

Paneloux sat down beside Rieux. It was obvious that he was deeply moved.

"Yes, yes," he said, "you, too, are working for man's salvation."

Rieux tried to smile.

"Salvation's much too big a word for me. I don't aim so high. I'm concerned with man's health; and for me his health comes first."

Paneloux seemed to hesitate. "Doctor . . ." he began, then fell silent. Down his face, too, sweat was trickling. Murmuring, "Good-bye for the present," he rose. His eyes were moist. When he turned to go, Rieux, who had seemed lost in thought, suddenly rose and took a step towards him.

"Again, please forgive me. I can promise there won't be another outburst of that kind."

Paneloux held out his hand, saying regretfully:

"And yet—I haven't convinced you!"

"What does it matter? What I hate is death and disease—as you well know. And whether you wish it or not, we're allies, facing them and fighting them together." Rieux was still holding Paneloux's hand. "So you see"—but he refrained from meeting the priest's eyes—"God Himself can't part us now."

The problem of evil that faces the atheistic humanist is not put with quite the same concentration by Camus, but it arises on various occasions, particularly in his plays. *Caligula*, for example, is a study of the quite insupportable human consequences of taking the absurd to its apparently logical conclusions. Caligula himself, by instituting an arbitrary reign of terror, is following out—and ultimately disproving—Ivan Karamazov's contention that "if God does not exist, everything is permitted." Seconds before he is assassinated Caligula cries: "But killing is not the solution. . . . I have chosen a wrong path, a path that leads to nothing. My freedom isn't the right one." In a program note for the Hébertot production in Paris, Camus commented:

> If his [Caligula's] integrity consists in his denial of the gods, his fault is to be found in his denial of men. One cannot destroy everything without destroying oneself. This is why Caligula depopulates the world around him and then, in keeping with his own logic, does what is necessary to arm against himself those who will ultimately kill him. Caligula's story is that of a high-minded type of suicide. It is an account of the most human and most tragic of mistakes. Caligula is faithless towards humanity in order to keep faith with himself. He consents to die, having learned that no man can save himself alone and that one cannot be free by working against mankind.

The problem of evil therefore prompts Camus to search for an alternative both to the Christian reaction (which justifies suffering in terms of a hidden divine purpose) and to the humanist—and particularly Marxist—response (which justifies political injustice and murder with the promise of an eventual social millennium). He objects to both answers because they attempt to justify means that involve human suffering by reference to distant and abstract ends. They undervalue our actual life in favor of another life which they promise but locate in the future. In a word, Camus is unable to accept the vertical transcendence (faith in God) taught by Christianity and is horrified by the cruelty resulting from horizontal transcendence (faith in historical inevitability) which characterizes certain political doctrines.

The case against horizontal, historical transcendence is repeatedly argued by Camus. It finds its strongest expression in the long politico-philosophical essay *L'Homme révolté*. It is here that Camus claims to show that Marxism derives from the Judaic-Christian tradition and that it is flawed, formally at least, by the same kind of weakness—an obsession with an apocalypse which discounts human suffering as relatively unimportant. Christianity was dominant during that period of history which Camus calls *le sacré*—a religious phase when the majority of men did not seriously question their condition but accepted the official answers given to their questions by priests and theologians. But we have been living for more than a century now in a world which is increasingly *un monde désacralisé*—a phase of metaphysical doubt and revolt against the God of traditional Christian teaching. What Marxist theory amounts to, then, is the replacement of God (a vestige of the religious phase) by historical process (the divinity of the secular age). The Judaic-Christian belief in a Second Coming remains in outline, but, with the "death of God," the millennium is brought within the confines of the historical process. From this it is a short step to what Wilfrid Sheed has called "the refusal of men as they are in the name of men as they shall be." This deification of historical futurity has led to the murderous ideologies of the last century and of our own. It explains for Camus the fact that both the French and Russian revolutions, which enthroned reason and history respectively, began with high humanitarian ideals but ended in turn with the guillotine and the police state. The desacralization of modern life has not lessened ideological murder. Wars of religion have been replaced by secular ideological conflicts that are equally brutal but ironically fought in the name of man, not God. Revolutions begun on man's behalf have turned lethally against man. Referring to Europe's recent past, Camus writes in *Actuelles II:* "Do you know that over a period of twenty-five years, between 1922 and 1947, 70 million Europeans—men, women and children—have been uprooted, deported and killed?" Camus even says that the political and economic fatalities of our age "seem more terrible than divine whims." At the same time he does not confine himself to condemnation of non-Christian or anti-Christian revolutionaries. He rightly takes the Church to task for its frequent collusion with inhuman political behavior. In his lecture given at the Dominican Monastery of Latour-Maubourg in 1948 he said:

> What the world expects of Christians is that Christians should speak out, loud and clear, and that they should voice their condemnation in such a way that never a doubt, never the slightest doubt, could rise in the heart of the simplest man. That they should get away from abstraction and confront the blood-stained face that history has taken on today. . . . When a Spanish bishop blesses political executions, he ceases to be a bishop or a Christian or even a man; he is a dog just like the one who, backed by an ideology, orders that execution without doing the dirty work himself.

I think one must say at this point that, however admirable Camus' rigorous moral tone may be, he oversimplified the problems encountered in the contemporary political scene. He is absolutely right, of course, to call for greater humanity in public life and to stigmatize ideological violence, but in the concrete situation there is often a moral ambiguity which even the most resolute ethical campaigner finds difficult to unravel. One can share his condemnation of the Spanish bishop mentioned in the last quotation and still believe that there are other situations which, by their very nature, make it impossible for the Church to speak with clarity and certainty on all points. There are conflicts in our own day in which the politico-strategic problem is so inextricably linked with a moral dilemma that a judgment made in purely political or purely moral terms amounts to an unreal and unhelpful oversimplification of reality. The Christian, or indeed anyone who holds firmly to certain ethical principles, must fight with determination in a way he believes will ensure the eventual triumph of these principles. But this is not to say that they can be easily or unerringly distinguished at a glance. Thus one may feel a glow of moral approval when Camus writes that "without freedom heavy industry can be perfected, but not justice and truth." Nevertheless, heavy industry is a necessity and cannot simply be placed in an either/or relationship with freedom, justice, and truth.

This is the kind of problem which led to the bitter controversy between Camus and Sartre which was carried on, largely in the pages of *Les Temps Modernes*, in 1952. Sartre opted for the efficacy of collectivist political solutions—always at the risk of mistakes and failures—and for the creation of human values through action in time. He argued that such values can exist in a meaningful way only through being fashioned by political activity. Camus, on the contrary, found his values in human consciousness, independent of action and history. He claimed that they are not absolutes but genuinely human values, and he held that they are degraded by collective historical development. The choice, then, is between Sartre's acceptance of guilt in the service of the revolution and Camus' moral austerity. We feel that Sartre is telling us what we *can* do, Camus what we *ought* to do. And if, on occasions, Sartre appears to lack moral concern, it is equally true that there are moments when Camus lacks practicality. As regards the weight of purely intellectual argument, Sartre is impressive. He rightly insists that we cannot, from a thoroughly humane position, choose either unlimited violence or integral pacifism; it is in the world of moral ambiguity between these two extremes that we find ourselves called upon to operate. But Camus is justified, in my view, when he upbraids Sartre for his partial, left-wing humanity. Demonstrations in the name of humanity are rightly made, for example, on behalf of imprisoned and tortured black African leaders. But the same sense of humanity should evoke equal concern and outrage at the murder of white missionaries. One could only suspect the humanity of the democrat who argued against French colonialism in Algeria yet remained silent about the Chinese invasion of Tibet.

Given his strictures against the Marxist deification of history and his inability to accept Christian beliefs, Camus' problem—as he himself put it in an interview as early as 1945—is "how to act when one believes neither in God nor [in] reason." A passage from one of his essays collected in *L'Eté* outlines the task which he set himself and the path which he attempted to follow:

> I do not believe firmly enough in reason to subscribe to the idea of progress or some philosophy of history. But at least I believe that men have not ceased to make progress in becoming aware of their own situation. We have not risen above our human condition, but we understand it better. We know that we are the victims of a dilemma; that we must refuse to accept it and do what is necessary to eradicate it. Our task as men is to find some formulas and pacify the great anguish of human kind. We must put together what has been torn apart, make justice a possibility in an obviously unjust world, render happiness meaningful to peoples poisoned by the sufferings of our age. This is of course a superhuman task, yet one simply calls "superhuman" those tasks which men take a very long time to accomplish.

Camus' death in an automobile accident at the age of forty-six left him insufficient time to complete this "superhuman task." But by the time of his death he had at least drawn the main outlines of that "new humanism" which he offered as an alternative to both Christianity and Marxism—a humanism of which freedom, justice, and happiness were to be the cornerstones. One is reminded of Tarrou's statements in *La Peste*: "What interests me is learning how to become a saint. . . . Can one be a saint without God?—that's the problem, in fact the only problem, I'm up against today."

The humanism which Camus proposes is implied in the criticisms he made previously. It is, as the term no doubt implies, man-centered and not theistic. It emphasizes nature rather than history, moderation rather than extremism, human concern rather than abstract ideology, the dialogue rather than the directive. In fact, it rests on those Mediterranean values which the Algerian in Camus sets above Nordic dreams of intemperance. His is a humanism, then, which refuses either to bend or to illuminate human nature in accordance with the demands of an *a priori* framework—whether theistic or historical. It is also a humanism which offers no precise program of action but attempts, in moral terms, to put first things first. It seeks primarily to make reforms in the nature and the attitudes of men, believing that it is only through this apparently indirect approach that society will be genuinely improved and human suffering effectively reduced. But above all it recognizes that the fight for justice and happiness must be unending. There is no earthly millennium. To be a human being means maintaining revolt indefinitely on behalf of man's highest ideal of himself.

No doubt Camus is thinking mainly of Marxism when he regrets the distortion of justice into "that terrible abstract passion which has mutilated so many men" and defines it as "both a concept and a warmth of the soul." Nevertheless, it would be quite wrong to assume that this opposition to the Sartrean type of progressive rationalist, intoxicated by historicism, makes Camus a Christian in all but name. He stands quite distinctly in a relationship of tension to Christianity, and this is one of the main aspects of the continuing interest and relevance of his position. What makes Camus so significant, and in many ways representative, a figure of his own generation is the fact that he experienced a religious need in its widest sense yet was unable to accept religious belief. The same fact guided his exemplary—if ultimately wrong-headed—quest for sainthood without God. He attempted to teach his contemporaries that it is both possible and vital to arrive at a rigorous personal and social ethic starting from the premises of doubt and despair and independently of dogmatic *a priori* foundations.

Jean Genet and Scapegoat Drama

by

John Killinger

A WORLD TURNED UPSIDE DOWN TO EXALT CRIMINALS, PEDERASTS, AND traitors; a dramaturgy so artful and convincing as to confuse the spectator and make him wonder which way is really up and whether, in the last analysis, it is he or the actors who are only playing; a religious style to put one in mind of Claudel, but dedicated instead to the powers of darkness and evil: that is the forceful and unusual theater of Jean Genet.

Accused at the age of ten of being a thief, Genet decided to exist as a thief, to be in himself what he appeared to be for others. "Abandoned by my family," he says, "I felt it was natural to aggravate this condition by a preference for boys, and this preference by theft, and theft by crime or a complacent attitude in regard to crime. Hence, I resolutely rejected a world which had rejected me."[1] By the time he was thirty he was devoted to a life of degradation and had been in and out of a number of prisons.

He began writing to indulge his fantasy-world, to create a mythology of evil to reinforce the dream he had chosen. His first poem, a strange, incantatory elegy entitled "Le Condamné à mort," he dedicated "à la mémoire de mon ami Maurice Pilorge dont le corps et le visage radieux hantent mes nuits sans sommeil."[2] As Martin Esslin has noted, the same incantatory quality, as of "the dark splendor of a religious act,"[3] characterizes the four prose works Genet then wrote between 1940 and 1948: Notre-Dame-des-Fleurs, *Miracle de la rose*, *Pompes funèbres*, and *Querelle de Brest*. They are hardly novels, for they have little plot and most of their characters are mere adumbrations of the author's dream world. They are more like litanies or prose meditations celebrating the loveliness of male bodies, the lurid fascination of the scatological, the hollow beauty of evil. They transport the reader into a whole new realm of values and experiences. "Passa l'Eternel sous forme de mac," says Notre-Dame-des-Fleurs—"The Eternal passed by in the form of a pimp." Genet has stood the universe on its head. He has not merely glorified crime and sodomy, he has provided them with a *Weltbilt*, an order of being, an ontological depth; he has bestowed mythological status upon them.

Genet's first play, *Haute surveillance* (*Deathwatch*), emerged from this background. Set in a prison cell, it turns on the relationships of three cellmates: a murderer named Yeux-Verts (Green Eyes), a thief named Lefranc, and a teen-ager named Maurice. A fourth prisoner, a Negro named Boule-de-Neige (Snowball), is never seen, but exerts an obvious influence over the others as the most important figure in their hierarchy of crime and desire. Lefranc calls him a king and describes his walk down the corridors as if it were the royal way of a monarch in his palace. After all, "prison offers the same feeling of security to the convict as does a royal palace to a king's guest. They are the two buildings constructed with the most faith, those which give the greatest certainty of being what they are."[4] Green Eyes is number two and is therefore adored by his cellmates, who are jealous of his least attention. Lefranc finally kills Maurice in the attempt to become a real criminal and win the respect of his idol. But Green Eyes refuses to have anything to do with him, saying that the crime must choose the man, not the man the crime. One wonders whether perhaps Lefranc does not in some way represent Genet himself, who, despite his protestations, was always a philosophical criminal, a man who emulated thieves and perverts in the wish to belong to them, but who never quite had the sense of being naturally constituted as they were.

Genet's second play, the first to be produced, moves out of the world of derelicts and into a society more familiar to play-goers. *Les Bonnes* (*The Maids*), as Sartre notes, is structurally similar to *Haute surveillance* in that there are three principals (two maids and their mistress) and an invisible fourth person (the mistress' lover). The play opens with a scene between Madame and a maid named Claire, in which Claire becomes increasingly insolent and at last slaps Madame; but then we discover that Madame is not Madame at all, but the real Claire, and that Claire is not Claire at all, but the second maid, Solange. Whenever Madame is away, the maids play the game of being mistress and servant, with the servant punishing and abusing the mistress. At the end of the play Claire takes an overdose of tranquilizers intended for Madame and thus dies in her place. Although he capitulated to the better judgment of Louis Jouvet, who first produced *Les Bonnes*, Genet originally insisted that the parts of the three women be played by transvested men: he would have turned the illusion to a still higher notch.

There is a remote, somnambulistic quality about both of these early plays, as though they were taking place in a dream. The author explicitly directed that *Haute surveillance* be performed "as in a dream," with the actors deadening the timbre of their voices and using either very heavy or very rapid movements. The whole thing is not far from the realm of ballet, especially in one scene when Green Eyes actually begins to dance. A similar effect is accomplished in *Les Bonnes* by the use of a kind of ritualism which builds through the entire play to a climax in the immolation of Claire when she drinks the poisoned cup. Genet cleverly uses an alarm clock which the maids have set to remind them of Madame's return, along with other techniques, to recall us to the ordinary world from time to time, but the interruptions serve mainly to mark the movements in the play and to permit a still greater intensification of interest and emotion.[5] Sartre is correct in calling the ritual a Black Mass.[6] The maids are fully conscious of this. Solange says to Claire, "It's God Who's listening to us. We know that it's for Him that the last act is to be performed, but we mustn't forewarn Him. We'll play it to the hilt."[7]

Two factors at least are responsible for Genet's use of ceremony in his attempt to fix the invertedness of the world and make it the property of prisoners and domestics, of people without status. One is the attraction he has always felt for the Roman Mass. He writes in his *Journal* of having once taken communion in a state of mortal sin, of having dared his soul against "a sickening impression of mystery" he felt in the service: "In the shadow of the church, facing the priest in his chasuble, I was frightened. But as the kneeling hidalgos beside me did not shrink from my rags, as they received the same host on the tips of their tongues, knowing full well that its power manifests itself within our souls and not elsewhere, in order to catch its imposture in *flagrante delicto* and make it my accomplice, I mentally cursed it as I chewed it."[8] He says he believes "that the idea of God is something I harbor in my bowels."[9] And he could never get away from the notion that the elevation of the Host in the Mass is the highest dramatic moment the Western world has known for two thousand years—hence his own reinforcement of his fantasy world by the use of ritual and inverted Christian symbolism, resulting in what Tom F. Driver has called his "spiritual diabolism."[10]

The second factor in his employment of ceremonial is one noted by

Sartre in his elaborate study of Genet.[11] From Mircea Eliade's *Myth of the Eternal Return*, Sartre appropriates the idea that rites are necessary to the securing of reality: we participate in certain rituals in order to fix the being of something, to reify it, to substantiate it. Incantation, dance, and a sense of liturgy help Genet to achieve what he calls "the Fable where all creation is possible."[12] As Joseph McMahon has put it, "he is seeking myth in the renewed sense of that weakened word—as a means of expressing imagistically that which cannot be adequately wrought discursively—and he is seeking to do this by relying on what has been the most potent conveyor of myth: its immersion in ceremony."[13] He can believe in the world he has created if he can satisfy the aesthetic and ceremonial demands of his soul through the liturgies mythologizing that world.

In both *Les Bonnes* and *Haute surveillance* Genet is content with the drama itself, with the more or less private experience of ritual. In *Le Balcon* (*The Balcony*) he widens his dimensions and invades the world of the general theater public. Performing the Black Mass might be enough for a mere devotee; but he wants something more: to expose the thinness of what passes for religious belief and justice and patriotism among those who belong to acceptable society. So *Le Balcon* opens with three scenes featuring, respectively, a bishop, a judge, and a general, each of whom is wearing cothurni and padding, in addition to traditional costumery, so that he is bigger than life. The bishop is accoutered as a churchman, and he talks like a churchman, especially one made cynical by the long possession of authority; yet before the scene is over, we know that he is no bishop at all, but a gasman dressed up as a bishop and spending an hour with a girl in a room in a bordello. Similarly with the judge and the general: each is masquerading in a role, enjoying the fantasies of sex and power here in The Grand Balcony, a brothel managed by a madam named Irma, who alone is free of illusions because she understands the nature of illusions and spends her life providing for the illusions of others. The French have a name for brothels: *les maisons d'illusions*. And The Grand Balcony goes all out to provide everything to enhance the illusions of its patrons. Once in the play Irma enumerates the personages represented in the fantasies of her house:

"There are two kings of France with coronation ceremonies and different rituals, an admiral at the stern of his sinking destroyer, a bishop during the perpetual adoration, a judge performing his functions, a general on horseback, a dey of Algiers surrendering, a fireman putting out a fire, a goat attached to a stake, a housewife returning from market, a pickpocket, a robbed man who's bound and beaten up, a Saint Sebastian, a farmer in his barn . . . but no chief of police . . . nor colonial administrator, though there *is* a missionary dying on the cross, and Christ in person."[14]

The allusion to the policeman is to the Chief of Police of the play, whose consuming desire is to be enshrined in a role, to become the object of emulation by men who frequent the brothel; and the reference to the colonial administrator anticipates Genet's disdainful use of colonials in a later play, *Les Paravents* (*The Screens*).

The counterpoint to the activity at The Grand Balcony is provided by a revolution going on in the city, for revolutionaries are in the main extremely serious persons who wish to have no illusions. Their chief illusion, in fact, is that they have no illusions; and they are bent upon destroying all who openly indulge their fantasies. In the course of the insurrection the Queen and her retinue are killed, and Irma and her false bishop, judge, and general are asked to take their places before the populace; after all, the populace cannot do without its illusions. "So I'll be real?" asks Irma. "The rest of the world will be a copy of what I'll be?"[15] How easily the black chesspieces are interchanged with the white! The fears which Irma and her friends entertain at first about posturing as the royal court are soon dispelled in the first magic moments before the crowds, who are evidently unable to recognize the difference between figureheads and genuine celebrities.

Soon the false bishop, the false judge, and the false general begin to merge their personalities with their new functions. The bishop, like Anouilh's Becket, decides that he will be more than the symbolic head of his country's church; he will be its actual head. The judge becomes absorbed in his appointments with the magistrates. And the general says, "By Jove, I no longer dream."[16]

Finally disillusioned about revolutions, the rebels are routed, and Roger, the most devoted of the anarchists, shows up at The Grand Balcony and asks to play the role of the Chief of Police. The Chief, afraid he would never be apotheosized, has had a gigantic memorial constructed for himself in the form of a phallus and is about to entomb himself in it when Roger appears. Overjoyed, he joins Irma at the special portholes through which she observes the dramas taking place in her establishment and watches as Roger and his assistants perform the rite in which Roger "becomes" the object of his fantasy. At a climactic moment Roger unexpectedly takes out a knife and castrates himself. The Chief instinctively reaches to see whether he is still whole and finds that he is. It is his *image* that will be castrated in every brothel in the world. With a feeling of satisfaction he enters his phallic mausoleum, prepared to remain there for the next two thousand years. It has taken a revolutionary acting out of his role to reveal to him what it is that police do not have: they are without phalluses and so can come and go in the bordellos. Now he can enter a role like the others and dream of sex and power.

As the play ends, Irma reassumes her position as the madam and begins again to distribute roles to others. She even has a word for the members of the audience about theirs: "You must now go home," she says, "where everything—you can be quite sure—will be even falser than here."[17] This is the *expositio* of the sermon Genet has been preaching— and there can be no doubt that it has sunk home.

Genet's theater, as Bernard Dort has observed,[18] differs fundamentally from that of such playwrights as Calderon and Pirandello. Whereas they work at developing the character of a being, Genet tries to demonstrate the sheer impossibility of the enterprise. Pirandello's Henry IV, for example, recovers a stance, a position, even in his fictive personality. Not so Genet's heroes; they never arrive at a "coherent ensemble," at a real system of values. Genet does not criticize them—his bishop is not sacrilegious in the manner of a bishop by Ghelderode; he only presents them in such a way as to make it obvious that they are mere phantasms and never more. He shows the spectators their images and then smashes them, leaving them with nothing to cling to. They are surer of falsehood and illusion than of faith and reason, and Genet has accomplished his mission of making his own world more real by making theirs less real. Far from experiencing what Tillich calls "the shock of being," they now experience a kind of ontological dizziness, a sense of remoteness from reality, as though nothing were sure or real any more. In Sartre's words, Genet has shown them the "whirligig," and has made "the *nothing* shimmer at the surface of the all."[19] They know now, if they did not know before, that the world is a whorehouse, a place of illusions, where men purchase what reality they have by playing roles and performing ceremonies.

If *Le Balcon* invaded the citadels of its viewers' private lives, Genet's next play, *Les Nègres* (*The Blacks*), constitutes what one interpreter calls "a genuine act of aggression."[20] The ambiguities of this play are even more complicated, if possible, than those of the earlier one. The key is struck in the author's brief Foreword: "One evening an actor asked me to write a play for an all-black cast. But what exactly is a black? First of all, what's his color?" What is black, indeed! The play apparently springs out of racial resentments and antagonisms. But the "white" court which sits on a high platform on the stage to judge the Negroes—a Court composed of the white Queen, her valet, the Governor, the Judge, and the Missionary—is obviously being impersonated by blacks wearing white masks. Again we are to have "phantasms within phantasms."[21] Genet is determined to play contraries off against each other. In his second Foreword to the play he says that the play is intended for a white audience and that if it should ever happen that the audience is all black, at least one white man should be invited and a spotlight focused on him through the entire performance. "But what if no white person accepted? Then let white masks be distributed to the black spectators as they enter the theater."

The kind of cabalism or voodooism detected so strongly in *Les Bonnes* and *Haute surveillance* really comes into its own in this play, where the accents of both jungle and civilization are merged into a perfect cacophony of language and emotion. There is an organizer, a kind of sacerdotal figure, named Archibald, who introduces the entertainment for the evening: the blacks will restage the murder of a white woman in front of the "white" Court and audience. Addressing the spectators, Archibald says:

> "This evening we shall perform for you. But, in order that you may remain comfortably settled in your seats in the presence of the drama that is already unfolding here, in order that you be assured that there is no danger of such a drama's working its way into your precious lives, we shall even have the decency—a decency learned from you—to make communication impossible. We shall increase the distance that separates us—a distance that is basic—by our pomp, our manners, our insolence—for we are also actors."[22]

Theoretically, then, the actors will handle their parts with what Brecht called the *Verfremdung* technique, alienating themselves from the characters they portray, so that the audience does not forget that it is only witnessing a play; but in fact it happens again that Genet confuses us about what is play and what is life, and we find ourselves looking into the kaleidoscope where racial relationships and emotive patterns are distorted and spun out again into new and frightening configurations. It is the whirligig again, this time operating at the level of genetic interplay and preconception.

A catafalque stands on stage, supposedly bearing the body of the white woman recently killed. A Negro man, a priest named Diouf, is elected to play the part of the white woman in the re-enactment; Village, the murderer, will play himself. Slowly, rhythmically the ceremony evolves. Through sarcasm and irony the Negroes vent their hatred and resentment of the whites; and the "white" Court mirrors the reaction of the whites, or the reaction as Negroes expect it to be. Once Archibald instructs Diouf: "Politeness must be raised to such a pitch that it becomes monstrous. It must arouse fear. We're being observed by spectators. Sir, if you have any intention of presenting even the most trivial of their ideas without caricaturing it, then get out! Beat it!"[23]

As Village plays the part expected of him by the whites, it is of a supple, sexually arrogant creature of the night, who gets his way by sleight and cunning and murder. "So it's always murder that we dream about?" he asks, feeling his way in the part. "Always," says Archibald, "and get going!"[24] As for the members of the Court, they play to the Negroes' expectations and are stuffy, disdainful, publicly frigid, privately debased. The Queen herself secretly desires to be the woman seduced by the Negro with the "singing" thighs.

The rhythm intensifies; the murder is done. As the Court begins to discuss the issues, the audience is given hints that some more ultimate action is being performed elsewhere, that the ceremony here is only a blind for another murder, another trial, another conflict. At last word comes that the other action is accomplished: a Negro traitor has been tried and executed while the mock trial has been going on. Whirligig! Shakespeare used the play-within-a-play in *Hamlet* to illuminate the real action; Genet has reversed the emphasis and uses the real action, as reported, to intensify the play itself. A subtle trick is being played on the mind of the audience. Discounting the off-stage action in favor of the play it has witnessed, it unconsciously attributes more reality to the play; and by transference the play is made more significant than the private life, the real life, of the audience. As at the end of *Le Balcon*, the spectator is made to doubt the authenticity of the role to which he must return. In Fernandez' words, this is truly "le théâtre magique."[25] It is like the experience of the Oriental who dreamed that he was a butterfly and when he awoke did not know whether he was a man who had dreamed he was a butterfly or a butterfly dreaming he was a man. One does not know whether the real whorehouse is inside the bordello or outside it.

It is frightening to have one's categories and values suddenly disarranged, to lose the centralizing ability of one's intelligence in the midst of the shattered pieces of his world outlook. Ionesco had to flee the theater before the performance was over. For *Les Nègres* is not merely an exercise in black-white relations. It is provocative on that subject, to be sure. But Genet is both too subtle and too complex to be caught issuing mere racial propaganda. The whole register of his experience is in this play. As Susan Taubes has said, "The drama of *The Blacks* is thus the drama of the 'rejected zone,' whether of the psyche, or of society, or of the dominant civilization; it is the zone of the 'totally other,' of the repressed; it is the domain of outcasts, criminals, children and prisoners as well as Negroes, with which Genet identifies himself."[26] Genet asks the question, "Who is Cain?" and he does not dismiss Abel from among the possibilities.

In *Les Paravents* (*The Screens*) Genet transfers the conflict between oppressor and oppressed, colonial and native, to the controversial Algerian scene. And this time he portrays the most abject and despicable character of all his dramas, the spineless and dirty native Saïd. Saïd is the epitome of the rejected ones; and, as it is with Genet himself, he is rejected partly because he chooses to be rejected. By a strange twist of fate, near the end of the play Saïd is accepted by the soldiers and invited to become one of them. It is his first real bid to respectability. There is a contest or argument between the soldiers and one of the old whores who wants to "protect his squalidness." Saïd is grandly aloof from it all. Surveying the square where they are arguing, he says oracularly, "À la vielle, aux soldats, à tous, je vous dis merde." "Merde" no longer elicits the shock it did when Jarry's Ubu stepped onto the boards and uttered it at the end of the last century, but the sentence does bear a distinct odor of finality!

Les Paravents is truly brilliant in theatrical technique and is scabrous comedy all the way through. The situation is delicate for French audiences, as it concerns an explosive political topic, the relationship of French colonialism to native unrest in Algeria; and Genet, who continues to think of France as his country only because he prefers the French language, does not spare any feelings of patriotism.[27] The colonials are mere caricatures, like haughty Sir Harold, who replies to a query about whether they ought not to evacuate the country with the statement, "I have a son. And to save my son's patrimony, I'd sacrifice my son."[28] The Arabs are basically what Arabs are in the minds of colonials—shameless, filthy animals, fit for only labor and copulation. The main conflict, again as in *Le Balcon* and *Les Nègres*, is in the form of a revolution; but the central issue remains one of values and ideals.

The screens noted in the title are tabloids of various sizes equipped with rubber-tired wheels and drawn across the back of the stage to provide the different settings of the play. Strindberg, Tennessee Williams, and others have employed this Oriental convention, but rarely with the ingenuity of Genet. At one point in the play the Arabs perform an oblation to evil in which they draw on blank screens representations of what they have contributed to the revolution. One draws revolvers; another, who has disemboweled three of the colonials' cows, draws the horns of the cattle; another puts up the bloodstain from the rape of a colonial's daughter; another, a house in flames; and so on. The entire affair is ceremonial and is reminiscent of the providing of gifts during the Mass. Because it is to be a Black Mass, the element of sacrilege must be made clear. An elderly man adds to the offerings a prayer he once made. Kadidja, the stage manager for the rite, says:

> Thank you, father. Get God in on it. Let him commit his crimes right and left, let him kill, let him pulverize, let him destroy. Go. Write your prayer on the wall. If you can't find any more crimes, steal crimes from heaven, it's bursting with them! Wangle the murders of the gods, their rapes, their fires, their incest, their lies, their butcheries! Wangle them and bring them![29]

One of the principal devices of illusion in this play is the way Genet keeps both the dead and the living on the stage at the same time by simply transferring the dead to a series of parapets above the other action. From their slight remove, the dead continue to comment on the proceedings and even to influence them, like the gods of a Greek play. By the end of the drama, more of the principals are among the dead than among the living. But all of them, living or dead, are intensely concerned about the decision of Saïd, who is given the chance to become one of the soldiers and improve his lot in the world. His mother, now among the dead, urges him:

> "Make a getaway. Don't let yourself be conned by either the old girl or the soldiers. Don't serve either of them, don't serve any purpose whatever. I think they're going to make up a song about you. The words have been written. People are humming it. It's in the air. Saïd, squelch the inspiration, shit on them!"[30]

The point seems to be that Saïd's freedom lies in his being himself, vulgar, filthy, unprincipled—and unadmired.

Probably Genet intentionally made Saïd analogous to himself, who, having once chosen degradation as a way of life, now found himself pardoned by the President of the Republic and lionized as a literary figure. As Roger Blin, the first to produce Les Nègres and Les Paravents, points out,[31] Genet is not a reformer; he hates society but does not wish to change it; and, most especially, he does not wish to be taken in by society, to be forgiven and robbed of his identity at the same time. Once the Cadi in the play says to Saïd, "I could play a dirty trick on you: I could acquit you of each of your crimes. I'd deliver sentence in the name of God and the people." "You'd be killing me," says Saïd.[32] It is ironic when the little boy who has scribbled obscenities on the sidewalk is punished by being praised for what he has done; and Genet evidently feels that this is the case with him.

This may account in part for the fact that Les Paravents is riper with scatological humor and anal eroticism than Genet's other plays; he appears to be intensifying the more objectionable elements in an attempt to revert from the enfant gâté to the enfant terrible. The play documents rather well the claim of Time magazine that "beside him, Henry Miller is but a cheerfully smutty college sophomore, Sade a dilettante aristocrat of eccentric habits, Gide a genteel old lady sedately cultivating nightshade in her little kitchen garden."[33] This is evidently what Genet wants. As Joseph McMahon has deduced:

> What Genet has had to examine is his role as a revolutionary, and the best available way of measuring that is to determine if the waves of shock sent out by his plays are still creating dramatic oscillations on the receiving equipment. The equipment seems to have built up overly responsive pulses; its components do not seem to have been quite so jarred as they should be. Other revolutionaries, seeing this as the surest indication that their ideas were becoming everyone's, would be cheered. Not so with Jean Genet. For him success offers no sweet smell, but only a fetid stench; for him, too, revolt can have no surcease. It must be ongoing, essential, unchanging, and unconsoling.[34]

But we are deceived if we think this is all that Genet is attempting here. Actually he is still at work trying to dissolve our old categories and prejudices. As our sympathies go to Saïd and the outcasts, we accept unconsciously the preference for their ways over those of the colonials—even down to their scurrility and eroticism. Our own standards have been quietly and deftly undermined; and the sabotage is all the better if we have been diverted from the real intention of the saboteur.

Once again Genet supports his inversion of values by the use of ritual. Roger Blin discerns four ceremonials integral to the movement of the play: the first is in the brothel, where the whores are making themselves up; the second begins when the Arabs commence drawing on the screens; the third occurs in the pinning of medals on the manikins, when we are introduced to the colonials; and the fourth begins when the French lieutenant is struck by a stray bullet and climaxes in the comic rite where the soldiers take turns squatting and releasing "un petit air de France" over his face.[35]

The relation of ceremonial to theater is of course as old as theater itself, many theorists holding that drama began in the sacred rites of the mystery religions or in primitive ceremonies of sympathetic magic. No less eminent a figure than Francis Fergusson has corroborated the notion of the English classicists that the form of ancient Greek tragedy embodied the ritual of the *Enniautos-Daimon*, or seasonal god. Fergusson elaborates the connection in his own discussion of Sophocles' *Oedipus Rex*, in which he says that Oedipus "fulfills all the requirements of the scapegoat, the dismembered king or god-figure."[36] One advantage of the theory is that it would explain how the ancient dramatists managed to continue to interest the audiences in presentations of a plot already known to them from earlier plays: the performances were themselves religious rituals in which the spectators found cleansing through the suffering of the protagonist or scapegoat.

Genet manages in a remarkable way to reunite ceremonials and scapegoat figures to the theater in our own day. He does it not with noble characters, to be sure, but with their opposite. It is his outcasts who bear the sins of the world. Evil is really the only thing they have. As Ommu says in *Les Paravents*, "Do sins scare you? We've nothing else to live but sins, we've got to live them. I have nothing against God, but he can see that all he's left us is sins."[37] The words of Leila, Saïd's wife, are the key to what happens to all the outcasts: "I know where we're going, Saïd, and why we're going there. It's not just to go somewhere, but so that those who are sending us there remain tranquil, on a tranquil shore. We're here, and we're here so that those who are sending us here realize that they're not here."[38] This is precisely the use that audiences make of reprobates and scapegoats.

Sartre says it is the way society used Genet himself, Genet the foundling, Genet the castoff. Society made him a monster and sent him away with its own evil on him. The so-called "decent folk" "made of a child their scapegoat."[39] "Even before he emerged from his mother's womb, they had already reserved beds for him in all the prisons of Europe and places for him in all shipments of criminals. He had only to go to the trouble of being born; the gentle, inexorable hands of the Law will conduct him from the National Foundling Society to the penal colony."[40]

And Genet accepted this deportment from society, this reification of evil in himself. Willingly he would become what the fraternity willed him to be. He writes in his *Journal:*

> The atmosphere of the planet Uranus is said to be so heavy that the ferns there are creepers; the animals drag along, crushed by the weight of the gases. I want to mingle with these humiliated creatures which are always on their bellies. If metempsychosis should grant me a new dwelling-place, I choose that forlorn planet. I inhabit it with the convicts of my race. Amidst hideous reptiles, I pursue an eternal, miserable death in a darkness where the leaves will be black, the waters of the marshes thick and cold. Sleep will be denied me. On the contrary, more lucid than ever, I recognize the unclean fraternity of the smiling alligators.[41]

It is also clear from the *Journal* that Genet identifies the significance of his sordid existence with that of the life of Christ:

> Jesus became man. He expiated. Later, like God, after creating men, He delivered them from their sins: He was whipped, spat upon, mocked, nailed. That is the meaning of the expression: "He suffers in his flesh." Let us ignore the theologians. "Taking upon Himself the sins of the world" means quite exactly: experiencing potentially and in their effects all sins; it means having subscribed to evil.[42]

The sole basis of saintliness, which Genet professes to be seeking, he takes to be renunciation—even the renunciation of morality and religion. Through the muck and the mire, through perversion and crime and betrayal, he will accomplish the generosity of renunciation necessary to become a saint. He will give up everything in order to have all. He will be the scapegoat.[43]

As Genet then reincarnates in each of his dramas the role of the humiliated one he understands so intimately, he provides us again and again with the necessary scapegoat, the one so steeped in evil, so utterly betrayed to it, that we are innocent by comparison. Thus we behold them at their dark rituals—the homosexual criminals of *Haute surveillance,* the perverted domestics of *Les Bonnes,* the whores and *poseurs* of *Le Balcon,* the voodooish blacks and white-blacks of *Les Nègres,* the verminous Arabs of *Les Paravents.* These are no mere anti-heroes such as step from the *anti-romans* and anti-plays of the period; they are the effluvia from the world's slime pits. They are untouchables. They nauseate and disgust us. And at the same time they attract us and intrigue us, for we cannot avoid the magnet of kinship that draws us to them—or that at least draws our darker natures to them. So we watch them. Better than that, we participate in them: we share in their saturnine ceremonials. Our evil is infused with theirs. We have communion with them. And when it is over, when the Black Mass is done, we have gotten something out of our systems; we are cleaner, purer, lighter. It is not entirely unlike what happened in the drama of the Greeks, or in the drama of the Roman Mass, for that matter; Oedipus or Christ or Saïd, there is a sense in which we have heard the cry of the goat being shredded in the wilderness by Azazel, the demon that destroys the creature bearing sin.

What this says is that we can hardly dismiss Genet as a mere pornographer or as a cheap illusionist, as some would ask us to.[44] That would be too quick and easy. We may find the world he pictures repugnant at times—perhaps indeed most of the time. But what disturbs us is likely to be, as Sartre suggests is probably the case with M. Mauriac, not what we see there in Genet but what we see there in ourselves. What horrifies us is our recognition of things, the automatic way in which we receive the signs and respond to them. Suddenly we know—we can no longer fool ourselves—that we are not strangers to this evil, that something in us rushes out to meet it, to embrace it, to identify with it.

No, Genet must be reckoned with on other grounds. And perhaps Sartre has led the way in pointing us to his saintliness. There is a fact that Christians have never grown used to but have always had to face, and that is that the Gospel is really a gospel for outcasts. It is always the derelicts who win in the accounts of the ministry of Christ—those who have so little and expect so little that they can still be formed to the Kingdom. They alone live with the kind of indifference necessary to true saintliness. Could it be that Genet, with the special attraction he has always felt for the Christian religion, has said something we need to hear about the nature of grace?

At the very least he has, in these prophylactic times, renewed and intensified our appreciation of the meaning of evil. He has put on the stage the end result of the kind of titanism Melville and Hawthorne and Dostoevsky were writing about in the last century. Only in Genet the blackness is worse, for it is not out there, it is not cosmic—it is human. Of all the absurdists, he is most concerned with human beings. Not that he always seems to regard man as being real—sometimes he speaks of him as a means to the end which is the achievement of poetry and beauty. But evil is real,[45] and evil is in human beings. Beckett is not much interested in us. He pities us—much more than Genet does. But we are only partly there in his burned-over world. And Ionesco is not quite sure he does not prefer the furniture and animals in his plays to the human beings they crowd to the periphery of things. There is something more biblical in Genet, a feeling for what St. Paul called "the body of this death." Evil exists in man. The dark rituals speak of the powers of the air and of this world and remind us of the real forces at work in us.

The importance of any kind of role-playing diminishes in the face of this agony of being and being evil. Both attribute and function fade before our terror. And if this sounds somewhat existentialist, we are reminded that Genet avoids being caught where the existentialists end up, in the posturing of authenticity itself.[46] He is a final and complete anarchist, opposed, as Roger Blin said, to any kind of order, even that of the existentialist faith. The world as he sees it can never be reformed, for reform itself is merely another illusion. Only grace can speak to such a world. Man cannot rely on himself or on his function. The posture of the saint who casts away everything is the only tenable one; all others should be exposed and abandoned.

It is significant that Genet does not reject the possibility of communication among men as some absurdists do. He does not trouble to demonstrate the inadequacy of language. The reason is that he believes in communion—the kind of communion men have by virtue of their living in a community of evil. Men are necessarily dependent on one another in such a community; they cannot go it alone. The prisoners in *Haute surveillance* must have their fellowship in order to exist; Lefranc's cry at the end, "I really am alone," is the real confession of doom. Claire and Solange in *Les Bonnes* are complementary personae, changing places, fading into one another, throughout the play; and even Madame is necessary to them, as they assume her role, become her, even to the point of dying in her place. The judge, or play-judge, in *Le Balcon* calls the thief who grovels before him and the executioner who carries out his sentences, "my two perfect complements." "My being a judge," he says to the thief, "is an emanation of your being a thief."[47] The blacks and the whites in *Les Nègres* are likewise only interdependent parts of the same being; the fact that each exists only as the other conceives him underscores their essential unity. Nor could the colonials and the Arabs in *Les Paravents* begin to imagine an existence apart from one another; they are indissolubly wedded.

In a sense, then, Genet preaches a doctrine of tolerance. Men must necessarily accept each other in such a world. From what false eminence can one man judge another? The world is a whorehouse, and patrons of the whorehouse do not accuse each other of indiscretions. The Cadi, or village judge, in *Les Paravents* sees what human judging really amounts to. Three offenders have been brought before him: a beggar who has outraged passersby by blowing a flute with each nostril; a man who was caught urinating against a young laurel at the edge of a public soccer field; and a woman who claims she did not really do anything but wishes to have ten blows with a stick as her punishment. "I'm fed up," says the Cadi. "Think of the nonsensical problems laid before me. I'm judge of a village where ghastly crimes are probably being committed every minute —or is anything a crime?—and the world offers up to God only one or two charming trifles."[48] His suspicion that perhaps nothing is a crime is based on the understanding that all men are both more innocent and more guilty than they realize. It is splitting hairs to talk of the guilt of one without talking of the guilt of all. The bishop has a real theological insight in The Grand Balcony when he says, "Here there's no possibility of doing evil. You live in evil. In the absence of remorse, how could you do evil?"[49] Here is a sense of the magnitude of sin and the acceptance of sinners uncommon among even bona fide churchmen.

Genet has clearly tried to be Christ to this mixed-up world. Not like those fanatics who always talk about a cross and try to imitate the stigmata on their bodies. But he has abased himself, has excluded himself from society, even from the living;[50] he has taken to slime and filth, denying his own sex, reveling in crime, choosing to be an outcast and an object of disgust. He is the paradigm of all sensitive persons who wish to be Christ to the world, to atone for the world; and, failing that, he renounces the world, denies it, choosing over it the reality of the evil in which it is immersed.

In his Journal he says that no thief ever sides with the devil because he knows that God will be the victor.[51] Exactly! And Genet never sides with evil. He is a moralist, and he wants to destroy man who is permeated with evil, who is indistinguishable from it, who gives it its substance and makes possible its existence. He wants to destroy himself, to put himself out of the way, just as he does his abject characters in the plays, ending every ritual with an immolation. Poor Genet! For his passion is, after all, the fundamental Christian passion. But without a proper sense of the efficacy of Christ's atonement, he must keep sacrificing, keep facing us with wonder and terror.

Notes

[1] *The Thief's Journal*, trans. Bernard Frechtman (Evanston, Ill., 1965), pp. 92–93.

[2] Genet, *Oeuvres Complètes* (Paris, 1951), II, 186.

[3] *The Theatre of the Absurd* (New York, 1961), p. 142.

[4] *The Thief's Journal*, p. 93.

[5] O. F. Pucciani, in an excellent analysis of the play, discerns five main movements: from the beginning of the play to the ringing of the alarm clock; from the ringing of the clock to the ringing of the telephone; from the ringing of the telephone to the arrival of Madame; from the arrival of Madame to her departure; and from her departure to the end of the play. The drama is a nearly perfect tragedy in the classical French tradition, says Pucciani, with five acts implicit in the five movements and with all the unities strictly observed. The only convention violated is that calling for noble *dramatis personae*, and it has been purposely violated. "Tragedy, Genet and *The Maids*," *Tulane Drama Review*, VII (Spring 1963), 42–59.

[6] Introduction to *The Maids*, trans. Bernard Frechtman (New York, 1954), p. 23.

[7] *The Maids*, p. 84.

[8] *The Thief's Journal*, p. 185.

[9] *Ibid.*, p. 186.

[10] Tom F. Driver, "The Spiritual Diabolism of Jean Genet," *Christian Century*, November 20, 1963, pp. 1433–1435.

[11] *Saint Genet, Actor and Martyr*, trans. Bernard Frechtman (New York, 1963), pp. 328–329.

[12] *The Thief's Journal*, p. 180.

[13] Joseph McMahon, *The Imagination of Jean Genet* (New Haven, 1963), p. 62.

[14] *The Balcony*, trans. Bernard Frechtman (New York, 1958), p. 44.

[15] *Ibid.*, p. 78.

[16] *Ibid.*, p. 96.

[17] *Ibid.*, p. 115.

[18] "Le Jeu de Genet," *Les Temps Moderne*, XV (June 1960), 1875–1884.

[19] Introduction to *The Maids*, p. 29.

[20] David I. Grossvogel, *The Blasphemers* (Ithaca, N.Y., 1965), p. 138.

[21] Jacques Guicharnaud, *Modern French Theatre from Giraudoux to Beckett* (New Haven, 1961), p. 169.

[22] *The Blacks, A Clown Show*, trans. Bernard Frechtman (New York, 1960), p. 12.

[23] *Ibid.*, p. 33.

[24] *Ibid.*, p. 41.

[25] Dominique Fernandez, "Claudel et Genet," *La Nouvelle Revue Française*, XV (January 1960), 122.

[26] "The White Mask Falls," *Tulane Drama Review*, VII (Spring 1963), 86–87.

[27] Cf. this diatribe of the Lieutenant: "France is watching us. She's sending us out to die. . . . Or half-die, that is, return crippled, armless, legless, broken and bent, balls torn off, noses eaten away, faces blasted. . . . That's very fine too. Painful, but very fine. Thus, in the image of its rotting warriors France will be able to watch itself rot. . . . But conquer? . . . And conquer what? Or whom? You've seen them dragging in the mud, living on peelings. . . . Conquer that!" *The Screens*, trans. Bernard Frechtman (New York, 1962), pp. 117–118.

[28] *Ibid.*, pp. 74–75.

[29] *Ibid.,* p. 102.

[30] *Ibid.,* p. 199.

[31] Bettina Knapp, "An Interview with Roger Blin," *Tulane Drama Review,* VII (Spring 1963), 111–124.

[32] *The Screens,* p. 52.

[33] "The Case of Jean Genet," *Time,* October 11, 1963, p. 114.

[34] *The Imagination of Jean Genet,* pp. 202–203.

[35] Knapp, *loc. cit.*

[36] *The Idea of a Theater* (Princeton, 1949), p. 39.

[37] *The Screens,* p. 133.

[38] *Ibid.,* p. 109.

[39] *Saint Genet,* p. 23.

[40] *Ibid.,* p. 31.

[41] *The Thief's Journal,* p. 47.

[42] *Ibid.,* p. 223. Cf. the Christological references to both Kadidja and Saïd in *The Screens,* p. 105 ("sponge and vinegar") and p. 189 ("between heaven and earth"), respectively.

[43] Sartre wisely observes that Genet decided to become a saint because he was not a son (*Saint Genet,* p. 11). That, I think, is a sound conclusion. The son, because he feels secure, does not need sainthood. But the foundling, or the son who thinks of himself as a foundling, must achieve his security. By becoming a saint, by refusing to use the world's riches, he renders those riches useless and proves himself superior to them. Sartre said he once had in his hands a copy of *Pompes funèbres* on whose flyleaf Genet had inscribed, "Jean Genet, the weakest of all and the strongest." Like Saïd in *Les Paravents,* he was weakest by virtue of having nothing, of being nothing; but he was also strongest in that he was free, that his role imposed no demands on him, or at least none of the conventional demands. He could reply "Merde" to them all.

[44] Mauriac and Marcel have led in raising the moralists' objections in France. In America negative response has generally been more ambiguous. Cf. J. M. Svendson, "Corydon Revisited: A Reminder on Genet," *Tulane Drama Review,* VII (Spring 1963), 98–110; Christopher

Ricks, "Dejecta," *New Statesman,* January 10, 1964, pp. 46–47; and Driver, *op. cit.*

[45] Cf. the invocation in *Les Paravents:* "Evil, wonderful evil, you who remain when all goes to pot, miraculous evil, you're going to help me. I beg of you, evil, and I beg you standing upright, impregnate my people." *The Screens,* p. 97.

[46] Cf. Benjamin Nelson, "*The Balcony* and Parisian Existentialism," *Tulane Drama Review,* VII (Spring 1963), 60–79.

[47] *The Balcony,* p. 14.

[48] *The Screens,* p. 51.

[49] *The Balcony,* p. 4.

[50] Cf. Sartre, *Saint Genet,* p. 20: "Time is only a tedious illusion, everything is already there, his future is only an eternal present and, since his death is at the end of it—his death, his sole release—since he is already dead, in short, already guillotined, it's better to get it over with right away. . . . Genet will henceforth date subsequent events from the day of his suicide. And later, in the dismal ceremonies which will restore the original crisis, the primary rite will be that of death."

[51] *The Thief's Journal,* p. 227.

The Devil and Saul Bellow

by

Robert H. Fossum

> Well, given time, we all catch up with legends, more or less.
> —Saul Bellow, *The Adventures of Augie March*

> Keep your hands off my soul!
> —James Purdy, *Malcolm*

IT WOULD SURELY BE STRETCHING A POINT TO CALL SAUL BELLOW A religious writer. Professing no allegiance to any theological system, he deals in his novels with problems which are not, in the strict sense, religious; most of his protagonists are Jews, but Judaism is not of much importance in their lives; and, while admitting that certain kinds of humanism—the "spilt religion" of romanticism, say—suffer from a distasteful "dampness," Bellow finds a "bottled religion"[1] such as that of T. E. Hulme and his followers equally unpalatable. He has not been attracted by the themes of alienation, abandonment, the *Deus absconditus*, which seem to preoccupy so many of the religious minds of our time. Nor, as Chester E. Eisinger has observed, is Bellow willing to go along with those modern theologians who would emphasize the "omnipresent evil and . . . innate depravity"[2] of man and reality. Instead, he has consistently affirmed man's desire for goodness and celebrated what the late Martin Buber called "joy in the world as it is, life as it is."

And yet, despite his apparent indifference to the more fashionable aspects of the current "revival of religion" among literary men, Bellow's novels reveal that he is just as deeply concerned, in his own way, with matters of the spirit as some of his more manifestly religious contemporaries. No less than a Julian Green, a François Mauriac, a J. F. Powers, Saul Bellow is concerned with the state of a man's soul. Indeed, from the Joseph of *Dangling Man*, his first slim book of fiction, to the Moses E. Herzog of his latest, incredibly rich novel, Bellow's protagonists are all (to paraphrase Jung) modern men in search of their souls; they are men occupied with the question: "How should a good man live; what ought he to do?" (*DM*, p. 39). Most important, they are men who discover— sometimes with great agony of spirit—that both "Good and Evil are real" (*H*, p. 165). For while believing, with his Joseph, that it is narrow and cowardly to regard the world as totally evil, Bellow also believes that "those who believe in a wholly good world . . . do not understand depravity" (*DM*, p. 29). Similarly, he suggests that if there is not exactly "a diabolic part" to man, there is certainly a "general, poor, human devil" (*DM*, p. 77) within each of us, a devil which we must exorcise if we are to become "good men."

Bellow's protagonists all come to understand depravity. And depravity means to Bellow that which would rob a man of his soul, the essence of his being, and turn him into an object, a thing to be manipulated, thereby preventing him from being a person "responsible for his own salvation, which is his greatness" (*DM*, p. 89). For in Bellow's view man is man only when he is free to develop the self which governs his fate: "Chance must not govern it, incident must not govern it. It is our humanity that we are responsible for it" (*DM*, p. 167). Anyone who denies this, for himself or others, is doing the work of the devil. So it is with those who think of men only in terms of *types* or *categories* rather than as personalities. So it is with those who subordinate men to theories about mankind. And so it is, most particularly, with the man who would, as Augie March says, "recruit other people to play a supporting role and sustain him in his make-believe" (*AM*, p. 402), who would try to attain being for himself by possessing and living through another person. Bellow's "good men," on the other hand, are those who accept the burden and the blessing of their humanity, who struggle to be persons and to effect a true meeting with other persons. Only in this way can a man truly "seek grace" (*DM*, p. 154).

Thus in *Dangling Man* Joseph struggles to "know what I myself am" (*DM*, p. 119), to understand what it means "to be held accountable for myself," before the Army's "supervision of the spirit" relieves him of "self-determination, freedom canceled" (*DM*, p. 191). This is why he must force acknowledgment of his identity from a Communist friend who would like to deny it to one who has not sold his soul to the Party. This is why he must refuse money offered him by his brother Amos, who wants only to make Joseph a respectable part of himself.[3] This is why he is so repelled by his friend Morris Abt, who in hypnotizing a woman at a party gains temporary possession of her. And this is why he must renounce those "ideal constructions" which some men substitute for reality, because they can exhaust a man and "become his enemy" (*DM*, p. 141).

In *The Victim* Bellow personifies the evil which he implicitly defined in his first novel. And he does so by endowing the anti-Semite Kirby Allbee with traits and a physical appearance typically associated with the Prince of Darkness. An actor and a liar, always "mystifyingly off center and precarious" (V, p. 74), Allbee—with his "sensational, terrible look of pain" (V, p. 293), his "suffering anger and hate" (V, p. 142), his "naked malice" (V, p. 219)—obviously suggests evil incarnate. Member of a once proud New England family, Allbee has come down in the world and now wants others to share his "fallen nature" (V, p. 271). As he says to Asa Leventhal: "You're in the empyrean . . . and I'm in the pit. And I have been in your position but you have never been in mine" (V, p. 69). Therefore, fastening himself on Leventhal, who has until now kept his "spirit under lock and key" (V, p. 146), he tries to lure his not-so-innocent victim into that darkness which "is as real as sunshine" (V, p. 146). As Eisinger puts it, Allbee commits the Hawthornean sin: he tries "to violate the sanctity of the human heart, to destroy the integrity and privacy of Asa's inner being."[4]

Allbee's technique is devilish indeed. On the one hand, he tries to convince Leventhal that men are "only creatures" and not, as Asa believes, "accountable in spite of many weaknesses" (V, p. 154) for what they are and what they will become; on the other hand, he suggests subtly that since Asa is apparently "not for God," then he might as well be "for the Old Scratch" (V, p. 266) and "sign on with the devil and . . . the powers of darkness" (V, p. 99). In short, Allbee's job is to convince Asa that he is basically as corrupt as Allbee himself and should admit it.

He almost succeeds. For Leventhal has in fact tried to shut his eyes to evil, the evil in the world and the evil in himself; and consequently, his soul—grown "fat like his body" (V, p. 169)—is unprepared to deal with it when it swims "toward him out of a depth of life in which he himself would be lost, choked, ended." In one sense, then, Allbee is Leventhal's tutor, his initiation guide into a knowledge of "horror, evil, all that he had kept himself from" (V, p. 277). But he is also, in a Dostoevskian way, Leventhal's double, an objectification of the "indifference and neglect"

(V, p. 158) of which Asa, too, has been guilty but which he has refused to confront. Thus it is that Asa sees something in Allbee's eyes "which he could not doubt was the double of something in his own" (V, p. 169) and that, looking at his corrupted counterpart, he is sometimes "singularly drawn with a kind of affection. It oppressed him, it was repellent. . . . Still, he welcomed it, too" (V, p. 224). Thus it is, too, that when his friend Harkavy says Allbee has sold him a bill of goods, Leventhal replies: "I must have wanted to buy" (V, p. 261).

By confronting evil without allowing it to possess his being, by accepting responsibility for himself, his actions, and his involvement with others, Leventhal ultimately succeeds in exorcising the "spell of confusion and despair" (V, p. 299) which Allbee has cast over him. Still, Leventhal has had his vision of evil, and, as Henry James might have put it, he will never again be as he was.

The Adventures of Augie March is a much more lighthearted book than either Dangling Man or The Victim. It is a book devoted, in fact, to a Whitmanian celebration of life. Nonetheless, it is not a book which ignores evil. As in the first two novels, evil is defined as that which would possess a man's soul and turn him from a subject into an object; in addition, it is seen as that which would deny life its divine vitality and diversity by reducing it to a series of forms or categories. Both of these are, as it were, activities of the Spirit of Denial, of what Bellow elsewhere calls the "anti-life" (DM, p. 165).

Because he is for life and man, Augie March resists as many forms and categories as he can. Although he realizes that "some version or other" (AM, p. 521) of life may help a man to survive, he also realizes that one runs a risk of "becoming them in the process" (AM, p. 303). Similarly, Augie manages throughout the novel to elude those people who would capture him and attain their own being by living through him. So Augie resists the efforts of his brother Simon (who has sold himself to money and the Magnuses) to turn Augie into another version of himself.[5] He turns his back on Mrs. Renling, who wants to adopt him, because he realizes she is merely trying to "consolidate what she affirmed she was" while turning him "into one of these people who didn't know who they themselves were" (AM, p. 151). He fights for his very life against Basteshaw, who has made himself barren "in order to become the man of his ideas" (AM, p. 512) and would make Augie an instrument in his scheme to create a new brotherhood of men by injecting them with a serum. He even breaks with the redoubtable Thea, because she would turn him into a pet to be possessed, trained, controlled, and he would be forced to "accept her version of everything" (AM, p. 316); he would become like "a fielder in a demon's game and . . . gallop here and there and catch burning stone in the air" (*AM*, p. 321).[6] To give himself up to any of these persons, to believe that they have "more power of being" (*AM*, p. 401) than himself, would be to sell them his soul and die the great death. For, as Augie says, "That's what death is about," that "we should no more be persons" (*AM*, p. 519).

Of all Bellow's protagonists, the one who comes closest to selling his soul is Tommy Wilhelm, the pathetic salesman of *Seize the Day*. In this novelette Bellow not only creates his most striking personification of evil, the charlatan Tamkin, but by means of (probably unintentional) parody, he makes an ironic comment on the character of temptation in our time. A matter of ironic correspondences rather than of conscious influence, no doubt, *Seize the Day* is nevertheless in many respects a parody of Goethe's *Faust:* Tommy Wilhelm a ludicrously inverted modern version of Goethe's great hero, Tamkin a shabby counterpart of Mephistopheles, the devil's agent.

Now at first glance there seems to be little resemblance between the timid, nerve-shaken Wilhelm and the magnificent Goethean rebel. Consider Faust, the scholar so sated with worldly knowledge that he turns in cynical boredom to a world beyond the human, and Wilhelm, the uneducated, unemployed salesman who spends his life *avoiding* knowledge; Faust, contemptuous of humanity and thinking himself a superman, and Wilhelm, alienated from others by his sense of failure and inferiority and yet desperately dependent on them; Faust, prototype of rebellious individualism, and Wilhelm, the conformist so frightened of being an outsider that he has dropped his Jewish name and renounced his identity; Faust, loved and sustained by the faithful Gretchen-Margaret, and Wilhelm, whose estranged wife, Margaret, is concerned only with money; Faust, whose goals are at least grandiose, and Wilhelm, who dreams only of easy money, social acceptance, and "peace of mind." And yet, if in a sense Faust represents mankind, is there not something of Faust even in Tommy Wilhelm? Are not the temptations of contemporary, post-Faustian man, however cheapened, counterparts of those to which Faust was exposed? If Faust was the embodiment of an age which glorified rebellion and individualism, is it not perhaps the pitifully compliant nonentity Wilhelm who epitomizes our age and its aims? In short, isn't Faust Inverted a frighteningly appropriate myth for our time?

The ironic parallels and inversions may be seen at the very beginning of the action, for the dark-carpeted Gloriana Hotel is suggestive of the Heaven which introduces Goethe's poem; Wilhelm's trip in the elevator is like a descent into Hell; the cafeteria where he eats is painted in gold and purple, looking—as does its food—like what it is not; and the elderly women he sees there, "rouged and mascaraed and hennaed . . . stared . . . with expressions that did not belong to their age" (*STD*, p. 91). Under the gilt and phony glamour, Tommy Wilhelm's Heaven is really Hell, a place of deceit and corruption; and Wilhelm, like Faust, is surrounded by "smoke and rot, animals' skeletons and dead men's bones" (*Faust*). The city outside is less carefully disguised. "Hot stony odors rose from the subway grating in the street" (*STD*, p. 101); in Columbus Circle "the mouth of midtown stood open" (*STD*, p. 100)—like the pit of Hell—and even the air was infected by "gas . . . from the bursting buses" (*STD*, p. 74). New York, once the earthly paradise of an immigrant's dream, is now a nightmarish inferno, "the end of the world, with its complexity and machinery, bricks and tubes, wires and stones, holes and heights" (*STD*, p. 83).[7]

New York is pandemonium in another sense as well: its inhabitants are unable to communicate with one another. To Wilhelm it is "the punishment of hell itself not to understand or be understood. . . . You had to talk with yourself in the daytime and reason with yourself at night. Who else was there to talk to in a city like New York?" (*STD*, pp. 83–84). Wilhelm suffers particularly from this torment, as suggested by his thickness of speech and persistent feelings of suffocation. Unlike the poetic Faust, Bellow's salesman cannot "bring his awful feelings forth" (*STD*, p. 53), and ever since his days as a movie extra he has suffered from "chest weakness." The malady reaches its height near the end of the story when, in a telephone booth (the ironic analogue of Faust's study), he feels that "he had scarcely enough air in his lungs to speak in a whisper" (*STD*, p. 114). Whatever communication does take place has to do with money. In the brokerage office Wilhelm meets and talks with those lost creatures who have sold their souls for money, whose very being has in fact become money: Rowland, a bachelor, retired from his law practice since his mother gave him twenty shares of steel; old Rappaport, the walking skeleton, with eyes which are "beyond remedy by glasses . . . smoky and faded" (*STD*, p. 86); and above all Tamkin, Bellow's Mephisto, with his easy-money scheme to tempt Wilhelm and his blood bond consisting of the power of attorney.

That Tamkin is a devil in modern dress is immediately evident. He has a "bald skull" and "handsome eyebrows"; his shoulders have "pagoda-like points," and he is pigeon-toed; his nails are clawlike, and there is a "hypnotic power in his eyes" (*STD*, pp. 62–63). He seems to have been everywhere and to know a little about everything—including the "guilt-aggression cycle" (*STD*, p. 64) which, he says, lies behind market speculation. Furthermore, Tamkin, like his Goethean counterpart, delights in parading his knowledge. He displays the proper books, and he speaks the jargon of scientism: "Of course, for simplification purposes, I have spoken of the soul; it isn't a scientific term, but it helps you to understand it" (*STD*, p. 71). Faust was beguiled by magic; today's victim is beguiled by a benighted faith in "science."

Nevertheless, Tamkin's statements, like those of Mephisto (and, one might add, like those of Allbee in *The Victim* and Thea in *Augie March*), are often partially true. For instance, he says to Wilhelm: "Fools, hard-hearted criminals, and murderers have millions to squander. They burn up the world . . . and suck even the earth and sky" (*STD*, p. 80). But this remark is not intended to persuade Wilhelm that money can corrupt, but rather to suggest that Wilhelm should put his fate in Tamkin's hands. "The world belongs to he who is noble and is swift to seize," says Goethe's Mephisto; Tamkin says, "Thou art king" and "all creations art thy just. . . ." (*STD*, p. 75)—if Wilhelm will only take his advice. In fact, it disturbs him that nowadays so many find damnation without his help, that he hasn't "even been able to practice [his] profession" (*STD*, p. 9). He is partly right in saying that everybody in the hotel is mentally disturbed, but he neglects to mention that he is the carrier, not the curer, of the disease. (He mentions that he has treated a girl who wore a broomstick skirt and suffered seizures and a man who howled like a wolf, but he doesn't say that he cured them!) He is also quite right in urging that Tommy have the "courage to be"—but under the guidance of the very one who would control that being.

For instance, Wilhelm suffers from a fear of failure. His Hollywood venture "unfitted him somehow for trades and business" (*STD*, p. 7): the agent Maurice Venice, a minor devil who is as much victim as tempter,[8] played upon Wilhelm's fear of "lagging"[9] and upon his typically American thirst for neon-lighted fame and the fast buck. Even Wilhelm's father despises his son not because he is morally confused, spiritually empty, and will-less, but because he is a financial failure. Tamkin, too, tempts Wilhelm with "success." For like Mephisto, Tamkin's illusory picture of "realized potential" includes money and "social power." It does not include self-possession.

But the principal prize Tamkin offers is neither financial nor social success; it is psychological tranquility. Here the parodic parallel to Goethe's *Faust* becomes most significant. As Bellow's title indicates, the novelette is centrally concerned with Tamkin's attempt to persuade Tommy that to find the good life he must "seize the day" and live in the here and now. Likewise, in Goethe's poem Faust agrees that Mephisto may possess his soul only when, perfectly satisfied with the present moment ("Stay, thou art so fair!"), he renounces responsibility for past mistakes and disregards future possibilities, that is, when he denies that life is a trial-and-error process leading toward either salvation or damnation. As D. J. Enright has noted, the technique of Goethe's devil "is not to provoke [Faust] into some enormity of evil but to confuse him, deaden his critical faculties, and so drown him in the lesser sensual pleasures and the specious showpieces of black magic that . . . he will in weary complacency call on the passing moment to halt and remain."[10] Tamkin is also a "confuser of the imagination" (STD, p. 93), whose emphasis on guilt-free expression of the instincts corresponds to Mephisto's offer of sensual delights; whose financial system and cheap psychology correspond to Mephisto's magic; and whose exhortations to "seize the day" echo Mephisto's. As he says to Wilhelm: "I am at my most efficient when I don't need the fee. . . . The spiritual compensation is what I look for. Bringing people into the here and now. . . . That's the present moment." And when Wilhelm has a choking spell, Tamkin says: "You should try some of my 'here and now' mental exercises. It stops you from thinking so much about the future and the past and cuts down the confusion" (STD, p. 89). According to Tamkin, these exercises produce serenity and put one in the "cradle of eternity." Indeed, they do. But to gain such serenity, one must anesthetize himself, morally and intellectually. The promised "eternity" is eternal damnation; the cradle, a coffin: for, as Goethe puts it in the Prologue to Faust, man gives in to evil when "unqualified repose too soon he learns to crave."

Just as Faust was visited by the Tempter (and Leventhal by Allbee) at the moment when he was most susceptible, so Tamkin seems to know that his victim is ripe for plucking. He knows about Wilhelm's Coca-Cola and pills (those modern equivalents of Faust's "strange potions"), and he knows, as did Mephisto, that death and damnation are the consequences of such sterile activities as Wilhelm has always practiced. For Wilhelm has been only a movie extra, not a creative actor; a hospital orderly, not a doctor; not an inventor, but a salesman—who has sold his soul piece by piece and seems willing to "buy it and sell it; sell it and buy it again" (STD, p. 8), hoping that the electronic bookkeeping machine will keep him out of debt. He is a man who wants success without risk, salvation without the agonies of selfhood and free choice.

Nevertheless, Wilhelm sometimes realizes, as Faust did, that he has the power to save himself, that devils are only effectual insofar as they arouse the evil *within* their victims. Like Asa Leventhal, Tommy is dimly aware that he has chosen to submit to that evil: "And so, from the moment when he tasted the peculiar flavor of fatality in Dr. Tamkin, he could no longer keep back the money" (*STD*, p. 58). He also senses that if he should resist, Tamkin would back down, that his devil is not carrying him, but that he is carrying the devil: "I was the man beneath; Tamkin was riding on my back . . . with hoofs and claws" (*STD*, p. 105). But whereas Faust was fully aware that one of the "two souls struggling for undivided reign" within him had to win, Wilhelm has been led by Tamkin to believe that neither should win; that they must be kept in equilibrium, because repose rather than struggle leads to redemption. Only occasionally does the force of truth in Wilhelm assert itself, and then it is soon forgotten. At one time it suggests to him that perhaps the real business of life is "to carry his peculiar burden," to struggle, to make mistakes, and to suffer the agonies of the will. It asserts itself again in the subway tunnel where he sees a warning sign, "Do Not Eat the Pig," and shortly after feels love for all the "imperfect and lurid-looking people" (*STD*, p. 84) who, like himself, are parts of humanity. Until the end of the story, however, such epiphanies are short-lived.

As in *Faust*, the conflict in *Seize the Day* is resolved at a funeral. Emerging from the last of his "descents into hell," a Turkish bath, Wilhelm is pushed by the pressure of a crowd into a chapel. He has been looking for Tamkin, but instead he sees his own image in the face of the corpse. The vision saves him. Here is the "serenity" and "cradle of eternity" which Tamkin promised—but it is death, not life. Life is activity and struggle, the natural elements of man which Faust came to believe in. It is a process, not a series of disconnected instants to be seized and held. Finally, although Wilhelm weeps partly out of self-pity, he weeps also out of love and compassion for all the poor creatures who, like himself, labor, spend, strive, design, love, cling, uphold, give way, envy, long, scorn, hide, want, die. Like Faust, he has spoken with the Devil and with Care, and the result is, as for Faust, "reintegration on a higher plane . . . self-love which grows until it embraces all humanity."[11] These are the things which Saul Bellow's inverted Faust hears in the funeral music as, "hidden . . . in the center of the crowd," he moves toward the "consummation of his heart's ultimate need" (*STD*, p. 118): understanding of himself; acceptance of the fact that responsibility for one's self is both the burden and the blessing of being human; and sympathy for the rest of the human family.

Like Tommy Wilhelm, the protagonist of Bellow's latest novel, *Herzog*,[12] has reached a point in his life where he feels that he has "mismanaged everything" (*H*, p. 3), that he has "a fatal attraction to the 'City of Destruction'" (*H*, p. 6), and that, as his brother Will says, he has a "talent for making a fatal choice" (*H*, p. 338). Moses Herzog's choice has been to believe in persons in an age of depersonalization, to believe in the human spirit in "an age of spiritual exhaustion" (*H*, p. 234). And, as he says, in a society where "personalities are good only for comic relief" (*H*, p. 149), anyone who "takes dignity seriously, old-fashioned individual dignity, is bound to get the business" (*H*, p. 193). Herzog does indeed get the business. Abandoned by his wife, Madeleine, and cuckolded by his best friend, Valentine Gersbach, Herzog sets out on a solitary quest to "discover what it means to be a man" (*H*, p. 201). He sets out, like all Bellow's men of good will, to rediscover and liberate that "primitive self-attachment of the human creature, that sweet instinct for the self" (*H*, p. 159) without which any true meeting with others is impossible.

Unfortunately, Bellow's Moses is taken to no mountaintop and shown no promised land. He is, indeed, susceptible to the very disease he has so keenly diagnosed. Although at one time he declares, "*I* am Herzog. I have to be that man" (*H*, p. 67), at another time he suspects that the "uniqueness of the Self" is the "last of the Romantic errors," a vestige of the worn-out "old Western, Faustian ideology" (*H*, p. 39). If this is true, then surely he is no more than a result of early traumata and a ridiculous figure whose assumption that his soul is his own is patent nonsense. Seeking relief from the "bone-breaking burden of selfhood" (*H*, pp. 92–93), he has tried to find salvation in other people—in friends and, most especially (in good American fashion), in women: in Daisy, the perfectly patient bourgeoise whose way of life is typified by the straight seams of her stockings; in Sono, the perfectly passive Japanese; in Madeleine, the emancipated, emasculating, culture-clutching female incubus who demands that Herzog's love assume the "flavor of subjugation" (*H*, p. 8) and who wants to take over Herzog's role of scholar-professor; and in Ramona, a theoretician of sex who, using a characteristic Mephistophelean ploy, offers Herzog not only a "life of pleasure" but "metaphysical transcendent pleasure—pleasure which answered the riddle of human existence" (*H*, p. 150), and who demands in return that Herzog say, "You belong to me . . . to me only" (*H*, p. 204).

Although Herzog seems at times to be as un-Faustian as Wilhelm, to be just as ready to place the fate of his being in the hands of another, he is never quite so passive and imperceptive as the poor salesman. He is frequently aware, that is, that Madeleine as well as others is trying to destroy "his pretensions to a personal life so that he might disintegrate and suffer . . . not on anything so distinguished as a cross, but down in the mire of post-Renaissance, post-humanistic, post-Cartesian dissolution, next door to the Void" (*H*, p. 93). He is also aware that "the man who shops from woman to woman . . . has entered the feminine realm" (*H*, p. 188). Most of all, he is aware that to try to attain being by living through another is to join the devil's party.

Ironically, he is made most aware of this through the man who cuckolds him, Valentine Gersbach. Gersbach, with his "fiery-dark depths" (*H*, p. 60) of hair, his "deep, hot eyes" (*H*, p. 19), and his look of "a man who had risen from terrible defeat, the survivor of sufferings few could comprehend" (*H*, p. 61)—this man of "molten sorrow" (*H*, p. 62) is the human analogue of the Father of Deceit who lives on the soul's blood of others. Like Tamkin, he is a charlatan, making "all sorts of people feel that he has exactly what they've been looking for . . . : whatever your heart desires" (*H*, p. 215); perverting religious doctrine and using it for his own ends;[18] giving lectures which are "a parody of the intellectual's desire for higher meaning, depth, quality" (*H*, p. 60); playing "a tremendous variety of roles with a lot of coarse energy" (*H*, p. 216); and appropriating "all the emotions about him, as if by divine or spiritual right," since, believing he "could do more with them . . . he simply took them over" (*H*, p. 61). When Herzog realizes that Gersbach was trying to possess him through Madeleine, he also becomes fully aware of the evil he must himself avoid at all costs: that of living on and through others.

Like all Bellow's protagonists, Herzog has learned that if "brotherhood is what makes a man human" (*H*, p. 272), brotherhood is possible only when man recognizes and accepts responsibility for himself as a "simple, separate person." Only when he realizes that he must "play the instrument he's got" (*H*, p. 330), his own soul, can a man attain independence that is not isolation, salvation that is not damnation in disguise.

Notes

¹ Saul Bellow, *Herzog* (New York, 1964), p. 129. Hereafter page number references to Bellow's novels appear in parentheses after the quoted passages. Abbreviations and the editions to which they refer are as follows: *DM, Dangling Man* (London, 1946); *V, The Victim* (New York, 1956); *AM, The Adventures of Augie March* (New York, 1953); *STD, Seize the Day* (New York, 1956); *H, Herzog*, edition cited above.

² Chester E. Eisinger, *Fiction of the Forties* (Chicago, 1963), p. 342.

³ Ironically, Joseph is as guilty as anyone else in the book of trying to possess and mold another person's soul. He tries to do so to Iva, his wife, only to discover finally that "she is as far as ever from what I once desired to make her" (*DM*, p. 152).

⁴ Eisinger, p. 353.

⁵ At one point in the novel Simon, though hardly a personification of thoroughgoing evil, is nonetheless implicitly compared to the "prince of . . . force and darkness," to "Apollyon with his horrible scales and bear's feet" (*AM*, p. 424).

⁶ Thea herself explains to Augie what other people want of him: "They haven't got anything of their own and they'll leave you nothing for yourself. They want to put themselves in your thoughts and in your mind. . . . They live through observation by the ones around them, and they want you to live like that, too" (*AM*, p. 318).

⁷ The metaphor of the city as Hell is employed frequently in Bellow's fiction (see, for example, *V*, pp. 183–184; *AM*, pp. 474–475; and *H*, pp. 32–33). It is a place in which people are herded together but never meet; in which they are subjected to smoke and heat and per-

petual, chaotic movement; in which a man is never alone and yet is almost always lonely, almost always anonymous.

[8] Venice is eventually sent to prison for the Mephistophelean act of pandering for a movie starlet, America's equivalent of a budding Helen of Troy.

[9] Joseph (in *DM*, p. 89) says: "The fear of lagging pursues and maddens us. The fear lies in us like a cloud. It makes an inner climate of darkness."

[10] D. J. Enright, *Commentary on Goethe's Faust* (New York, 1949), p. 45.

[11] Gusta Barfield Nance, "The Philosophy of Goethe's *Faust*," *Southwest Goethe Festival* (Dallas, 1949), p. 84.

[12] *Henderson the Rain King*, published in 1959, is in its own way fully as rich as *The Adventures of Augie March* and *Herzog*, but it is not particularly relevant to my topic.

[13] For example, Gersbach lectures Herzog on Martin Buber and the sin of making "a man (a subject) into a thing (an object)," while at the same time rearranging Herzog's life, cuckolding him, and making "out his budget for years to come" (*H*, p. 64).

The Curse of Christ in Flannery O'Connor's Fiction

by

Robert Detweiler

FLANNERY O'CONNOR ONCE SAID THAT THE SOUTH IS NOT CHRIST-CENTERED but Christ-haunted and that "ghosts cast strange shadows, very fierce shadows, particularly in our literature."[1] She could scarcely have chosen a better image to describe her own fiction, for it is there, in her stories and novels, that the specters of sin, guilt, and judgment are incarnated and quickened in violent, perverse, and monstrous form to plague our uneasy, godless era. Her art illustrates the observation of Paul Tillich that "Now, in the old age of our secular world, we have seen the most horrible manifestation of these daemonic images; we have looked more deeply into the mystery of evil than most generations before us; we have seen the unconditional devotion of millions to a satanic image; we feel our period's sickness unto death."[2]

To note that Miss O'Connor's stories are permeated by religious material and attitude is to make neither a theological nor a literary discovery. But although theological interpretations of her work abound, much of the spade work remains to be done. Most of the studies speculate—and often speculate well—upon the religious orientation of her fiction but without the literary underpinnings, and it is precisely in those that the locus of her power is found. I intend to show how four of the main constituents of fiction as they are employed by Miss O'Connor are informed and determined by corresponding religious elements, and how she, simultaneously, converts those elements into the structure and content of good literary art.

The novel or short story is created first of all through the manipulation of language and image. In Miss O'Connor's fiction, language and image encounter and often blend with the components of religious exhortation and worship: the revealed word, sacrament, and ritual. Fiction occurs, second, within a particular context composed of the physical and cultural setting of the story, but also (as is too often forgotten) of the implied cultural background of the author himself. Miss O'Connor's stories are located almost exclusively in a setting calculated to produce strong religious colorations that reflect her own acquaintance and ultimately her own spiritual position. Third, fiction is carried by action (or, in more formal terms, by the imitation of action) and necessarily moves from a basic situation through conflict to a climax and a resolution. In Miss O'Connor's novels and tales, most of the situations become a paradigm of the human awareness and assumption of individual guilt and the struggle to find grace, so that the structure of action corresponds to the encounter with guilt and the attempt to rid oneself of it. Fourth, fiction employs language and image, setting, and action to arrive at the thematic relationships that constitute the meaning and purpose of a particular story. Miss O'Connor projects her characters regularly into situations of ambiguity, whereby she works with the grotesque, with irony, and with paradox to describe man's spiritual dilemma that is her central concern.

Turning first to language and image, one discovers in the simple dialogue and description a wealth of characterizing revivalist phraseology. At the beginning of the novel *Wise Blood* Haze Motes, the protagonist, says aggressively to a fellow passenger, "I reckon you think you been redeemed" (p. 12), and has the blind ex-evangelist remark about him, "I can hear the urge for Jesus in his voice" (p. 31). In the short story "The River" the evangelist tells the crowd assembled on the banks of the stream, "If you ain't come for Jesus, you ain't come for me. . . . There ain't but one river and that's the River of Life, made out of Jesus' Blood. That's the river you have to lay your pain in, in the River of Faith, in the River of Life, in the River of Love, in the rich red river of Jesus' Blood, you people" (p. 151).[3]

Sometimes the revivalist idiom becomes a discordant blend of King James English and backwoods red-neck utterance. In the story "The Displaced Person" the indignant Mrs. Shortley in an inner monologue mutters about the priest who has induced her employer to hire a Pole as farmhand: "Here he was, leading foreigners over in hoards to places that were not theirs, to cause disputes, to uproot niggers, to plant the Whore of Babylon in the midst of the righteous" (p. 276). In the novel *The*

Violent Bear It Away young Tarwater uses an image from a New Testament parable to tell his schoolteacher-uncle which one of them has been cursed by Pentecostalism: "It's you the seed fell in. . . . It ain't a thing you can do about it. It fell on bad ground but it fell in deep. With me . . . it fell on rock and the wind carried it away" (p. 416). And in "A View of the Woods" old Mark Fortune shouts in confusion at his granddaughter, "Jedge not . . . lest ye be not jedged" (p. 64).

One can collect further a startling array of ambivalent profanity from the fiction. "My Jesus," "Sweet Jesus Christ Crucified," "Christ nailed," and "Jesus hep me" appear as curses in *Wise Blood;* "Jesus God Almighty damn!" is a particularly effective one from "Parker's Back." But the religious cursing can also come close to prayerful expression, and Miss O'Connor is in fact careful to describe that possibility of ambiguity. In "A Good Man Is Hard to Find" the grandmother, facing death at the hands of the escaped convict, "found herself saying, 'Jesus, Jesus,' meaning Jesus will help you, but the way she was saying it, it sounded as if she might be cursing" (pp. 141–142). In "The River" the boy Harry has always unconsciously assumed that the divine name is just profanity: "If he had thought about it before, he would have thought Jesus Christ was a word like 'oh' or 'damn' or 'God' " (p. 149). In "Parker's Back," when Parker's shirt is lifted to reveal the incredible Byzantine Jesus tattoo, the single word uttered in the pool room expresses recognition, wonder, and derision all at once.

On a more subtle level are the images, often similes or extended metaphors, with distinct Old and New Testament connotations. Haze's mother in *Wise Blood* has "a cross-shaped face." Mrs. Flood, Haze's landlady, fancies Haze "going backwards to Bethlehem." In "The Displaced Person" Mrs. Shortley's husband sits abruptly up in bed "like Lazarus from the tomb." Old Testament images function in the same manner. Three boys who have started the forest burning in "A Circle in the Fire" are likened to "the prophets . . . dancing in the fiery furnace, in the circle the angels had cleared for them," an obvious reference to Daniel 3 (p. 232). When young Tarwater throws a fit in *The Violent Bear It Away,* "he might have been Jonah clinging to the whale's tongue" (p. 432); later, as he is approaching final madness, his eyes "looked as if touched with a coal like the lips of the prophet," as described by the writer of Isaiah 6 (p. 442).

Certain of these images deepen into reflections of sacrament or religious ritual. Baptism and the Eucharist appear in a combination of literal action without intentional sacramental intent and, simultaneously, with unmistakable imagistic implication. In "The River" and *The Vio-*

lent *Bear It Away* two drownings are associated with baptism. In "A Temple of the Holy Ghost" after the celebration of the Mass, the sun is described as "a huge red ball like an elevated Host drenched in blood" (p. 194). In *The Violent Bear It Away* the schoolteacher experiencing the exploitation of the child revivalist feels "the taste of his own childhood pain laid against his tongue like a bitter wafer" (p. 382). Later in the same novel young Tarwater, after arguing with a shopkeeper about "the Resurrection and the Life," suddenly demands of her, "Sell me a purple drink" (p. 438). Ritualistic action with religious undertones pervades everything Miss O'Connor wrote. Haze Motes sleeps with a strand of barbed wire wrapped around him three times; the Misfit in "A Good Man Is Hard to Find" shoots the grandmother through the chest three times; the seduction of Hulga, the Ph.D. with a wooden leg, by the Bible salesman in "Good Country People" proceeds with ritualistic precision; in "The River" Harry's baptism is preceded and accompanied by a name-changing rite; in *The Violent Bear It Away* young Tarwater's spasm is the ritual prelude to his insane prophetic destiny; in "Judgment Day" old Tanner's preparations for his burial are ritualistically directed.[4]

Why pay such close attention to the religious involvement of language and image? Here lies, for one, the most cogent reason for Miss O'Connor's so-called graceless style. That gracelessness is in reality limited to dialogue and interior monologue and is the result of her fine accomplishment in creating the illusion of reproduced backwoods speech. I say "illusion" because she makes no attempt at actual verisimilitude in the exhaustively detailed naturalistic mode. Rather, through the nuance of the occasional ungrammatical word or construction, she gives the impression of the coarseness and clumsiness of the dialect without submitting to its spirit. What are the religious implications of that style? It initiates two elements that are developed through other aspects of her writing. First, the combination of revivalist term and phrase with "normal" speech reflects the subjugation of the religious spirit to selfish modes of existence. Miss O'Connor did recognize, as did Sinclair Lewis (*Elmer Gantry*), John Steinbeck (*The Grapes of Wrath*), and Erskine Caldwell (*The Journeyman*) before her, the tendency of American revivalism toward rendering the religious impulse as a means of egotistical satisfaction. That perversion of religion by the ego is a major theme of Miss O'Connor's fiction, reflected most essentially in language and image. Second, the conjunction of biblical and backwoods English indicates the same impulse, in the domestication and profanation of the majestic language, but at the same time the jarring incongruity reveals the immense gulf between the divine and the human, and here a second major theme is introduced. In Miss O'Connor's language there is an analogy to the Incarnation itself: the Word become flesh. In the shock of disparate language and image (even aside from its function as conveyor of spiritual situations through setting, action, and symbol) there is something akin to the paradox and scandal of Christ. The language is prophetic, kerygmatic, existential, and sacramental. It is prophetic in the Old Testament sense: in the mixture of formal poetic speech with rough-hewn, violent, and homely expression intended to expose evil and call to repentance; in the use of images with direct Old Testament connotations. It is kerygmatic in the sense of the New Testament gospel: within the trappings of myth, parable, and metaphor is the core of a message that demands interpretation and receives immediate interpretation through the juxtaposing with familiar, popular, even banal discourse. It is existential in its constant leaning toward dialogic form, in its innate insistence upon stark extremes that allow for no aesthetic compromise but call to belief—not yet belief in a Christian vision but a more elementary acceptance of the believability of the language itself.[5] The call to faith that leads to grace or judgment, in other words, is anticipated in the language: one either accepts the grotesque speech and description as a true artistic representation of the human condition or rejects it as a sham construction coming with signs and wonders that are false claims to good art. The language is sacramental, finally, in the most literal sense. The word is the instrument of transformational power that, like the Logos of faith, provides the vital form of idea. Words like "blood," "bread," "water" become charged with dynamic meaning that shakes the reader's self-awareness and compels him to consider the potential of grace. The word patterns, further, echo the sequential repetition of human thoughts and actions that settle into ritual—set formulas of word and act seeking to impose order upon existence. The formality and rigidity of much of Miss O'Connor's language in dialogue and depiction of action reveals the human dependence upon specifically religious patterns as denominators of meaning.

Yet Miss O'Connor's art, analyzed from the perspective of language and image, is anything but Christian fiction as the term is popularly understood. She does not preach; she does not write propaganda; she does not seduce the reader into an acceptance of Christianity by a bland mixture of the sensual and the spiritual; she does not even employ her characters as mouthpieces for little homilies on sin, guilt, and salvation. Instead, her art embodies, incorporates the Christian understanding of life, translates it honestly and forthrightly into the elements of fiction.

The discussion of the religious import of language and image provides a natural introduction to the religious settings that form the background and often enough the foreground of Miss O'Connor's stories. One finds a strong sense of locale in her art; yet although the settings are more or less geographically definable, they depend less upon depiction of physical place than upon the pervasion of spiritual moods. Her fictional world is predominantly backwoods Bible Belt, but against that Pentecostal landscape are drawn also the configurations of Roman Catholicism and of the militant atheists whose fervor is religious in itself, while here and there a sketch of "the world," the religiously unconcerned and uncommitted, is filled in. Within the atmosphere created by all these there are tensions and contrasts that determine character, precipitate action, and inform most of the symbolism. One can classify the characters, major and minor, according to four categories.

The largest body is the first one, the Pentecostal fanatics, who are possessed by a kind of inborn and inbred religious zeal. More often than not they are self-styled evangelists, such as Haze Motes' grandfather and old, blind Asa Hawkes in *Wise Blood* and Bevel, the healer in "The River." Sometimes they are rabid lay-members, such as Mrs. Commins in "The River" and Mrs. Shortley in "The Displaced Person." All of them have an obsession to convert and baptize; all of them, in one form or another, are patently and destructively crazy. A fascinating aberration of this group is the religious manipulator, who does not believe in the Pentecostal gospel but who exploits it toward his own ends. Hoover Shoats and Solace Layfield are two of these in *Wise Blood*. They preach the Church Without Christ in competition with Haze Motes solely to make a fast buck. The boy who goes under the name of Manley Pointer in "Good Country People" is another one. He sells Bibles ostensibly in the name of "Christian service" but is really out for sexual conquests and their trophies, such as the woman's glass eye he once garnered and the wooden leg he carries away from Hulga Hopewell.

The second group working in and out of the Pentecostal setting is the militant atheists. These are the ones who most literally feel the curse of Christ upon them. They are not content simply to disbelieve; they disbelieve with a passion and have given their lives to an aggressive denial of the reality of Christ. Haze Motes in *Wise Blood* insists that "Nothing matters but that Jesus don't exist" (p. 33). The Misfit in "A Good Man Is Hard to Find" blames his life of crime on the fact that "Jesus thrown everything off balance" (p. 142). Hulga Hopewell, the crippled Ph.D. in "Good Country People," has a philosophically based belief in Nothing; Rayber, the schoolteacher in *The Violent Bear It Away*, is a behaviorist who has rationalized his own Pentecostal childhood in terms of psychological patterns. But none can escape the curse. Haze finally dies in his insane attempts to purge himself of the nagging possibility of Christ's truth. The Misfit's dedication to murder leaves him jaded and empty. Hulga is grotesquely duped by the Bible salesman. Rayber has his rationality shaken and his idiot son drowned by the demented young Tarwater.

The religiously unconcerned form the third group. These are the ones on whom the fervor of Pentecostalism is lost, not because they are enemies of it but because they do not care about it. To them it seems ridiculous, unbalanced, and absurd. Harry's parents, particularly his mother, in "The River" are examples of these "worldly" people. Sophisticated, alcoholic, and bored, Harry's mother is mildly amused by Mrs. Commins' religion, but also mildly suspicious of it. Yet she and her husband both suffer from it as their confused and neglected son drowns trying to find the Kingdom of God. Mrs. McIntyre, owner of the farm in "The Displaced Person," is one of the uncommitted who are caught between Pentecostalism on the one hand and Catholicism on the other. Both Mrs. Shortley and the priest make their demands upon her. She gives in to neither, but at last her farm and her spirit are destroyed by the tensions between the two. Sheppard, the good-hearted social worker in "The Lame Shall Enter First," tries to disenchant his motherless son of notions about a literal heaven and hell; but the boy, driven by the satanic Rufus Johnson, hangs himself in a desperate search for his dead mother.

The members of the fourth group, the conventionally religious, lack both the color and the zeal of the Pentecostals and the atheists and the worldly wisdom of the unconcerned. They function clumsily and helplessly in Miss O'Connor's fiction. Mrs. Cope in "A Circle in the Fire" mouths Christian platitudes but is incapable of dealing with evil. Mrs. Hopewell in "Good Country People" is unable to fathom or challenge her daughter's intellectual atheism. Father Flynn, the priest in "The Displaced Person," serves the church with a half-senile tenacity, and Father Finn in "The Enduring Chill" displays a knack for delivering the exactly right religious cliché at the wrong time.

What do these four embodiments of religion and irreligion contribute to Miss O'Connor's fiction? They establish one thing: the inescapability, on whatever level of existence, of the individual's confrontation with God and, at the same time, the impossibility of ever finding God on one's own terms. So where does that leave us? Miss O'Connor herself was Roman Catholic, and one must therefore consider the possibility that she is saying "*extra ecclesiam nulla salus est*"; yet even if that is her final position, it is not so easily derived. Rather, the four groups stand in specific relationships to the New Testament Christ. They attempt either to manipulate Him (unconsciously or purposefully), to deny Him, to ignore Him, or to accommodate Him. The setting, consequently, is essentially a spiritual context: the sense of potential judgment that is not so much the heavy hand of God as it is the individual willing, actively or passively willing, to condemn himself in the name of his ego, to corner himself in such a manner that there is at last only senseless violence, insanity, self-destruction, or—possibly—grace.

The inevitability of the encounter with Christ in Miss O'Connor's fiction takes form in the individual assumption of guilt and the struggle to rid oneself of it. That process can best be described in terms of action, for in her art the structure of action usually imitates the pattern of spiritual action that involves judgment or grace.

For Haze Motes in *Wise Blood* the sequence of action corresponds exactly to the workings of grace and judgment upon him. The basic situation at the beginning of the novel finds Haze just released from the army and about to begin his career as sidewalk preacher to establish the Church Without Christ. But what really impels Haze is the sense of guilt gnawing at him, the result of childhood and adolescent experiences with sex and the Pentecostal gospel that have left him feeling unclean. The conflict that ensues is essentially within Haze himself; he strives to throw off the sense of guilt by insisting that sin does not exist and thus that there is no need for redemption through Christ; yet the inner conflict becomes crystallized through an external situation. Haze soon meets preaching competition through Hoover Shoats and Solace Layfield, who also begin recruiting for the Church Without Christ in front of the same movie theater, but with an eye toward collections instead of salvation from needless guilt. Haze is left without even the integrity of his blasphemy; driven to his wit's end, he kills Layfield, his alter ego, in the climactic scene of the novel; then, frustrated in his attempt to flee the town (his old car is destroyed by a policeman), he returns to the boarding house and blinds himself with lime. Miss O'Connor remarked that her characters always receive a moment of grace.[6] For Haze that moment comes when, back at the boarding house, sick, helpless, and trying madly to exorcise his guilt through self-torture, he receives an offer from Mrs. Flood, his landlady, to marry him and care for him. That final gesture of mercy is lost upon him. Haze rejects the offer and leaves the boarding house; he is found unconscious in a ditch the next day, is beaten by a policeman, and dies on the way back to the boarding house. Because he has tried to live without grace, he must die without it.[7]

In "A Good Man Is Hard to Find" occurs a still more intricate interaction of grace and judgment. What begins as a harmless pleasure trip for a Georgia family ends, through the irresponsibility of the grandmother and the guilt of the escaped convict, in six murders. The conflict is between the convict (The Misfit) and society, represented by the varying ages (from very old to very young) of the traveling family, but it deepens into a conflict between The Misfit and Christ. Here again, as in *Wise Blood*, is the curious presence of the alter ego which precipitates the climax of the action. The Misfit's alter ego is Christ Himself, his object of both comparison and condemnation. Like Christ, he has suffered unjust punishment, he says, yet Christ is at fault for throwing the world out of kilter. "If He did what He said, then it's nothing for you to do but throw away everything and follow Him, and if He didn't, then it's nothing for you to do but enjoy the few minutes you got left the best way you can—by killing somebody or burning down his house or doing some other meanness to him. No pleasure but meanness" (p. 142). Right there are grace and judgment in stark, unequivocal terms. But The Misfit becomes an alter ego in his own right. For the old lady in her demented fright, he becomes one of her own children. The moment of grace comes for both of them in the chilling decisive scene. Having judged herself by denying Christ in a last desperate attempt to save her life ("Maybe He didn't raise the dead," she says), she makes a gesture of confused love toward the criminal. "She saw the man's face twisted close to her own as if he were going to cry and she murmured, 'Why you're one of my babies. You're one of my own children.' She reached out and touched him on the shoulder. The Misfit sprang back as if a snake had bitten him and shot her three times through the chest" (p. 143). The grandmother dies groping toward love and forgiveness; that is a situation in which grace may abound. For The Misfit, his rejection of love amounts to a rejection of grace. Even if he escapes the law, he has judged himself finally and irrevocably. "It's no real pleasure in life," are his last words. He has damned himself to meaninglessness.

Other of the stories present similar patterns of redemptive and condemnatory action, with a similar presence of an alter ego and the moment of grace. In "The River" the boy Harry has the faith healer Bevel as his double and even assumes his name. Judgment descends upon his parents as they lose their son through their neglect of him; the boy himself finds grace in his drowning. Searching angrily and despairingly for the Kingdom of God under water, as the preacher has promised he will find it, he experiences an inner peace as he dies. In "The Displaced Person" Mr. Guizac, the Pole, has Christ as his alter ego. Somewhat like The Misfit, he upsets the balance at Mrs. McIntyre's farm by innocently arranging to have a female relative come from Poland to marry a Negro farmhand. Mrs. McIntyre has her moment of grace when she has a chance to save the Pole from death under the wheels of the tractor. She does not act. With the death of Guizac, her farm and her own health and her personality disintegrate. In *The Violent Bear It Away* Rayber, the schoolteacher, finds his alter ego in young Tarwater, his nephew, who is obsessed with the Pentecostal call to prophesy and baptize. Rayber sees in him his own fanatical adolescence from which he is still trying to escape. Grace and judgment come together when Tarwater kills Rayber's idiot son, baptizing him and drowning him all at once. Rayber does nothing to prevent the death. For him it means release from the burden of his son and his own tortured past, but it also means a deliverance into the terrible void of senseless life.

The patterns of action in Miss O'Connor's fiction are telescoped versions of the New Testament message. As in the study of language and image, so one finds through the analysis of action a perfect artistic parallel with the prophetic, kerygmatic, existential, and sacramental aspects of the Christian gospel, presented in a swift, abrupt, compressed economy of movement that has the concentrated force and impact of expressionist drama. There is always a character present at the beginning of the story to establish the basic situation in the prophetic mode: the warning, however distorted by its conveyor, that grace or judgment will inevitably ensue through the encounter with a representative of the Word. The conflict in the action is invariably kerygmatic; the alternatives of redemption or damnation are embodied in the confrontation of two characters, usually the protagonist and his alter ego, and their acceptance or rejection of each other. The moment of grace that corresponds with the climax is existential. In it the individual in his uniqueness is faced for at least an instant with the wholly other who becomes, through the mysterious potential of love, the way to himself. In that instant of decision he creates his freedom or his bondage. The resolution is bound up in sacrament, whether it be the vehicle of grace or the despairing motions of a lost chance; a baptismal drowning, a last partaking of food or drink, the ritualistic gestures of sex, disfiguration, or murder are the postlude to the attempts to satisfy or destroy the individual religious obsession. The whole pattern of action in many of Miss O'Connor's stories becomes, on the deepest level, a dynamic metaphor that mirrors the charismatic-anathematic structure of the New Testament understanding of life.

Finally, in trying to ascertain the thematic statement of Miss O'Connor's fiction, one discovers how she deals in ambiguity. Out of that ambiguity emerge two constituent elements: the grotesque and paradox.

Each of these in turn has its component pairs. The grotesque results from the combination of the comic and the tragic. Paradox grows from the blending of symbol and irony.

The grotesque, abstractly understood, consists of distortion and incongruity. In Miss O'Connor's stories distortion and incongruity appear in language and image, setting and action, to create the opposing poles of the comic and the tragic. In *Wise Blood* (which Miss O'Connor herself labeled a comic novel), Haze Motes' brief career is infused with aspects of distortion and incongruity that join comedy and tragedy to produce the grotesque. The concept of the Church Without Christ itself is a distortion of the basic idea of Christianity, incongruous in its insistence upon a "new jesus" who will preach and redeem through a Christless gospel. It is comic through Haze's speech and appearance (he wears a big black preacher's hat and a bright blue suit with the price tag still attached), through the cantankerous, rat-colored old Essex he drives and preaches from, through his sexual adventures, through the mix-ups with the competing evangelists in front of the movie house. It is tragic through his murder of Layfield, through his blinding of himself (including the overtones of Oedipus putting his eyes out), through his self-torture and eventual death. In "The River" comedy occurs when Harry lets out the hogs at Mrs. Commins' farm and where the faith healer prays for the "affliction" of Harry's mother that turns out to be a hangover; but all that shifts to tragedy when Harry drowns himself in the stream. In "A Good Man Is Hard to Find" comedy engenders tragedy, as the grandmother's cat, hidden in the car, springs upon Bailey the driver and causes an accident which leaves the family at the mercy of The Misfit, who shows no mercy and kills them all. The grotesque *must* result in Miss O'Connor's fictional world because personalities are distorted and lives incongruous; any moment existence can veer off into the comic or the tragic because there is no reconciliation between the two. In a world which rejects the presence of grace there can be only abnormality, only extremes; and if reading Miss O'Connor's fiction is often like watching a freak show, that is because her art insists that man without God is a sad joke, ridiculously absurd in his efforts to cope with life on his own terms or shockingly monstrous in his dedication to evil.[8]

Paradox develops through the merging of symbol and irony. In many of her stories there is a secondary level of meaning which, once interpreted, reveals an irony that deepens into paradox. In *Wise Blood* Haze Motes' call for a "new jesus" is accompanied by an obscene travesty of the Incarnation of Christ. Enoch Emery steals a three-foot-long mummy from the museum and brings it to Sabbath Hawkes, the old evangelist's daughter who sleeps with Haze. In a fantastic scene Sabbath cradles the mummy in her arms, in a parody of the Madonna–Child Jesus pictures, before Haze grabs it, literally knocks the stuffing out of it, and throws it out the window. In that instinctive action Haze rids himself frantically of any reminders of Christ. The irony of it is that in destroying Christ, symbolically or intellectually, Haze destroys himself. The paradox is that, in Christian theology, only by allowing Christ to die for one does one gain life; Haze will not accept that, and it is a final symbolic irony that he dies under the Law. Found at last unconscious in a ditch by two policemen, he is beaten by one with a billy club and dies in the squad car.

In the same novel Enoch Emery's adventures with the gorilla skin have symbolic, ironic, and paradoxical meaning. Enoch forcibly takes the skin off the man who is wearing it to promote a movie in town. In an elaborate ceremony at night Enoch takes off his clothes, buries them, and dresses in the gorilla skin. The overtones of St. Paul's putting off the old man and putting on the new are unmistakable; the irony is in the inversion of the process: Enoch dresses like a beast in order to become more human. The paradox is that only by really giving himself up in the genuine Pauline sense could he at last become himself.

In "The Displaced Person" the Polish refugee functions on Mrs. McIntyre's farm in a role akin to Christ's work in Judea. In a beautifully ironic scene, the priest and Mrs. McIntyre are talking past each other: Mrs. McIntyre, thinking of old Guizac, says, "He didn't have to come in the first place." The priest, thinking of Christ, says, "He came to redeem us." The irony of the story is that Mrs. McIntyre allows Guizac to be killed and through his death finds her farm ruined. The paradox is that only by accepting Guizac's radically different concept of life could the woman have saved herself; only by allowing for the possibility of her livelihood being destroyed could she have salvaged it. "He who loses his life for my sake shall find it."

Speaking of the overworked concept of "the death of God," Miss O'Connor remarked that our stifled religiosity has "gone underground and come out in distorted forms."[9] Those distorted forms pervade her fiction; they are not there for the sake of sensationalism but for literary-theological interpretation. Through them one discovers that a life without grace is altogether possible, perhaps even probable, yet it will always result in a substitute, secondary existence that becomes a relentless search or a void. The curse of Christ is that He has appeared so unequivocally. The reverse side of grace is judgment. Miss O'Connor's fiction functions in the tension and as the tension between grace and judgment. Hers is the artist's view of reality that becomes transparent to the gospel itself.

Notes

[1] The quotation is taken from page 11 of a pamphlet entitled *Recent Southern Fiction*, which contains the proceedings of a panel discussion held at Wesleyan College, Macon, Georgia, on October 28, 1960. Participants were Katherine Anne Porter, Flannery O'Connor, Caroline Gordon, Madison Jones, and Louis D. Rubin. No date of publication is given.

[2] Paul Tillich, *The Shaking of the Foundations* (New York, 1948), p. 181.

[3] All quotations from Miss O'Connor's fiction are taken from the paperback collection, *Three by Flannery O'Connor* (Signet Books, New York, 1964), and from the posthumously published collection, *Everything That Rises Must Converge* (New York, 1965). Of the stories I discuss, "A View of the Woods," "The Enduring Chill," "The Lame Shall Enter First," "Parker's Back," and "Judgment Day" appear in the more recent collection; the two novels and the other stories are in the 1964 paperback collection. The page numbers in parentheses refer to the pages in the two texts.

[4] Jonathan Baumbach, in "The Creed of God's Grace: The Fiction of Flannery O'Connor," *The Georgia Review* (Fall 1963), discusses ritual in terms of character and action. "The ritual configuration is, in a sense, a reversal of the *rite de passage*; that is, her central characters do not fall from innocence. They are fallen at the outset and more, doomed, through an infested world of proliferating evil until at the heart of darkness they discover light (or God) and through renunciation and extreme penance achieve redemption for themselves and, in extension, for all of us" (p. 334). As becomes obvious through the rest of my study, I do not agree with Baumbach that very many of Miss O'Connor's characters achieve personal redemption or effect it vicariously.

⁵ Cf. Robert Fitzgerald's comment, in the Introduction to *Everything That Rises Must Converge*, p. xxvi, on *Wise Blood* as a conscious but serious parody of existentialism. Fitzgerald's biographical-critical Introduction, incidentally, is the most enlightening study of Flannery O'Connor that I have read to date.

⁶ For this information I am indebted to Mr. M. Smith Kirkpatrick, creative writing teacher at the University of Florida. Cf. also Fitzgerald's mention (*Everything That Rises Must Converge*, pp. xi–xii), of the moments of natural beauty and beautiful actions in the stories that offset the violence and perversity.

⁷ Mr. Baumbach states ("The Creed of God's Grace," p. 334) that Haze achieves redemption and that "his redemption is therefore intended as exemplary; that is, it makes possible the redemption of his world." I would agree rather with Ihab Hassan, who writes in *Radical Innocence* (Princeton, 1961), p. 79, that Haze "gives up his very salvation though he blinds his eyes with quick lime, wears barbed wire next to his chest, and walks with broken glass in his shoes. . . . The victim of a grotesque nihilism remains the pinpoint of light in a society too smug both in its skepticism and belief."

⁸ Cf. Robert Drake's brief but valuable discussion of the grotesque in "The Harrowing Evangel of Flannery O'Connor," *The Christian Century*, September 30, 1964, pp. 1200–1202.

⁹ *Recent Southern Fiction*, p. 12.

J. D. Salinger and the Russian Pilgrim

by

George A. Panichas

CRITICAL ESTIMATES OF J. D. SALINGER's *Franny and Zooey* INVARIABLY contain references to the profound influence made on Franny Glass by a little book of Russian Orthodox spirituality, *The Way of a Pilgrim*.[1] It is obvious that Salinger attaches much significance to this work of Russian piety, as is clearly registered in his depiction of Franny's response to the book. This influence, however, does not necessarily prove distinct structural affinities or parallels, but rather reveals a sensitive recognition on Salinger's part of the moving spirit and message of *The Way of a Pilgrim*. That is to say, Salinger, in showing the influence of this book on Franny, confesses at the same time a decidedly sympathetic and intuitive understanding of the Russian work. He seems to have found in it what might be called a transcending religious meaning and experience; and in his characterization of Franny he re-creates the form, direction, and power of such an experience.

The difficulties and the doubts that Salinger must have experienced in order to achieve a positive realization of *The Way of a Pilgrim* are readily seen at the beginning of *Franny and Zooey*, where allusions to the Russian book are couched in obscure and even suspicious terms. Like Franny, Salinger seems at first somewhat ashamed of the "small pea-green clothbound book," which Lane Coutell notices Franny carrying in her left hand when he meets her on the station platform. She has come to join him for "the weekend of the Yale game." He questions her about the book, but she avoids discussing it and quickly stuffs it into her handbag. Yet, by the end of Salinger's book, *The Way of a Pilgrim* is freed from this preliminary obscurity and suspicion. Gradually, its title and content are referred to freely and fearlessly, and its growing significance becomes incontestable. Indeed, at the conclusion of *Franny and Zooey* the spirit and inspiration of *The Way of a Pilgrim* have become convincing and impelling, and the earlier process of grudging discovery is transformed into an undoubting triumph of affirmation. *The Way of a Pilgrim*, thus, is no longer "just something," but the way to redemption and the very beauty and wisdom that Franny desperately and painfully longed for.

It would be best at this point to say a few things about *The Way of a Pilgrim* before going on to appraise its significance in Salinger's work. The complete title of the book is *The Way of a Pilgrim and The Pilgrim Continues His Way*, translated from the Russian by R. M. French. The first translation of *The Way of a Pilgrim* was published in 1930, and its sequel, *The Pilgrim Continues His Way*, was published separately at a later date; in 1941 both were published for the first time as a continuous narrative in one volume. The Pilgrim's story was first discovered in manuscript form at a Greek Orthodox monastery on Mt. Athos by a Russian abbot, who copied the manuscript, on the basis of which a book was published in Kazan in 1884. This volume narrates the experiences of a Russian wanderer over the steppes and fields of Russia at some time prior to the liberation of the serfs in 1861. In particular it is the story of the Pilgrim's practicing a way of prayer which arises out of his desire to understand the words "Pray without ceasing," from the first Epistle of St. Paul to the Thessalonians. In the process of learning the meaning of "unceasing interior prayer," the Pilgrim seeks the advice of a monk (*starets*) known for his wisdom and spiritual counsel. "Learn first to acquire the power of prayer," he is advised, "and you will easily practise all the other virtues" (p. 8). The monk also tells him that the essence of the prayer is found in the words "Lord Jesus Christ, have mercy on me." Soon the Pilgrim obtains a copy of the *Philokalia*, or *The Love of Spiritual Beauty*, a collection of mystical and ascetic writings by the Fathers of the Eastern Orthodox Church. Compiled in the eighteenth century, the Greek *Philokalia* was first published in Venice in 1782; in the nineteenth century it was translated into Russian (*Dobrotolubiye*), and this translation was to play an important role in Russian religious life and thought.

Often described as "the foremost and best manual of the contemplative spiritual life," the *Philokalia* was to be for the Pilgrim a major guide in his attaining purification and in his comprehending more fully the Jesus Prayer. This achievement was to be no easy matter, for the Pilgrim was to experience the inevitable assaults of laziness, boredom, and distraction. It was not merely a matter of learning and repeating the Jesus Prayer, but of making it become a "self-acting spiritual prayer." Constant effort and stern self-discipline are necessary for the Pilgrim to purge his soul. In the end, with the understanding and assistance of his *starets*, the Pilgrim discovers the mystery of prayer. He gradually reaches a state of happiness and innocence, free from evil-thinking and from an ego-tainted consciousness. Although he is only thirty-three years of age, the Pilgrim is a widower. He has a withered left arm. His sole worldly possessions are a knapsack containing some dried bread, a Bible, and the *Philokalia*. Nevertheless, in his arduous travels and in his encounters with all kinds of persons, he meets with success; for the Jesus Prayer has become an organic part of his life and purpose, enabling him to see and feel God everywhere.

From all this it should not be inferred that Salinger has adopted Russian mysticism as a kind of religious prop or that he has been experimenting with Eastern Orthodoxy as a means of religious conversion. On the contrary, his approach is entirely nonsectarian: it is mainly a search for religious meaning and for spiritual vision on higher levels of experience. It is expressed in a pre-eminently modern idiom and context. The fact remains that *Franny and Zooey* is not a "devotional manual," but rather a creative work of art that transcends religious doctrine, creed, and so-called theological dimensions. Its preoccupation is with religious sensibility, with vital emotions, responses, and instincts outside the pale of the rational and the empirical. Any attempt to treat Salinger's work on a religious plane should be detached from the strictly theological and homiletic. Religion, *not* religiosity, is what distinguishes *Franny and Zooey*; and it is religion in the spirit of Alfred North Whitehead's admirable definition which sees it as

> the vision of something which stands beyond, behind, and within the passing flux of immediate things; something which is real, and yet waiting to be realised; something which is a remote possibility, and yet the greatest of present facts; something that gives meaning to all that passes, and yet eludes apprehension; something whose possession is the final good, and yet is beyond all reach; something which is the ultimate ideal, and the hopeless quest.[2]

Let us turn again to *Franny and Zooey* and particularly to the first scene. In it we find Franny and her boy friend, Lane Coutell, sitting at a table in a downtown restaurant called Sickler's, an eating place specializing in snails—"a highly favored place among, chiefly, the intellectual fringe of students at the college." This setting is identified by what Salinger describes as college students "talking in voices that, almost without exception, sounded collegiately dogmatic." Lane Coutell personifies this haughty dogmatism and pseudo-sophistication; he is very much a product of an educational system that, Salinger charges, is "all the most incredible farce." In the words of Franny's brother Zooey, Lane is "a charm boy and a fake," and "it's paid off!" He even reminds Franny of "pedants and conceited little tearer-downers," a potential "section man" with "his little button-down-collar shirt and striped tie." Franny becomes ill in the course of their conversation—a conversation that inevitably reveals to her the crassness and impoverishment of Lane's state. Upon finishing with the words "I'm sick of just liking people. I wish to God I could meet somebody I could respect . . . ," she excuses herself and goes to the ladies' room. Here *The Way of a Pilgrim* comes into view a second time, directly after Franny has gone into "the farthest and anonymous-looking" enclosure: "She cried without trying to suppress any of the noisier manifestations of grief and confusion, with all the convulsive throat sounds that a hysterical child makes when the breath is trying to get up through a partly closed epiglottis" (p. 22). Then she "picked up her handbag from the floor, opened it, and took out the small pea-green clothbound book," that is, *The Way of a Pilgrim*. "She picked up the book, raised it chest-high, and pressed it to her—firmly, and quite briefly" (p. 22). Then she returned the book to her handbag, stood up and came out of the enclosure. After washing her face, applying fresh lipstick, and combing her hair, she left the room. "She looked quite stunning as she walked across the dining room to the table, not at all unlike a girl on the *qui vive* appropriate to a big college weekend" (p. 23).

As if strengthened by the "small pea-green clothbound book," Franny returns to the table. From the menu she selects a chicken sandwich and a glass of milk, much to the surprise of Lane. "This is going to be a real little doll of a weekend," he exclaims ominously. A moment later he orders frogs' legs, snails, and a salad for himself. Their conversation continues as Lane confidently outlines plans that include meeting his college friend Wally Campbell for a drink and then going to the stadium for the football game. Franny's immediate response is none too favorable: she begins to condemn a society flooded with Wally Campbells:

"I don't mean there's anything horrible about him or anything like that. It's just that for four solid years I've kept seeing Wally

Campbells wherever I go. I know when they're going to be *charming*, I know when they're going to start telling you some really nasty gossip about some girl that lives in your dorm, I know when they're going to ask me what I did over the summer, I know when they're going to pull up a chair and straddle it backward and start bragging in a terribly, terribly quiet voice—or *name*-dropping in a terribly quiet, *casual* voice" (p. 25).

To Lane this outcry sounds incredible—although it makes little appreciable difference in his enjoyment of the snails that he is relishing while he listens to an increasingly pale and haggard Franny. When he learns, however, that she has abandoned all her interests in drama and the theater, he is perturbed. The reason for Franny's decision, in spite of the fact that she has had notable acting success, especially in summer stock, is made explicit in her remark that she is "just sick of ego, ego, ego. My own and everybody else's. I'm sick of everybody that wants to get somewhere, do something distinguished and all, be something interesting" (p. 29). To this assertion Lane reacts with a smugness typical of his kind, and he glibly implies that Franny is afraid of competing. He proclaims that her statements would reveal something very serious to a psychoanalyst! Franny's rejoinder rings with honesty. "That's why I quit the Theatre Department," she declares with feeling and resolution. "Just because I'm so horribly conditioned to accept everybody else's values, and just because I like applause and people to rave about me, doesn't make it right. I'm ashamed of it. I'm sick of it. I'm sick of not having the courage to be an absolute nobody. I'm sick of myself and everybody else that wants to make some kind of a splash" (p. 30). As she utters these words, her forehead is perspiring conspicuously, and she unloads a few things from her handbag in order to find some Kleenex. In "the disorderly little pile of handbag freight on the tablecloth," there comes into view again "the little clothbound book," *The Way of a Pilgrim*.

The third appearance of the book is in every way apocalyptic: No longer is *The Way of a Pilgrim* a shadowy form hovering sadly in the background, but it is an immanent, living force. Indeed, all that has been said up to this point has had as a silent but compassionate witness the Russian Pilgrim. Doubtless he has been kept undercover, hidden from actual sight, and Franny's handbag has been like a gray, oppressive shroud imprisoning a spirit of enlightenment and joy. Bowing at last to Lane's demands, Franny begins to explain the history and meaning of *The Way of a Pilgrim*. Her summary of it becomes increasingly enthusiastic, in spite of occasional interruptions by Lane as he eats his frogs' legs, which he even admonishes at one time to hold still. "I hate to mention it," he breaks in to say, "but I'm going to reek of garlic." Bravely Franny continues with her exposition of *The Way of a Pilgrim*, even when Lane blatantly interferes again to ask Franny whether she will read in the near future a psychoanalytic paper of his on Flaubert, which his instructor had suggested was publishable. Franny, very tolerant and patient, agrees to do so as she watches him butter another piece of bread. "You might like this book," she suddenly says. "It's so simple, I mean" (p. 35). Nonchalantly, he opines that it "sounds interesting," at the same time asking, "You don't want your butter, do you?" But despite the gross indifference that captivates a self-centered Lane, who is now smoking as he sits rather slouched in his chair, Franny goes on to give special emphasis to the Jesus Prayer. She notes that the power of this prayer is no less effective than the words, "Namu Amida Butsu," in praise of Buddha. The same thing happens, she says, in "The Cloud of Unknowing" with the word "God."

Lane's reaction is in keeping with the character and malady of a negator. "You actually believe that stuff, or what?" he inquires. What, he demands to know, are the concrete results of "All this synchronization business and mumbo-jumbo." Accustomed as he is to supra-rational formulas, to inviolable answers and systems of thought, he discloses a condition of mind that automatically suspects experiences and responses which are of a visionary and intuitive nature. Nevertheless, Franny is in no way wholly discouraged or frightened by Lane's cold and calculating doubts and questions. Her reply to him has an enhancing grace and simplicity; in its innocence it is both lovely and touching: "You get to see God. Something happens in some absolutely nonphysical part of the heart—where the Hindus say that Atman resides . . . and you see God, that's all" (p. 39). Lane responds with the question, "You want some dessert, or coffee?" noticing, too, that Franny has not touched her chicken sandwich. He also looks at his watch and states that there isn't much time left to get to the game. And only then does he in any way attempt to refer to Franny's impassionate remarks on "seeing God." He notes condescendingly, and with the kind of toleration which masks a sinister sneering and a heartrending insolence, that what Franny has been saying is perhaps "interesting" but doesn't "leave any margin for the most elementary psychology."

It is evident that Franny has been unsuccessful in communicating with Lane, and it is the brutal realization of an unshared sensibility that drives her once again from the table. She walks briskly through the dining room and stops short at the small bar at the far end of the room. Here she faints and collapses to the floor. Five minutes later she finds herself on a couch in the manager's office, with Lane sitting beside her. Now when she realizes that they have missed the cocktail party and the football game, she apologizes. Lane shrugs it off with the advice that she should return to her lodgings and get some rest—after all "that's the important thing." Likewise, he tells her that once she has rested and regained her strength, she will be in good condition to meet him that night. Getting to her will be no problem: A man of wide experience and accomplishment, he can easily find out about some back staircase. "His hot little ivy league intellect," after all, should be able to come up with something! (Remember, too, he handles martinis as easily as he does Flaubert!) His real purpose, finally, becomes crystal clear in the remark that then follows, and reveals, concurrently, a creatureliness with only one thing in mind: "You know how long it's been?" he asks. "When was that Friday night? Way the hell early last month, wasn't it? . . . That's no good. Too goddam long between drinks. To put it crassly" (p. 42). Soon he leaves the room, and an agonized Franny lies very still, looking at the ceiling. And when the first part of the book concludes, we have a vivid picture of Franny, her lips tremblingly "forming soundless words"— the words of the Jesus Prayer: "Lord Jesus Christ, have mercy on me."

The first part of *Franny and Zooey* may be likened to a momentous encounter achieved on a creative scale and proportion no less effective or dramatic than, for example, F. M. Dostoevsky's depiction of the meetings between Ivan and the Devil or between Christ and the Grand Inquisitor in *The Brothers Karamazov*. On the one hand, Lane Coutell represents a degenerated consciousness that is irrevocably insensitive and contaminated. On the other hand, Franny represents a consciousness that, even when faltering and fearful, seeks for purposive meanings in human relationships. In her encounter with Lane, therefore, Salinger is attempting to show the difference between what is debased and what is potentially good. Franny embodies the potentiality for good, and Lane personifies the spirit of ruin. He will utilize every devious device and means at his command to achieve his aims. He can be considerate and charming, but his manner hides an ulterior purpose. He has many other weapons at his disposal: derision, cajolery, innuendo, deception, slander. Before such awesome power, Franny appears somewhat limp and overmatched. And yet, we can say that at the end of the first stage of her pilgrimage, Franny has managed to survive the attacks brought to bear on her. This is not to claim that she is triumphant, but rather that she has succeeded in confronting the real nature of debasement. Concerning Franny's triumph we must look to the second, longer part of Salinger's work.

This second part, "Zooey," serves as a kind of sequel to the first story. The time is a November morning in 1955, and the setting is an old but not unfashionable apartment house in the East Seventies of Manhattan. Here we come face to face with Franny's brother Zooey and her mother, Bessie. We also derive information about the other members of the Glass family: Seymour, the eldest and most brilliant brother who had committed suicide; Buddy, a writer-in-residence in a girls' junior college in upstate New York; Boo-Boo, the mother of three children; and the twins, Walt and Waker, the former of whom had been accidentally killed in Japan while serving with the army of occupation. Concerning Mr. Glass, we learn that "He thinks anything peculiar or unpleasant will just go away if he turns on the radio and some little schnook starts singing" (p. 82). We learn, too, that all the Glass children, during the period 1927–1943, participated on a popular radio quiz program, "It's a Wise Child." For the most part, however, it is Zooey, a handsome twenty-five-year-old television actor and leading man, who occupies the central place in this story. His role, however, is closely interlinked with Franny's: for they both respond to the problems of life with an intensity, even a desperation, that makes them allies and fellow-sufferers. When Franny at one point tells him that "we're not bothered by exactly the same things, but by the same kind of things . . . and for the same reasons" (p. 143), she is emphasizing a truth that becomes increasingly clear by the end of the book.

Now, the most painful and serious problem confronting Zooey is that of ego. Zooey is without doubt an egoistic young man with strong and violent prejudices and dislikes. Extremely intelligent, he holds an M.A. in mathematics and could easily go on to obtain a Ph.D. in Greek that would permit him to become a member of what Salinger speaks of as "a brass-hat, brass-mortarboard world." He is a quick thinker and a ruthless conversationalist. But, as he himself admits, "We don't talk, we hold forth. We don't converse, we expound" (p. 139). He lacks an active and energizing humanity, not because he is innately bad but because he is too arrogantly intellectualized to allow his instinctive goodness to blossom forth naturally. "If you don't like somebody in two minutes, you're done with them forever," Mrs. Glass declares to him on one occasion (p. 99). Defiant and impatient in his approach to human relationships, Zooey needs above all to be schooled in lessons of humility. He has lost a sense of wonder that would help him overcome his deep-seated bitterness and cynicism. And yet these are negative traits that he has adopted through the years as a defensive mechanism. His deficiency is understandable when we recall that the Glass children were always in the public eye, were always looked on as young geniuses, and as such were expected to provide answers and solutions to "alternately deadly-bookish and deadly-cute questions" sent in by listeners. Moreover, all seven of the children "had been fair game for the kind of child psychologist or professional educator who takes a special interest in extra-precocious children" (p. 54). Zooey, who had the "most precocious wit and fancy," had especially been the victim of examinations and research, one diagnosis concluding that at the age of twelve he "had an English vocabulary on an exact par with Mary Baker Eddy's, if he could be urged to use it" (p. 55). No wonder that he describes both Franny and himself as "freaks."

Nevertheless, Zooey's ego is essentially a disguise; like Franny, he would like to renounce this disguise and to rediscover that inmost part of his being which still retains its humanity, its naturalness. Zooey's awareness of his own condition becomes clear in proportion to his recognition of the spiritual metamorphosis in Franny, who has now left college and returned home. According to her mother, she is continually "crying" and "mumbling" and has become a "run-down, overwrought little college girl that's been reading too many religious books." Zooey's mounting concern for Franny is self-concern as well: he senses that her agony mirrors the same kind of deep inner turmoil that he is suffering. Not without reason, therefore, he comes to Franny's defense when Mrs. Glass is critical of her daughter's behavior and implies that her present state is unnatural and abnormal. She suggests that it would be helpful to consult "a very devout Catholic psychoanalyst" who might "save" Franny. To this suggestion Zooey replies in words that not only throb with imprecation but also indict a conditioned response to an age that is characterized by an imperious psychology with its manufactured panaceas and bedside beneficence:

> "You just do that [Zooey cries to his mother]. You just call in some analyst who's experienced in adjusting people to the joys of television, and *Life* magazine every Wednesday, and European travel, and the H-bomb, and Presidential elections, and the front page of the *Times*, and the responsibilities of the Westport and Oyster Bay Parent-Teacher Association, and God knows what else that's gloriously normal—you just do that, and I swear to you, in not more than a year Franny'll either be in a *nut* ward or she'll be wandering off into some goddam desert with a burning cross in her hands" (pp. 107–108).

It is characteristic of Zooey that his vocabulary drips with spleen not only when he is speaking to his mother but also when he is counselling

Franny. "You're beginning to give off a little stink of piousness"; "all this hysteria business is unattractive as hell"; "this [is a] little snotty crusade you think you're leading against everybody" (p. 160)—these are statements which comprise Zooey's criticism of Franny's religious crisis. Strongly critical of Franny's use of the Jesus Prayer, he questions her motives. He accuses her of using the prayer as a means of laying up "some kind of treasure" and even making it "as negotiable as all those other, more material things." "As a matter of simple logic," he says to Franny, "there's no difference at all, that *I* can see, between the man who's greedy for material treasure—or even intellectual treasure—and the man who's greedy for spiritual treasure" (p. 147).

But Franny's honesty and integrity are her greatest strengths in her pilgrimage. She makes no attempt to find all the answers to the great problems and enigmas of life. Nor does she try to be presumptuous or cute in her discussions with her brother. She has, as she confesses, definite human weaknesses. For example, she admits to her brother that she abhors the man who has been teaching her in a religion seminar, a Professor Tupper. She sarcastically describes him as being "charming and Oxfordish," "on lend-lease or something from Oxford." What she mainly dislikes about him is that "He has no enthusiasm whatever for his subject. Ego, yes. Enthusiasm, no" (p. 127). To her he represents a false teacher who is comparable to a false poet—one of those poets who, she asserts, "get published and anthologized all over the place," but who fail "to do something beautiful," "to *leave* something beautiful after you get off the page and everything." The whole problem of education is for Franny a crucial one. The pursuit of knowledge for the sake of knowledge, she charges, is one of the worst faults of the modern educational system. "I don't think it would have all got me quite so down," she cries, "if just *once* in a while—just *once* in a while—there was at least some polite little perfunctory implication that knowledge *should* lead to wisdom, and that if it *doesn't*, it's just a disgusting waste of time" (pp. 145–146).

Consequently, Franny's chief problem is that of reconciling her ostensible lack of charity for people with her earnest efforts to purify her outlook on life. Zooey recognizes her dilemma and understandably then he summarizes his case against Franny when he criticizes the way she talks about others. "I mean," he says to her, "you don't just despise what they represent—you despise *them*" (p. 161). What Zooey fails to perceive at first is that Franny has an intrinsic awareness of her dilemma. She does see that somehow she must overcome the personal limitations of her response to people. She does see that if the Jesus Prayer is to be really effective and redeeming, she must struggle to overcome these short-comings. After all, she cries out to Zooey, one of the reasons for her agony is that she has been worrying all along "about my motives for saying the prayer." "That's exactly what's *bothering* me so," she remarks. "Just because I'm choosy about what I want—in this case, en*light*enment, or peace, instead of money or pres*tige* or *fame* or any of those things— doesn't mean I'm not as egotistical and self-seeking as everybody else. If anything, I'm more so" (p. 148). When she realizes, finally, that Zooey is not able to help her, she balefully asks to talk to her brother Seymour, who has been dead for seven years. And indeed, we have at this point a concomitant feeling of gloom and despair: Both Franny and Zooey are precariously groping for a restorative religious meaning and experience.

In spite of all the gloom, there occurs in the course of their conversation an episode that contains a saving grace and foreshadows an ultimate note of affirmation. This episode reveals that Zooey is not beyond the reach of those glad moments in life that suddenly burst forth to sustain faith in humanity. It takes place after Franny's frantic request to talk to Seymour. Dazed and puzzled by what has preceded, Zooey lets his attention be drawn "to a little scene that was being acted out sublimely, unhampered by writers and directors and producers, five stories below the window and across the street" (p. 150). There he notices a girl of seven or eight hiding behind a maple tree in front of a girls' private school. Some fifteen feet away her dog is scurrying and sniffing to find her. The anguish of separation is scarcely bearable for him. When he finds the little girl, he gives a little yelp, then cringes, "shimmying with ecstasy, till his mistress . . . stepped hurriedly over the wire guard surrounding the tree and picked him up" (p. 151). Zooey is profoundly stirred by the charm and beauty of this scene; in a very deep sense it conveys to him a message of hope—of hope reborn. It also demonstrates that he has an essential sensibility that is not doomed or dead but is capable of being aroused and energized. "God damn it," he says, "there are *nice* things in the world—and I mean nice things. We're all such morons to get so sidetracked. Always, always, always referring every goddam thing that has happened right back to our lousy little egos" (p. 151).

Zooey's experience, in this respect, is comparable to Franny's reactions to a family that the Russian Pilgrim meets in *The Way of a Pilgrim*. It is a family, as Franny said to Lane Coutell at the beginning of the book, that she loved more than anybody she had ever read about. As an "instructive experience" in the wanderings of the Russian Pilgrim, this scene takes place one day as he is seen passing through a poor village, where he stops to pray at a small wooden church. At the side of the church, he sees two little children who cry out to him, "Dear little beggar! Dear little beggar! Stop!" The two youngsters then run after him and take him by the hand to their house, where their mother greets him warmly and with her own hands takes off his knapsack and offers him the hospitality of her home and family. She then asks him to join her family in attending church on the following day, Sunday, and to share their meal after the services. What impresses the Pilgrim most during this scene is the meal that he shares at the dining table not only with the family but also with four other women guests who are present. He learns that the four, who are treated as sisters by the mistress of the house, are respectively the cook, the coachman's wife, the woman who has charge of the keys, and the maid. To Franny this meal in *The Way of a Pilgrim* serves as a memorable picture of simplicity and harmony. It is truly a "feast of love," undefiled by any artificiality. Taken together, then, both episodes comprise for Franny and Zooey what can be termed as brilliant gleams of illumination, those "graces of light," as François Mauriac has called them, that are given to man "at moments of tribulations and uncertainty —at the hour, as it were, of darkness."[3]

Doubtless, it is not easy for Zooey to realize the profundity of Franny's religious sensibility, or to fathom the influence on her by *The Way of a Pilgrim*. Often and too quickly, therefore, he tends to ignore and dismiss the manifestations of these influences and to subject them to cruel rational dialectic. Zooey's reactions are, as a result, a reflection of the atrophy of his own sensibility. In short, he has for too long subjected the meaning of *all* religious experience to an intellectualized, forensic process and has subordinated it to the irritability and pettiness that often condition and inform his response. The result is that he is really unprepared and unable to appreciate Franny's efforts to respond to the voices of "the emotional soul," "the spontaneous, living, individual soul," and to embrace a "gentle faith in life," to quote D. H. Lawrence's terminology. This is especially noticeable in his reactions to the Jesus Prayer. He does *know*, to be sure, what the Prayer is, but he does not comprehend the delicacy and sensitivity of the feelings behind it. Thus he reflects the acquired hardness and harshness all too common in modern technological civilization.

In the main Franny's conduct is at all times an offshoot of what she has read and reverenced in *The Way of a Pilgrim*, just as the Russian Pilgrim himself had been immensely influenced by his study and absorption of the *Philokalia*. When, therefore, Franny refuses to eat very much, she is merely doing something that the Russian Pilgrim does as a result of the instruction of St. Gregory of Sinai that "the practiser of silence should always be starved, never allowing himself to eat his fill" (*Philokalia*, p. 78).[4] When Franny is seen weeping, she, like the Russian Pilgrim, is adhering to the instruction that "a man striving to attain pure prayer in silence must proceed towards it with great trepidation . . . constantly shedding tears for his sins, in sorrowful contrition" (*Philokalia*, p. 82). Indeed, Franny's self-imposed silence and solitude parallel the Russian Pilgrim's response to the injunction "sit silently in your cell and it will teach you everything" (p. 224). Beyond this, Franny's silence is completely in line with the spirit of *The Way of a Pilgrim* which stresses that "the silent recluse teaches by his very silence, and by his very life he benefits, edifies and persuades to the search of God" (p. 226). Even Franny's relationship to Zooey, for that matter, is at all times epitomized by an unerring faith in the saying that "*spirit can give to spirit*" (p. 230), a saying that is the very essence of the Russian Pilgrim's travels and that becomes the supreme inspiration of one's attempt "to reach the harbor of the good father" (*Philokalia*, p. 98).

Although Zooey is not in complete *rapport* with these phases of Franny's religious sensibility, he is not able to repudiate their sincerity. Ultimately, this sincerity is communicated to him. In sharp contrast to a Lane Coutell, he is not an uncompromising negator of the marvels and mysteries that distinguish the development of "self and soul." Inevitably, the form and substance of this communication progress into a greater vision of life. It remains, then, for the ending of Salinger's book to depict the process and achievement of this vision, as well as to underline the concept that "spirit can give to spirit."

We should stop to recall here that in the final phase of his conversation with Franny, Zooey had accused her of misapplying the Jesus Prayer by "using it to ask for a world full of dolls and saints and no Professor Tuppers." Surely, there was much truth in Zooey's diagnosis—and Franny knew it was true. She knew, furthermore, that spiritual egotism is as onerous a condition as evil itself. But Zooey's diagnosis was rooted in disheartenment and led, in turn, to abstraction from life. It was this disheartenment that Franny sensed in her brother's attempt to counsel her, and it was *this* disheartenment, and not her brother, that she rejected. Of necessity, then, Zooey leaves Franny on a note of failure—a failure that "had suddenly filled the room with its invariably sickening smell."

Not long after this conversation takes place, Zooey goes into his brothers' old room. It is obvious that he is now deeply disturbed by his inability to help Franny in her problems. He is undergoing much self-questioning, and he realizes that if he is able to help Franny, he will also be helping himself. Soon we find him taking up the telephone on Buddy's old desk to call Franny, who answers on the telephone in her parents' bedroom. Zooey begins by saying that it is Buddy who is speaking, and Franny seems unaware of the impersonation. However, it does not take long for her to realize that it is Zooey who is speaking: his celebrated verbal stunts finally give him away. But she also realizes that Zooey's usual bravado is missing, that even reconciliation and atoning echo in his words. By the conclusion of his telephone call, Zooey is able to describe to his sister an incident which informs the conversation with a redeeming magnanimity. He relates that as a youngster appearing on "It's a Wise Child," he had on one occasion acted very hostile after being told by his eldest brother, Seymour, to shine his shoes before the program was to begin. His immediate reaction to this request was furious, and he recalled: "The studio audience were all morons, and I just damn well wasn't going to shine my shoes for them . . ." (pp. 198–199). Seymour told him to shine them anyway—to shine them for the Fat Lady. Although Seymour didn't tell him who the Fat Lady was, Zooey did shine his shoes finally and continued to do so on later programs. He envisaged the Fat Lady as a person suffering from cancer, sitting on her porch all day, swatting flies, and listening to her radio playing full-blast from morning to night. Zooey then goes on to tell Franny "a terrible secret," namely, "*There isn't anyone out there who isn't Seymour's Fat Lady*" (p. 200)—including even Professor Tupper. Indeed, he asserts, the Fat Lady is Christ Himself!

To Zooey's final comment, Franny reacts with instantaneous and ecstatic gladness. She is "filled with joy" at "the good news," for Zooey's remark is in every possible way a victory over his disheartenment, a vindication of the Jesus Prayer itself. Franny has, in fact, been waiting and praying for this all along, and now she "rises upward," as it were, purged of the engulfing spirit of negation and cynicism. This is the moment of victory in the lives of two young people when both are released from "the abyss of hell even before death" (*Philokalia*, p. 63). It is a moment that testifies to the message and inspiration which Franny received through her study of and meditation on the life of the Russian Pilgrim. Like the Russian Pilgrim she has been on a pilgrimage that has taken her from death into life. Like him she has grasped the tremendous implications of the Jesus Prayer. At the end of the book we are able to feel the serenity and beauty that accompany this affirmation. We also discover the joy and wonder of having reached at last "the royal road." When, therefore, Salinger's book concludes with Franny's falling "into a deep, dreamless sleep," we too are blessed with the sweet slumber that comes at the end of a long journey into the very heart of human existence. And, in effect, we become Pilgrims in Eternity.

Notes

[1] J. D. Salinger, *Franny and Zooey* (Boston, 1961); *The Way of a Pilgrim and The Pilgrim Continues His Way*, trans. R. M. French (London, 1961). All page references are included in the text.

[2] Alfred North Whitehead, *Science and the Modern World* (Cambridge, England, 1926), pp. 267–268.

[3] François Mauriac, *Cain, Where Is Your Brother?* (New York, 1962).

[4] *Writings from the Philokalia on Prayer of the Heart*, trans. E. Kadloubovsky and G. E. H. Palmer (London, 1951).

NOTES ON CONTRIBUTORS

MILTON BIRNBAUM is now Chairman of the Department of English at American International College, Springfield, Massachusetts. His interest in Huxley goes back many years: he wrote his master's thesis (New York University) on the literary friendship of Huxley and D. H. Lawrence and his doctoral dissertation (New York University) on Huxley's search for values. In addition to giving courses in twentieth-century British and American fiction and in contemporary European drama, he lectures frequently on literature and philosophy before literary and church groups. He also contributes to religious and professional journals.

VINCENT FERRER BLEHL, S.J., Associate Professor of English Literature and Co-Director of the Center of Newman Studies at Fordham University, New York, was born in New York in 1921. Ordained a priest of the Society of Jesus in June 1952, he holds an M.A. from Fordham University and a Ph.D. from Harvard. He helped to launch and edit the definitive edition of Newman's letters and is the editor of *The Essential John Henry Newman*. His discovery of original documents on Newman solved the mystery surrounding Newman's failure to be made a bishop in 1854.

JOHN CRUICKSHANK was born in Northern Ireland in 1924. During World War II he was a cryptographer in British Military Intelligence. In 1948 he was graduated from Trinity College, Dublin, with First Class Honors in Modern Languages (French and German). After a year at the Ecole Normale Supérieure in Paris, he was appointed a lecturer in French at the University of Southampton. In 1962 he was appointed to his present post as Professor of French at the University of Sussex, where he is also Vice-Dean of the University's School of European Studies. The author of *Albert Camus and the Literature of Revolt*, *Critical Readings in the Modern French Novel*, and *Montherlant*, he edited and contributed to *The Novelist as Philosopher* and is at present editing and contributing some chapters to *French Literature and Its Background*.

ROBERT DETWEILER studied at the University of Hamburg, Germany, Goshen College, and the University of Florida. A post-doctoral research fellow at the University of Florida, he is at present teaching at Florida Presbyterian College. He is the author of *Four Spiritual Crises in Mid-Century American Fiction* and has contributed articles to *American Quarterly*, *American Literature*, *Monatshefte*, *Modern Fiction Studies*, *The Christian Scholar*, *Theology Today*, *The Journal of Bible and Religion*, and *The Personalist*. He is now at work on a critical study of John Updike.

FREDERICK W. DILLISTONE, born in England in 1903, was graduated from Oxford University with Honors in mathematics in 1924. Proceeding to the study of theology, he became B.D. in 1933, D.D. in 1951. Ordained to the ministry of the Church of England, he has taught in theological colleges in Oxford, Toronto, and Cambridge, Massachusetts. In 1956–1963 he was Dean of Liverpool. Now he is a Fellow and Chaplain of Oriel College, Oxford. His writings, which relate Christian doctrine to the symbolic forms of other religions and of the arts, include *Christianity and Symbolism* and *The Novelist and the Passion Story*.

GEORGES FLOROVSKY, perhaps the most distinguished living Eastern Orthodox theologian and church historian, was born near Odessa, Russia, in 1893. In 1926 he was invited by the late Russian philosopher Nicholas Berdyaev to join in ecumenical conversations along with Jacques Maritain, Gabriel Marcel, Winifred Monod, Marc Boegner, Sergius Bulgakov, and, occasionally, Père Lebreton, Etienne Gilson, and Edouard Leroy. In 1926–1948 he was a professor of patristics at the famous Orthodox Theological Institute in Paris. In 1952 he helped to found *St. Vladimir's Seminary Quarterly*. He has been awarded honorary doctorates by St. Andrew's University, Boston University, and the University of Salonica; he is a member of the Academic Council of the Ecumenical Institute established (1965) by Pope Paul VI in Jerusalem; he was elected to the Royal Academy of Athens (along with Augustin Cardinal Bea and Dr. Albert Schweitzer) in 1965 and, later, to the American Academy of Arts and Sciences. He is the author of *The Ways of Russian Theology*, *Eastern Fathers of the Fourth Century*, *Byzantine Fathers of the Fifth to Eighth Centuries* (all in Russian). Emeritus professor at Harvard, he is Visiting Senior Fellow of the Council of Humanities and Visting Professor of History and of Slavic Languages at Princeton.

ROBERT H. FOSSUM was born in Beloit, Wisconsin, in 1923. Awarded degrees by Beloit College (B.A.), the University of Southern California (M.A.), and Claremont Graduate School (Ph.D.), he has taught at Beloit College, the University of Southern California, California State College at Los Angeles, and Harvey Mudd College. At present he is an Associate Professor of English and Acting Chairman of the Humanities Committee at Claremont Men's College. He is finishing a book on the problem of time in Hawthorne's fiction and has published articles and reviews in *The Christian Scholar*, *The Chicago Review*, *The Claremont Quarterly*, *The Explicator*, and *Nineteenth-Century Fiction*.

THOMAS L. HANNA was born in Waco, Texas, in 1928. He was granted a B.A. in philosophy from Texas Christian University in 1949. From the University of Chicago he received a B.D. in 1954 and a Ph.D. in 1959. At present he is teaching at the University of Florida (Gainesville), where he is Chairman of the Department of Philosophy. His interests are centered on phenomenology in nineteenth- and twentieth-century Continental philosophy. He has written *The Thought and Art of Albert Camus* and *The Lyrical Existentialists* and has edited *The Bergsonian Heritage*.

MARTIN JARRETT-KERR, C.R., born in England in 1912, was educated at Oxford University, where he received an Honors degree in English language and literature and a Dipl. Theol. He was ordained deacon in 1936, priest in 1937. In 1943 he joined the Anglican religious order Community of the Resurrection. He was Vice-Principal of the Theological College of the Resurrection in Yorkshire in 1949–1952 and served in Johannesburg, South Africa in 1952–1959. His books include *D. H. Lawrence and Human Existence, François Mauriac, The Secular Promise,* and *Studies in Literature and Belief.*

JOHN KILLINGER, an ordained Baptist minister, was born in Germantown, Kentucky, in 1933. He studied at Baylor University, the University of Kentucky, Harvard University, and Princeton Theological Seminary. An Associate Professor of Preaching at the Divinity School, Vanderbilt University, he is the author of *Hemingway and the Dead Gods, The Failure of Theology in Modern Literature,* and *The Thickness of Glory;* his articles and reviews have appeared in the *Saturday Review, Religion in Life, The Journal of Religion, The Southwestern Journal of Theology,* and *The Princeton Seminary Bulletin.*

G. WILSON KNIGHT was born in Sutton, Surrey, England, in 1897. In 1916–1920 he served in the armed forces in Mesopotamia, Persia, and India. He received a B.A. and an M.A. from Oxford University. Chancellors' Professor of English, Trinity College, University of Toronto in 1931–1940, he was Reader and later Professor of English at the University of Leeds (1946–1962) and subsequently Emeritus Professor there. He gave the Clark lectures at Cambridge University in 1962 and the Festival Seminars at Stratford, Ontario, in 1963. His well-known critical studies on Shakespeare include *The Imperial Theme, The Crown of Life, The Shakespearian Tempest, The Sovereign Flower,* and *The Mutual Flame.* He has also written books on other poets: *The*

Burning Oracle (Milton, Swift, Pope, Byron), *The Starlit Dome* (Wordsworth, Coleridge, Shelley, Keats), *Chariot of Wrath* (Milton, prose and poetry), *Laureate of Peace* (Pope), *Lord Byron: Christian Virtues*, and *Lord Byron's Marriage*. On the subject of poetry and religion he has written *The Christian Renaissance* and *Christ and Nietzsche*. He is a Fellow of the International Institute of Arts and Letters and a Fellow of the Royal Society of Literature. In 1966 he was awarded an Honorary Doctor of Letters by the University of Sheffield.

WILLIAM A. MADDEN is an Associate Professor and Assistant Chairman in the Department of English, Indiana University. He helped to found *Victorian Studies* and serves on that journal's editorial board. He has published articles on Chaucer, Kafka, and various Victorian authors; he is co-editor of, and a contributor to, *1859: Entering an Age of Crisis*. He has a forthcoming book on Matthew Arnold. Currently he is editing, with George Levine, a collection of essays on prose style.

THOMAS MERTON was born on January 31, 1915 in Prades, France, near the mountainous borders of Spain. As a youth, he lived in Flushing, Long Island, as well as in Paris, in London, in Genoa, and in other major European cities. He spent his freshman year at Cambridge University and then transferred to Columbia University (B.A., 1938; M.A., 1939), where he was interested in literature, in modern art, and in jazz sessions. At the age of twenty-six, he converted to Roman Catholicism and subsequently entered a Trappist monastery. In his autobiography, *Seven Storey Mountain* (1948), he describes his conversionary experience: "I had come, like the Jews, through the Red Sea of Baptism. I was entering into a desert . . . [that] would lead me to a land I could not imagine or understand." He elaborates on some of these themes in a companion volume on Trappist life, *The Waters of Siloe* (1949). Today, an ordained priest known as Father M. Louis O.C.S.O., he is Master of Novices in the Abbey of Our Lady of Gethsemani, Trappist, Kentucky. He has written over thirty religious books, as well as several volumes of poetry, including *Figures for an Apocalypse* (1947) and *Tears of the Blind Lions* (1949).

J. HILLIS MILLER was born in 1928 and educated at Oberlin College and Harvard University. After one year of teaching at Williams College, he went to The Johns Hopkins University, where he is now a professor of English and Chairman of the Department. He is the author of *Charles Dickens: The World of His Novels*; *The Disappearance of God: Five Nineteenth-Century Writers*; and *Poets of Reality: Six Twentieth-*

Century Writers. In 1965–1966 he was in London on a Guggenheim Fellowship working on a book on Victorian fiction.

CHARLES MOELLER was born in Brussels in 1912. He received a doctorate in theology from the University of Louvain in 1942. In 1942–1954 he was a professor at the Institut de Saint Pierre. Now he teaches at the University of Louvain. He has contributed numerous articles on the encounter between the Christian faith and contemporary literature to journals in Belgium, France, Spain, and the United States. Among his books are *Litterature du XXe Siècle et Christianisme, Simone de Beauvoir und die Situation der Frau,* and *The Theology of Grace and the Oecumenical Movement.*

EDWIN M. MOSELEY, Dean of Faculty and Professor of English at Skidmore College, has written and lectured extensively on the Renaissance, the history of the novel, and contemporary literature. With Robert P. Ashley he edited *Elizabethan Fiction* and has contributed both fiction and criticism to *Accent, University of Kansas City Review, College English, Shenandoah,* and many other journals. His *Pseudonyms of Christ in the Modern Novel: Motifs and Methods* (1963) was widely reviewed as a significant piece of literary criticism.

GEORGE A. PANICHAS was born in Springfield, Massachusetts, in 1930. In 1962 he received his Ph.D. from the University of Nottingham, England. He is now an Associate Professor of English at the University of Maryland. Many of his writings, on literature and religion and on literature and philosophy, have appeared in scholarly publications in the United States and abroad. He is the author of *Adventure in Consciousness: The Meaning of D. H. Lawrence's Religious Quest* and *Epicurus.*

VIVIAN DE SOLA PINTO was born in Hampstead, London, in 1895. He was educated at University College School in London and at Christ Church, Oxford, where he was graduated with First Class Honors in 1921 and was subsequently awarded the degree of D.Phil. He taught for a year at the Sorbonne and was Professor of English at University College, Southampton, in 1926–1938 and at the University of Nottingham in 1938–1961, retiring with the title of Emeritus Professor. He has lectured in many countries; during the academic year 1965–1966, he was Distinguished Visiting Professor at the University of California (Davis). He served in the British army in both World Wars and is a Fellow of the Royal Society of Literature. His publications include *Enthusiast in Wit: Por-*

trait of *John Wilmot, Earl of Rochester;* an edition of Rochester's poems; *The English Renaissance; Crisis in English Poetry, 1880–1940; The Restoration Court Poets;* and a selection from William Blake's writings. He has also contributed to many learned periodicals and collections. One of his chief literary interests has long been the work of D. H. Lawrence. In 1960 he organized a Lawrence exhibition at Nottingham. In collaboration with Warren Roberts he edited *The Complete Poems of D. H. Lawrence.*

DEREK STANFORD was born at Lampton in Middlesex, England, in 1918, and educated at Upper Latymer School near Hammersmith. For a while he studied law, but later decided to follow the profession of letters. After working on the land at Cambridge, he spent five years in khaki in a noncombatant capacity during World War II. During this time he contributed to many little magazines and wrote the introductory essays to two numbers of the anthology *New Road.* His first book of verse, *Music for Statues,* was published in 1948, along with his first book of literary criticism, *The Freedom of Poetry.* Specializing in the 1890's, he has written *The Poets of the 'Nineties, Short Stories of the 'Nineties,* and *Beardsley's Erotic Universe.* In addition, he has published books on Dylan Thomas, Christopher Fry, John Betjeman, and Emily and Anne Brontë, as well as editing a selection of Fénelon's letters and a collection of John Henry Newman's correspondence. He is a Fellow of the Royal Society of Literature.

HYATT H. WAGGONER, Professor of English and Chairman of the American Civilization Program at Brown University, is best known for his Hawthorne studies. He has edited *Selected Tales and Sketches* and *The House of the Seven Gables,* the latter with a new text based on the manuscript. He has written *Hawthorne: A Critical Study, The Heel of Elohim, William Faulkner: From Jefferson to the World,* and a pamphlet on Hawthorne; and he is responsible for Hawthorne in the annual *American Literary Scholarship.*

INDEX

INDEX PREPARED BY SIDNEY AND ALICE MASON